A POPULAR HISTORY OF
IDI AMIN'S UGANDA

A POPULAR HISTORY OF IDI AMIN'S UGANDA

DEREK R. PETERSON

Yale

UNIVERSITY PRESS

New Haven and London

Yale University Press books may be purchased in quantity for educational, business, or promotional use. For information, please e-mail sales.press@yale.edu (U.S. office) or sales@yaleup.co.uk (U.K. office).

Set in Janson type by IDS Infotech Ltd.
Printed in the United States of America.

ISBN 978-0-300-27838-5 (hardcover : alk. paper)
Library of Congress Control Number: 2024950209
A catalogue record for this book is available from the British Library.

Authorized Representative in the EU: Easy Access System Europe, Mustamäe tee 50, 10621 Tallinn, Estonia, gpsr.requests@easproject.com

10 9 8 7 6 5 4 3 2 1

For my parents

Contents

Preface and Acknowledgments   ix

Introduction   1

1. A Nervous State: Uganda in the 1960s   25
2. The Second Republic   59
3. The Transistor Revolution   77
4. A Government of Action   99
5. The Economic War   119
6. Violence and Public Life   139
7. The Front Lines   159
8. Governing Religion   185
9. Making History   207
10. Living Off the Grid: The Rwenzururu Kingdom   229
11. Liberating Uganda?   253

Notes   271
Bibliography   323
Index   343

Preface and Acknowledgments

Idi amin was africa's most notorious dictator, infamous for his blustering demagoguery and for the awful violence of his regime. He was also a pioneering leader of Black economic empowerment, a vocal opponent of South Africa's apartheid regime, chairman of the Organization of African Unity and the host of its 1975 convention, and a supporter of liberation movements in Asia, Europe, and the Americas. In March 1977, shortly after the archbishop of Uganda's Anglican church was murdered by Amin's men, *Time* magazine featured a picture of Amin on its cover, titling him "The Wild Man of Africa." A delegation of Black Americans brought a copy of *Time* with them when they visited northern Uganda later that month. A cameraman captured the moment when one of the visitors held his copy of *Time* aloft before a public assembly. Indignation was written on his face. The magazine was "malicious propaganda," he said. The following day, on 21 March, the *Voice of Uganda* newspaper showcased the visitor's speech in a front-page report.

Idi Amin was the creator of a myth that was both manifestly untrue and, for many people, extraordinarily compelling: that Uganda, a landlocked country far from the front lines of conflict, was at the forefront of the global struggle against colonialism, apartheid, and racial injustice. For many Africans, and for some Black Americans, he was a champion of African liberation.

That is why I have styled this book *A Popular History of Idi Amin's Uganda*. It is often said that Idi Amin ruled at the point of a gun, intimidating Ugandans into cowed acquiescence. Here, by contrast, I argue that his regime was founded on its popular appeal. Like the great historian Howard Zinn—whose *People's History of the United States* is a source of

Black American journalists display a copy of *Time* magazine in Gulu,
northern Uganda, March 1977 (Courtesy of the Uganda Broadcasting
Corporation)

orientation—I aim to bring the lives of marginal people into focus. The
people who are the protagonists of this book worked in the provinces, far
away from the center of power in Kampala, Uganda's capital. They were
low-level bureaucrats, museum curators, radio engineers, petty bureaucrats, and self-nominated proprietors of institutions. They thought of
themselves as actors in the great work of racial and political liberation.
They sacrificed themselves—their talent, their time, their energy—to
make the promises of Idi Amin's government real. I admire their tenacity,
but I do not subscribe to their politics. The Americans about whom Zinn
wrote were inspiring architects of popular democracy. The protagonists

in this book, by contrast, were oftentimes chauvinists, misogynists, and busybodies. Their demagoguery was enabled by their profound sense of patriotic duty. This book explains why so many earnest, knowledgeable people placed themselves in the service of a military dictatorship whose violence was widely known. In inquiring into the popular foundations of Idi Amin's government, the book offers insights into our current place and time, as democracies everywhere confront a new generation of popular demagogues.

This book rests on the labor of a great many people who have—over the past fifteen years—rescued, rehabilitated, organized, and digitized the hitherto hidden archives of Idi Amin's government. I've worked especially closely with colleagues at Mountains of the Moon University in Fort Portal, who have created a comprehensive digital archive of the provincial and district government records of western Uganda. I thank the former board chairman, Hon. Tom Butime, and the former vice chancellor, Dr. John Kasenene. Their visionary leadership has made MMU a continental leader in the management of electronic archives. The hard work was carried out by Moses Akugizibwe, Evarist Ngabirano, and other colleagues, to whom many thanks. The Cooperative Africana Materials Project of the Center for Research Libraries and the African Studies Center at the University of Michigan furnished the funding for this work. I owe an equal debt of gratitude to colleagues and friends at the Uganda Broadcasting Corporation, with whom I've been working to digitize photographic negatives, cinema films, sound recordings, and other analog media assets. Former board chairman Simon Kaheru, current board chairman James Tumusiime, managing director Winston Abaga, and deputy managing director Maurice Mugisha have been supportive from the start; and the team that runs the UBC archives—Malachi Kabaale, Dean Kibirige, and formerly Jacob Noowe—have worked with dedication and commitment. The digitization of the UBC photographic collection was carried off by Edmond Mulindwa, Jimmy Kikwata, and Edgar Taylor, with the advice of Tom Bray. My thanks to all of them. Particular thanks to my friend Dr. Richard Vokes, of the University of Western Australia, who has helped to organize and fund all the work at the UBC.

A team from the University of Michigan and Kabale University organized and inventoried the archives of Kabale District in 2013. I thank Ashley Rockenbach, whose talent for the work made that project possible, and Martin Tushabe, the district's records officer, who lent us his advice and insight. The archives of Jinja District were rescued from a watery doom in 2015 by a large team from the University of Michigan, the British Institute of Eastern Africa, and Busoga University, led by Ashley Rockenbach and Riley Linebaugh and guided by Mr. George Nabida, the district's records officer. In 2018 a team from Michigan began working with the Judiciary of Uganda to rescue and catalogue the legal archives of the High Court; once that work was complete, the team turned its attention to the archives of the Mengo Court, the highest appeals court within the legal system of the kingdom of Buganda. The team was led by Sauda Nabukenya, whose indomitable energy sustained the whole undertaking. I thank the former permanent secretary, Kagole Kivumbi, the current permanent secretary, Pius Bigirimana, and the former chief justice, Bart Katureebe, who immediately saw the point of this important work. In 2011 and 2012 a team from Michigan collaborated with colleagues from the National Archives to put their collections in order; and in 2016 the collection was moved from Entebbe to Kampala, where it now inhabits a wonderful new building. My thanks to the commissioner for archives, Lilian Ariso, and the national archivist, Justine Nalwoga. Under their stewardship the newly created Uganda National Records Centre and Archives has become a source of hope for all of us who study Uganda's history.

This book has largely been written at the University of Michigan, a congenial place from which to think critically about Africa's past and future. I thank Gabrielle Hecht, Nancy Rose Hunt, Butch Ware, Raevin Jimenez, Jason Young, Carina Ray, Rebecca Scott, Anne Pitcher, Martin Murray, Adam Ashforth, Omolade Adunbi, and other Michigan colleagues for the insight, advice, and knowledge they have given me. The African Studies Center has supported my work in a great number of ways, and I have particularly benefited from my long involvement in the African Heritage Initiative. My thanks to Ray Silverman, Judy Irvine, Kelly Askew, Ciraj Rassool, Kodzo Gavua, Geoff Emberling, Henrike Florusbosch, and others who have helped me think creatively about memory, museums, and the making of history. I've had the tremendous good fortune to work with a number of talented, smart, principled Ph.D. students: Chris Tounsel, Edgar Taylor, Ashley Rockenbach, Doreen Kembabazi, Benedito Machava, Sara Katz, Nana Quarshie, Tara Weinberg, Lamin Manneh, Emma Park, Kevin Donovan, Sauda Nabukenya, Kristen Connor, and latterly Comfort Mtotha, Jessie Bakitunda, Norah Langat, Dennis Simiyu, Inhae Yap, and Talitha Pam. All these talented people have read this book in part or in whole and given me their ideas and their criticism. Working with them in their studies has been one of my greatest pleasures.

I've presented chapters drawn from the manuscript before a number of engaging audiences. My thanks to the conveners and participants at lectures and seminars organized by the Department of History at Duke University; the Interdisciplinary Center for the Study of Global Change at the University of Minnesota; the Program of African Studies at Northwestern University; the Department of Religious Studies at Lafayette College; the Wits Institute for Social and Economic Research; the Department of History at Emory University; the Department of History at the Johns Hopkins University; the Re:Work Institute at Humboldt University in Berlin; the Centre of African Studies at Cambridge University; the Centre for the History of Colonialisms at the University of Kent; the Centre for Humanities Research at the University of the Western Cape; the Royal Historical Society; the Institute for Religion, Culture and Public Life at Columbia University; and the Center for African Studies at Harvard University. Ten years ago the Mellon Foundation awarded the African Studies Center at Michigan and the Wits Institute for Social and Economic Research in Johannesburg a joint grant to enable academic exchange between our two institutions; and over the course of time I've greatly benefited from the workshops that WiSER and Michigan have together organized. I thank Keith Breckenridge, Hlonipha Mokoena, Sarah Nuttall, and other Wits colleagues who have enriched this exchange.

Ezron Muhumuza worked with me to conduct interviews among now elderly Rwenzururu veterans in Kasese, Bundibugyo, and other parts of the Rwenzori Mountains. I am grateful to him for his knowledge and his commitment. The late Tom Stacey gave me access to his important collection of papers and photographs concerning the Rwenzururu movement, and I am thankful that his family has allowed me to reprint a few of the photos here. Colleagues at Makerere University in Kampala have been charitable and welcoming. Over the course of years I've presented material drawn from this book at lectures organized by the Makerere Institute for Social Research, the Department of History, and the College of Humanities and Social Sciences. At Makerere I was for several years a research associate at the Makerere Institute for Social Research. I thank Prof. Nakanyike Musisi, Dr. Frederick Golooba-Mutebi, and Prof. Mahmood Mamdani, the institute's directors, for standing behind me. Latterly the School of Social Sciences welcomed me, and I am grateful to Prof. Andrew

State, who made me a research associate. The Department of History and Heritage Studies has been an intellectual home, and I am thankful to the department's leaders: Drs. Deo Katono, Simon Rutabajuka, Godfrey Asiimwe, Pamela Khanakwa, and Charlotte Mafumbo. Thanks also to Edgar Taylor and Christopher Muhoozi, who are among my most valued interlocutors and friends. For your generosity and goodwill: thank you to all my Makerere colleagues.

My work in Uganda has been made much more pleasant by Godfrey and Joyce Asiimwe, Andrew and Eliz State, Daudi Ngendo Tshimba, Simon and Jophine Kaheru, Daudi Mpanga, Anna Adima, and other friends. James Tumusime has been a constant source of advice and insight. Many thanks to Simon Mpanga, who has worked hard to make me into a competent speaker of Luganda. Many thanks also to Mayimuna Amin and Jaffar Amin, who over the space of time have shared their personal memories of their father with me.

I am grateful to the Kellogg Institute for International Studies at the University of Notre Dame, which made me a visiting fellow in 2014, and the Re:Work Institute at Humboldt University, which made me a visiting fellow in 2019. The American Council of Learned Societies awarded me a fellowship in 2016, and in the same year the John Simon Guggenheim Foundation made me a fellow in African Studies. I thank both these institutions. In 2017 I was made a MacArthur fellow. Support from the MacArthur Foundation has been particularly consequential for me, and I am hugely thankful to Cecilia Conrad and the foundation's leadership for their investment in my work.

In 2019 and 2020 I had the pleasure of working with Richard Vokes, Nelson Abiti, and Edgar Taylor in the curation of *The Unseen Archive of Idi Amin: Photographs from the Uganda Broadcasting Corporation*, an exhibition that was on show for eight months at the Uganda Museum in Kampala. Later I worked with Pamela Khanakwa, Edgar Taylor, and David Ngendo Tshimba to put on *Uganda at 60: An Exhibition of National History*, which opened at the Uganda Museum in October 2022. Rose Mwanja Nkaale, the Commissioner for Monuments and Museums, and her successor Jackline Nyiracyiza supported both exhibitions. I am grateful to all of these talented people. They helped me see how historical work can enable civil discourse.

Jaya Chatterjee, Amanda Gerstenfeld, Erica Hanson, and their colleagues at Yale University Press have taken great care over this book, and

I thank them. Gabriel Moss prepared the map. Parts of Chapter 8 have been published in Jacob Olupona, ed., *Evangelical Christianity and the Transformation of Africa* (Georgetown University Press, 2025).

My colleague and friend David Ngendo Tshimba read the whole of this manuscript and generously gave me his trenchant criticisms. Jean Allman—formerly my teacher, now my co-editor and friend—read through parts of the book and gave me advice. So did Tim Parsons, fellow historian, valued friend, and insightful advocate for popular history. Over the years I have benefited from the insight of Darren Walhof, Julian Murchison, Carina Ray, Ben Fortson, Pierre LeMorvan, Felicity Wong, Karin Barber, Harri Englund, and other friends. Allen Isaacman has long been a mentor and an adviser, and I am thankful for his support for my work. John Lonsdale has been my most consistent, most charitable, and most insightful reader, and I remain tremendously grateful for his mentorship and his friendship.

It has taken me almost fifteen years to write this book, and through it all my closest and dearest critics have been Rebecca Peterson and Adeline Mbabazi Peterson. They have helped me see that historical thinking—like all intellectual life—happens in the middle of everything. I have loved living through the pressures and the joys of our time in their company. I dedicate this book to my parents, Rodney and Linda Peterson. Their love for each other and their love for the world have been a constant example for me. This book is for them.

A POPULAR HISTORY OF IDI AMIN'S UGANDA

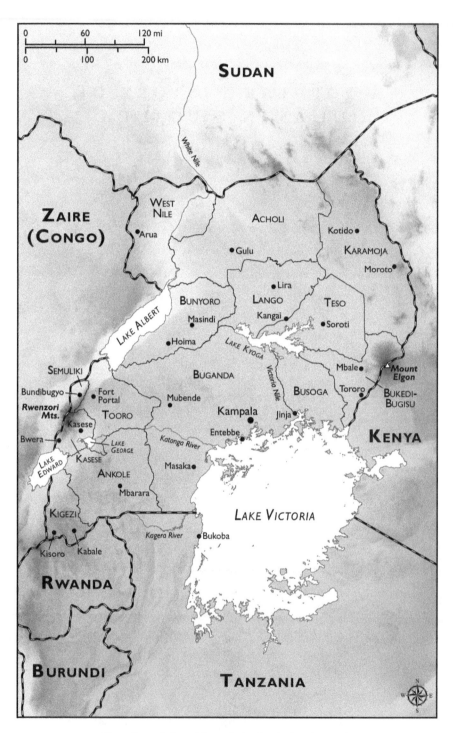

Uganda and East Africa (Map by Gabriel Moss)

Introduction

IN THE LAST DAYS of 1974 the artist Eli Kyeyune was hard at work in Lugogo Stadium. He was putting together an exhibition showcasing the art of Uganda's painters and sculptors. Earlier that year the International Commission of Jurists had issued a report accusing the government of Idi Amin—who had ruled Uganda since 1971—of causing the deaths of tens of thousands of innocent people.[1] As Kyeyune worked, a commission of inquiry was collecting evidence concerning the fate of people who had disappeared. Hundreds of courageous, grieving men and women were filing before the commissioners to testify against the powerful people who had wronged them.[2]

Eli Kyeyune must have known about all of this, but his life's work was there, on the grounds of Lugogo Stadium, and it demanded all his energy. President Amin's government had promised his committee a budget of 400,000 shillings, and with the money Kyeyune and his colleagues had hoped to purchase Uganda's "best and most outstanding artistic treasures" from the British Museum, which held thousands of objects acquired from Uganda in colonial times. They had also hoped to commission three hundred artworks from contemporary painters and sculptors. All these ambitious plans came to nothing. At the last minute, the government had reduced the project's budget to a bare 10,000 shillings.[3] With the opening of the exhibition just days away, Kyeyune commandeered a vehicle and drove from one end of Uganda to the other, pleading with artists to donate their work. On 30 December he called his committee to the stadium to lay out the show.[4] There was only one wall, a flimsy partition that Kyeyune had erected in the edge of the football pitch. Over the course of several hours the committee sketched out a rough plan. They packed as many paintings as possible onto the partition and placed the pottery in a semicircle in front of the wall. Less consequential works were placed on tables around the edge of the field. Kyeyune slept at the stadium for four nights, laboring long hours to assemble the exhibition. It was, he reported, a time of "exhaustion caused by hard work and sleeplessness."[5]

Idi Amin was one of the twentieth century's most menacing monsters, a byword for inhumanity and brutality. Journalists, activists, and historians have composed dozens of damning reports that illuminate the florid violence of his regime. These books bear sensational titles, likening the Amin government to the awful history of twentieth-century Europe: *Idi Amin: Hitler in Africa; Idi Amin: Death-Light of Africa; Uganda Holocaust.*[6] In his own time Amin was called "Africa's Most Evil Man."[7] When the curators at Madame Tussauds in London surveyed their two million visitors in 1976, they found Amin to be the second most hated figure in the whole of their museum, behind Adolf Hitler.[8] Today Amin is an inescapable figure in books and film documentaries about the most evil characters in world history. In the children's book series "History's Villains," Amin appears in the company of Attila the Hun and the conquistador Francisco Pizarro. In the Netflix documentary series *How to Become a Tyrant*—to which I was an on-camera contributor—he's third in the list of exemplary dictators, behind Hitler and Stalin.[9]

In a time of pervasive violence, how did Eli Kyeyune have time for art? He was a man of great skill, a painter who—according to one Kenyan critic—had "more talent in his little finger than half of the other artists in Nairobi put together."[10] Another Kenyan critic thought that his early works were "definitely the best paintings an East African has yet done," and called him "probably the finest colorist in East Africa."[11] American connoisseurs held him in similarly high esteem. In 1969 his paintings were showcased in New York, at the first American exhibition of the Society of East African Artists.[12] In 1970 the scholarly journal *African Arts* awarded him a prize and printed two of his paintings on its pages.[13] He regarded himself as a man of principle. "I have become the African expressionist of the Uhuru [Freedom] era," he told an audience. "I express myself with confidence because my people are confident people, since they are their own masters."[14]

Like many other patriotic, talented people, Eli Kyeyune was convinced that Idi Amin's regime heralded a new era of justice and liberation. He was acting with the eyes of history upon him. When the Amin government removed the statue of King George VI from its pedestal in Kampala, Kyeyune published an editorial letter calling it a "symbol of the cultural revolution."[15] The toppling of Britain's king marked a

> turning point, whereby colonial symbols have inevitably to give way to indigenous African symbols. Ugandans have been fed up with a dying colonial policy, which destroyed Ugandan culture and turned a few Ugandans into black Europeans. . . . Uganda has many heroes, ranging from ancient kings and chiefs, to religious martyrs, to world famous sportsmen, and to great modern African statesmen.

He called for new monuments honoring the heroes of old, for galleries where Uganda's history could be recounted and celebrated, and for books celebrating Uganda's art and culture. "This is not a remote call for action in a country where action does not exist," Kyeyune concluded. "If at any time there is action anywhere in the world, it is right here in Uganda."

Uganda had won its national independence in 1962 under the leadership of a politician named Milton Obote. There was no war fought to secure Ugandans' freedom from British colonists. No mass movement propelled Milton Obote to power. There were no martyrs to lament, and neither were there heroes to hymn. Uganda's decolonization was boringly undramatic: it was won in a series of stage-managed elections. The first time Obote stood for election was in 1957, when he sought a seat on the colonial legislature. He won his home district by a vote of 48 to 7.[16] By 1960 he had maneuvered himself into the leadership of Uganda People's Congress, a political party that had been patched together out of the wreckage of several older organizations. Unlike many of his contemporaries among Africa's nationalist leaders, Obote was never imprisoned by British authorities. His party came to power out of a back-room deal struck with the leading politicians of Buganda, Uganda's most prosperous and most powerful kingdom. In October 1962, after a national election, Milton Obote became independent Uganda's first prime minister and leader of government business, but the president and head of state was Frederick Muteesa, king of Buganda.

Obote's government was among the weakest in Africa. Under the constitution that brought independence to Uganda there were five kingdoms that enjoyed a measure of political autonomy. The most powerful kingdom—Buganda—had its own police force, court system, and king. In May 1966, Obote, determined to build up his authority, sent in the military to crush the palace of Buganda's king. More than a thousand people are said to have been killed in the ensuing melee. Buganda's king, who barely escaped the cataclysm, went into an unhappy exile in London. Having abolished Uganda's kingdoms, Obote pushed a new constitution through Parliament, centralized the court system, and installed himself as president. It was, he declared, a victory for national unity.

General Idi Amin rose to prominence in public life as an indispensable instrument of Milton Obote's government. He was in command that day in May 1966 when the Uganda Army assaulted the king's palace. Observers saw him clubbing a prostrate old man over the head. In the years that followed, General Amin avidly crushed opposition in Buganda and other parts of the country. On 25 January 1971, while Obote was attending a conference in Singapore, Amin summoned the army, seized the seat of government, and installed himself as president of the Second Republic of Uganda.

Over the course of his years in power, President Amin's government faced overwhelming economic challenges: a global depression, spiraling inflation, worldwide shortages in agricultural commodities. He also faced serious political opposition. Julius Nyerere, president of neighboring Tanzania, offered asylum to Milton Obote and harbored militias that were intent on overthrowing Amin's regime. Within Uganda there was opposition, too. Kampala was brimming with coups, plots, and schemes foretelling the imminent overthrow of Amin's regime. There was an attempted coup in April 1972, when disaffected army officers planned an insurrection; another in March 1974, when Christian officers in the Uganda Army raised a mutiny, broke into State House, and nearly killed the president; a third in February 1975, when Amin, riding in his Maserati, survived a nighttime ambush; a fourth in June 1976, when assailants lobbed three grenades into a crowd that President Amin was addressing, killing his bodyguard; a fifth in January 1977, when disgruntled soldiers planned to shoot Amin during the ceremonies marking the anniversary of the coup that brought him to power.[17] According to one account Amin survived seven assassination attempts during his first three years in power. Predicting the downfall of Amin's government became a favorite pastime for journalists in the United States and Europe. "Uganda's Amin Living on Borrowed Time" was the headline of an article published in 1975.[18]

Idi Amin remained in power until April 1979. In the end, it was not popular discontent or political opposition that brought his rule to a close. President Amin was ousted because a foreign adversary—Tanzania—sent its regular army across the border and, after several months of fighting, drove Amin and his army from the country.

How, in the face of overwhelming adversity, did Idi Amin hold power in Uganda for eight long years? It is often said that he governed through terror, using public displays of violence to intimidate people and crush opposition. This book—by contrast—focuses on motivated people like Eli Kyeyune who, whether out of an earnest sense of duty or a belief in historic destiny, made government work. Thousands of ordinary people served Idi Amin's government. They were not soldiers or menacing intelligence operatives. They were clerks, bureaucrats, curators, musicians, priests, teachers, and businessmen. They worked hard to impose order, even in unlikely circumstances. One prominent critic famously called Idi Amin's Uganda a "state of blood."[19] I argue, by contrast, that it was a government of action.

The singular accomplishment of the Amin regime was this: to transform the boring, technical work of government into a thrilling battle for racial and political liberation. Amin's regime invited Ugandans to see themselves as frontline soldiers in a global war against the forces of oppression. The field of public administration became an arena where people could fight for their freedom. The door to politics—hitherto closed to all but a small class of experts—was suddenly opened wide. In Uganda as in many other places, the 1970s were a time of economic crisis, as worldwide shortages in commodities crippled industries and drove price inflation. The building blocks of governance were in short supply, and infrastructures of all kinds were breaking down. Ordinary people were quite suddenly called into service. Matters that had formerly been the responsibility of government technicians were, all at once, made into campaigns that Ugandans mobilized around. Cotton production needed to be doubled, then doubled again; city streets needed to be cleaned up; businesses needed to be liberated from outsiders' ownership; cultures needed to be freed from the vestiges of colonialism. History needed to be remade, too. Revolutionary curators transformed a host of otherwise unremarkable sites into sacred grounds and made heroes of previously nondescript characters. Idi Amin's regime was built on the idealism, knowledge, and energy of ordinary people, who responded to the urgent demands of their time by sacrificing their time, energy, and treasure to make government work.

Time was in especially short supply. Radio Uganda—the national broadcaster—set the pace of public life. Over the airwaves Amin announced policy, buttonholed individuals and groups, and imposed obligations upon them. Categories of people who had not previously existed in public life were suddenly summoned to take on new responsibilities. Even the most obscure administrative questions became matters of consequence. For many people it was a cause for inspiration, a source of orientation and excitement. It could inspire works of great personal commitment. Here was the fuel with which the Amin government operated: it channeled and directed commoners' talents, their proprietary sense of responsibility, their prejudices and enmities, their energy and commitment.

This book brings the political logic of Amin's regime into view. It is not a chronicle of dysfunction and death. Neither is it a biography of Idi Amin. This book explains how, in a time of spectacular violence in public life, patriotic men and women found reason to invest their energies in serving Africa's most brutal dictatorship.

It is a good time for all of us, whoever and wherever we are, to study the history of Idi Amin's dictatorship. All over the world, populist majorities are on the march, repossessing cultural and political properties that they regard as their own. The racial logic of economic and cultural liberation has now become a mortal threat to democratic governments in Africa, Europe, and the United States. American democracy is imperiled by right-wing demagogues who have mobilized to "take our country back" from immigrants and other racial outsiders. In Africa there is a new enthusiasm for military rulers and their authoritarian efficiency. In Burkina Faso and Gabon, soldiers have overthrown corrupt civilian governments, vowing to push back the lingering colonial influences and reclaim national patrimonies. In Guinea and Mali ascendant soldiers have pledged to nationalize mines owned by French firms, while in Burkina Faso the new military government has adopted constitutional provisions that displace French from its status as a national language.

In these and in many other places autocratic leaders promise to restore lost freedoms, reclaim lost properties, and empower a majority that has been dispossessed by outsiders and interlopers. They manufacture grievance by contrasting the enrichment of an outsider minority with the impoverishment of the majority. In so doing they make their followers foresee their destiny: to win back their inheritance, to exorcise the invidious influence of foreigners.

That is one of the ironies of the story I am about to unfold. One of history's most infamous dictators was regarded, in his own time, as a hero of cultural and economic liberation.

In Uganda today there are very few places that honor the memory of those who suffered and died during the 1970s. The buildings that were once central to the Amin regime's power have been leveled or re-purposed. "Command Post," which was Idi Amin's residence in Kampala, now houses the North Korean embassy. Nile Mansions, where hundreds of men and women were tortured and murdered, has been made into a high-end hotel. Uganda's national museum is empty of displays that deal with the events of the 1960s and '70s. The history books that secondary school students are assigned say very little about their country's most infamous ruler. Very few people have been held to account for their deeds.

In the absence of a memorial infrastructure, the work of assessing the Amin era has fallen largely to private individuals. Almost as soon as Idi Amin was overthrown, Ugandans began publishing earnest scholarship that analyzed the reasons for his disastrous government. Answers were urgently needed. The evils of the old regime needed to be identified, then put to rest. It fell to historians to act as prosecutor, judge, and jury. "What went wrong with our independence?" asked Semakula Kiwanuka in his book *Amin and the Tragedy of Uganda*, published in 1979. "How can we prevent a recurrence of such tragedies?"[20] Samwiri Karugire titled his book *The Roots of Instability in Uganda*.[21] Mahmood Mamdani vowed to "dissect every nerve and muscle of fascism" in order to "identify the conditions and forces" that upheld Amin's regime; while Phares Mutibwa similarly promised to "dissect . . . every nerve and muscle" of Amin's malign regime "so as to identify the conditions that made it possible."[22]

It was as if historians were coroners. Many Ugandan scholars worked on behalf of institutions that were rebuilding the country after years of devastating conflict. Professor Mamdani's research was sponsored by the World Council of Churches. The economist Will Kaberuka, the author of a book in 1990 about "colonialism and underdevelopment," was economic adviser to Uganda's new government.[23] Professor Karugire was director-general of Uganda's customs agency.[24] Phares Mutibwa was a member of the committee charged with composing a new constitution for Uganda. These scholars wrote history to advance the work of political reconstruction. It was a way to harness their skills in the service of the nation. They differed in their political commitments, but they shared an underlying conviction that the "social origins of violence" could be found in Uganda's past. Abdu Kasozi, for instance, set out to "locate the structural weaknesses in Uganda's society on which dictators and men of violence thrive."[25] His book ended with a conclusion listing the means by which Uganda's political malignancies could be rectified. Kiwanuka concluded his 1979 book by urging Ugandans to "remove the roots" of dictatorship and misgovernment; Professor Mamdani likewise sought to "explain" the reasons for people's suffering, in order to "be in a position to build a movement to identify, isolate and defeat" social and political forces working against the common good.[26]

That was the role that Uganda's historians claimed in the wake of Idi Amin's ouster. The past had bequeathed an unstable foundation for public life. Working in the service of the new regime, historians saw it as their duty to identify failures in the making of their country, evaluate and adjudicate inadequacies in the national fabric, and point toward remedies.

Since that first wave of writing there has been relatively little scholarly work on Uganda's postcolonial history. The space for historical evaluation was closed by Uganda's current president, Yoweri Museveni, who came to power in 1986 promising to turn the page on his country's violent past. His government encouraged Ugandans to look toward the promising future, not to a bloody and forgettable history. The traumas of Uganda's history had to be pushed out of view. Shortly after it came to power, the Museveni government set up a Commission of Inquiry into Violations of Human Rights. The commission was empowered to look into the period between 9 October 1962 (the date of Uganda's independence) and 25 January 1986 (when Museveni's army had marched into Kampala).[27] Commissioners were meant to investigate a huge range of crimes: arbitrary arrests, detention without trial, torture, the "displacement of people," and the "subjection to discriminatory treatment by virtue of race, tribe, place of origin, political opinion, creed, or sex." The commission was chaired by Arthur Oder, justice of the Supreme Court; the six members included a lawyer, a medical doctor, and a professor of history.

Oder initially hoped that he would be given powers proportionate to the task before him: he asked the government to extradite Idi Amin and Milton Obote, both of whom were living in exile, on charges of violating human rights.[28] Nothing came of this request, but Oder and his colleagues were full of confidence about their work. As Oder argued:

Ugandans should not think that the incidents which concern
them happened so long ago that it is useless to raise [them] now.
They may say "What is the use of digging up the past"? Ugandans should not let bygones be bygones. . . . I would like people
to be positive and to come forward and talk about their human
rights because that is the only way to prevent the possible viola-
tion of human rights again.[29]

The commission held hearings in virtually every region of the country,
and 608 people gave oral evidence. The written record of the testimony
ran to eighteen large volumes. It was full of specific, graphic, and often
horrifying descriptions of violence committed against Uganda's people
by agents of Idi Amin and Milton Obote.

All of this was a way of miniaturizing the traumas of the past, of wrangling imposing questions into a manageable container, of pushing historical controversy out of view. Provisions from government were lamentably
small. Commissioners' salaries were paid infrequently, and they were constantly short of pens, paper, and file covers.[30] In 1988—two years after Justice Oder's commission began taking evidence—a journalist purchased
some tomatoes at one of Kampala's markets. They were wrapped in a page
recording the testimony of the former minister of economic planning in
Amin's government.[31] Other vendors were using typed paperwork from the
commission's secretariat to wrap biscuits, peanuts, and other items for sale.

Justice Oder's report was finally published in 1994. It attracted almost
no attention, and today it is hard to find copies of the report in Uganda.[32]
Only five people were prosecuted for crimes they committed under Idi
Amin's regime, and as far as I know only two people were convicted.
Most of the killers faced no legal punishment for their bloody deeds. In
1987 the government declared a general amnesty for "those who were
members of former armies and fighting groups . . . and who by their past
activities would be liable for prosecution."[33] Several thousand people who
had served Amin's government took advantage of this blanket amnesty.
That is how democratic discussion over the lessons of history was fore-
stalled, how Uganda's government closed off claims for justice, compensation, and restitution. The investigation the earnest commissioners
pursued—so full of detail, replete with actionable evidence—had virtually
no consequences.

In the absence of a social and political consensus, it has been hard for
contemporary historians to know what to say about Idi Amin's regime.

The most recent national history of Uganda is largely silent about Amin's regime, acknowledging that the subject "remains shrouded in fear, guilt and simply ignorance."[34] A new biography of Amin—while full of insight—is based almost entirely on the published accounts of journalists, diplomats, and historians.[35] Some writers have been busy refurbishing the reputation of Uganda's second president. One new book is titled *The Other Side of Idi Amin;* another, co-authored by Amin's son, has the title *Idi Amin: Hero or Villain?*[36]

========

The archives of Kabarole District in western Uganda were until recently kept in the "Boma," a cavernous building that had once been the headquarters of the local government. When I visited the attic repository in 2005, I found that wasps had fully occupied the place. Their nests were everywhere—on the flaps of the cardboard boxes, on the bottom of the wooden shelves, on the files themselves. It took more than a week to clear the attic of its inhospitable residents. One memorable morning I found myself standing back-to-back with a valiant records officer, cans of insecticide in both hands, spraying waves of angry bugs as they surged toward us. We went through five cans of "Doom," two cans of "Kill," and one can of "Bop." None of it worked particularly well. I spent several months reading files in the attic repository, and every day I had to contend with wasps who were determined to leave their mark on me.

It took a great amount of work to redeem the Kabarole archive from its dereliction. In 2009 colleagues and I moved the papers to the campus of Mountains of the Moon University, a new institution supported by the local government council. We hired and trained a small team of university graduates to do the work; local carpenters constructed the desks and shelves; file folders, brushes, and other cleaning supplies were sourced from Kampala. Acid-free boxes had to be brought in from India. Over the course of several months the team removed the files from their decaying folders, extracted staples, clips, and other bits of metal, cleaned the papers of dirt and dust, and placed them into new file covers. Then the team set to work reboxing and inventorying the collection. In 2011 we purchased several scanners and computers, and over the ensuing year the team digitized the whole archive.

Once the Kabarole District collection had been digitized we brought other local government archives into the university's working room. First was the archive of the Tooro kingdom, which was kept in a basement

below the local council chamber in Fort Portal. The recovery of that archive required an archaeologist's skill, for the historical papers had been
buried in layers of discarded bureaucratic paraphernalia. The top layer
consisted of old bicycles, broken circulating fans, broken parts of photo-
copiers, and disused desktop computer terminals. Below that was a layer
of dot-matrix paperwork from the 1980s. The oldest files—handwritten,
dating to the 1930s and '40s—could be found at the bottom of the pile.
The team unearthed, organized, and digitized those papers, then started
work on another project, focused on the archives of Hoima District.
There we found the papers piled high on shelves in a mechanic's shed
behind the local government offices.

After more than a decade of work, the archivists at Mountains of the
Moon University have created a digital collection of 500,000 scans. It is, as far
as we know, the largest digital archive of government documents in Africa.[37]

As the digitizing of western Uganda's provincial archives has gone
along, I've also been working with colleagues in other parts of the country to rehabilitate the paper archives of Uganda's government. In 2011
and 2012 a team of graduate students from Michigan and Makerere University organized the material in the Uganda National Archives. Most of
the collection had been piled on shelves in a warren of basement rooms
below a government building in Entebbe. The team put the files into
order and created a catalogue of nine volumes to describe the collection.
In 2013 we organized and inventoried the substantial archive of Kabale
District, in Uganda's south. That archive is now held in a sunlit attic
above the district headquarters. In 2015 we salvaged the waterlogged archives of Jinja District. The papers had been kept in a basement that had
flooded during the seasonal rains. We brought the papers above ground,
dried everything out, scraped off the mud, organized the files, and created an inventory. In 2018 a large team from Michigan and the Judiciary
of Uganda organized the archives of the High Court. The files had been
kept in the basement of an old court building in the center of Kampala.[38]
Most recently we worked with the judiciary to rehabilitate the archives
of the Mengo Court. It was once the highest court of appeal in the Buganda kingdom's legal system and one of the oldest venues for jurispru-
dential reasoning in eastern Africa. After Milton Obote abolished
Uganda's kingdoms in 1967, the Buganda court system was dissolved,
and all the case files were piled into a storeroom in the basement. The
building was repurposed as a government magistrate's court. By 2019,
when we began to work on the archive, a substantial number of papers

had disappeared, as prisoners awaiting trial would reach through the ventilation grate and withdraw papers to use in a nearby toilet. It took months of hard work to put the archive of the Mengo Court in order. Like many of the collections we have organized, it is now on deposit in the newly built repository of the National Records Centre and Archives in Kampala.[39]

All this labor has brought to light a profuse assortment of paperwork created by people who served Idi Amin's regime. As it turns out, government authorities of the 1970s were prolific correspondents, inveterate writers of reports, compulsive keepers of records, and avid contributors to news media. When in 1975 the government official responsible for Rwenzori District was transferred to another place, he made a point of emphasizing—in a meeting with his colleagues—that his deeds should be remembered. "Be it therefore recorded in the annals of Rwenzori District that whatever I did and whatever the Pioneer District Officers . . . did was done for God and Our Country," he said.[40] Where else did the annals of Rwenzori District—or any other place—reside except in the files of local government? Today district archives all over Uganda bulge with papers authored by low-level government servants, who duplicated and distributed their reports to fellow officials. In August 1976, for instance, the government's agriculture officer in Bundibugyo made dozens of copies of an unremarkable letter addressed to one of his subordinates. He mailed it out to all of Uganda's district agriculture officers.[41] Marooned in a remote province and lacking petroleum to fuel his motorcycle, the officer had not left his office for five months. By distributing his correspondence to colleagues across Uganda, he found a means to make his labors visible. The archives of the Amin government are full of paperwork produced by men who, like the official in remote Bundibugyo, felt the need to broadcast evidence of their work.

For the people who served Idi Amin's regime the circulation of paperwork was a means to ensure that their deeds would be noticed, credited, and rewarded. It was also a passport to longevity. In 1977, the new government archivist proclaimed that archives were "the instruments from which the present and future generations can learn about the history of this nation in its correct perspective."[42] The documents "depict our national heritage," she argued. She ordered that archive files be stored in rooms without leaky roofs, in places free of insects. The following year President Amin retained the services of a consultant from UNESCO to assess Uganda's archives service. He was J. M. Akita, for-

merly the chief archivist of Ghana. In his report Mr. Akita recommended
a dramatic expansion of Uganda's archival infrastructure. He wanted the
national archives to be moved from their remote location in Entebbe to
a new building in Kampala. He recommended the creation of a conservation laboratory where damaged files could be properly restored, and he
suggested that the staff establishment be expanded to sixty people.[43]

Mr. Akita's plan never came to fruition, for Idi Amin was overthrown
before it could be put into effect. Even so, his ambitious plan helps us see
how much hope the patriots of the 1970s placed in the archives. Their
impressive commitment to record-keeping reflected the uncertainties of
their position, their constant need to impress the authorities in the center. In insecure and dangerous times it was a way of proving their commitment, of gaining traction with higher-ups in Kampala, of making
themselves exemplary. It also reflected a core conviction: that their work
deserved to be noticed, honored, and remembered by Uganda's people.
Idi Amin's dictatorship was documented from the bottom up, by men
and women whose marginality in public life drove them to create written
evidence of their industriousness.

Not everyone got into the archive, because not everyone wanted to
be noticed by the authorities of Amin's government. Some people lived
off the grid, away from centers of power and beyond the reach of officials, soldiers, and agents of Amin's intelligence service. Being undocumented was a license for a kind of freedom. One such character was a
man named Rwemutwe. In 1973 a government chief in southern Uganda
reported that he had been found hiding in one of the valleys of a mountainous parish. After being imprisoned for tax delinquency, he had taken
up a peripatetic life, moving from place to place. Rwemutwe "changes his
name every now and then and even his proper home cannot be traced,"
the chief reported.[44] He found means of making himself inaccessible.
Rwemutwe's life-on-the-move was an extreme instance of a more general
lifestyle strategy. All over Uganda there were determined efforts to in-
habit unreachable places, forgotten corners, mountainous hideaways, and
hidden crannies. Thousands of people moved into Uganda's forests. In
the Semuliki forest, settlers put up houses of stone and set to work cultivating plantains, coffee, and cocoa.[45] By the late 1970s there were large
communities living in the Kibaale, Kisangi, and Rwenzori forests.[46]
Many people wanted to be unreachable.

The unexpected richness of local government archives gives
substance to this book. To find undocumented people like the itinerate

Rwemutwe, though, I have had to look outside the archives that Amin's regime created. I conducted months of research in the Rwenzori Mountains, on the remote border with Congo, talking with people who were loyalists of the "Rwenzururu" movement. Rwenzururu was founded by men and women who fought to defend mountain people's independence against the enfolding power of the government of Uganda. In the 1960s they created a government bureaucracy, a court system, a king, and an archive of their own. In the 1970s the Rwenzururu kingdom was the only place in Uganda where people could be free of Idi Amin's dictatorship. As I argue in Chapter 10, their independence was upheld by their archive, a constant source of inspiration and a fortification for Rwenzururu's particular patriotism.

Most people did not, and could not, live in an independent state. For most people Idi Amin's regime could not be ignored. Broadcast over the airwaves of Radio Uganda, the president's voice set the tempo of public life. Amin's regime was an enclosure from which it was hard to escape. It was also a forum in which patriotic people discovered a vocation.

This book focuses on people who worked—inside and outside the official bureaucracy—to make the Amin regime function. The protagonists are people whom I call "commoners." Few of them wielded substantial power. All of them had to navigate the uncertain relationship between the capital and the periphery. They worked in overlooked places, distant from the center of Amin's regime. That is why they created so much paperwork. They had to make up for their political marginality through constant acts of archival self-documentation.

Many of the enthusiasts who served Amin's regime were demagogues. Others were earnest patriots. Most of them were men. They regarded independent women—their fashion, their sexuality, their freedom—as a danger to their people's integrity. None of them were "willing executioners," as Daniel Goldhagen termed the ordinary Germans who supported Hitler's extermination of the Jews.[47] The ordinary Ugandans on whom this book focuses were not driven by an "eliminationist" ideology; neither were their minds defined by a single way of seeing the world. There was no uniform creed that drove Ugandans to work for Amin's regime. Some of these ordinary Ugandans were working to build trans-African alliances and create continental solidarity. Others were earnest proprietors of endangered cultures and traditions, looking for resources to defend a way of life. Still others were professionals, habituated in routines, proud of their mastery over technologies and fields of knowledge. All of these people were caught up in the great drama of their day. They saw themselves as actors in a global war for racial and cultural justice.

I do not make judgments on the people whose lives I study in this book. The curators, bureaucrats, culture workers, scholars, and entrepreneurs described here had good reasons for their enthusiasm. I share some of the principles that they sought to advance. Perhaps you do, too. At the core of Idi Amin's program was the "Economic War," a government-run campaign to secure the commanding heights of Uganda's economy for black people. It involved a great amount of inhumanity: the expulsion of Uganda's Indian and Pakistani community; the execution of innocent people who fell afoul of government rules. But the ideas that lay behind the Economic War were widely resonant, both inside and outside Uganda. Black American activists were engaged, in those days, in building entirely new cities that were meant to create space for flourishing Black businesses.[48] American advocates for Black economic empowerment were among the most urgent supporters of Uganda's "Economic War"; and over the course of the 1970s a constant stream of pilgrims from the United States visited Uganda to learn from Idi Amin's example. Today there are ongoing efforts to rectify the racial injustices of our capitalist world economy, to carve out space and opportunity for the enrichment of people of color.[49] Idi Amin's Economic War revolted many Ugandans, and its inhumanity was legendary, but the injustices it aimed to address are enduringly relevant in our contemporary world.

Amin's war on colonial culture has likewise remained relevant. The idea that Africans should overturn the mythology of European colonialism and write their own history was foundational to the Amin regime's political program. As we shall see, it animated creative, principled work on Uganda's museums and archives. It sent curators and historians on a desperate search for new heroes to honor, new martyrs to hymn, new monuments to build. Today there is new urgency around decolonizing institutions and curricula. Activists are toppling monuments to the Confederacy in Richmond, Virginia, dragging statues of slave traders through the streets of Bristol, England, and making Cecil Rhodes fall in Cape Town and Oxford. In Uganda there are continuing efforts to re-engineer public space, to make African heroes more visible, and to push memorials to colonial heroes out of view. The culture war launched in Idi Amin's Uganda was tied up into the fabric of the ongoing world-historical struggle against racism.

The more malevolent aspects of Amin's government are likewise a continuing presence in our contemporary world. Anyone who has lived

through Donald Trump's presidency will immediately recognize my account of Idi Amin's Uganda. It is not only the braggadocio, the self-
regard, the love for military ceremony. Anyone who has spent sleepless
hours monitoring Trump's social media feed will feel sympathy for the
Uganda civil servants who had to organize their schedules around Idi
Amin's radio broadcasts. Any American will likewise recognize the bellicose demagoguery of Idi Amin's government. The demonization of social
and racial minorities, the targeting of immigrants, the sidelining of ex-
pert authorities: all of this is a continuing part of politics in the United
States, Europe, and Africa.

Idi Amin's Uganda was not a singular episode in a faraway place. It
was a premonition of our contemporary times.

═════

Democracy, as recent scholarly work shows, has an infrastructure.[50] So
does dictatorship. At the center of this book is the history of Radio
Uganda. With its power to (apparently) bridge geographical distance and
project a signal to far distant places, radio was a novelty in Uganda's public life. Radio helped make Idi Amin a dictator. That is the first of the
major themes that orient this book. Radio was a megaphone by which the
Amin regime could admonish, instruct, and mobilize constituencies that
were otherwise outside its reach. Technologies of communication shape
politics: they make some kinds of communities thinkable while foreclos-
ing others.[51] In Amin's Uganda the immediacy of radio broadcasting was
transformative. It stripped away time for dialogue and imparted an urgency to government work. Social and political constituencies that had
been cloudy and hard to define were, quite suddenly, spurred into action.
There was no mechanism for feedback, for argument, or for debate.
There were goals that had to be met. People had to be mobilized. That is
what Idi Amin's government-by-radio entailed: a greatly enlarged demand for public service; a greatly heightened tempo in civic affairs.

However powerful the signal seemed to be, however pressing the demands were, it was human labor that made the government work. All the
infrastructures on which the Amin government rested needed constant
superintendence from skillful, committed people. That is the irony that
underlays Amin's dictatorship. Amin's regime was upheld by the energy
and commitment of ordinary people who, voluntarily or through com-
pulsion, sacrificed their time and energy to serve the public interest. People had to work to overcome shortfalls in the mechanics, to ensure that

the broadcast was smooth and uninterrupted, that the monument did not crack and fall, that the performance was authentic. People had to stand in for infrastructures that could not carry the political weight assigned to them.[52] They had to fill in gaps, overcome blockages, cover up insufficiencies.

The protagonists of this book are people who made Idi Amin's government of action function. They were engaged in maintenance, ensuring that technologies, buildings, and routines did not decay with time. Their work was rarely compensated; ordinarily, it was invisible. That is how culture works: it makes the vexed process of its construction invisible. No one sees the stagehand in a musical performance, just as no one watches the musicians practicing and perfecting their art. No one sees the curator assembling exhibitions, organizing displays, crafting a storyline. No one hears from the engineer who gets the broadcast on the air. In these and in other arenas of culture the backstage is screened off.

This book brings the hidden machinery of cultural and political life in Amin's Uganda into focus. One chapter is about an earnest man named John Tumusiime, a government "culture officer" in southern Uganda, who spent years building a memorial to the end of the First World War at an inconspicuous and inappropriate place. Another chapter is about John Mbiti, theologian and philosopher, who spent the early 1970s sorting out the elements of African Traditional Religion, even as the world around him fell apart. A further chapter focuses on Peter Wankulu, a worker at a sugarcane factory who created a series of remarkable collages to advocate for pan-African unity. These and other men devoted their time and their energy to making the promises of the era real. They were creative, talented people who, out of an earnest sense of responsibility, dedicated themselves to fighting Idi Amin's culture wars.

Was their enthusiasm for the Amin regime a charade, masking their real views on public life? It is hard to know. Over the course of more than a decade I have helped to put together three museum exhibitions to encourage public deliberation around the events of the 1970s. The first exhibition, which was shown at Uganda's national museum, featured previously hidden photographs made by government cameramen; the second, which marked the sixtieth anniversary of Uganda's independence, featured archival documents, memorabilia, and artifacts; the third, convened in the precincts of the Catholic cathedral, was about the history of the church. Through this work I've come to know some of the leading figures in Idi Amin's regime. The man who was once Amin's private secretary helped me identify the individuals pictured in the government photographs. The man who was Amin's minister of provincial administrations was the guest of honor when we opened the photographic exhibition in northwest Uganda, close to Amin's hometown. The man who was Amin's minister of education is now the chancellor of the provincial university that houses the digitized archive I've helped to create. Some of the soldiers who served in Amin's army came to see the photographic exhibition when it was on show. Idi Amin's children were, for a time, keen participants in exhibition planning. I spent several days in their company, listening to their reminiscences about their father as they went through some of the pictures we'd assembled.

Today very few of the many people who served Idi Amin's government will admit that they were once his supporters. The regime has been discredited. It is in no one's interest to express overt enthusiasm for a government that is now a byword for inhumanity. Even Amin's children equivocate about their father: they acknowledge the brutality of certain agents of his government while stressing his personal discipline and charity.

The surest proof of the sincerity of people's enthusiasm for the Amin regime can be found in their work. An astonishingly wide range of civic institutions were made to function through the self-sacrificing labor of ordinary people. People built roads and stadiums, kept monuments in order, funded Olympic athletes, and sponsored anti-apartheid activists. They made personal sacrifices to close the gap between the promise and the capacity of the state to deliver. That is how all civil institutions work: through the unremunerated work of public-spirited people. It was particularly essential in Uganda, where the demands of the day far outstripped what the machinery of government could possibly deliver.

From where did these ordinary Ugandans draw their inspiration? They thought themselves living on the front lines of the global war against racism and imperialism. That is a second theme that orients this book. In scholarship as in contemporary global diplomacy Africa is ordinarily shunted into a marginal place, a remote province far from the global center of things. That is not how Idi Amin saw the world. He wanted the headquarters of the United Nations moved to Kampala, at the geographic and political heart of the world. He put himself forward as chair of the Commonwealth. He carried on a one-way correspondence with American presidents. He offered to mediate between the recalcitrant Scots and the British crown. He launched a campaign to renovate Uganda's economy, expelling hundreds of thousands of prosperous people of Indian and Pakistani descent and handing their properties over to black Ugandans. To outside observers the expulsion of Uganda's "Asian" community was an act of inhumanity. For a great many Ugandans it was a war of liberation, a historically consequential struggle to win economic sovereignty for Africa's native people. Amin was inviting Ugandans to act as though they were at the center of things.

The distance between the locality in which commoners lived and the front line in the global war against imperialism was radically compressed. Even the most mundane aspects of civic life were made to seem important. Idi Amin's campaigns lent meaning, direction, and importance to trivial matters. At a time when foreign exchange was scarce and opportunities for international travel were strictly limited, Ugandans found it possible to live lives of worldwide importance. Some of these self-made global citizens were interlopers, inspired by Amin's government to take an active interest in matters about which they had no particular expertise. Others were visionary idealists, patching together an imaginary new world that they hoped to create in real life. Still others were vigilantes, committed to fighting battles that were not their own. All of them were self-nominated, self-propelled, and self-financed. That is what the times demanded.

Curatorial institutions played the key role in making otherwise routine civic work seem consequential. This is the third of the book's major themes. For patriotic men and women the monument, the archive, and the museum were a source of confidence and hope. Their power was this: to confer on otherwise forgettable events and otherwise fragile memories a concrete solidity, a passport to longevity.

The struggle to free Uganda's culture and history from foreign influences was one of several wars of liberation that patriotic people pursued under Idi Amin's direction. The terrain was uncertain and shifting, for rituals, music, and other performance routines were always changing in response to new tastes. That made the practice of conservation essential. Patriotic people created inventories for endangered cultural assets and built monuments to remember the achievements of newly recognized heroes. All over Uganda there was a rapid expansion in monumental architecture, as otherwise unnoticed places were turned into sites of national significance. Museum curators embraced a vastly expanded sense of mission, avidly seeking out objects that could testify to the accomplishments of the heroes of old. The instruments of curatorship were the weapons by which patriotic people could fight and win the war of cultural liberation.

Patriotic people acted in the sure conviction that the eye of history was upon them. New fronts were being opened up, new campaigns were being launched, new wars were being fought. There were new martyrs that needed to be hymned, new victories that needed to be sung. Curators, scholars, and archivists were called into service. It was their task to ensure that valorous deeds did not go unremembered. That is how the dedication and self-sacrifice of commoners were made to seem justified. There, in the archive or in the shade of the monument, it was possible to see one's private travails and personal sacrifices as chapters in an encompassing history that led toward freedom.

The tragedy of Idi Amin's Uganda is this: the wars that patriotic people fought in those years were generally fought against other Ugandans. The war of economic liberation was won by exiling Ugandan Asians, whose property was taken away and whose businesses were made into state property. The struggle against cultural imperialism was won at the expense of Baha'is, Pentecostals, Baptists, and other nonconformists, whose religious lives were foreclosed. The earnest struggle to preserve cultural property and guard African traditions was conducted through the suppression of Ugandan women's sexual and social freedom. The campaign to advance black people's economic power involved the imprisonment and execution of smugglers, cheaters, and other people who were guilty of what Idi Amin called "economic crimes." The building of national unity involved the closing down of alternative ways of life, the sidelining of royalists, and the use of military force against recalcitrant separatists.

Some Ugandans were summoned to serve in the great struggles of their day. Other Ugandans were made into unwitting targets of state-authorized violence. That is how Idi Amin's government of action worked: by naming and identifying whole communities as enemies of the state, by advancing the majority's interest at the expense of disentitled minorities.

———

This book is put together in a broadly chronological manner. The first two chapters set out a context for Idi Amin's rise to power, showing that the political tumult of decolonization made Uganda's rulers ever more reliant on military force to uphold their authority.

In the last years of British colonial rule there was a protracted and violent struggle over the country's very fabric. The prospect of majority rule terrified a great many people: it foretold a future in which a dominant group would impose its language and its interests on cultural and political minorities. Chapter 1 begins with Augustine Kamya, incendiary spokesman for the impoverished urban crowd. In December 1960 he and his unruly men pushed the leaders of the kingdom of Buganda to declare independence from Uganda. Kamya's demagoguery helped to define the architecture of the new Ugandan republic. Under the constitution that brought Uganda to independence in October 1962 the political autonomy of the Buganda kingdom was enshrined in law, and Prime Minister Milton Obote came to power as leader of one of Africa's weakest central governments. Obote set out to consolidate his authority by forcibly closing down public space.[53] In 1966 the prime minister sent the Uganda Army to crush the palace of the king of Buganda, and thereafter he pushed through a new constitution that centralized power in his hands. All at once, rituals and routines that had formerly been valued aspects of culture and community were rendered illegal. By the late 1960s, Obote's government had to depend on coercive military force to defend against the dangers that popular activists posed. That is how Idi Amin came to occupy a central place in Uganda's politics. Raised up through the ranks of the Uganda Army, he was the indispensable tool of Milton Obote's war against his own people.

On 25 January 1971, General Amin organized a coup, ousted Obote from his seat, and brought in the Second Republic of Uganda. For many people—especially in the defunct kingdom of Buganda—it was a liberation. Over the course of Amin's first year in power, though, Ganda patriots found the space of freedom dramatically constrained. In October 1971, Amin announced that none of Uganda's kingdoms would be restored. Buganda's royalists were obliged to move underground. As Chapter 2 shows, they were to become the leading critics of Amin's regime, and the most voluble members of the exile community.

The following four chapters bring the infrastructure of Idi Amin's revolutionary government into view. Amin's regime made otherwise mundane aspects of civil administration into urgent political questions needing immediate action. It commandeered people's passion and energy, dragooning them into projects and campaigns, demanding their attention and loyalty. All of it was full of violence, for the campaigning energy of the Amin government relied on the motivational power of fear. But there was also reason for enthusiasm and idealism.

Chapter 3 draws on the sound, photographic, and film archives of the Uganda Broadcasting Corporation—which I've been working to organize and preserve—to reconstruct the history of radio broadcasting in Uganda. Prior to independence, African-language newspapers had set the tempo of public life. Edited in Kampala, these newspapers were engaged with the specific contexts in which people lived. Over the course of the 1960s the space for independent newspapers was shuttered. Nervous about the influence that urban rabble-rousers exercised, the government of Milton Obote built a uniquely powerful radio service. It was a way of making the president's word definitive and inescapable. That is how, when he came to power in 1971, Idi Amin accidentally inherited one of Africa's most powerful broadcasting services.

Radio was the crucial technology through which Amin's dictatorship worked. It quickened the pace of public life, stripping away time for discussion, making the president's directives imperative. At the same time, the infrastructure for civil administration was radically constrained: shortages of paper, file covers, and petroleum made it impossible for the authorities to exert control. In conditions of dire austerity, it was commoners' passion that subsidized government work. Chapter 4 focuses on the entrepreneurs and vigilantes who sacrificed their time and their resources to meet the demands of the moment. Amin's regime was a do-it-yourself government, and a great many self-interested people developed a proprietary feeling of responsibility over matters that were far distant from their own fields of knowledge. That is how uncredentialed people came to exercise power in civil administration.

The most consequential of Idi Amin's many campaigns was the Economic War, which was launched by radio announcement in August 1972. That is the subject of Chapter 5. More than 50,000 people of Indian and Pakistani descent were given a spare three months to tie up their affairs and leave the country. For its many supporters the Economic War was a war of liberation, freeing the country's people from outsiders' control. For Uganda's "Asians"—as they were called—it was a disaster. A great many black Ugandans suffered, too. The chapter focuses on the "Economic Crimes Tribunal," by which otherwise innocent Ugandans were put on trial, before military judges, for minor infractions against the official rules that governed the buying and selling of commodities. The penalty for conviction was death. Their punishment helped to establish the Amin government's moral role: as liberator of Uganda's people from thralldom to petty self-interest.

Idi Amin's government went to war against a great many people. Many of them were Uganda's own citizens. Chapter 6 unpacks the social logic of violence. Much of the inhumanity of the Amin years grew out of the militarization of previously technical questions. Some people suffered and died because they were typified as enemies of Amin's regime. More often, though, Ugandans suffered a social death. Soldiers used their elevated position to make profits, to exact revenge, to gain immoderate leverage in their personal lives. Cultured people regarded unlettered soldiers' authority as a danger to social order. Their outrage fed their disgust with Amin's government, and their defiant effort to defend civil order was the starting place for oppositional politics.

The third part of the book showcases the passionate work that patriotic people did to liberate Uganda's culture. Under Amin's regime a host of properties had to be reorganized and freed from foreign influence. Amin's regime put Ugandans on the front line of the global struggle to defend Africa's religions, cultures, and history. For Uganda's commoners, it made difficult work seem surpassingly important.

Chapter 7 focuses on an otherwise unremarkable worker at a sugarcane factory: a man named Peter Wankulu, who made himself into a pioneering advocate of pan-African unity. In the 1960s he had written a series of essays calling on Africa's youth to unite under his leadership. In 1974 and 1975 he found a new vocation: as a collage artist, creator of visually compelling posters that made it easy to see what unity looked like. His creativity was occasioned by the Organization of African Unity, which met in Kampala in July 1975 under Idi Amin's chairmanship. Wankulu was not directly involved in the O.A.U. meeting, but like many other Ugandans, he was inspired by the global possibilities that the Amin regime opened up. From an unlikely place, he made himself into a central actor in one of the pressing matters of his time.

The Amin regime's effort to govern the unsettled world of culture is the subject of Chapter 8. There was an urgent search for cultural traditions that Ugandans could claim as their national property. Religion was one of several arenas that had to be freed from outside management. In 1973, in 1975, and again in 1977, Amin's government banned minority religious groups, seized their property, and dispersed or imprisoned their congregations. Only three religious organizations—the Catholic Church, the Anglican Church, and the Muslim Supreme Council—were permitted to operate in the country. The space for idiosyncratic or dissident religion was sharply constrained, and religious life was brought under state management. For the theologian John Mbiti—whose work is the subject of the chapter—it was a source of inspiration. He saw the consolidation of religious institutions as a welcome move toward Christian solidarity. Here, under Amin's rule, was an opening toward religious unity.

History, like religion, had to be reworked and placed under African management. New heroes had to be named and celebrated. Chapter 9 highlights the work that curators and archivists did to reorient Uganda's history. The chapter focuses on one creator of historical mythology: John Tumusiime, a government culture officer in a remote district in southern Uganda. He invested his time and energy in two sites of memory—a monument and a local history museum—that placed local people at the center of world historical events. Building monuments in the 1970s was by no means straightforward, and Tumusiime struggled to find concrete, wood, and other resources necessary to make his creations solid and lasting. His ambitious work shows us that the making of national myths depended on commoners' ingenuity, dedication, and sense of vocation.

Chapter 10 takes the reader to the outer limit of Idi Amin's Uganda. The subject is the Rwenzururu kingdom, the most sustained and most successful movement of opposition to Amin's government. Its architects fought for more than twenty years to secure their freedom. Rwenzururu partisans learned how to stand back from the information economy of Amin's Uganda, how to listen critically to radio, how to honor their own heroes. In the eyes of Ugandan authorities, they were criminals with delusions of grandeur. Their rebellion rested on their disciplined refusal to be dragooned into the political campaigns of the 1970s. They insisted on composing their own account of history. As we shall see, they were to author their political future, too.

This book is grounded in archival materials that have, until very recently, lain beyond reach. It widens the historical record to include people who, despite their marginality, felt that they were at the center of things. It brings into view people who, even at a time of social and political upset, expected their self-sacrificial work to be recognized and honored. The book asks you, the reader, to see their industrious, earnest patriotism side-by-side with the calamity that Amin's regime brought upon Uganda's people. The victories that patriotic people won in Idi Amin's cultural and economic wars were won at the expense of other Ugandans. The earnest work that civil servants and self-appointed experts did to keep institutions functioning was done in the service of a dictatorship. The cultural and religious liberation that patriotic people achieved was won at the expense of other Ugandans' ways of life. That is what Idi Amin's regime demanded: earnest self-sacrifice and malevolent demagoguery, hopeful idealism and indignant self-righteousness, shared effort and morally justified enmity.

CHAPTER ONE

A Nervous State

Uganda in the 1960s

I N 1961 AND 1962, British authorities organized a series of conferences to establish the legal framework for an independent, African-run government in Uganda. Delegates representing each of Uganda's provinces gathered in London, where they spent weeks hammering out the details of the new constitution. In the conference room it was easy to see the country's future as a tidy legal matter. But outside the halls of Lancaster House, Ugandans were mobilizing around different kinds of questions. The legal negotiations masked an important reality: Uganda was coming apart at the seams. A great many people saw themselves as freedom fighters, liberating their people from foreign oppressors. But the oppressors they challenged were not British colonists; and the freedom they sought was not the independence of Uganda.

Mid-twentieth-century Uganda was overflowing with noisy, assertive, creative activists. Some were cultural minorities. Others were rowdy urban commoners, scorned by the polite and polished men who administered the government bureaucracy. British authorities attempted to impose order on these restive activists by reinforcing the power of Uganda's kings. Five ancient kingdoms—Buganda, Bunyoro, Ankole, Tooro, and Busoga—had been folded into the structures of colonial government. The kings of colonial Uganda exercised wide powers. In the Buganda kingdom, for example, the government of the Kabaka—Buganda's king—had its own police force, its own legal system, and its own parliament.

Kings' authority was grounded in the customary deference that man-
nered people were meant to show to their social betters. It was also
grounded in the law. In the last years of colonial rule the British negotiated a series of agreements with Uganda's kingdoms, formalizing their
powers and cementing their prestige. The bargains that the British
struck with traditional rulers shaped the legal architecture of Uganda, for
after independence in October 1962, kings' powers were written into the
constitution.

But even as the political elite deliberated over the terms of independence, unruly people were making new demands. All over the colony oppressed minorities were convinced that the incoming tide of political
change would make them subject to foreign oppression. In the far west,
on the border with the Congo, indignant mountaineers rejected the authority of the Tooro kingdom, arguing that Tooro lowlanders had killed
their ancestors and suppressed their culture and language. In 1962—just
as Uganda was about to achieve national independence—they founded a
separate kingdom called Rwenzururu, and over the ensuing years they
conducted a long war of independence against the governments of Milton Obote and Idi Amin. At the center of Uganda, angry patriots of the
Buganda kingdom similarly fought to defend their endangered homeland. They were convinced that rule-by-majority in independent Uganda
would spell the end of their unique civilization. Buganda's parliament
voted to declare the kingdom's independence in December 1960; and
over the years that followed patriotic Ganda people staged a constant
struggle to expand their kingdom's powers.

The end of British government in Uganda did not involve a heroic
fight for national independence. There was no mass movement that
brought Ugandans together to challenge colonial rule. There were no
national martyrs. No blood was shed on behalf of Uganda's new government. Instead, in the last months of British colonial government there
was a protracted, bloody, and controversial struggle over the makeup of
the country itself.

Prime Minister Milton Obote came to power in October 1962 as independent Uganda's first chief executive. He inherited from British authorities a host of irresolvable questions about the very nature of the new
country he purported to lead. Determined to build up power in his own
hands, he sent the Uganda Army to destroy the palace of the king of Buganda in May 1966. The following year he abolished all of the ancient
monarchies and rewrote the constitution to make himself the unchal-

lenged head of state. Public life was sharply transformed. All at once, whole ways of life—habits of conversation, styles of attire, rituals, ceremonial occasions of all kinds—were made illegal. Quite suddenly, aspects of collective life that had once upheld royal authority were classified as matters of state security. There was a vastly expanded field for intelligence gathering. There were new government bureaucracies to keep watch over public life and collect information. Everyone, it seemed, had evidence to contribute, and everywhere there was proof of plotting.

In this way the government of Milton Obote became a nervous state: watchful of political activism, guarded about information, paranoid about dissent, severed from the taproot of historical legitimacy, increasingly reliant on a swiftly growing security apparatus to keep control over public life.[1] Having gone to war against ways of life that many Ugandans deeply valued, Obote's government found itself surrounded by enemies on all sides. That is how, after the bloody events of May 1966, General Idi Amin, the commanding officer of the Uganda Army, came to be indispensable, an essential instrument in the maintenance of order, a bulwark against an apparently limitless threat of subversion.

—————

The largest and loudest of the angry crowds of colonial Uganda was in Kampala. By 1960 the city's population numbered more than 100,000 people. Two-thirds of residents lived outside the municipal boundaries to the west and south, in a neighborhood called the Kibuga (Luganda: "the city"). Much of the land was formerly a swamp. The roads were of earth, and during the rainy season they turned to mud. The sewers were open, and noxious odors pervaded the place.[2] Thirty percent of the Kibuga's residents were under sixteen years of age. Only one person in twenty lived in a building with brick walls and a concrete floor, and most people slept six or eight to a room.[3] Many people lived on less than fifty shillings a month, at a time when the minimum living wage was estimated at eighty shillings.[4]

On 28 February 1959, the angry people of the Kibuga burst into the political theater, when an activist named Augustine Kamya organized a rally at the bus park and launched a trade boycott against Indian-owned businesses. A crowd of 2,500 people listened to thirty-five speeches over the course of the day. Kamya told the crowd that nothing was to be bought from Indian-owned shops. European-style beer should not be sold in African bars; buses—which were mostly owned by Indians—should be boycotted.[5] The boycott that followed was full of violence.

Government placed the whole of Kampala under emergency management and deployed the army.[6] Officials estimated that 3,500 people lost
their jobs as the urban economy slowed.[7]

Who was Augustine Kamya? He was a bricklayer from Katwe, one of
the slums on Kampala's outskirts. The American consul, who met him in
1961, was impressed: his face was lined and expressive, his eyes burning
and deep set. There was a "compelling and even magnetic quality in his
appearance," reported the American, "that renders his reported ability to
sway the masses fully understandable."[8] In the view of British officials,
Kamya was a "political wide boy," a "thoroughly ugly customer," and "a
bad piece of business."[9] The Kabaka—ruler of the Buganda kingdom—
called him one of the "back room boys," someone who was best kept out
of the public view.[10] The Kabaka and his ministers took a hard line
against the boycott that Kamya organized. "All forms of criminality re-
tard our progress and delay our independence," said the Kabaka in a
statement.[11] But the boycotters would not bend the knee to the royal
will. When the Kabaka paid a visit to one urban neighborhood, the residents shouted "Freedom!" at him. "There [is] a hostile feeling towards
government and authority in Kampala," the Kabaka reported. "Something [has] to be done to clean up the Kibuga."[12]

Kampala's urban crowd gave the boycott energy, but it was the
Ganda-language newspapers that gave it logic and momentum.[13] The
1950s were a high tide for African-language newspaper publishing in
Uganda: ten newspapers had been launched in the years just before the
boycott. Most had their offices in Katwe, at the center of Kampala's slums.
They shared space, paper, typewriters, and office staff with the political
organizations on which they reported. In the newspapers people could
read about the exemplary work that other people were doing and draw inspiration for their own actions. *Uganda Empya* reported that children at
Aggrey School had refused to buy peanuts from an Indian wholesaler.
"Even the Young Are Nationalists," read the headline.[14] A correspondent
wrote to *Obugagga* to describe how, one morning, two men had bought
corrugated iron sheets from an Indian-owned shop. When they exited the
shop, "people came out and looked at them in the face. No one said anything at all." One of the men set off on his bicycle, but he toppled over,
injured his knee, and bit his tongue. The men decided that the iron sheets
were cursed and returned them to the Indian seller.[15]

Newspapermen made unremarkable transactions into public events.
Police reported that boycott organizers stood outside boycotted shops

with a camera, giving shoppers the impression that they were being photographed.[16] Everyone, it seemed, was subject to surveillance. One of the most prolific pamphleteers was named "Muzinge," a pseudonymous writer who styled himself as chairman of the "Uganda Underground Movement." In the Ganda language "Muzinge" is a peacock, the king of birds; and like a king, the writer Muzinge dictated to other people about their conduct. The flyers he signed threatened specific individuals with punishment for breaking the boycott. In April 1959 a man wrote to *Uganda Empya* to apologize "to all his friends over the difficulties which his children brought him." His children had innocently bought some sweets from an Indian-owned shop, and his business—he ran a restaurant—had therefore been made subject to the boycott.[17]

That was the editors' role: identifying traitors, naming patriots, making martyrs. On 1 May 1959, *Munnansi* ran a front-page photograph picturing a woman bleeding profusely from her head. The headline read, "Omusaayi! Omusaayi! Omusaayi!" (Blood! Blood! Blood!) in capital letters of increasing size. "Do you see how the blood flows?" read the caption. The article described how the woman had been kicked by a government policeman during a pro-boycott protest.[18] An official investigator who looked into the matter found that the newspaper's editors had doctored the photograph: they had drawn the blood, with ink, onto the picture of the woman's face.[19] The activists of the Kibuga were inflating the facts, trying to generate outrage and passion. The lawyer Godfrey Binaisa clipped the article and sent it to a sympathetic British parliamentarian, calling it "conclusive evidence of what happened two days ago." The incident "[demolished] our confidence in British justice and democracy," he wrote.[20]

The boycott of 1959–60 expanded the political field. New categories of people found a voice. There were new techniques with which they could work, and new instruments by which they could exert pressure. Even as the British sought to engineer a decorous and democratic exit from Uganda, the unruly crowds of the Kibuga were setting the terms for Uganda's decolonization.

In August 1960 the colonial government began to register voters in anticipation of colony-wide elections, which were to be held in March 1961. Colonial authorities had come to regard Uganda's independence as a necessary historical development, the fruit—in the governor's view—of "our progressive educational policies."[21] Officials hoped for the "quick evolution of one or two strong political parties," and surreptitiously offered financial and logistical support to promising party leaders.[22] All of it—the cultivation of political parties, the development of a representative legislature, the selective enfranchisement of Africans—was called "decolonization." "We respect your desire to move forward toward self-government," the governor told the Legislative Council. "Our task, jointly with you, is to build up Uganda into a strong, happy and prosperous country which, when the time for self-government comes, can take its proper place in the world."[23]

To patriotic people in the Buganda kingdom British plans for an independent Uganda foretold a disastrous future. They feared that—under majority rule—the country's disparate peoples and cultures would be forcibly amalgamated, and Buganda's civilization would be swept away. Ugandan independence, in this view, was a pathway toward cultural and political disempowerment. There was "evidence from all over Africa," warned Buganda's prime minister, of the "harm which politicians could do to the existing or traditional regimes of the country."[24] Ganda patriots pointed toward Ghana, where the nationalist Kwame Nkrumah had sidelined his country's hereditary rulers and created a government "under the control and command of a dictator."[25] In September 1960, Buganda's legislature adopted a resolution calling for a separate independence for their kingdom. The resolution argued:

> It would be asking too much of the Baganda to trust the destiny of their country to the hands of political party leaders. . . . This could be extremely risky in light of recent history which has shown clearly that politicians in emergent countries use parliamentary democracy as a springboard to virtual dictatorship.[26]

The kingdom's independence day was set for 31 December 1960. For the kingdom's well-connected elite, the prospect of a separate independence was a means of protecting the power and privileges they enjoyed. The copy of the petition they sent to the Colonial Office was handsomely presented, encased in a blue cardboard cover with gold lettering. The pages and binding were held together with a broad black-and-gold striped ribbon, secured with a wax seal bearing the imprint of a shield and two spears.[27] Two delegations of the Buganda government visited the American consul in Kampala. Both of them presented copies of the memorandum and politely inquired whether the United States would open diplomatic relations with an independent Buganda.[28]

While the elite negotiated, Augustine Kamya and other restive populists set the pace for Buganda's separate independence. In November
1960 Kamya formed an organization called Omwoyo gw'Egwanga, the
"Heart of the Nation." In this new party were several people with whom
he had organized the boycott of 1959–60. They mobilized crews of volunteers to bring in building materials for triumphant arches and a speaking platform outside the kingdom's parliament, where the ceremony of
independence would be held.[29] The editor Obadiah Tamusange set about
recruiting and equipping an army for the breakaway kingdom. It was on
Tamusange's press that the flyer outlining a "Buganda Defence Force"
was printed.[30] The aim was to "teach people the art of defending themselves." Ganda men registered at the offices of Tamusange's newspaper,
where they were asked to sign a declaration promising to serve the
Kabaka.[31]

British officials thought Kamya, Tamusange, and their colleagues
were a "noisy group of narrow-minded irresponsible Baganda tribalist
self-seekers, none of whom merits the title of African Nationalist Politician."[32] The leaders of Uganda's political parties—who stood to inherit
power from British officials—agreed with this assessment. The president
of the Uganda National Party, the lawyer Apollo Kironde, called the secession campaign "a fine example of the power and unpredictability of
mob rule."[33] Milton Obote, the leader of the Uganda People's Congress,
vowed that "if the Kabaka tries to interfere in the government of the
country he will be exiled to Moroto."[34] In the last days of December
1960 nervous British officials drafted police from other parts of Uganda,
brought in a full battalion of the King's African Rifles to maintain order,
and paraded them, carrying their weapons, through the center of Kampala.[35] It was called "Operation Mistletoe."

On 30 December 1960—when the Buganda kingdom's legislature gathered to decide whether or not to declare the kingdom's independence—the
gallery overlooking the assembly hall was packed with Augustine Kamya's
men. They were "men without steady employment, who had been frustrated
or failed to gain an education," an irritated parliamentarian told an
American diplomat. They cheered boisterously for any speaker who
advocated for Buganda's independence and loudly booed parliamentarians
who spoke against secession.[36] The Kabaka tried desperately to avert a deci-
sive vote for independence: at the last minute he sent a message to the
Speaker of parliament, telling him to adjourn the session. The Speaker
refused, saying that a delay "would have meant the overthrow of the

Kabaka."[37] When the vote was called, the measure passed with a 79 to 8 majority.

Against the will of Buganda's elite, and against the interests of British officials, riotous activists had pushed their kingdom to independence. In the first months of 1961 they looked for ways to make that independence effective. Augustine Kamya thought patriotic Ganda people should refuse to pay taxes to the Uganda government. Buganda should issue its own driver's licenses; people imprisoned by the Uganda government should be freed; and all government buildings should display the kingdom's flag, not the flag of colonial Uganda.[38] He threatened to launch a new boycott if Buganda's independence was not made real in these ways. There was a vigorous discussion in the vernacular press about specific measures that Ganda patriots could take to establish their independence. Two men from Kyaggwe wrote to suggest that the heading on tax tickets be altered to read "Buganda Kingdom" in place of "Uganda Protectorate."[39] A Ganda priest, visiting Athens on behalf of his church, organized a spur-of-the-moment visit to the Foreign Ministry and asked Greece's government to open diplomatic ties to independent Buganda.[40]

What did it mean, in the age of Uganda's decolonization, for the Buganda kingdom to be independent? In law as in administration Buganda remained within the Protectorate of Uganda. The kingdom's independence was a kind of shadow theater. "They had in their own minds actually seceded and they were entirely independent," recounted a British official, "whereas in fact we were going around dictating all the work in their own territory."[41] In February an earnest Ganda bureaucrat put together a five-year plan that aimed to "convert Buganda from an agrarian and weak country into an industrial and powerful country, fully independent of the caprices of world capitalism."[42] The plan called for the creation of large, state-run farms to promote development. In April the Buganda parliament resolved that the seat of Uganda's government should be removed from the city of Kampala, which Ganda politicians claimed as their national territory.[43] Ganda parliamentarians also demanded that Uganda's name be changed, since it sounded too much like the name of their kingdom.

The Buganda kingdom did not have the military, financial, or political wherewithal to enforce its independence on Uganda. It fell therefore to individuals—their decisions, their actions, their deeds—to make Buganda independent. People were obliged to give evidence of their kingdom's sovereignty by their disconnection from Uganda. Buganda's independence was a matter of personal choice. That is why—in the leadup to Uganda's national independence—the separate independence of the Buganda kingdom involved a violent contest over people's loyalty.

=======

Uganda's first colony-wide elections were held in March 1961. They pitted the Democratic Party, led by the Catholic politician Benedicto Kiwanuka, against Milton Obote's Uganda People's Congress. The franchise was wide: anyone who was at least twenty-one years old and who could meet qualifications as to property-holding, wealth, or education could register. Wives of qualified voters were entitled to vote, as were newcomers to Uganda who had lived in a constituency for at least six months.[44] Altogether 1.3 million people across Uganda—75 percent of the potential electorate—registered to vote in the 1961 election.[45]

Buganda's activists insisted that patriotic Ganda people boycott the 1961 election. "War is at hand between the Kabaka and the outlaws," they wrote in a pamphlet. "Whoever shall register [to vote] shall be committing high treason."[46] The menacing characters born during the 1959– 60 boycott reappeared in public life. There were several flyers from Muzinge, the pamphleteer who had reported on blacklegs who broke the boycott. He threatened to pluck out the eyes of individuals who dared to cast ballots in the election.[47] When the votes were counted, the number of voters in Buganda was vanishingly small: in one county 158 people voted; in another there were 188 voters.[48] Almost all of this tiny electorate voted for the Catholic-run Democratic Party. On the strength of their victory in Buganda—where nineteen seats were awarded—the Democratic Party won a majority of seats in Uganda's Legislative Council. The election brought party leader Benedicto Kiwanuka to power as chief minister of a self-governing, but not yet independent, Uganda.[49]

In the months that followed the 1961 election Buganda's activists launched a violent campaign against Kiwanuka's administration. Buganda's parliament expelled Democratic Party members from its ranks and voted to break off relations with Kiwanuka's administration.[50] Activists took a harder line. An intimidating letter arrived bearing the signature Nnaganga Nnamuzisa, Muzukulu wa Walumbe. It was a terrifying pseudonym: "the Plague that Cannot Be Cured," the very "Grandson of Death."[51] There was a bone-chilling drawing of Nnamuzisa himself, a demonic character with sharpened teeth and a goatee. There was a drawing of a gun. "This gun releases 12 bullets every 14 seconds. It is manufactured in Russia," read the caption. The author warned, "The bombs and guns that I have brought have never been in this country." He gave the British governor twenty-four hours to declare, over the radio, that Benedicto Kiwanuka, winner of the 1961 election, would not become the prime minister over independent Uganda.

One of several personas that Ganda activists created in those years, Nnaganga Nnamuzisa could not be reasoned with. There was no room for negotiation, no call for diplomacy, no need for discussion. Ganda activists believed electoral democracy threatened their very existence. "What sort of Ganda person are you who allows Benedicto Kiwanuka or any other person whatever to sit over the Lion, His Highness the Kabaka of Buganda?" asked the authors of another pamphlet.[52] They vowed to exterminate Kiwanuka and his followers using a "new Atomic Bomb."

There was no atomic bomb for Ganda activists to deploy. Neither did they possess a rapid-fire machine gun from Russia. It was exciting to fantasize about the extermination of their political antagonists, just as it was exciting to act as though their kingdom was an independent state. In fact, Ganda activists had to work within a political system that constrained their room for maneuver. That is why—in the months that followed—they formed a political party. On 10 June 1961, 3,000 people gathered at the stadium near the Kabaka's palace.[53] Many of them bore flags and pennants with the words "Kabaka Yekka." The phrase meant the "Kabaka Alone."[54] A leading organizer told a police detective that their goal was to "unite the Baganda into a party determined to secure independence for Buganda."[55] Kabaka Yekka was an uneasy alliance between the polished, polite, prosperous elite and the gritty urban populists. More than half of the founding members—there were several dozen of them—were small traders, transporters, and political activists who lived in and around Kampala. Many of them had been at the center of the 1959–60 boycott.[56] They were convinced that political leadership over Uganda was their manifest destiny. One of them compared Ganda people to eagles, penned together with chickens. "Eagle, you are an eagle, look up to your place in the sky and fly," he wrote.[57]

Kabaka Yekka was registered as a political party in February 1962. Its leaders formed an alliance with the Uganda People's Congress, the party that Milton Obote led. It was, from the start, an ill-fated relationship. Obote's party envisioned an independent Uganda with universal adult suffrage, a wholly elected parliament, and a council of ministers who would be accountable to the legislature.[58] There was little space, in this view of the political future, for an independent Buganda kingdom. African nationalism "hates small states," Obote had said in 1960. If Buganda sought a separate independence, he would "crush Buganda."[59] But in the first months of 1962, Uganda's national independence was close at hand. The elections that would bring an independent African government to power were scheduled to take place in April. With his party's loss in the 1961 elections in view, a chastened Milton Obote paid a courteous visit to the Kabaka of Buganda. He and his colleagues agreed to withdraw UPC candidates in Buganda, in return for which Kabaka Yekka would form a coalition government with the UPC after the election. To cement the deal Obote offered five ministerial posts to Ganda politicians.[60] He also agreed that Muteesa II, the Kabaka of Buganda, would be independent Uganda's first head of state.[61]

Milton Obote's political biography was undistinguished. Born in Lango District, by 1956 he was working in Nairobi for Standard Vacuum Oil Company.[62] Shortly after his return to Uganda he was elected to the Legislative Council as the member for Lango District. The British thought he was a "mob orator of some skill. . . . bitterly and childishly anti-European."[63] In his speeches he made a point of taunting the police and courting prison. "Going to [prison] is of no importance," he told a crowd in 1958. "Dr. Nkrumah went to [prison] and now Europeans are his servants."[64] But Obote was never himself imprisoned for his political convictions, a fact his political opponents were keen to point out. Augustine Kamya pointedly told a newspaperman that he considered ex-prisoners to be the only suitable candidates for head of state, since "such a person would understand the needs of common people better than one who has never suffered for the good of the people."[65]

Voting tallies from the April 1962 election highlight a widespread absence of enthusiasm for Obote's leadership. In Teso, in Uganda's east, less than half the electorate cast votes. Many people withheld their votes, regarding the UPC's alliance with Kabaka Yekka as an unholy bargain.[66] In West Nile District, in the country's northwest, voters dropped abusive letters or leaves into the ballot boxes.[67] In Kampala only 60 percent of eligible voters cast ballots.[68] Even in Lango District, where Milton Obote was from, the number of voters was relatively small: only 61 percent of the electorate cast votes.[69]

In Buganda, by contrast, the 1962 election campaign was a cause célèbre. Encouraged by the activists of Kabaka Yekka, 769,651 people registered to vote, a vast increase over the 36,000 who had registered for the 1961 election.[70] Members of the Democratic Party, the winners of the boycotted 1961 election, were targeted in hundreds of cases of arson, looting, robbery, and assault.[71] When the votes in the 1962 election were counted, the Uganda People's Congress had won thirty-seven seats in Uganda's new parliament. Kabaka Yekka won nineteen of the seats available in Buganda. The Democratic Party won only twenty-two seats across the whole of Uganda. In the aftermath of the election Milton Obote's Uganda People's Congress duly formed a coalition government with Kabaka Yekka, and prepared to usher Uganda to independence.

That is how Milton Obote came to power. He was not the head of a unified people. He was not an inspiring martyr in the cause of freedom and independence. He was not even head of state: under the terms of Uganda's new constitution, that ceremonial position belonged to Muteesa II, the Kabaka of Buganda. He was hedged in on all sides by activists who demanded recognition, power, and sovereignty. The Ugandan polity he led was partible, and in the most consequential part of the country—the Buganda kingdom—a great many people regarded themselves as citizens of an entirely separate, independent state.

The struggle for Uganda's sovereignty was displaced. Weighty, imposing questions about the very fabric of the country were effectively put off. Milton Obote's government was obliged to spend the rest of the 1960s wresting power from the passionate activists of the Buganda kingdom.

═══

The Sovereign State of Uganda—as the newly independent nation was called—was patched together in haste. In the space of a few weeks Uganda's legislature passed bills concerning citizenship and immigration control, a bill establishing the national army, and a bill defining the official flag and armorial design. The legal code was borrowed word-for-word from Tanganyika, a neighboring territory that had celebrated its independence one year before.[72] The tune for the national anthem was selected at a meeting of Milton Obote's cabinet, when the police band director brought in a tape player and went through several recordings.[73] It was harder to get everyone to agree on the words. Three weeks before the independence ceremonies, Milton Obote was wrangling over the text with the Anglican bishop, who complained that God was not mentioned in the first verse.[74] The initial draft had struck a republican note: "Oh Uganda, thy people praise thee" was the first line. At the bishop's insistence the wording was changed to "Oh Uganda, may God uphold thee."

Independence Day arrived on 9 October 1962. The day was full of ceremony, with teams of musicians from northern Uganda, pipers from the Scots Guards, and a dancing team from India.[75] The printed program included a message from Ghanaian president Kwame Nkrumah. "The salvation of Africa lies only in unity, and Local Associations and Regional groups are no substitute for the vital goal of African unity," he wrote.[76] But all the pomp and ceremony could not cover up the basic questions that needed to be resolved. For many Ugandans Nkrumah's slogan— "the salvation of Africa lies only in unity"—was a cover-up, disguising the injustices that urgently needed to be addressed.

Among the leading critics of Uganda's independence was Augustine Kamya, the architect of the boycott of 1959–60 against Indian-owned businesses. Two months after the independence celebrations, Kamya demanded the ouster of Kampala's mayor, who was Indian. "I need to have a black African mayor since Uganda is a country for blacks," he told a crowd. He set a deadline of Christmas Eve for the mayor's resignation.[77] The following month Kamya and his boisterous colleagues formed a new organization—the "Uganda African National Farmers and Traders Movement"—and demanded that Africans take over coffee factories, cotton ginneries, and business enterprises from Indian and Pakistani proprietors.[78] Kamya told the thousands of people who attended their rallies that "they did not wish to see another Bombay in Uganda." He called for a new boycott of Asian-owned businesses: growers of coffee and cotton were to sell their produce to African brokers, not to Asian intermediaries.

On 1 February, Milton Obote's new government designated Kamya's boycott as illegal activity under the law. "We may be new amongst the nations of the world," said the Ministry of Justice press release, "but the Uganda government will protect the lives, property, and livelihood of all the country's inhabitants." The boycott would "shake the confidence of investors, who are essential to our economy."[79] Privately the prime minister of the Buganda kingdom warned Milton Obote that "people of balanced thinking" were "very much worried by certain hot heads like Kamya," who were going about the country advocating for a new boycott. He urged Obote's government to act quickly, before "this fire eats us all."[80]

Milton Obote could agree with the leaders of the Buganda kingdom about the threat that Augustine Kamya posed to the ruling order. Within the year, though, the alliance that joined his party with Kabaka Yekka— the party of Buganda's royalists—had fallen apart. At issue were the "Lost

Counties," a vast swath of fertile, productive land that lay across the middle part of the new country. In ancient times the land had been a central part of the Bunyoro kingdom, and the tombs of Bunyoro's kings lay within its precincts. In the late nineteenth century, the British—having defeated Bunyoro in a long and bloody war—carved the territory out of their adversary's domain and handed it to the Buganda kingdom to govern.[81] It was a reward for faithful service, a recognition of Britain's dependence on the military and political power of the Buganda kingdom. For Bunyoro's leaders the "Lost Counties," as the territory came to be called, were a constant reminder of their political and cultural disempowerment. In the months directly around Uganda's independence they authored a series of petitions that exposed Buganda's misgovernment and highlighted the disputed region's close connection with Bunyoro.[82]

Prime Minister Obote kept notes on the Lost Counties close at hand, in a file labeled "P.M. 1."[83] He read the petitions closely, making marks in the margins and underlining text. In August 1964 he announced that his government would hold a referendum to determine whether Lost Counties residents wished to be governed by Bunyoro or Buganda. The results of the referendum were announced on 6 November. In one county 86 percent of 13,000 people voted to return to Bunyoro, while in another nearly 70 percent of 9,600 voters favored Bunyoro.[84] In the days immediately following the referendum there were riots in Buganda. Activists put up roadblocks around Kampala, refusing to allow people who were not from Buganda to pass and throwing rocks at motorists.[85] "All Baganda are ashamed on account of the loss of their counties," a petitioner wrote in an angry letter to the Kabaka. "How is it that a small tribe like Bunyoro has taken over the two counties?"[86] For Ganda patriots the political future had never seemed more fragile.

That is why—in the weeks before the referendum—Ganda activists began to plumb the mind of Milton Obote. In September 1964 a document titled "This Is My Secret Plan of Ruling Uganda" began to circulate, supposedly composed by Obote himself. In it, the pseudonymous author laid out, under thirty-three headings, his dark schemes. "I will visit Sudan, Egypt, Russia, China and other countries where there are no kings and get advice to remove all kings in Uganda," he wrote. The author vowed to "demolish all rich people who are owning ginneries, factories, garages, and big gardens and landlords." Through these means the "population of Buganda will be intangibly reduced because they are beggars, they are too selfish, and therefore I must keep them as slaves and will never let them free." All of these dystopic schemes and plotting calculations came under the ironic heading "These Will Be My Happy Days." The document purported to give Ganda people insights into the darkest corners of Obote's supposedly twisted mind. It forecast a future in which the very foundations of the Ganda political community would be swept away. The creators of the document thought it deserved a wide readership. They distributed it to the Anglican Church, the Catholic Church, and several government offices.[87]

There were many other "secret plans" that came to light in the latter part of 1964. Many of them were composed by pseudonymous authors claiming to write from the innards of the Obote regime. "That Man Has This Plan" was the title of a document received in the Catholic mission in Fort Portal in late 1964.[88] The paper laid out Obote's secret agenda for Buganda, foretelling a day when his confederates would govern all of Uganda's kingdoms. Kabaka Muteesa was to be branded a criminal and deported to Ghana; thousands of Ganda people were likewise to be deported and replaced with immigrants whom Obote would bring in to settle the land. "That Man Has This Plan" was a horoscope predicting the incoming tide of change. The authors claimed to reveal the inner workings of the political machine. They helped Ganda people see a pattern to things.

For his part, Obote regarded the Lost Counties referendum as an opportunity to launch a new, sovereign, and unified Uganda. Here, at last, was a war of independence to fight and win. He was determined, he said, not to allow the "interests of any Owekitibwa [Luganda: "Honored Sir"] or Bwana [Swahili: "Boss"] to outweigh those of the Common Man." The crisis was a "struggle between the interests of the common man and those persons who are highly placed and occupy positions of influence."[89] Prime Minister Obote came before Uganda's National Assembly on 15 April 1966 and announced the abrogation of Uganda's constitution of 1962. The new constitution unified the court system, deprived the Buganda government of its budgetary subsidy, and eliminated the ceremonial presidency, which had been occupied by Buganda's king.[90] In response the Buganda parliament accused Obote of attempting to "assume dictatorial powers and disturb the country's peace, traditions, and institutions, rocking the very bottom of our foundations and leading us back into slavery."[91] On 20 May the Buganda parliament resolved that Milton Obote and the Uganda government should remove itself from the kingdom's soil.[92] Obote declared a state of emergency, and on the morning of 24 May he sent the army to arrest Buganda's king at his palace at the center of Kampala.

The attack began at dawn, when Uganda Army soldiers machine-gunned down a group of elderly volunteers, who were sleeping on the roadway outside the palace. Over the ensuing hours the king's bodyguard, 160 men strong, fought back with rifles and the sixteen submachine guns they had in their armory.[93] By two in the afternoon the Uganda Army had overrun the palace. The carnage was—in the words of the British officer who had trained the Kabaka's police force—"brutal, murderous, and unnecessary."[94] Soldiers slaughtered men who were trying to surrender; unarmed passersby were shot down without reason. There were bodies everywhere, so many that two police officers who inspected the scene were overcome with nausea. Some estimates had it that 1,000 people were killed. For days afterward army trucks ferried dead bodies to communal graves.[95] The king himself escaped. During a sudden rainstorm he climbed over the palace wall and fled to the Catholic cathedral, and from thence to Burundi. On 23 June the Kabaka of Buganda and two aides flew, in a freight airplane, into exile in London.[96]

In the wake of the demolition of Buganda's administrative center the kingdom was split into four districts, each reporting directly to the central government. The kingdom's legal system was abolished, and its police force was disbanded.[97] The palace was wrecked. When journalists visited the site in early June, they found the buildings blackened with fire and the interiors ransacked.[98] The kingdom's regalia was a spoil of war: on the fateful day of the assault a historian at Makerere University saw drunken soldiers of the Uganda Army carry off the kingdom's ceremonial spears and drums.[99] The following year, in 1967, Obote pushed a new constitution through the National Assembly. It concentrated power in his hands, making him Uganda's president and giving him the right to dissolve the legislature, detain people without trial, and appoint and dismiss public officials.[100]

All at once the ancient monarchies were cast into the dustbin of history. Royalties that had—in the older order—wielded immense cultural and political powers were unceremoniously ousted from their seats. In Lira, the Won Nyaci, leader of the Langi people, was given two weeks to vacate his official residence. His robes, regalia, and furniture were left behind for local officials to deal with.[101] In Kabale, in southern Uganda, the Rutakirwa—formerly the cultural leader of the district—was forced to turn his car and his office furniture over to the government.[102] The

Omukama of the Tooro kingdom in western Uganda was allowed to stay on in his palace for a few weeks after the abolition of his kingdom, on the condition that he agreed to "live there quietly and avoid drawing attention to himself or his position."[103] The regalia of his office was stored in the safe of the district government's engineer.

Milton Obote saw the events of 1966 as a turning point in Uganda's history. In the wake of the kingdoms' abolition his government adopted the "Common Man's Charter" as its guiding political philosophy. It set a course toward state-led socialism. At a rally in Lugogo Stadium in December 1969, Obote hymned the centralization of state power before an audience of 1,000 delegates:

> The fragmentation of Uganda has now ... been relegated to the fertile archives of history. . . . Having rid herself of her numerous kings and miniature kings, Ugandans can now realize that they are individuals, with rights which they can exercise in nation building and the strengthening of their "one country, one people, one parliament and one government."[104]

Here, at last, was an opportunity for Milton Obote to take on a historically consequential role. Some of the printed placards that members of the crowd carried that memorable day called him "Hero of Uganda." Other placards called him "Founder of the Uganda Republic."[105]

Late that evening, as he was departing the stadium, Milton Obote was shot. The would-be assassin fired three times; one bullet passed through Obote's mouth, scoring his teeth and piercing his tongue.[106] Obote was rushed from the scene. The army fanned out through the city of Kampala, and as many as twenty-five people were killed and more than one hundred wounded in the ensuing crackdown.[107] Police investigators arrested six men for the attempted murder. All of them were Ganda people.[108] All of them came from the urban underground around Kampala. One was a taxi driver; three were farm workers; another was a motor mechanic.[109]

———

In an earlier time confident activists had mobilized Buganda's urban masses by pioneering new techniques of political discipline and developing new means of exposing the secret evils of governmental power. In Milton Obote's "Secret Plan" and other pseudonymous texts they had revealed the design behind public policy, outraging readers and making political action seem essential. Now, in the wake of their kingdom's violent demolition, protesters could rely on techniques they had developed earlier. Confronting a regime that was apparently intent on their cultural and political destruction, Ganda activists spirited secret information out of the halls of power, using it to bolster their campaign against Obote's dictatorship.

In the immediate aftermath of the assault on Buganda's palace, activists distributed pamphlets around Kampala calling on Ganda people to join in a "war against northerners."[110] The characters whom activists had invented during the 1959–60 boycott reappeared in public life. Among them was Muzinge, the pseudonymous author who had issued the orders that set the tempo of the boycott. Writing on behalf of a movement that he claimed numbered three and a half million people, Muzinge ordered Ganda people to forgo funerals and to boycott post offices, dances, the electrical company, bars, football matches, and other institutions that upheld government power. Those who broke the boycott, he warned, would be "dealt with accordingly by General Muzinge's merciless long arms one by one until the whole home of the defaulter is exterminated."[111] "Why should we rejoice and indulge in merriments when our country is at stake?" asked the boycott's organizers.[112] They reminded their followers of the "thousands of our relatives, children, husbands, wives and friends killed during the [assault on the Kabaka's palace]."

Campaigners were inspired by starkly ethnocentric convictions. "Buganda is the most enlightened, the most developed, the most evangelized and socially developed with endowed natural resources while the rest of the surrounding tribes are still barbaric today," argued activists in a document circulated around the city.[113] Obote's attack on the Buganda kingdom was in this view a form of regression. "You yourself happen to come from one of the most backward societies in Uganda," activists told Obote in an open letter. "The simplest explanation [for the attack on the palace] we can think of is that you and your fellow backward tribes are jealous of Buganda."[114]

Behind the popular campaign opposing Obote's government were the same people who had, in an earlier time, driven the movement for an independent Buganda. One of them was Obadiah Tamusange, owner and editor of the newspaper *Ddembe* (Luganda: "Freedom"). In 1960 Tamusange had offered his office as a recruitment center for the kingdom's newly formed army. In 1967 he was arrested by Milton Obote's police and accused of plotting against the state.[115] Another campaigner was Kasane Mulindwa, who in the early 1960s was a leading figure in the effort to equip and train the Buganda kingdom's new military. On May 1966 he was at the head of the demonstrations protesting Milton Obote's new constitution.[116] Men and women like Tamusange and Mulindwa could draw upon networks, resources, and ideas that they had honed in an earlier time to contest their kingdom's untimely end.

On paper, though, the people behind the campaign said nothing about their identities. There were no petitions, with long lists of signatories imploring Obote's government to rectify the wrongs that it had done. The campaigners did not purport to speak on behalf of interest groups, or organizations, or constituencies. They wrote, instead, on behalf of a shadowy organization: the "Secret Council." This was a strategy, of course, a means of protecting themselves from Obote's security service. But their anonymity was also a productive place from which to write. It gave activists a foothold in unlikely places. The return address for most of the Secret Council's circulars was given as P.O. Box 5, Entebbe—the mailbox of Uganda's prime minister. Other circulars listed the return address as "Lira, Lango, Uganda," which was President Obote's home constituency. In print, activists could disguise their real identities and write from the innermost sanctum of power.

It was not the first time Ganda campaigners claimed that they had access to the secrets of Uganda's government. During the 1961 election campaign the pseudonymous Nnaganga Nnamuzisa—the "Plague that Cannot Be Cured"—had written an intimidating letter describing the havoc he would visit on the enemies of Buganda. The return address he gave was P.O. Box 1, Entebbe, the address of the British governor. In 1961 as during the 1966 campaign against Obote's tyranny, Ganda activists seemed to be writing from the very heart of Uganda's government, enlightening the Ugandan public about the malevolent design of official policy.

Their role was thrust on them by necessity, campaigners insisted, because the press under Obote had deprived citizens of necessary information. "Journalism in Uganda today is a false picture of Uganda, thrown upon a lighted screen in a darkened room so that the real Uganda and Buganda at that is not seen!" they argued.

We now live under SECRET GOVERNMENT, conducted by a secret process called dictatorial [sic] imbued with a wanted desire and sole intent to annihilate the BUGANDA ENTITY to give room [to] BARBARIC NILOTES to assert themselves politically supreme NOT a man amongst us dare NOW utter his honest opinion. Would you utter it, you well know beforehand that it would never appear in print.[117]

The civic role of journalism—to alert the public to abuses of power, to act as a platform for criticism and complaint—had been squelched under Obote, depriving people of the information they needed to act in their own interests. "We are marionettes," activists wrote. "All our capacities are all at the mercy and are all the usurped property of this wanton apostle." Ganda activists felt compelled to expose the wrongs of Obote's regime. The Secret Council's trademark was a pair of spectacles—rounded frames, sometimes with earpieces. The authors drew the spectacles at the top of many of the letters they composed.[118] They made the council's public role apparent. The Secret Council saw things that other Ugandans did not see. They made hidden things visible. They exposed wrongs and made the opaque and shrouded back channels of public life transparent.

All of the Secret Council's circulars were carbon-copied to a wide set of recipients. "Protest No. 4," for instance, named the U.N. secretary-general U Thant, the president of the United States, Pope Paul VI, the secretary-general of the Organization of African Unity, Senator Robert Kennedy, the prime minister of Sudan, and "The Press" as recipients. The circulars were sometimes distributed via the postal service, in addressed envelopes. On other occasions activists personally delivered their incendiary missives into diplomats' hands.[119] I have found correspondence from the Secret Council in diplomatic archives in Jerusalem, Dar es Salaam, London, Ottawa, and Washington, D.C. But most of the Secret Council's correspondence was not distributed through the postal system. It followed a more circuitous route. Letters were exchanged between acquaintances and friends, handed on surreptitiously, or left in conspicuous places for interested readers to find. Secret Council paperwork piggybacked on the social and commercial networks that Ganda people cultivated across Uganda. The authors of one pamphlet assured their readers that they had put one million copies of the pamphlet in circulation, to "give chance to all people in Buganda to read it."[120]

The imagined readership for Secret Council publications was wide. What brought them together was the experience of cultural and political endangerment. One pamphlet concluded by reminding readers of what they shared:

> Let everyone play his role, for we did not commit any wrong. Thousands of people have been killed, houses set on fire. All kingships, not only in Buganda, are facing their end. Most people are scared to go out of their houses stricken by terror. . . . Is there anyone who did not lose a relative or a friend?[121]

It was a scare tactic. Activists had to impress their readers with the desperation of their situation to motivate them to act.

That is how, in the latter months of 1968, a rewritten version of Milton Obote's "Secret Plan" came into circulation. The "Secret Plan" had been composed in 1964, as part of the campaign by Ganda critics against the Lost Counties referendum. Four years later, the document was redrafted and recirculated to spark outrage across the entire Ugandan people. Supposedly penned by an elder from Lango District—he called himself Okello Apello—this new letter laid out a seventeen-point plan for Obote's government. "It is only [people from Lango] who are capable of leading the rest," wrote the pseudonymous author. He instructed Obote to install men from Lango at the head of the Public Service Commission, the Uganda Development Corporation, the national parks, and other vital positions. In this way, wrote the author, "it will give the impression that the Langi are the only leaders of the country, and if anyone wants good ideas, they should always get it from Lango."[122]

The "Lango Letter," as it came to be called, was the most successful and most widely read of the many publications created by the indignant campaigners of the late 1960s. The authors preserved the trick that had given the "Secret Plan" its power. The letter was supposedly written from inside the inner sanctum of Milton Obote's government. But in contrast with the "Secret Plan," which had exposed Obote's dark plans for one segment of the country—the Buganda kingdom—the "Lango Letter" revealed a wide-ranging plot that gave a broad range of Ugandans reason to feel outrage. American intelligence experts worried that it would aggravate "long standing tribal friction among groups in northern Uganda" by showing the government's plans to "ensure the domination of Ugandan politics by President Milton Obote's tribe."[123]

Searching for ways to make bigger and more diverse communities feel oppressed by Obote's malevolent regime, activists experimented with authorial voice. Pseudonymity—the trick of writing under a false name—was the means by which Ganda activists made their vendetta against Obote into a nationwide problem, bringing to light secrets that could offend, aggravate, and mobilize a growing number of Uganda's people.

═══════

In February 1967 police arrested seven Ganda people who were said to be plotting with rebels in South Sudan to overthrow the Obote regime. The plotters hoped that the deposed king of Buganda would return to Uganda with a Sudanese army at his back. On that happy day they intended to put Milton Obote in a zoo.[124] In 1969 security agents were investigating a different conspiracy, involving Kabaka Yekka activists who planned to kidnap President Obote. They evidently had an informant—a "senior government official"—who had told them where the president slept at night.[125] In September 1970 police in western Uganda discovered that Ganda workers in the local mine were planning to assassinate Obote. The perpetrators had very modest qualifications: one was the personnel officer in the mine, another was a shop owner.[126]

We know about these and other plots because Milton Obote's intelligence officers reported on them. Today, their reports lie in the newly catalogued archives of the Obote presidency. Never before had intelligence seemed so necessary, so urgently important. In the eyes of Obote's government, the campaign protesting the Kabaka's overthrow was criminal activity. That is how Uganda's intelligence service was born: as a means to control the creative activism of indignant Ganda patriots.

The General Service Department was established in 1964. It was a counter-intelligence operation, designed to limit the flow of secret information. Every government department was supposed to have an officer whose job it was to secure vital materials from public view.[127] Uganda's intelligence service grew in proportion to the threats—real and imaginary—that Obote's government faced. In March 1967, in the midst of the furor surrounding the destruction of the Buganda kingdom, Obote's head of intelligence warned the cabinet about an "immediate need for the expansion of the security services." Meetings of the Secret Council had taken place "in broad daylight and within five miles of Kampala," he reported. The cabinet duly resolved that "Uganda should move toward a more scientific method of getting information."[128] Intelligence committees were set up in every district to report on events in their localities. There was a standard form for their reports. The first heading was for "Internal Subversive Activities," with subheadings focused on "Tribal Unrest," "Subversive Activities by Religious Organizations," and "Foreign Propaganda."

Intelligence gathering was consolidated in the hands of Akena Adoko, who was Milton Obote's cousin and head of the General Service Department. The American ambassador thought him "smooth and polished, amusing and probably ruthless."[129] Adoko was a public figure, not a spook. He hosted a current affairs program on Uganda's television service.[130] He published a column in the ruling party's newspaper. He gave lectures at Makerere University. He was president of the Uganda Law Society. And he was the author of the book *Uganda Crisis* in 1967. It was an account, in blank verse, of the circumstances leading up to the confrontation with the Buganda kingdom. Adoko's long poem built toward a verse set in bold type:

We have learnt one great lesson;
All hereditary rules
Are indeed rule by Corpses.
No dead man has any right
To rule over the living
Directly through his own ghost
Or indirectly through his heirs.[131]

He went on to liken Milton Obote to "A giant among dwarves," a "Cyclops among men," and to "Elgon or Ruwenzori in a big sea of ant hills."[132]

Adoko's operatives were ambitious young men, prospective politicians, unskilled in the practical art of intelligence gathering.[133] Adoko set high standards for them: he wanted men, he wrote,

Who united the qualities
Of deep learning
To the highest quality
Of Apostles:
Men who were neither hypocritical
Nor avaricious, nor fearful
But dedicated
To the demolition of idols
And the purification of sanctity.

Men of sincerity
And adventurous courage
Who would dare to defend right
When right was miscalled wrong.[134]

Intelligence gathering—in this account—was a high calling, not a shadowy back-room enterprise. The men whom Adoko recruited as operatives were public figures. One of them was a young academic named
Picho Ali, who had studied in Moscow and published academic articles
on the judiciary. Another was Aggrey Awori, who had studied at Harvard,
worked as registrar at Makerere University, and later became the first African director of Uganda's television service.[135] Ruhakana Rugunda and
Masette Kuuya joined Adoko's department while enrolled as students at
Makerere. They paid occasional visits to the American ambassador,
where they quizzed him about American foreign policy.[136] These men
were political climbers. They did not possess a grassroots network from
which to withdraw information. That was Adoko's intention. Obote's
government was so popular, he wrote, that "it could safely afford to place
its security in the hands of the populace." What was needed were security officers who were "completely exposed to the public," so that ordinary people would feel free to report to them.[137]

Intelligence gathering in Obote's Uganda was indiscriminate. His
operatives collected intelligence from commonplace sources: hearsay,
rumor, bits of conversation. One operative composed his report—which
concerned the threat posed by the disgruntled activists of Buganda—
based on his "tours through bars, night clubs, and other places where
through listening, arguing and discussion etc. most of the prevailing at-
mosphere has come out."[138] In another report an intelligence officer
summarized a conversation he had overheard at a snack bar in southern
Uganda.[139] The officer acknowledged that "they were just talking among
themselves while drinking." Nonetheless, he put the whole conversation
into his report, which was carbon-copied to the minister of internal affairs, the secretary of the cabinet, the office of the president, and many
other high officials in Obote's government. Even the most ordinary
people could become informants, possessing material that was relevant
to government policy-making. That is why the General Service
Organization—as it came to be called—had its own schools where operatives were taught shorthand and speed typing.[140] There was so much
that needed to be reported.

To opponents of the regime Obote's intelligence operation was a tool of oppression. In 1969 an editorialist complained:

> There are political spies in virtually every place of employment—in Government, in parastatal bodies as well as in private firms. Bars are perpetually patronized by Government informers, and all efforts are being made to appoint spies in every little village in the country. To the Government plots against the state are being hatched in practically every private conversation, in every house and bar and, we are told, in every forest![141]

As I read through the reports, though, I am struck by how uncertain Obote's officers were about their work. A great amount of energy was expended in sifting through information that was, by any standard, valueless. In November 1966, an intelligence officer reported on a meeting with a man named Stanley Magunda. Magunda was an entirely unremarkable fellow: he did not speak for a community, and he did not have expertise or access to special knowledge. He simply wanted to say that it was impossible for candidates from Obote's party to win an open election for Buganda's parliament. The government officer who interviewed Mr. Magunda faithfully transcribed his words and sent them on to the permanent secretary of Obote's cabinet.[142] This and other reports were produced at a time when, quite suddenly, areas of politics that had formerly been basic to the constitution of civil life were defined as subversion. It was hard to know exactly what counted as subversive activity.

All of this opened up opportunities for grifters. Knowing that intelligence operatives were unsure about where their focus ought to be, informants drove up the price of the information they provided. One informant—a man named Nsereko—told his handler that he had identified Kabaka Yekka men who were collecting weapons. They arranged to meet alongside a roadway at seven o'clock one evening in April 1968, but when the agent searched a van that Nsereko claimed was secretly transporting guns, he found furniture piled inside. Nsereko, undeterred, promised the agent that "he knew where the arms were kept but could not lead us to the place because we had no proper cover." He was angry, he said, because "the department had failed to make him happy" after an earlier job. Nsereko asked his handler for money for beer, and demanded better pay in compensation for the information he provided.[143]

Men like Nsereko could furnish Akena Adoko with information about
a wide range of plots. Even so, sometimes intelligence operatives needed
to fabricate evidence. In the Uganda National Archives there is a file with
a green cover labeled "Mr. Akena Adoko."[144] In it are a series of reports,
dating to 1968 and 1969, from a man named B. W. Bato, an officer of the
police Special Branch. Officer Bato was reporting on a conspiracy involving some of the most eminent people in Buganda. Abubakar Mayanja, formerly a cabinet minister in the Buganda kingdom, was supposedly
involved. So was Benedicto Kiwanuka, leader of the Democratic Party,
and the eminent Catholic politician Paulo Ssemogerere. Officer Bato
quoted the plotters, word-for-word, as they laid out their plans. He did
not condense or summarize any part of their conversation. In one report a
plotter lays out a scheme for Obote's assassination: two Somalis from Nairobi had already agreed to do the job during the sixth anniversary of
Ugandan independence.[145] Mayanja reminds his colleagues to be careful.
There were too many new faces at their meeting. Badru Kakungulu, uncle
to the Kabaka of Buganda, says—as if on cue—that "everyone should do
everything possible to overthrow Obote's government." The parliamentarian Charles Ssembeguya suggests that the Somali assassins ambush
Obote on Ring Road, where his car could be seen out in the open. In Officer Bato's report everyone verbally assents—one after the other—to the
group's plans. Everyone is present, responsible, implicated, incriminated.

The file that contains Officer Bato's extraordinary report bears no
reference number. Other files in the archive have a "ladder" on the cover,
listing the reference numbers of files containing related information. Officer Bato's file cover is unmarked. It was not part of a series of other
files. There were no cross references. It was not compared with other information. The file was kept separate from the ordinary machinery of
government bureaucracy. It was very likely part of a small collection that
President Obote kept in his personal possession. Obote's secretary,
Henry Kyemba, reported that in the late 1960s,

> File after file of foiled "Obote assassination attempts" were
> compiled and delivered to me for passing on to him. Every day
> he would receive the [General Service] Unit's green folders—
> sometimes containing many sheets, sometimes one typewritten
> page, sometimes a handwritten note. For a time, Obote kept
> them to himself, but after several weeks this clearly became
> impossible and he began to turn them over to me for filing.[146]

Officer Bato's carefully composed reports seem to have been written with a specific purpose in view: they were meant to incriminate Obote's political enemies. Even as the popular campaigners of the Secret Council were inventing evidence of Obote's malignancy, so too was Obote's own government creating documents that could prove plotters' criminality. That was the purpose of the file. That is why it had to be kept close at hand. It furnished actionable evidence that could prove the guilt of the regime's opponents.

In September 1969 government police came to Benedicto Kiwanuka's house, roused him from his sick bed, and arrested him on charges of criminal libel and sedition.[147] As evidence the charge sheet pointed to a Democratic Party press statement.[148] It is hard to take the charges seriously: the press statement was issued six months before Kiwanuka was arrested. What occasioned the arrest of Benedicto Kiwanuka—and doubtless many other people—was the secret information accumulating in Milton Obote's files. Most of it was scurrilous, self-interested, and partisan. Much of it was rumor or hearsay. Some of it was fabricated. Nonetheless, it allowed government officers to see political campaigns as plots, activism as subversion, Ganda patriotism as treason.

Obote's regime had come to view a whole sector of Uganda's political life as subversive. There was an inflationary pressure for information, as officials in government cast about for data that could incriminate their political opponents. Intelligence reports—composed over the signature of evidently reliable sources—were the currency with which Prime Minister Obote pursued his political and legal campaign of nation-building.

———

The Obote government's paranoia over subversion fed the growth of a security service that was preoccupied with the pursuit of internal enemies and largely unaccountable to the common good. That is how Idi Amin rose to prominence in public life: as an architect of state security.

At the time of Uganda's independence, the Uganda Rifles—as the army was then called—stood at 1,058 men. In mid-1963 Milton Obote's government began to recruit a second battalion.[149] There were plans for a third battalion, but in January 1964 soldiers angry about their conditions of service raised a mutiny in the barracks in Jinja. The mutiny was part of a series of uprisings by rebellious soldiers across eastern Africa.[150] Prime Minister Obote called in British troops to support his government, and in an evening the mutinous battalion was disarmed. Three hundred soldiers were dismissed from the service, and Obote's cabinet

Lieutenants Shaban Opolot (left) and Idi Amin (right) with Sir Frederick
Crawford at Government House, Entebbe, August 1961 (Courtesy of the
Uganda Broadcasting Corporation)

resolved that the mutineers should be barred from future employment in
government jobs.[151] That was the only punishment imposed on them.

In the wake of the mutiny Obote endorsed dramatic pay raises for
Uganda's soldiery.[152] At the same time government rolled back educational qualifications for enlisted men. The cabinet resolved that the sole
qualifications for enlistment were "physical fitness, ability and the determination to serve."[153] African officers were promoted to command the
two battalions of the Uganda Rifles, replacing the units' British officers.
Those newly promoted officers were Majors Shaban Opolot and Idi
Amin, both of whom were made lieutenant colonels.

Who was Idi Amin, who rose so suddenly to importance after the 1964 mutiny? He was a skillful creator of myths about his early life.[154] His father was a policeman from Koboko, in West Nile District, on the border between Sudan and Uganda. He was a Kakwa, a minority ethnic group often regarded by cultured southerners as backward and primitive. Aware of the scorn other men might have for his parentage, Amin often claimed a more distinguished background. In the archives of the Uganda Broadcasting Corporation there are several sound recordings wherein Amin—speaking competent but not fluid Luganda—tells audiences that he had been born in Buganda, in a police barracks at the center of Kampala.[155] The young Amin enlisted in the colonial military around 1946. He was, in the view of the British soldier who was once his commanding officer, a

> splendid man by any standards, held in great respect and affection by his British colleagues. He is tough and in the judgment of everybody completely reliable. Against this he is not very bright and will probably find difficulty in dealing with the administrative side of command.[156]

Lieutenant Colonel Amin's first assignment as battalion commander was in western Uganda, where two companies under his command were deployed a few weeks following the 1964 army mutiny. A group of dissident mountaineers had launched an insurgency, fighting to achieve the political and cultural independence of a kingdom they called Rwenzururu. The threat posed by the insurgents was small: theirs was a movement of conviction, and their soldiers carried spears, not firearms. Yet Amin's men pursued the campaign against Rwenzururu loyalists with aggression and inhumanity. An army patrol stopped a fisheries officer on the road, dragged him from his car, and beat him with the butt of a rifle.[157] His assistants were "kicked and slapped with pangas, beaten with rifle ends." In early April a Uganda Rifles company raided a village of fishermen, ostensibly searching for Rwenzururu rebels. They rounded up a thousand people, and many of them—according to police investigators—were "manhandled, slapped, kicked, punched, and struck with rifle butts." Eighteen women told the police that soldiers had raped them that day.[158] By June the local authorities were reporting on "unprecedented scenes of violence" in the region.[159] The army was burning houses on the mountainsides, turning hundreds of people into refugees. Some of the fleeing people described how soldiers had speared babies carried on their mothers' backs.

That is how men in power redirected the mutinous energy in the ranks of the Uganda Army: by targeting the hapless people of western Uganda. British diplomats—who were distant from the scene of the violence—considered this small-scale campaign a "very satisfactory internal security operation." The deployment had got the mutinous troops out of their barracks and kept them occupied.[160] Only a few government officials worried about the breakdown of discipline. In mid-April the minister of internal affairs wrote to the army's commanding officer, warning that "if officers ... are incapable of exercising discipline over their troops, or are too frightened to do so," then they ought to be dismissed from service.[161] He threatened to disband the units if discipline did not improve. A week later the government's chief secretary warned that "the behavior of some of these troops appears to bear a most disturbing resemblance to that of the Congolese Army." He warned the army commander of the "damage that is done ... to the public image of the Army and the Government" by instances of indiscipline.[162]

But in Uganda's new government there was very little political will to impose order on the army. Wilson Oryema, the head of the police force, wrote to Obote's cabinet suggesting the creation of a force of military police. "There appears to be considerable indiscipline in the Army," he noted. "Instead of having a disciplined organization, [we] have a large number of heavily armed men who will not do as they are told."[163] Oryema wanted a small, well-trained, well-educated army, whose energy would be focused on curbing the cattle rustlers in the northern part of the country. His suggestions—sensible as they were—came to nothing. Obote was facing a tide of resentment in Buganda. Everywhere there were schemes, plots, and potential insurrections. No one in government had an interest in imposing discipline on the men of the military.

Obote made Idi Amin deputy commander in the Uganda Army in September 1964. The following year Shaban Opolot, the army's commander, wrote to complain that Amin was "making personal contacts with individuals of higher and lower ranks, campaigning against other tribes and showing that he is the leader of the northern tribes." Opolot thought it was an outrage. "This Uganda Army is not meant to be for one particular tribe and particular region," he wrote.[164] Amin should "know that he is junior to me, and most of his military knowledge is from me." In February 1966, Obote relieved Opolot of his command, accusing him of conspiring with Buganda's king to mount a coup against the government. Obote contemplated making himself commander of Uganda's armed forces in Opolot's place. He had a military uniform specially made, with the intention of wearing it at the independence anniversary celebrations on 9 October 1966. At the last moment he changed his mind, fearing that he would appear ridiculous in military garb.[165] Instead, he promoted Idi Amin to brigadier general and made him commander of the Uganda Army.

Idi Amin rose to power as a willing instrument of Milton Obote's efforts to suppress the campaigners of the Buganda kingdom. On the fateful morning in May 1966, when the Uganda Army assaulted the palace of Buganda's king, Amin was the officer in command of the operation. A British policeman saw Amin at the palace gates, smashing an old Ganda man to the ground, dragging him across the road, and hurling him into a ditch.[166] A civil servant who met with him that afternoon reported that Amin was "in a jolly mood and obviously enjoying the fight."[167] Late in the day, after the battle was over, Amin came to Obote's office, bearing with him the Kabaka's presidential flag and the Kabaka's military uniform. They were trophies of the battle, spoils of a bloody conquest won against the recalcitrant kingdom of Buganda.

The ensuing campaign against Buganda's activists greatly enlarged General Amin's public role. Amin warned an audience in 1968 about "people who call themselves the Secret Council and the Buganda Liberation Army," who were scheming for the return of the Kabaka of Buganda.[168] For Amin, the uncoordinated and far-fetched plans of the Ganda activists were a license for the expansion of military power, an invitation to launch an ongoing and wide-ranging campaign against Uganda's civilians. Amin promised to "deal a blow which the so-called Liberation Army will not forget." Later in 1968 he demanded that the palace of Buganda's king—vacant since the events of May 1966—be allocated to the Uganda Army as a base. It was centrally located, he argued, and an ideal home therefore for a new battalion.[169]

In June 1969 the British embassy's defense adviser visited the headquarters of the Malire Regiment, the new unit created by General Amin, which was based on the grounds of the Kabaka's vacant palace. The palace building was full of holes made by artillery shells during the 1966 assault. There were tents scattered about on the grounds, and ramshackle platforms where parachutists could practice their technique.[170] In the center was a forlorn bandstand, formerly used by the Kabaka's musicians.

There were very few toilets. The government's health department warned that soldiers' health was endangered by the poor sanitation on the site.[171] It was here, at the derelict center of the defunct kingdom of Buganda, that General Amin based the Praetorian Guard of the newly expanded Uganda Army. The armaments of the Malire Mechanized Regiment were a hodgepodge: at the first occasion they went on parade there were armored personnel carriers from Czechoslovakia, anti-aircraft guns from the Soviet Union, anti-tank guns from Israel, and scout cars from Britain.[172] Diplomats reported that General Amin knew many of the soldiers in the regiment by name.[173] Many of them came from West Nile, his home district. President Obote, for his part, saw the new unit as the guarantor of Uganda's unity. At a review he lauded the men of the Malire Regiment as builders of the nation, faithful servants of a unified Republic of Uganda.[174]

In his pursuit of Ganda activists Idi Amin made the growth of the security services into a matter of national importance. Pope Paul VI visited Uganda in July 1969, the first time a pope had come to an African country. A few weeks before his arrival General Amin told Obote's cabinet that he had received a letter from the Secret Council.[175] It vowed that the deposed Kabaka of Buganda would return to Uganda at the head of a foreign army during the papal visit. The returned king was to replace President Obote's regime with a new government, with himself at its head. The cabinet hastily authorized General Amin's request for funding, and heavily armed troops were stationed at five provincial towns around Buganda.

It was a license for indiscriminate violence. In the view of Ganda patriots, the soldiers of the Uganda Army were an occupying force, and their relationship with civilians was tense. In the newly inventoried archives of the Ministry of Internal Affairs, there are thick files full of reports documenting soldiers' assaults on innocent people. In Mubende three privates assaulted the conductor of a bus, demanding to be given seats on the vehicle, which was fully occupied.[176] In Gulu a group of inebriated and aggressive soldiers assaulted the district's medical officer and two magistrates at the White Horse Bar, accusing them of disrespecting the military.[177] In March 1970 soldiers manning a roadblock roughed up the chief justice of Uganda while searching his car. In August that year the commander of the police force totaled up the incidents in which Uganda Army soldiers had attacked innocent people. The police had investigated 228 cases in 1968; 300 in 1969; and 195 during the first half of

President Obote (center) with Brigadier General Idi Amin (right) and Uganda Army officers at the "Tiger Battalion" barracks, Mubende, 1969 (Courtesy of the Uganda Broadcasting Corporation)

1970.[178] Soldiers very often disregarded court summons, refusing to respond when judicial officers called on them to answer to victimized civilians' accusations.

General Amin responded to these and other reports by defending the army's independence from civilian control. Even when soldiers were badly behaved, Amin argued, it was essential that "members of the public cooperate with the Armed Forces when the latter are going about their lawful duties."[179] That is what the campaign against Buganda's activists created: a military that was unaccountable to the common good, that regarded many of Uganda's people as enemies.

———

On 25 January 1971, while Milton Obote was returning from a meeting in Singapore, Idi Amin launched a coup, sent the Malire Regiment to secure the airport, and proclaimed himself president. The young soldier who announced the coup over the radio attributed the army's action to

Obote's misgovernment, complaining about the many people Obote had imprisoned. He spent several minutes excoriating Obote's intelligence chief, Akena Adoko.

In the hours after the announcement of the coup, diplomats reported, "a wave of hysteria has swept over the town. There are wild demonstrations in favor of the army."[180] Ganda people responded to the coup with "an explosion of relief and enthusiasm." In Mengo—formerly the capital of the kingdom of Buganda—there was dancing in the streets the morning that General Idi Amin came to power as president of the Second Republic of Uganda.[181]

CHAPTER TWO

The Second Republic

A T 3:45 P.M. ON 25 January 1971 a junior officer announced on Radio Uganda that the army had overthrown the government of President Milton Obote. He listed the iniquities of the old regime: the corruption of Obote and his ministers, the lack of free elections, the high prices that had crippled the Ugandan economy.[1] He emphasized Obote's ethnocentrism, his self-promoting efforts to advance men from Lango, his home district. As evidence he pointed to a document called the "Lango Development Master Plan." It showed that Obote had "decided that all key positions in Uganda's political, commercial, army and industrial life have to be occupied and controlled by people from . . . Lango District, at the expense of other areas of Uganda."[2]

The "Lango Development Master Plan" had a long history in Uganda's public life. It first came to light in 1968 as the "Lango Letter," one of a number of pseudonymous documents that supposedly revealed the inner workings of Milton Obote's malevolent government. Composed by the sharp-eyed men and women of the "Secret Council," this and other documents—purportedly stolen from the private files of government—had furnished critics with evidence of the hidden evils of Obote's regime. In 1971 the "Lango Letter" came back into circulation. Early in March the document was printed in the government newspaper.[3] Later that month it was published in an appendix to *The Birth of the Second Republic of Uganda*, a pamphlet that laid out a rationale for Amin's coup.[4] For Amin's new regime, as for the Ganda activists who had composed it, the

"Lango Letter" laid bare the consuming self-interest that had guided Milton Obote's regime. It was a revelation.

In contrast with the dark malevolence and plotting ethnocentrism of the old regime, President Amin promised an ethnically inclusive and politically transparent government. There would be no "Secret Plan" emerging from government under his presidency. "I am a man of truth," Amin said.

> I believe in open discussion of matters affecting our Country, whether they are against me or for me. . . . Anybody is free to see me and to address memoranda to me, setting out grievances or suggestions as to how we can develop our country.[5]

In the days following the coup the Amin government released the detainees whom President Obote had incarcerated. One of the liberated prisoners was Benedicto Kiwanuka, who had been incriminated by Officer Bato's reports. Also released were some of the leading figures in Buganda politics, imprisoned after the attack on the Kabaka's palace in 1966. Among them were Badru Kakungulu, uncle to the Kabaka, and Nalinya Ndagire, the Kabaka's chief sister.[6] In early February, 50,000 exultant people gathered on an airstrip in Kampala to watch Idi Amin take the oath of office. His ministers were given the choice to take the oath on one of three volumes: a large red Quran, a black-covered Bible, or a very large manual of military tactics. President Amin was reduced to tears during the twenty-one-gun salute; but even at the height of his emotion, he tugged on his uniform, making certain that it was hanging just right.[7]

In the first half of 1971, Amin barnstormed around the country, introducing himself before massive crowds that gathered in the provincial capitals. He announced a one-million-shilling reward for anyone returning Milton Obote alive to Uganda, where he was to answer for charges of corruption.[8] To many people, Amin's coup seemed to herald the restitution of old wrongs. In Kigezi District, in Uganda's south, Catholics felt oppressed by Protestants, who had dominated local politics under Obote's government. When Idi Amin visited he was greeted by a huge banner imploring him to "Save Kigezi from Discrimination."[9] In Acholi District, where the "Lango Letter" had convinced many people of Obote's malevolence, a young man came to a reception wearing a handwritten sign with an acrostic poem. It said:

President Amin visits Kabale, 1971 (Courtesy of the Uganda Broadcasting
Corporation)

Africans
Must enjoy the fruits of their
Independence
Not only a few.[10]

The most enthusiastic advocates of the coup were Ganda people.
They hoped that Amin's rise to power would bring about the revival of
their kingdom. During the heady days of late January and February 1971
men wearing Kabaka Yekka uniforms rode through the city streets on the
backs of trucks, singing the praise of their king.[11] "We wholeheartedly
support this take-over which has brought an end to a very ruthless dictatorship," wrote a group of Ganda politicians.[12] They asked Great Britain
to recognize Idi Amin's new government. President Amin, they said, realized that "no Ugandan leader can brush aside Buganda and what it
stands for . . . and expect to succeed for any length of time."

Some people had lost their kings. Others had lost their inheritance,
or their identity. Still others—hundreds or thousands of people targeted
by Obote's intelligence service—had lost their liberty. For dispossessed

people of all kinds, Amin's coup heralded a restoration. An enthusiastic civil servant compared the coup to the French Revolution:

> The events of our recent coup d'état are by no means unknown in the history of the world, and . . . we are following the pattern of trying to put right abuses and to establish our freedoms as individuals.[13]

That is why, in the months following the coup, so many people found reason to celebrate. They hoped for a rebalancing of the scales.

These hopes soon proved to be illusory. The freedoms that Ugandans were so eager to claim were foreclosed over the course of the first ten months of 1971. Amin set about consolidating public life: imported newspapers were banned; political organizing was outlawed. There was no room for kings or chiefs. New technologies—radio in particular—made it possible for officials in Kampala to communicate directly with people in the provinces, sidelining intermediaries and making Uganda into a dictatorship. Inherited hierarchies and ancestral traditions were made to seem outmoded, irrelevant, backward. There was no time for such antique rituals and archaic loyalties.

That was the fate of the patriotic activists who had—in the 1950s and 1960s—set the tempo of politics. Men and women who had been at the head of assertive movements for cultural and political self-determination were made to play a new role: as spokespersons for morality and tradition, as representatives of outmoded ways of life. They were curators of antique things. All at once, time seemed to pass them by.

━━━━

Under the old regime many Ugandans had come to see Obote's government as plotting against their interests. In the days following 25 January 1971 people felt free to pursue vendettas, enmities, and objectives that had been foreclosed under the old order. Passions and resentments that had been stoked in the former age could suddenly burst into flame.

In the weeks immediately following the coup there was a pogrom in the army. Soldiers from Lango—Obote's home district—were slaughtered mercilessly. A newspaper reporter who toured the barracks heard that Amin had ordered the execution of Langi soldiers holding a rank above corporal.[14] In Gulu, where the air force was headquartered, the reporter estimated that one hundred soldiers were killed; in Kampala 114 men were executed. Some bodies were buried in mass graves; others were thrown into the River Nile. By the end of March as many as five hundred officers and enlisted men—mostly from Lango District—had been murdered.[15]

People from Lango were being made to repay the moral and political debt that they supposedly owed to other Ugandans. The government administrator reported that Langi people greeted the news of Obote's ouster with "panic, doubtfulness, worry and even suppressed agitation." Educated Langi people "have, since the announcement of the takeover, tended to feel a noticeable sense of guilt and fear in their minds," while uneducated people have "openly displayed a sense of insecurity."[16] In March Langi politicians met with President Amin in their district's leading town, Lira. The delegation was made up of politically savvy men: there were four ex-chiefs, several local councilors, and Ben Otim, formerly the traditional ruler of the Langi people.[17] They spent their time refuting the "Lango Development Master Plan." "If Dr. Obote, a son of this tribe, had any plan to perpetuate his personal rule in the name of Lango people, we as a tribe have always been completely ignorant of such design," they argued. The "opportunists and hypocrites" who had supported Obote's regime had come "from all parts of Uganda and we all suffered equally at their collective hand." The elders argued that President Amin's campaign against the Obote government was unfairly targeting them. The "entire community [has] suddenly become filled with bereavement and [is] virtually dying in fear, but also with uncertainty for their future within this nation," they said.

On the day President Amin visited Lira there was no dancing. The men were dressed soberly, in suits and ties. In one photograph the elders of Lango stand in a line, their eyes downcast as they shake the president's hand.[18] No one smiles. In another photograph President Amin stands on a rostrum in front of a crowd.[19] The elders sit on chairs arranged at his feet. Several of them have notebooks on their laps. Were they writing down the president's admonitions? In the pictures the most distinguished men of the district look like truants who have been caught. Their role was foreordained: it was to apologize for the wrongs of the Obote era.

In Buganda, by contrast, the presidency of Idi Amin came as a liberation. Buganda's king, Frederick Muteesa, had died in exile in London in November 1969. President Obote had offered to fly Muteesa's remains back to Uganda for burial, but Muteesa's relatives indignantly refused. Some people speculated darkly that Obote planned to subject the

President Amin greets elders in Lango District, 1971 (Courtesy of the Uganda
Broadcasting Corporation)

deceased king's body to a symbolic court-martial, then incinerate it.[20]
Others were sure that Obote intended to chop up the body and bury it in
a prison cemetery.[21] Fearing these and other unhappy fates, Muteesa's
relatives had buried his body in a British tomb. After the coup, Idi Amin's
new government proposed that Muteesa's corpse be exhumed and trans-
ported to Kampala for a state funeral. A few people wondered whether
the time was right.[22] But most welcomed President Amin's invitation,
seeing it as a means of reinvigorating their kingdom.

The funeral was carefully organized. The Ministry of Health set up
first aid stations throughout the city to care for the hundreds of thousands of people who came to mourn the king's death.[23] The British government sent a contingent of ten men from the Grenadier Guards, and
the British high commissioner sat at the right hand of President Amin
when Muteesa's body arrived at the airport.[24] The funeral was held at the
Anglican cathedral; the choir sang "Abide with Me" and "Rock of Ages"
in Luganda. The body was taken to the traditional burial site for Buganda's kings, where it was laid to rest in a large tomb constructed for the

Funeral of Sir Edward Muteesa, late Kabaka of Buganda, 1971 (Courtesy of the
Uganda Broadcasting Corporation)

occasion.[25] There President Amin—wearing a tie bearing the outline of
the British Isles—laid a wreath at the coffin of the dead king. The American ambassador was impressed. He reported that President Amin had
"blended together elements to make him appear a proud leader of his
people, a weeping son of Uganda mourning the death of a President and
a thoughtful statesman."[26] A Canadian diplomat thought the funeral was
conducted with "a dignity and calmness that would be difficult to exceed
anywhere."[27] British officials felt uplifted by the occasion. In the months
following the funeral, the wife of the British high commissioner was—
according to an American diplomat—"bustling about escorting cabinet
wives hither and thither and generally acting like a middle-aged Vicar's
wife," behaving in the "slightly patronizing way" characteristic of British
people in former colonial territories.[28]

Beyond the diplomats' view, the funeral of Kabaka Muteesa II was
less polite, less polished, and much more volatile. When the body of
their king was helicoptered onto the airstrip, thousands of Ganda women
and men were gathered there clad in barkcloth, a sign of mourning. The

journalist Henry Lubega remembered that in the hours leading up to the
body's arrival women huddled in small groups, sobbing.[29] Lubega himself
collapsed in tears when he saw Muteesa's body, enclosed in a transparent
case. When the embalmed corpse was displayed for public viewing at the
Anglican cathedral, the line of people waiting to see the body stretched
for four miles.[30]

For Ganda patriots the return of Muteesa's body was an opportunity
to rectify the wrongs that Obote had done. In the "Lost Counties"—the
disputed territory severed from Buganda after the 1964 referendum—a
government official received a threatening letter written on behalf of the
region's Ganda residents.[31] "Whenever the Kabaka returns you [people
from Lango] will face it," warned the author. One rumor had it that
Muteesa was alive, living in Ethiopia, and that he would return on 31
March to reclaim his throne.[32] Another rumor had it that—on the day of
the king's burial—Langi people would be rounded up and buried in the
deceased king's tomb.[33] Langi people living in Buganda were—according
to their leaders—"hurriedly leaving their homes and properties behind
to seek, in desperate panic, refuge elsewhere because the sign of events
appears to them too foreboding to wait and see."[34] An American diplomat heard a rumor that as many as 8,000 foreigners living in the Buganda kingdom were stoned to death or immolated in open fires during
the week of Muteesa's funeral.[35] The minister of internal affairs privately
told his colleagues that a great many houses had been burned in Buganda. Most of them belonged to supporters of Obote's government.[36]

Ganda royalists regarded the funeral of their deceased Kabaka as
proof that the tides of time were finally shifting their way. A British military officer visited President Amin at his home one evening in March,
shortly before the funeral took place. Their conversation was interrupted
by a delegation of Ganda drummers and harpists, who danced into
Amin's living room bearing a large painted portrait of the president. It
pictured Amin in military uniform, with a colossal golden halo circling
his head.[37] That was what Muteesa's funeral did: it made Amin—for a
time—into a saint.

A few months after the funeral President Amin convened a meeting
at the International Conference Centre in Kampala to discuss the future
of the Buganda kingdom. More than 1,500 people attended. The young
heir of Muteesa II, Prince Ronald Mutebi, sat at Amin's side for the
whole meeting. One after another, forty of the kingdom's leading men
and women rose and asked for the restoration of their kingdom.[38] There

was Mayanja Nkangi, formerly the prime minister of Buganda. There was Kizito Bulwadda, formerly a taxi driver, who had been a leading activist pressing for the independence of the Buganda kingdom in 1960. There was Sarah Ndagire, who had been the first female member of the Buganda kingdom's parliament. The meeting lasted six and a half hours.[39] The Radio Uganda technicians who broadcast it used thirteen reels to record the proceedings.[40]

That was the high tide for Buganda's resurgent royalism. In the days following the president's meeting with Buganda's leaders there was a wave of criticism in the press. People from Lango, Ankole, and Kigezi Districts sent in petitions arguing against the restoration of Uganda's kingdoms. The former king of Ankole led a delegation to Kampala opposing the restoration of his own kingdom.[41] At Makerere University the students' union passed a resolution decrying the "surging wave of monarchist and feudalist activity and sentiment" among Ganda people.[42] In September, when a group of Ganda students organized a concert in the main hall and invited their prince, the young Ronald Mutebi, to be the guest of honor, the Makerere Students Guild banned the concert and called the Ganda students feudalists. Indignant students chased the audience out of the hall where the concert was to be held.[43] The civil servants who worked in Amin's administration were similarly wary of Buganda's royalism. A leading civil servant wrote to President Amin, reminding him that "we have firmly said that there will be no return to the kingdoms." Government needed to "watch carefully older royalist politicians who believe that they can gain political popularity by asking for the return of the kabakaship."[44]

Early in October 1971 a group of Ganda elders visited with Amin to discuss the restoration of the kingship. Amin instructed them "not to awaken the issue of Kabakaship at a time when Uganda is busy reorganizing herself and convalescing from political antagonism."[45] The following week the police arrested twenty members of a leading Ganda political party.[46] By mid-October Amin was emphatic about the matter: in a meeting with three Ganda activists he declared the question of kingship "COMPLETELY CLOSED."[47] At the celebrations of Uganda's independence anniversary he hymned the need for unity:

We Ugandans are determined to stand not as a collection of timid tribes but rather as a united nation, fully equipped materially, morally and otherwise to resist any temptation and aggression from any quarter.[48]

Later that month sixteen Ganda politicians were arrested and imprisoned, accused of holding an illegal political meeting.[49] The space for political organizing was dramatically narrowed. The "Suspension of Political Activities Decree," announced in the last months of 1971, banned political gatherings and outlawed the carrying of flags, the wearing of uniforms, and the distribution of literature on behalf of a party. It also outlawed the utterance of political slogans, forbade the collection of funds for political parties, and empowered police officers to enter buildings where political meetings were said to be taking place.[50]

Over the course of the years that followed a wide range of people were defined as enemies of Idi Amin's government. People from Lango and Acholi, Asians, Kenyans, Israelis, Pentecostals, Sikhs, Christian evangelicals, and many others were targeted. Some people were executed, others made into exiles. Buganda's royalists were the first of Uganda's political communities to be cast out of the body politic.

=====

For monarchists in Buganda it was a grave disappointment. After the events of October 1971 many Ganda royalists turned against President Amin's government. They returned to the political strategies and authorial tricks they had developed in earlier decades and remodeled them to serve a new purpose: staging a resistance to Idi Amin's government.

In mid-November 1971 police intelligence reported on a new organization, called "Sanyu lya Buganda," or the "Joy of Buganda."[51] Among its leaders was "Jolly Joe" Kiwanuka, a newspaperman who had helped to organize the campaign for Buganda's political independence in 1960. Sanyu lya Buganda claimed to be a religious group, but its meetings began with a prayer asking God for strength in "escaping [our kingdom] from the hands of its enemies." The organization's leaders had prepared a leaflet titled "There Can Be No Peace in Buganda Without the Kabaka." Their leaders traveled to Entebbe to meet with President Amin; when they did not find him, they presented his bemused wife with a white dress and a copy of the leaflet.

By 1972 the tide had turned. There was no "joy" in Buganda. It was time for new and more aggressive tactics. The "Secret Council"—the shadowy group that had circulated pamphlets revealing the hidden malevolence of Milton Obote's government—reappeared in January with a flyer that denounced "Amin's Rotten Regime."[52] The document highlighted Amin's misgovernment, decried the ongoing murders in the

Uganda Army, and predicted that Nigeria and Great Britain would soon send in their armies to crush Idi Amin. Over the ensuing years a range of organizations advocating the overthrow of Amin were formed. There was, for instance, "Uganda Popular Revenge," which published a series of sophisticated pamphlets detailing the malfeasances of the Amin regime. One document was composed as a charge sheet: in numerical order it accused Amin of "extravagance and dissipation," of "lowering the standard of education in Uganda," of promoting unqualified army officers, and of corruption.[53] Another document was composed in Luganda. It contrasted the desperation of ordinary Ugandans with the luxury that Idi Amin personally enjoyed.[54] A third document was circulated in Kampala by a group called the "Uganda Freedom Fighters." The authors outlined "more than 50 points why Amin and Co. should be overthrown," and concluded by reminding Ganda readers of the civilizational battle in which they were involved.

> [Act] now and not tomorrow, otherwise we shall be forced to leave our mother land Uganda to the Refugees, Amin and Co. What do we benefit from the Arabs? They are thugs. In 1900s they brought [venereal disease] and worse still used to trade our grand fathers [as slaves]. Today, they have started with bringing us poverty and taking our essential goods such as milk, sugar, meat etc.[55]

Ganda opponents of Idi Amin's government saw their struggle as a battle between order and savagery. In their partisan view Amin and his men were like the Arabs of old, despoiling civilization for their venal purposes.

Searching for meaningful alliances, Ganda royalists returned to their glorious history, hoping to persuade British monarchists to join, once again, in the work of renewing Uganda's civilization. Writing to the secretary-general of the Commonwealth in 1973, a group of authors claiming to represent the "Former members of the [Parliament of Buganda]" wrote that Uganda had "become a country of fear and [instability] where people are brutally killed." They asked for the renewal of the British colonial government over Uganda.[56] Another organization, headed by a Ganda exile, envisioned a post-Amin dispensation in which white Rhodesians would be enlisted to serve in Uganda's government.[57] The Ganda royal family had supposedly promised to allocate several islands in Lake

Victoria for the Rhodesians to farm. The organization claimed that apartheid South Africa would furnish military backing to bring about Amin's overthrow.

There were many other harebrained schemes dreamed up by Ganda exiles. Effective or not, Ganda schemes to overthrow Idi Amin highlight the enduring relevance of inherited political strategies. Even at a time of dramatic upheaval, Ganda activists' political theory was conservative. It rested on the presumption that Buganda's people were somehow entitled to rule over other Ugandans; and it called on Britain to honor the commitments that the crown had made to the protection of its Ganda subjects.

What happened to the kings and chiefs who, in a former time, had commanded vast cultural and political power? They were discredited, deprived of financial and cultural standing. The very existence of the ancestral chiefs, argued a government administrator in 1972, was "contrary to the Republican Constitution." He instructed hereditary chiefs to

> desist from interfering with public property, land, and also not to impersonate public officers by calling themselves chiefs. They should consider themselves civic leaders whenever such a situation called upon them to do so.[58]

Chiefs, kings, and other defunct potentates found it difficult to keep body and soul together. The queen mother of the Bunyoro kingdom—traditionally a personage of great importance—was obliged to apply to a local administrator for permission to live on her hereditary land. The administrator pared away four acres from the estate, reducing her holding to two acres. He warned Bunyoro's royal family that "Uganda is no longer a Protectorate, it is a Republic whereby the past is forgotten. To think of traditional offices is to hinder the progress of the nation."[59]

In 1975 the Amin government struck its most serious blow to the inherited power of chiefs and kings. The Land Reform Decree placed the disposal of all of Uganda's land in the hands of a government-run Land Commission, which was empowered to lease property to renters who could make it productive. All privately owned land—including properties owned by chiefs and kings—was made into government property.[60] The decree grew out of discussions in Amin's cabinet, where government ministers lamented that hereditary landholders could not "plan an effective use of the land" or "derive benefit from modern methods of farming."[61] The Land Commission set about reallocating agricultural land throughout Uganda, awarding it to farmers who possessed capital and know-how to cultivate on a large scale.

The political theory that guided the Land Reform Decree was captured in an editorial cartoon published in the government newspaper.[62] The cartoon depicts a confrontation between two men. The man on the left—wearing practical rubber boots and rolled-up pants—has arrived on the scene in a truck. On the bed of the truck is a modern house, fully equipped with a cooking stove, and a wife and two children. The man on the right—bare-chested, wielding a simple hoe—gestures wildly at the settler. "What do you want with my land Mr. Stranger??" he asks. At his back is the signpost that borders his land: "Matata and Sons Kibanja," it says. His name—"Matata"—is the Swahili word for "trouble." The landholding is said to be "5,000 by 7,000 km." It is an impractically huge expanse. Matata's land could not possibly be productive, farmed as it is by the simple tools that he carries in his hands. No wonder the settler wears a bemused expression on his face, as he tells his angry interlocutor, "Cool down old man. Haven't you heard of the new Land Decree?" The man has the wind of historical change behind him. Technology and expertise arrive here, on the bed of a lorry, ready to make Uganda's under-tilled land productive, ready also to make the obstinance of ancestral landholders obsolete.

The Land Reform Decree was a license for an abrupt transformation of older ways of life. To take one example: in 1977 the Land Commission granted a lease of three hundred hectares in western Uganda to a farmer named Labani Nyakaana. Nyakaana was one of Uganda's first trained economists, earning a doctorate for a dissertation in 1970 titled "Agriculture Development Planning and Policy in Uganda."[63] His dissertation had highlighted the difficulties hindering the transformation of agriculture from "semi-subsistence to commercial farming." Dr. Nyakaana intended to cultivate his newly acquired land intensively, using the techniques he'd studied in graduate school. He had little regard for the six hundred people who had lived on the land for decades prior to his arrival. He told the residents of the estate that they were "not human beings but animals."[64] Government officials were impressed with his vision, and they shared his disdain for the hereditary landholders who resided on the place. "Customary tenants do not have the means to develop their [gardens] except at a subsistence level," argued a group of officials who toured the estate. One of them told a crowd that government policy "was promulgated to ensure that land is used for productive purposes, rather than holding it traditionally as a symbol of prestige."[65]

That is how the men at the center saw things. They worked from the top down, allocating land in large chunks that could be cultivated at a large scale. The estates they defined were drawn on a surveyor's map. They did not acknowledge the claims that people made to land on the basis of custom and heredity. In January 1975 the commission allocated twenty hectares to a farmer named Yonasani Balinda. When government officers investigated his neighbors' complaints, they found that Balinda's barbed-wire fence had been erected only centimeters from the outer wall of one woman's home, making it impossible for her to access her banana farm.[66] Another person complained that Balinda had come—gun in his hand—to cut down his banana plantation and erect his fence.[67] The man had lived on the land for sixteen years, and had raised nine children on the farm. The people who lived on Balinda's estate knew nothing about the Land Reform Decree. Government authorities lamented that they "still adhere to their traditional belief that once a father or grandfather allocates land to anybody in his or her family then that land is regarded as his permanent land."[68]

The men of Idi Amin's regime had little time for sentimentality, tradition, or custom. Elizabeth Bagaya, the daughter of the former king of Tooro, exemplified the new posture that Uganda's royals were obliged to adopt. Educated at Cambridge University, she had a successful career as a lawyer and a model before becoming Amin's minister of foreign affairs in 1974. That year she told a Canadian diplomat that "she and many others of royal Ugandan ancestry had radically changed their lifestyles and no longer pursued selfishly elitist lifestyles."[69] She argued that President Amin's apparently irrational politics were in fact guided by an underlying commitment to equality and the common good.[70]

Inherited social position now counted for little. The passions and loyalties of the old era seemed suddenly passé. Memories of earlier injustices might inspire resentment and anger, but they did not shape public action. Joseph Kazairwe—who had formerly led the Bunyoro kingdom's campaign to reclaim the "Lost Counties"—wrote to President Amin in May 1971 to complain about the governance of the two counties that had been wrested away from Buganda.[71] In the 1960s, Kazairwe and his colleagues had organized mass rallies, incited public opinion, and mobilized evidence of Buganda's tyranny. In 1971, by contrast, Kazairwe's strategy of political engagement was restrained. He complained to President

Amin that he and his neighbors were governed by old and autocratic men from Bunyoro. Kazairwe asked that the two counties be carved out of Bunyoro and given a local government of their own. He furnished Amin with a list of twenty-nine people he hoped would be employed in government jobs. Heading the list was his own name, identified as a "medical assistant and sergeant in the King's African Rifles." He made no mention of his credentials as a political organizer and provocateur.

There was no campaign to back Kazairwe's advocacy. There were no rallies, or flags, or political pressure groups, or incendiary speeches. Kazairwe's petition did not have a public face. He and other activists of the "Lost Counties" had deep and wide experience in organizing: in former times they had been the architects of one of eastern Africa's longest-running political campaigns. They had tools, skills, and techniques that they might have worked with. But by 1971 the framework for political activism had shifted. The urgency of their patriotism was lost.

———

What was left for Joseph Kazairwe and the many other activists of the old order? Elderhood was the only framework in which cultural authority could be exercised in Idi Amin's Uganda. Men who had formerly stood at the head of rambunctious movements asserting their people's will were obliged to become respectable senior citizens.

From 1971 onward, as a matter of routine, President Amin met with committees of elders whenever he made a visit to one of Uganda's provincial localities. In some places there was a single figure—a "chief elder"—at the head of his colleagues. When the Uganda government formed a new "National Forum" for discussion about public policy, each district was required to nominate two "elders"—one man, one woman—along with two businesspeople, four religious leaders, and two schoolteachers to represent the district's interests.[72] There were no qualifications for eldership: no rituals, no inherited titles to validate their position. Some people were discomfited at being made—all at once—into relics. Elders in southern Uganda asked whether they might be given a badge, so that "wherever they are, say, attending certain functions, they are recognized as elders."[73] They wished for status, for the power that came with a formalized position. Elderhood was a holding cell where politically active people could be enclosed.

For some men, elderhood offered a congenial and productive career, a refuge from controversy, a calling, a vocation. At the time of his death

in 2020, Festo Karwemera was regarded by many as a "walking encyclopedia" of the culture and customs of southern Uganda's people.[74] In the
1960s, he had been a rabble-rousing politician: an active member of Milton Obote's Uganda People's Congress and editor of the party newspaper. In those years the politics of the UPC in Karwemera's home district
were contentious: there were two groups, called the "eaters of vegetables" and the "eaters of meat," who vied for supremacy in local politics.
Karwemera was an "eater of vegetables." In 1970 he was involved in a violent attack on the leader of the rival faction.[75] In April 1971, Amin's new
government put Festo Karwemera in prison.[76] Government intelligence
reported that Karwemera's friend and mentor, the politician Mukombe
Mpambara, was plotting to "assassinate [Idi Amin], cause economic chaos
by exporting goods to Zaire and Rwanda, [and] weaken people's interest
in the present government."[77] Mpambara fled into exile.[78] For Festo Karwemera it was a parting of the ways. In an interview he told me that his
arrest "caused me to doubt, and I asked God, if he was indeed alive and
risen, why he had allowed this to happen to me."[79]

He spent his time in prison preparing for a new vocation: he composed a series of book manuscripts concerned with the culture and
customs of his people, the Bakiga, the predominant ethnic group in
southwestern Uganda. In July—a few weeks after his release—Radio
Uganda's recording van visited his district to record broadcast material.
Most of the clubs, choirs, and personalities who came before the radio
engineers performed for less than an hour. Festo Karwemera spoke for a
full twelve hours before the microphone. He addressed an astonishingly
wide set of issues: the "coming of people" into his district; the "selling
and buying of cattle"; the biography of a prominent spirit medium.[80] The
month following his lengthy radio address Karwemera took a job with
the Language and Literature Committee, checking the spelling and or-
thography of Kiga language books.[81] By 1974 he was the chairman of the
district's newly established Cultural Committee.[82] He was vitally involved in the making of a new museum of Kiga culture, housed in the
Hindu temple, which was left vacant after Amin's government expelled
the Asian community. In 1977 he was one of several public figures involved in the fundraising committee to establish a new library.[83]

For Festo Karwemera and for many other people, Idi Amin's sudden
rise to power closed off the field of political activism. It was illegal to be a
member of a political party, to shout political slogans, or to wear a party
uniform. Some political activists spent the 1970s in exile in Tanzania,

Nairobi, or London, plotting against Amin's regime. Karwemera found his safe haven in culture. Under the old regime he had been a political man, actively engaged in the public affairs of his time. After Idi Amin came to power, though, he needed a way to lift himself out of the dangerous controversies of the 1960s, to identify and pursue a new vocation. That is how he became the most prolific, most well-regarded spokesman for southern Uganda's history and culture. When Yoweri Museveni's National Resistance Movement came to power in 1986, Karwemera was ready: at the first meeting of the newly established "Culture Executive Committee" he handed over a manuscript titled "Oshwera Abuuza," a play about marriage and custom. Over the ensuing decades he published more than two dozen books, most of them written in the vernacular language of southern Uganda.

In Karwemera's winding career we can see—in a small way—how the dynamics of military rule reshaped the cultural politics of Uganda. Activists who had riled up followers in defense of certain ways of life were obliged to become elders, safely enclosed within the gossamer bonds of nostalgia. It was a way of domesticating their persuasive power. The forms of collective action they had once pursued were revalued as culture. The ways of life they had once defended were made into museum pieces. The museum, the radio program, and the library helped to turn rambunctious activists into harmless senior citizens.

─────

After October 1971 there was only one place in Uganda where people could claim a culture, a way of life, and a king that was their own. That was Rwenzururu, a kingdom on the borderland between Uganda and Congo. Rwenzururu's partisans fought a long war to defend their homeland against the dictatorships of Milton Obote and Idi Amin. As we shall see in Chapter 10, they were the most consistent, most successful opponents of Idi Amin's tyranny.

Outside Rwenzururu the pace of public life was set from Kampala. There were new goals to pursue, and new forms of collective action. There were new media, too, that demanded everyone's attention.

CHAPTER THREE

The Transistor Revolution

T HE SOUND ARCHIVE OF the Uganda Broadcasting Corporation is stored at the corporation's headquarters on Nile Avenue in Kampala. There, neatly shelved in a stuffy room, are hundreds of 5-inch, 7½-inch, and 10-inch magnetic reels, carefully placed in boxes, labeled, and lined up by date. The archive reflects the meticulous care and paranoid precision with which radio technicians did their work. Magnetic tapes were expensive, and Radio Uganda had a limited supply of them: in 1969 there were only fifty 7½-inch reels and twenty-five 5-inch reels in the engineers' hands. Once they were played on the air, most of the tapes had to be erased and re-used. But a few tapes contained material of such importance that they deserved to be preserved for posterity. The procedure was laid out in 1969, when the chief engineer instructed the librarian to label historically important reels with a "distinctive number," then place the reel on the shelves.[1] For each archived tape the librarian had to type out a card, listing the speakers, the occasion, and the date. The card was inserted into a binder alongside other cards, allowing the librarian to locate the reel easily.

Many of the reels in the UBC's radio archive feature the voice of Idi Amin. There are 287 reels that record President Amin's on-air addresses from the year 1972 alone. All of them had to be dealt with carefully. On the back of one reel there is a handwritten note penned by an anxious technician. "There is a slight break in recording the President's speech," he nervously wrote, for one of the adapters to hold the spool was trying to come off and the tape had to be stopped to put the adapter back in its rightful place. Am sorry for this inevitable technical fault and any inconvenience caused due to this is regretted.[2]

For the technicians it was important to get every word on record.

Idi Amin came to power just as the transmitting capacity of Radio Uganda was undergoing a revolutionary expansion. In 1965 Ugandans—who numbered some six million people—owned 112,698 radio receiving sets.[3] A survey conducted that year found that eight of every ten Ugandans over the age of sixteen listened regularly to Radio Uganda.[4] In 1968 the Obote government signed a contract with a British firm, and construction began on four 100-kilowatt transmitting towers.[5] The radio expansion project was nearing completion when, in January 1971, General Amin overthrew Milton Obote's government. The first of the powerful new transmitters began broadcasting in November, ten months after Amin came to power.

Through a historical accident President Amin inherited one of the most powerful radio broadcasting services in Africa. Radio helped to make him a dictator. The peculiar quality of radio broadcasting is this: it is a one-way medium. There is no built-in mechanism by which listeners can talk back to the broadcaster. There is no channel for debate, for discussion or disagreement. Unlike Uganda's newspapers—which were stuffed with letters, editorials, and reports from a disparate assortment of authors—a radio broadcast was ordinarily a monologue. For President Amin, radio became a vehicle of public address, a megaphone by which officials in Kampala could impose themselves on an apparently attentive public. It allowed Amin to project his voice to the most remote parts of the country. It enabled him to issue directives to persons and groups that might otherwise be out of reach.

In fact, the reception of radio and other official media was not as ubiquitous as authorities imagined. Broadcasting equipment was fragile and easily broken, requiring constant superintendence from overburdened engineers. Interference from wind and weather limited Ugandans' ability to receive the signal. It took labor to made radio work. But radio never gives evidence of the limits of its listenership. There are no lists of individuals who do not, or cannot, receive the radio signal. That is how broadcasting works: there is no means of determining the limits of the audience.

For the Amin regime, the apparent universality of Radio Uganda's signal was a useful fiction. Regardless of their personal circumstances, irrespective of the hindrances they faced, Ugandans were obliged to pay heed to Radio Uganda's broadcasts. The radio schedule structured their time, imposed itself on their private lives, and compelled them to listen. It consolidated the president's authority, sidelining bureaucrats, experts, local authorities, and other intermediaries. Radio put Idi Amin at the center of every question.

=====

British officials in Uganda had conducted experiments with sound broadcasting as early as 1939, using wires to distribute a signal to speakers set up in government buildings. Officials worried about the ephemeral nature of sound broadcasts: as one of them wrote, the

> fleeting character of any message carried by sound waves … renders wireless propaganda particularly susceptible to distortion, benign as well as malignant, in the minds and by the tongues of listeners.[6]

The problem was particularly pronounced among Africans, whom colonial officials believed to be easily misled and inattentive. "The African can discount a bazaar rumour," wrote a government official, but "it may be some time before he can discredit an inaccurate and alarmist account of a broadcast which will be regarded at first as authoritative."[7] When the first wireless sets were distributed to Ugandans, officials handed them to trustworthy people—chiefs in Buganda, the kingdom's prime minister, missionaries, and district commissioners—who could reliably interpret the broadcast to audiences of listeners.[8]

The Uganda Broadcasting Service went on the air on 1 March 1954, broadcasting from a 7½-watt transmitter located in Kampala. The first programs lasted for an hour and a half, with an hour in Luganda and a half hour in English. All of it was pre-recorded. The service sent out vans to record music, lectures, and other material in Uganda's provinces.[9] A quarter hour of broadcasting time every week was allocated to an Anglican sermon, and another quarter hour to a Catholic homily.[10] By 1958 there were 55,000 shortwave receivers in use in Uganda.[11] The UBS was on the air five days a week, from 2:00 p.m. to 10:30 p.m. Producers filled the time with edifying news piped in from Uganda's districts. The quarter-hour program from Busoga District, for example, featured four-minute portraits of eminent personages from the district, together with longer talks about places and institutions in Busoga. The theme, as an official put it, was "the problems of the olden days and how they were solved; today's problems and how they can be solved by central government."[12] African politicians were barred from the airwaves. In officials' view "political parties had not yet developed to the point where their leaders could be allowed free access to radio broadcasts."[13]

Outside the doors of the radio station, on the streets of Kampala, Luganda newspapers were setting the pace of public life. African-run newspapers were produced in Katwe, at the heart of Buganda's urban populist movement, by men who were themselves actors in the dramas they reported on. Editors were mobilizing urban commoners to boycott Indian-owned businesses and demand a greater share of the economy. Radio broadcasts, by contrast, were composed by schoolteachers, veterinary officers, or medical assistants. It enraged some listeners, who saw the dull earnestness of the radio as a distraction from real and pressing matters. As a correspondent in the newspaper *Ndimugezi* wrote:

> It is wrong to listen to Kampala Radio all the time. There is a lot of indoctrination on the radio and this can only be avoided by reading newspapers. It is useless to say that I never read newspapers because I have a radio at home. Kampala Radio never fought for [the Kabaka], never pressed for elected members on the Legislative Council and never gave you fresh news.[14]

Radio broadcasts were deliberately disengaged from the politics of their time. On Tuesday 13 November 1960—just as Augustine Kamya and other urban rabble-rousers were organizing to win the independence of the kingdom of Buganda—radio listeners could hear a discussion in the Teso language titled "Our Children Learn from Us" and a selection of folk tales in Luganda from the historian Michael Nsimbi. On 18 November there was a lecture titled "Advice on Legal Proceedings" delivered in Luganda, and a talk about kwashiorkor.[15] Speakers addressed matters that were apparently above dispute. When the recording van visited southern Uganda, a schoolmaster named Y. Barigyira used the opportunity to record a talk titled "Native Beer to Be Drunk at the Proper Time." In it he complained that girls stayed in clubs all day long. "When are you going to go home to cook and who is going to take care of the home?" asked Barigyira. Barigyira's talk was deeply partisan: at a time when many Ugandan women were seeking out social and economic opportunities in Kampala and other urban centers, Barigyira treated women's independence as a problem that needed rectifying.[16] But he and other broadcasters did not acknowledge the partisanship of their broadcasts. That is how radio worked: by making the speaker invisible, radio also made controversial issues appear to be above argument.

That is why—after Uganda's independence—Milton Obote's government invested so much in the infrastructure of radio broadcasting. At a time when public life was full of acrimony, with scurrilous rumors about the government's secret plans all around, radio made politics sound harmonious. When the recording van visited Kigezi District in 1970, the engineers recorded a series of starchy programs: "Songs and Hymns from Schools and Clubs"; "Songs by the Native People"; "Traditional Dances"; and "Talks by Heads of Department."[17] Two teachers from the regional high school played the *endigiri*, a stringed instrument played with a bow. An eminent man—Paulo Ngologoza, formerly the district's leading administrator—spoke at length about a range of subjects, including "marriage, burials, tribal wars, movements, building, religion, culture etc." Radio Uganda instructed listeners on how to manage the mechanics of their lives.[18] For Obote's regime as for the colonial officials who came before, radio was a means of orienting public culture toward a higher plane, transforming the vernacular languages of ethnic populism into apolitical vehicles for promoting morality.

It required constant vigilance and careful attention, for there was much that could not be said on the air. On 24 May 1966, Obote sent the Uganda Army to crush the palace of Buganda's king. The day after the battle—while fires still burned in the Kabaka's wrecked palace—Obote's government directed that every program broadcast on Radio Uganda should be read out from an official script.[19] The script was to be reviewed by the controller of programs in advance of the broadcast. Music, too, needed careful supervision. A few months after the Kabaka's palace was sacked, the musician Simon Kate Nsubuga recorded a song in Luganda titled "What Happened in Africa?" "We got independence but there is no peace," Nsubuga sang. "Every nation is lamenting—people are crying—we killed ourselves—people are dying."[20] It was part of an album, released as a vinyl record and played, among many other places, on Radio Uganda. Officials were alarmed: "politically this record is doing a lot of harm to our party and the Government," wrote an administrator. The record was swiftly banned.

The legal and administrative powers of Uganda's kingdoms had been pruned away. With so much of public life closed off, the broadcasting studio became the sole arena where patriotic royalists could compete for attention, power, and a voice. It was in many ways an enclosure. In November 1968 a group of listeners wrote to complain that the Luganda news reader had "irritated us in the way he was reading the news."[21] His voice was "lagging, the words were unclear and we found it difficult to extract any meaning from what he was reading." The critics wondered "why such a man was allowed to read the news to the nation in such a state." They wanted the newsreader replaced with a more able colleague. Listeners exerted pressure on Radio Uganda's managers, demanding more airtime, more professionalism, more eloquence.

That was the impetus for the expansion of the radio service. Immediately after independence Radio Uganda increased the number of languages used in broadcasting from seven to fourteen. In 1967—even as Uganda's kingdoms were abolished—another ten languages were added to Radio Uganda's schedule.[22] The equipment had to be reconfigured to accommodate this enlargement of scale.[23] The government set out to build four new high-powered broadcast stations. Each site would be furnished with two 100-kilowatt medium-wave transmitters. During the daylight hours broadcasting would be conducted in English. In the evening, one of the two transmitters would drop out of the national network and broadcast locally produced programs, given in the African languages of the region. The English-language program was supposed to reflect "national policies and the life of the nation as a whole," while the vernacular programs were aimed at "keeping alive the language, customs and traditions of the region."[24] In December 1968 the Uganda government signed a £700,000 contract with the British firm Marconi to begin construction of the new broadcast stations.[25] The work began immediately.

In a former time activists had worked on the streets of Katwe and other urban neighborhoods, building alliances that challenged the government's hold on public life. After 1966 all of that organizing was rendered illegal, and airtime was opened up on Radio Uganda. Under government supervision, the architects of ethnic solidarity could speak in a new register: as disembodied arbiters of morality and custom, as defenders of a politically neutered ethnic heritage.

═══════

President Amin opens the Radio Uganda transmitting tower in Kabale, southern Uganda, 1974 (Courtesy of the Uganda Broadcasting Corporation)

The construction of Uganda's new radio network was well under way when, in January 1971, Idi Amin overthrew Milton Obote's government. The first of the new towers—located in Uganda's eastern region—began transmitting on 20 November 1971. The second new tower, sited in the north, opened the following year.

The new service proved to be tremendously popular. A survey in 1974 found that people in the most remote places were listening to radio broadcasts: in a county in the distant north there were 640 sets; in another there were 1,285.[26] For listeners all over Uganda the broadcasts of Radio Uganda were a source of fascination and pleasure. Writing from southwestern Uganda, a listener named Raphael Kangye told the chief engineer that—even in his remote locality—he could listen to Radio Uganda and "enjoy your good music." "Last Tuesday you made me very happy," he wrote, and "perhaps if you could have been nearer to me I could get you something to drink."[27] Another listener—a young woman named Lucy Apaco—was delighted by the music newly available on Radio Uganda. Writing from Gulu town, she reported that the morning hours were boring, for Radio Uganda was off the air and she was obliged to help her parents labor in the farm fields. But "I do enjoy the afternoons and evenings very much," she reported. "You know, I'm fond of records, and in addition to the records you have got a nice volume which reaches us nicely."[28]

The expansion of Radio Uganda was a government initiative, driven by the authorities' self-interest. It was also driven by listeners' excitement, enthusiasm, and eager involvement in the perfection of the technology. In the archives of the Uganda Broadcasting Corporation there are several thick files full of letters from listeners. They report on the strength of the signal, on the fluctuations in its reception, and on the content of the programs. From a small town in Ethiopia a listener reported that he had heard Radio Uganda's broadcast of Jim Reeves's music, and found "the reception was very good and clear," with no distortion of any kind.[29] From western Uganda, a listener reported that the signal could be "heard loud and clear" on his Sierra three-band radio, far outstripping the clarity of Radio Rwanda or the Voice of South Africa.[30] From the northwest, a schoolboy named James Uyana sent in a report on the variations of the Radio Uganda signal. On 13 May the broadcast had become inaudible within minutes, covered up by a rattling noise. On 17 May the 6:15 p.m. broadcast was unclear, while the late-night broadcast was inaudible up to 11:40 p.m. Uyana volunteered to send in daily reports on the reception of the radio.[31] He and other listeners had a proprietary view of Radio Uganda. They saw it as a public good.

Listeners from Asia, Europe, and America were likewise tracking the signal of Radio Uganda. After the erection of the new 100-kilowatt transmitters the Ugandan signal could be heard with clarity in far distant places. A fifteen-year-old German named Roland Dilmetz decorated a letter to Radio Uganda's manager with hand-drawn illustrations depicting a man jumping aloft in excitement, radio in hand. He reported that the signal from Kampala could be heard in Berlin, though there was occasional interference from Radio Yaoundé, which broadcast on a nearby frequency.[32] From Sweden a correspondent wrote to report on his reception of Radio Uganda's broadcast. He was forty-seven years old, a warehouse worker, and a longtime radio enthusiast.[33] Another man wrote from Champaign, Illinois, saying that he had received the Ugandan signal on his home-built Hallicrafters S-85 radio.[34] For listeners in Berlin and Illinois as for listeners in Gulu or Kabale, Radio Uganda was a fascinating new technology. Unlike newspapers, which relied on the transport infrastructure to reach readers, and unlike a letter, which took weeks to reach its addressee through the post, the radio signal could traverse vast distances in an instant, apparently unhindered by geography. It was a marvel.

Like many other people, Idi Amin was fascinated by radio's power to traverse geography and engage listeners in distant places. Within a few months of his coming to power Amin's cabinet decided to establish an external broadcasting service. It was, in his ministers' view, the "most important decision taken by the Government of the Second Republic of Uganda."[35] The minister of information and broadcasting was given a vast new mandate: it was his ministry's role to "create a vivid, alert and outward-looking society."[36] In February 1974 the government signed a contract with a Swiss firm for the construction of two 250-kilowatt transmitters, together with an array of antennas that would direct the signal to distant places.[37] President Amin could not wait for the legal formalities to be completed. On 19 January 1974, several weeks before the contract was signed, he laid the foundation stone for the building housing the powerful transmitters. There was a new four-story office block to house fifty-three new staff members; thirteen new studios had to be constructed for the recording of external programs.[38]

The external broadcasting service went on the air in 1975. In his introduction to the printed programing guide, President Amin wrote that Radio Uganda would "effectively fight colonialism, neo-colonialism, capitalism and racism even better especially when we shall be reaching right into the enemy's camp."[39] The signal was beamed toward South Africa in the late afternoon hours, then to western Africa, and then to northern Africa. Listeners were treated to a program featuring "Presidential Quotations with Musical Bridges," accompanied by a series of talks on subjects such as "African Solidarity," "Liberation and the Liberators," "Economic Emancipation in Africa," and "Uganda's Economic War." The external broadcasting service transposed Uganda—a landlocked, provincial place—into the middle of things. It was a way of making Uganda's politics exemplary. "Whatever we broadcast will be monitored, recorded and analyzed by foreign countries and news agencies," President Amin told a crowd. "We shall therefore be judged by the quality and contents of our broadcasts."[40]

Amin kept a very close eye on the news media. In his first year in power the cabinet rejected a proposal to establish privately run radio stations in Uganda. Everyone in the cabinet agreed that "the radio service was, in the present circumstances, the most powerful communications medium between the Government and the public." If private broadcasting stations were set up, cabinet members feared, they "might be used by enemies of the Government to broadcast subversive propaganda to the Nation."[41] Journalists had to be exceptionally careful about their reports. Newsmen should "write the gospel of truth," urged a government minister in a seminar with Ugandan reporters. Their role was to "unite Uganda as one country."[42] There was a new newspaper—the *Voice of Uganda*—published by Amin's government. In October 1973, the Amin government prohibited Kenyan newspapers from circulating in Uganda; the following year a number of British newspapers were banned.[43]

=====

The apparatus of official media was designed to give President Amin the final word on public affairs, but from the start the range and audibility of Radio Uganda's broadcasts were constrained. The technology was fragile, and frequently needed repairs. There were no solid state electronics in Idi Amin's Uganda. It required human initiative—creativity, attention, energy, dedication—to keep Radio Uganda on the air.[44]

The rate of breakage and decay often outran engineers' efforts at maintenance. By 1956—only two years after Radio Uganda went on the air—the transmitter in eastern Uganda had fallen into dereliction. The plot on which it sat was surrounded by a high barbed-wire fence, but the posts had been eaten by termites and the fence had collapsed. The door of the building where the transmitter was housed had been broken down. Vagrants made a habit of sleeping overnight on the premises, and there was a pervasive smell of urine around the place.[45] Breakdowns were constant. On one occasion Radio Uganda was off the air for two hours because an acrobatic frog managed to climb an eighteen-foot steel pole and lodge itself between an electrical winding and a ground wire, shorting the current that supplied the transmitter. That incident was reported by the Associated Press and printed—under the headline "Voice of Uganda Silenced for Two Hours by Baby Frog"—in several American newspapers.[46]

In the archives of the Uganda Broadcasting Corporation there are dozens of logbooks, bound with hard cardboard, which contain the handwritten notes of Radio Uganda's studio engineers. They testify to the constant need for human intervention in the operation of radio equipment. On one occasion Radio Uganda was off the air for several minutes because a technician pressed a button labeled S1A, jamming the signal from the broadcasting studio. He was supposed to have pressed button S1.[47] On another occasion the news in Karimojong was delayed for several minutes because someone had mistakenly turned a knob that regulated the impedance of the signal from the broadcast studio, making it impossible for the program to be transmitted.[48] On a third occasion the station sent engineers to a Kampala nightclub to record a live program of dance music. The signal they transmitted to the broadcast studio was exceedingly faint, and there was a loud hum. It took an hour for the engineers to sort out the fault and get the dance music on the air.[49]

People, like equipment, needed careful handling. Most programs ran for periods of less than fifteen minutes, meaning that the announcer had to pay close attention to what came next. The announcers were very often befuddled by the complexity of the day's program, and there was hardly a day when the announcer did not cause some kind of interruption. On 4 September 1965 there was no announcer at the station when it opened at 9:00 a.m.[50] Neither was there an announcer between 2:00 p.m. and 3:30 p.m. The following day, on 5 September, there was again no announcer to open the station. When it came time to read the news in Kuman at 3:00 p.m., no newsreader could be found. Five minutes after the program was to start a stranger barged into the studio, saying that he was meant to read the news. The engineers would not allow him on the air. "The habit of the Announcer to miss has grown mature and I don't know how to overcome this problem," noted the studio engineer.[51]

All of this placed heavy demands on Radio Uganda's engineers. They had to work long hours. There was little time for human convenience. At 2:00 one afternoon in 1971 a peckish engineer named Waliggo wrote:

> With the assumption that I was a human being or at least a living creature I took permission from the [engineer in charge] to go to canteen and feed as it is an obligation of all creatures if they are to live.[52]

By 2:07 he had returned to his post. "Back in this damn enclave," he wrote in the logbook. He was on duty that day until 5:00 p.m. He and other engineers lobbied management for amenities that would make their work easier. "Important: it is considered as a high degree of consideration to supply the [central control room] with soft comfortable chairs to make life relatively easy here, especially for the night shift," wrote an uncomfortable engineer in the logbook.[53] A few weeks later another engineer wrote to complain that the air conditioning system in the studios was not functioning. "I think no one is bothered about mental strain imposed on us due to the stuffiness caused by inadequate circulation of fresh air," he wrote in the logbook.[54] These and other complaints reflect the claustrophobic pressure that those who worked in the service of technology must have felt.

The shortages and upsets of Idi Amin's Uganda made it ever more difficult for engineers to manage the pressures that technology imposed on them. Living in dangerous and insecure times, many staff members found it impossible to do their jobs. One evening in May 1971 thieves broke into the house of a Radio Uganda engineer. The engineer awoke and pursued the burglars, and in the fracas that ensued he cut his foot badly. He was unable to work for several days.[55] For some time in 1975 the Arabic news program could not be broadcasted because the newsreader was in prison.[56] In 1978 the director of broadcasting prepared a document with the title "Some of the Failures in Transmission Emanating from Unreliable Transport at U.B.C."[57] The vehicle tasked to deliver staff members from their homes to Broadcasting House had a puncture, and the staff was obliged to walk to the studio. The director of broadcasting called this and other difficulties "demoralizing."

Like the engineers, the journalists who created reports for Radio Uganda's programs had to contend with shortfalls in equipment and material. Shortly after Amin came to power the government posted "information officers" to each of Uganda's districts.[58] Their task was to compose news reports on local affairs, which they relayed to Broadcasting House in Kampala over telephone or telex machines. The information officer in Jinja, the capital of eastern Uganda, had no office furniture, and there was no money even to pay for cutting the grass. "We cannot overemphasize the preponderous role being played by the Mass Media in the development of a nation," wrote one officer,

> without being flung by emotion to wonder over the ordeal of an Information Officer without transport, whose usefulness is thought of only when his pen and paper are required. Their condition of service leaves a lot to be desired.[59]

The information officer in Lira District, in Uganda's north, was a man named Obwona. He had no office and no telephone line.[60] When he had a story to file, he had to walk into town and use the post office call box. The telephone line from Lira to Kampala was full of static, especially during daylight hours. Mr. Obwona was obliged to spend a great many evenings at the post office, filing reports with the newsroom in Kampala.[61] Even when the line was operational, the newsmen in Kampala were often rude. As Mr. Obwona reported:

> Some of the headquarters staff treat we up country officers as their house boys who they can afford to do anything to. Sometimes when we get through to Kampala it is ridiculous that it should take a person receiving the story five to ten minutes to get a pen and some papers. Some of them direct us to ring later and just bang the receiver down.[62]

There were language problems, too. Mr. Obwona reported that headquarters staff had "fallen into the habit of showing off that they know every English word in the whole vocabulary." When an up-country information officer used an unfamiliar term, the man in Kampala would unctuously correct him, saying that "such and such a word does not exist when in fact it is him who doesn't know the meaning."[63]

It was a struggle to keep Radio Uganda on the air. Listeners likewise had to struggle to make Radio Uganda work. For many Ugandans the signal was irregular and hard to pick up. In the early 1970s—when the powerful new transmitters were installed—engineers shifted the station's signal from the shortwave to the medium-wave frequencies. The medium-wave transmissions could travel over a vast terrain, but rainy weather or cloud cover could interrupt transmission. Throughout the 1970s Radio Uganda's morning broadcasts were inaudible to many Ugandans, for medium-wave signals are constrained by sunlight. One listener—a student in northern Uganda—spent several days tuning his radio to Radio Uganda's frequencies. It was only during the evening hours, from seven to nine, that he could hear clearly.[64] Another listener, writing from West Nile, reported that he had to take great care in positioning his radio receiver: if it faced northward or southward the signal dissipated.[65] In 1974 the Ministry of Information sent three senior bureaucrats on a tour to assess the reception of radio and television broadcasting in the provinces. Everywhere the men from Kampala were confronted by frustrated listeners. In Busoga, in Uganda's east, a district councilor complained that "for two years his radio has not been serving him properly: at times the radio generates awkward noises which makes it difficult to receive radio programmes properly."[66] Why, wondered another councilor, could he receive the Voice of Kenya or Radio Rwanda more clearly than Radio Uganda? In reply, the Kampala officials explained that the soil in Busoga was unsuitable for medium-wave broadcasting, making it hard for the signal to propagate.

The shift to medium-wave broadcasting created new inequalities of access. Owners of shortwave radio sets—which were smaller and cheaper than medium-wave receivers—found themselves shut out of the airwaves. Writing from Lango District, a student noted that the new signal was "very good and clear and loud and we all like it very much indeed," but he and other students who owned shortwave radio receivers found it impossible to tune in.[67] He asked for a return to shortwave, so that "we poor people owning small radios with one band should enjoy the new transmission together with the people who are better off." Poverty likewise made it difficult for people to purchase the batteries that powered radio receivers. In a letter to President Amin a critic complained that "We buy one torch dry cell at Shgs 7 each and you tell the world that we are very well off in Uganda. Maybe you are very happy because you have many cars."[68] By the later 1970s, dry cell batteries were unavailable for purchase in the leading town in eastern Uganda, and local officials lamented that "the public are unable to listen to government policies on their radios."[69] They had to commandeer cartons of batteries for distribution to anxious citizens.

The trade language of the media business makes it seem as though in radio the broadcasters have all the initiative. Radio stations "broadcast," as if the program were effortlessly sent out into the wind. Listeners are called an "audience," as if the ear—not the hand—was all that was needed to receive a radio signal. The quality of the signal is called "reception," as if all the user had to do was to receive. In Amin's Uganda, though, receiving the radio signal was an active undertaking. The channels of distribution were never clear of interference. The path of the radio signal from transmitter to receiver was impeded by the weather, by landscape, by soil types, by the financial wherewithal of the listener, and by the listener's access to the technology of reception. There was a constant need to adjust the tuning and search for the signal. Listeners had to be aware of the changing patterns of wind and weather. They had to anticipate the advancing hours of darkness. They had to have batteries and medium-band receivers, at a time when such equipment was expensive and hard to find. Receiving the broadcast required creativity, connections, and constant attention.

═══════

The men who governed Idi Amin's Uganda could not acknowledge the work that was required to receive the signal. Standing at the edge of a new era in the history of communication, officials in Kampala treated the distribution of radio broadcasts as undifferentiated and universal. At a seminar in 1973 a longtime Ugandan journalist heralded the "transistor revolution." The "mass media," he said, "can reach enormous audiences. The radio does it regardless of climatic hazards, regardless of inappropriate communications through jungles, swamps or even storms at sea."[70] At the same seminar another speaker proclaimed radio to be a means of "reaching, simultaneously, millions of people of all classes in a matter of moments."[71]

Officials in government presumed that listeners were available, attentive, hanging on every word. At a briefing in Kampala on 14 May 1973, President Amin directed two students from each of Uganda's universities and colleges to meet him at State House at 8:30 p.m. the following day to discuss the prospect of a national language for Uganda.[72] There were no students physically present when Amin issued his directive. Neither was there a procedure by which students could select their representatives. But Amin was confident that, through the broadcast media, a specific constituency—the "students"—could be summoned. Government officers imagined an extensive, attentive audience for official media. When Radio Uganda in March 1973 announced its intention to launch broadcasts in Rwamba—a minority language in the far west of Uganda—a tiny column appeared in the *Voice of Uganda* newspaper, inviting people fluent in the language to report to the controller of programs, in Kampala, by 8:15 p.m. that very day.[73] It was a physical impossibility that a Rwamba speaker, at the far end of a long and broken road, could somehow make his or her way to Kampala in the course of a day. But government officers were not worried about geography or the transportation infrastructure. So long as the reporters gathered before them, any occasion, and any audience, was an opportunity to summon the whole Ugandan people.

At a time when paper was in short supply, when the postal system was increasingly inoperative and petroleum was prohibitively expensive, radio was the means by which government authorities communicated with Uganda's people. Idi Amin's speeches were full of directions for specific groups and constituencies. On one occasion—during the same broadcast in which he instructed students to attend an evening meeting regarding the choice of a national language—Amin also told government authorities to install a water supply in Arua; instructed the minister of commerce and industry to build a cement factory on the road from Moyo to Arua; directed the Yugoslav contractors building the Arua airport terminal to transfer their attention to the building of a hotel; accused the hotel management in the Paraa Lodge of tribalism and nepotism in the hiring of staff; condemned waiters for demanding tips from their customers; and suggested that people living in overpopulated areas of southern Uganda should move to unpopulated areas in the north.[74]

These speeches were tedious. An editorialist complained about the long reports that the government-run media produced.

> It is [as] tiresome to sit and yawn listening to a so-called bulletin of 30 minutes or more as it is discouraging to read a lengthy story on the front page and then see "turn to back page" two or three times on the same page. . . . Long verbatim reports . . . tire and discourage the reader, yet [journalists] get out of their professional conduct and ethics of journalism and print word for word. Absurd.[75]

Officials called it "government by radio announcement."[76] Local authorities had to budget their time to be present when broadcasts were on the air. Listeners in northern Uganda had to stay up late, past 11:00 p.m., to hear the local news, which was broadcast after President Amin's long and winding speeches had ended. They complained that it was difficult to find time for sleep.[77] Even so, radio was essential listening, and local authorities had to pay close attention. They took notes. On 29 August 1972, for instance, President Amin made an address at the International Conference Centre in Kampala that was broadcast on the radio. Amin announced the creation of nine new provinces in Uganda and banned teenagers' dances, reasoning that they have "sapped the energy of our young people and . . . encouraged drunkenness, laziness, disobedience to parents and other vices." He also announced new opening hours for bars and nightclubs.[78] Away in the provinces, the administrator in Kigezi District was listening carefully. The next day he typed up a summary of the speech for district officials.[79] He highlighted the presidential directive to "speed up services" and mentioned the new opening hours for bars. His transcription of the key points furnished local authorities with the information they needed to get in line with the president's speech.

Inattentive people could—quite suddenly—find new obligations thrust upon them. In a radio address on 4 February 1974, for example, Amin's government announced a summary ban on the wearing of wigs.[80] They made "our women look unAfrican and artificial," the president argued. Besides, the wigs were fabricated by "the callous imperialists from human hair mainly collected from the unfortunate victims of the miserable Vietnam war." Amin's decree came as a surprise. A woman named C. Kakembo listened to the news broadcast on Radio Uganda at eight that night. No mention was made of the directive, and she blithely went out for an evening drink. It was only during the 10:00 p.m. broadcast that the directive was announced. Ms. Kakembo reported that "those who heard the announcement and happened to be in public places had to pull off the wigs immediately to avoid being bullied, touched and embarrassed."[81] The announcement demanded the rapid revision of women's attire. Ms. Kakembo and many other women were obliged to find ribbons and cloths to tie over their heads in order to "look respectable enough in public."[82]

The irritation that Ms. Kakembo felt must have been shared by many Ugandans, who found themselves—unexpectedly—compelled to conform to government decrees. On 14 May 1973, President Amin announced on the radio that Ugandans should hold countrywide meetings about the design of the national flag. Shortly thereafter a county chief in eastern Uganda received a telephone call telling him to summon taxpayers to discuss the issue that very day.[83] The chief hurriedly typed out a missive to his subordinates, instructing them to bring representatives to his headquarters within the hour. The notices were delivered by messengers, and many of them did not reach their destinations until the early afternoon. The discussion had to happen in great haste. That evening the county chief—who was probably exhausted after all of the activity—typed up a report. His people preferred that the red color be replaced with green in the flag, he wrote, since red "shows us that Uganda will remain in blood shed" and therefore damaged the country's reputation abroad.[84]

All of this tells a familiar tale about the capriciousness of life under a dictatorial government. The point here is that arbitrariness has an infrastructure. It was possible for government officers to issue rapid-fire directives because they imagined that the whole of Uganda could be addressed through official media. With the Ugandan public apparently gathered before them, officials could compress the timescale on which government worked and make everyone act. That is why Ms. Kakembo found herself unwittingly exposed to censorious attention, and why the hapless chief had to hastily organize a meeting to discuss the national flag's design. That is how many Ugandans unknowingly and unexpectedly came to be categorized as enemies of the state, as whole categories of people were summoned, directed, and made subject to Amin's radio-borne directives.

Radio shortened the distance between Kampala and the provinces. It condensed lines of authority, sidelining chiefs, officials, and technical experts. It made every individual—regardless of circumstance and location—responsible for following directions.

———

Idi Amin occupied a great amount of space on Radio Uganda's airwaves, but there were other voices, too. The station's managers in Kampala depended on local authorities for news from the provinces, which they distilled and broadcast during regularly scheduled segments. Here was a platform that local authorities could use to curate their own political voice. It was a tool of administration, a means to address people and constituencies. It was also good advertising. In Radio Uganda local authorities found means by which to fashion themselves into spokesmen for Amin's regime.

By the mid-1970s, authorities in Uganda's provinces were using radio to conduct the most basic elements of their work. In the district archive in Kabale there are several files full of typed notices composed by local authorities, ready to be read out over the air. On 2 January 1975, for example, the education officer broadcast a message asking the headmasters of Nyarushenje Primary School and Kigezi High School to report to his office the following day to discuss school affairs.[85] The district commissioner announced that a meeting with government chiefs scheduled for 9 April had been rescheduled for 10 April.[86] The county chief in Ntoroko called on T. Bakahiiga to report to county headquarters to reclaim his cow, which had been seized because he had no permit for it.[87] Thousands of notices like these were broadcast on Uganda's radio network. They were not in the public interest. Their intended audience was tiny—members of a committee, a schoolmaster, the owner of a lost cow. Broadcasts like these served the purposes of government. They gave officials means to overcome deficits in the physical infrastructure of communication and allowed them to address people by name.

Even as they filled the airwaves with minutely specific reports, local government officials were keenly aware that their messages—even those meant for small, specific audiences—were audible to the generality of Ugandans. Over the course of time they became adept at using radio-borne reportage to burnish their reputations and prove their worth. Radio Uganda was full of reports from self-interested, self-aggrandizing local officials, who used the news to demonstrate their effectiveness. It was propaganda from below.

Perhaps the most industrious of Uganda's provincial self-propagandists was a Uganda Army sergeant who signed himself as William B. Baker. Over the course of six years he issued dozens of communiqués from his post as government chief in an obscure locality in Bundibugyo, one of Uganda's most remote regions. Baker issued his first report in December 1974. It was an amateurish production, full of platitudes about Christmas-tide cheer. "I checked in the police station, and no one was arrested," Baker wrote. "Please, keep in good spirit like that."[88] His reportorial voice became more confident over the course of time. In April 1977, Baker used his tour of Karugutu subcounty as the occasion around which to frame his report. The people with whom he met, their accomplishments or needs, the happenings in the locality—none of this found a place in Baker's report. Instead, Baker used his report to reiterate the directives he gave to the elders of the place:

1. As they are Elders they must not sit idle in their area, they must join hands with strong Cooperation with Government Officers to maintain law and order. . . .

2. Cotton must be cultivated in plenty, every Ugandan at least to cultivate one acre of cotton, not to take it as a Punishment you are given by chiefs. . . .

5. County Chief Ntoroko Mr. William B. Baker warned very, very seriously on those who are hiding robbers in their homes to attack their friends during the night. . . .

7. Tribalism must be stopped very very strictly. We are all Ugandans, our father is the Head of State.[89]

On the rare occasions when Baker gave other people a voice in his reports, they always spoke words of congratulation, like a Greek chorus.

When Baker reported on his inspection of the crews building roads in his county, for example, he described how the men had told him that "I, Sgt. William B. Baker, have been the first County Chief to make a meeting with road works and advise them on Government Policies. . . . They told me how they can't realize their mistakes unless they meet with an advisor like me."[90] It was Sergeant Baker's energy, and his fidelity, that was the subject of the report.

Why did this officer, posted in the distant marches of Idi Amin's Uganda, devote so much time to writing press reports? Like all local government officers in Amin's Uganda, Sergeant Baker was in a precarious position, always worried about his standing in the eyes of the authorities in Kampala. He worked to overcome this insecurity by inserting himself into as many radio broadcasts and as many archives as he could. His communiqués—addressed to the managers at Radio Uganda—were carbon-copied to a wider range of recipients: the provincial governor, the district commissioner, the district police commander, schoolteachers, elders, church ministers. Even if he did not always get his reports on the air, on paper Sergeant Baker projected himself outside his provincial locality.

In 1977 President Amin invited chiefs to nominate constituents who had "made a positive contribution towards the development of Uganda" for the award of a special medal. William Baker placed his own name at the top of his list of nominees.[91] He had made himself into a hero of Idi Amin's Uganda. The evidence could be found in the broadcasts of Radio Uganda, which he had so industriously populated with evidence of his spokesmanship.

———————

In February 1979, Radio Uganda's employees planned a celebration marking the twenty-fifth anniversary of the station.[92] The organizing committee planned for a "program production competition," in which teams of announcers would broadcast, in fifteen-minute intervals, from the top of Broadcasting House in Kampala. The challenge was to ensure that equipment, microphones, and personnel were all in place and that the broadcast went off smoothly. The engineering staff had a separate competition: they were to design and build a recorder using spare equipment in Radio Uganda's engineering shop. The winner of each of these games was to be awarded 50,000 shillings.

Radio Uganda's twenty-fifth anniversary was never celebrated. Even as the planning committee developed its plans, an invading army from

Tanzania was marching north, driving Amin's men before them. The Amin regime was overthrown before the festivities could take place. But the earnestness with which Radio Uganda's employees laid in plans to celebrate the jubilee reflects their investment in the technical work of radio. During the most tumultuous months of Uganda's history they looked for ways to celebrate and honor their vocation.

Radio Uganda helped organize political life. Coming to power at the edge of a new era in the history of technology, Idi Amin found in radio a vehicle by which to address the whole of Uganda's disparate people, all at once. Radio furnished the Amin government with a prosthetic infrastructure for government communication. It preempted Ugandans' disparate timetables, obliging everyone to act on short notice. There was no time for representation, for deliberative democracy.

Suddenly it became possible to think of government itself in a new way: a perpetual campaign. Here was an engine for a new form of politics.

CHAPTER FOUR

A Government of Action

IDI AMIN ENJOYED CALLING his regime a "government of action." It was a way of contrasting the energy and vigor of the Second Republic of Uganda with the lethargy that had crippled his predecessor's presidency. "If the army had not taken action, Uganda was about to be bogged down in a morass of political and economic stagnation," Amin told an audience after seizing the presidency. His aim was to "make Uganda move once again after she had been lagging behind for the last nine years."[1] By 1973 Amin could claim that his regime was "moving at supersonic speed." Government ministers and other politicians who "could not cope with the speed [have] got to be retired."[2]

Under Milton Obote's presidency paranoid officials had seen conspiracies all around. Under Idi Amin the insecurities of the old era gave way to a manful confidence about the role of government in society. Amin's officials saw themselves as taskmasters. Matters that had formerly stood outside the government's purview were, quite suddenly, targeted by official decree. Issues that had formerly been people's private concerns were thrown open and made into national priorities. Everywhere campaigns drafted people to serve in projects launched from Kampala. For many people it was exhausting. The campaigning momentum of government made strenuous claims on Ugandans' time, energy, and resources. For some, however, the campaigns that the Amin regime launched created a self-righteous sense of vocation, a call to duty.

The Amin regime's efforts to arouse the enthusiasm of Uganda's people grew in proportion to the shrinking of the state's capacity for governing. From 1973 onward global price inflation crippled the economy, rendering wage employment largely unprofitable and encouraging people to divest from the formal economy. Everywhere there were shortfalls that compromised the infrastructure of government work: shortages of paper made it difficult to collect taxes or keep records; shortages of petroleum made it impossible to inspect schools or conduct land surveys; shortages of cement and corrugated iron made it hard to construct new buildings. The many campaigns of the Amin government had to be pursued under conditions of austerity.

In a time of widespread shortage, commoners—people outside the formal institutions of the administration—were called upon to subsidize government administration. It was their self-sacrifice and their knowledge that made Idi Amin's campaigns work. Many people came to see themselves as proprietors of civic institutions, and a whole host of self-nominated busybodies came to play a role in public life.

═══════

Radio allowed Idi Amin and other officials in Kampala to stand outside the complicated material world and issue directives. Over the radio, matters that had previously been outside the government's supervision—the cleanliness of homes, the cultivation of gardens, the planting of trees, the disposal of waste—could be taken out of private citizens' hands and made into programmatic activities. There were new goals, new standards, new guidelines, and new metrics for evaluation, as previously unremarkable activities were made into contests around which people had to mobilize.

One of the first of these contests was the "Double Production" campaign, meant to increase the harvest of food crops. For every county the government set production targets. Each tractor in Uganda was to plow ten acres per day, with farmers clearing out stumps and brush in advance. The campaign's advocates saw themselves as clear-sighted pioneers, manfully pushing Uganda's agriculture forward. "We are now engaged in a dynamic programme to ensure that the standard of living for our people in the countryside is improved," wrote an agriculture officer. "We have the land and the brains. What we need now is determination and willpower. CHESTS FORWARD, HEADS UP AND MOVE STRAIGHT TO THE FARMER."[3] There was a form that local authorities were obliged to fill in on an annual basis, listing twenty-eight different crops in a column, with spaces to fill in "acres under production" and "gross quantity produced."[4] Targets had to be met. Committees of officials went out to rural parishes to address farmers about "possible ways of accelerating and doubling both food and cash crops," stressing "early land preparation, timely planting, correct spacing, early weeding, proper thinning and timely harvesting of crops."[5]

Cotton was a crop that was particularly easy to supervise.[6] President Amin himself prepared a "Nine Point Plan" which was copied and delivered to agriculture officers throughout the country. It contained very specific guidance. Amin directed cotton farmers to "increase the yield per acre by planting your cotton correctly spaced. Two feet apart in rows, with planting holes one foot apart."[7] Seeds were to be planted five to a hole. Amin himself kept a close eye on the weather, and when it began to rain heavily, he issued a statement exhorting Ugandans to "go out in full force and ensure that Double Production of food and cash crops is achieved during these rains."[8] There was a "President's Cotton Production Cup," whose judges toured cotton farms throughout Uganda. The answer to "How much cotton was planted in the recommended time?" earned contestants up to twenty points, while "How much was planted with the recommended spacing?" was worth ten points.[9]

All these plans—precise and exacting though they were—made it seem as though cotton cultivation was a straightforward mathematical matter. In reality Ugandan farms could not be run by mathematical equations. When government officials surveyed people in western Uganda about cotton they received a litany of complaints.[10] Water was scarce because wells had not been maintained. There was no transport to bring the cotton crop to purchasing agents. Neither were there storage facilities in cooperative buildings. Farmers were therefore obliged to store their cotton in their private homes. Officials urged people to take matters into their own hands: roads could be improved through uncompensated labor; stores for cotton could be built if local people volunteered their time to construct them.[11] Even so, in many places the environmental conditions were simply not conducive to cotton cultivation. In Kasese, in the mid-west, the soil was thin; plants grew spindly and tall, and they bore little crop.[12]

The authorities in Kampala could not acknowledge any of this. They established the standards, drew up the regulations, and imposed them on Uganda's localities. It was a way of paring down complicated and vexing problems, of making things manageable. The National Tree Planting campaign, for example, was launched in 1978, with official guidelines set out in a neatly typed document. In Omwanguhya parish the census reported a population of 8,955 people; and therefore 8,955 trees were to be grown in the parish nursery. In Kisusu trading center there were 477 people, and 477 trees were therefore to be grown.[13] The statisticians in Kampala used these estimates to work out the amount of seed that was to be distributed to each parish: Omwanguhya was to receive 190 grams, Kisusu 20 grams. The Ministry of Agriculture supplied hoes in proportion to the number of trees being cultivated. The rest—spades, watering cans, rakes, soil, labor time—was to be provided by each parish on a "self-help" basis. That is how the government campaigns worked. No one in Kampala was worried about soil quality, weather, or topography in the places where the trees were to be planted. There was no discussion about the local availability of land, or about the labor burdens that people bore.

Government authorities saw themselves as drill sergeants. It was their role to get people into line and ensure that the targets were met. In 1978, Alex Owor, the governor of Western Province, toured the district surrounding Kasese town. He did not have expertise in any of the several fields of government work on which he was invited to comment, but he had in mind quantifiable criteria by which to evaluate, judge, and correct his subordinates.[14] About the infrastructure for health care, Owor "instructed the chiefs to mobilize the masses and erect aid posts" and commanded the district's nursing officer to "immediately begin the supply of medicine." About education Owor decreed that "all teachers must be clean shaven, they must trim their hair short and their finger nails, must not drink excessively, must not dress in torn clothes or shoes, or come to duty drunk." There were dozens of directives issued in Owor's fifty-page report. Each directive was marked in the margin with capital letters: "CHIEFS TO NOTE," for example, or "TEACHERS TO NOTE." His report was a set of marching orders.

It was as if all Uganda were on parade. Suddenly a whole range of activities—formerly outside officials' purview—were subject to inspection and oversight. In western Uganda government officials began collecting school fees from parents. If the parent was unable or unwilling to pay cash, officials confiscated property and auctioned it off to raise money. In northern Uganda government chiefs were instructed to send in reports about the behavior of their people. Individuals who were "moving rumours, thieves, guerillas, strangers, people who have magic, and who bewitch their friends" were all supposed to be reported to higher authorities.[15] One county chief—a man named Keresi Amini—made a list of the offenses for which he imprisoned people. The criteria were extensive.

1. Kondo [hooliganism]
2. Pregnating [*sic*] school girls and giving no help.
3. One refusing to pay one's due. . . .
5. One to marry a wife of someone illegally.
6. A person telling false information against the Government.
7. Raping a woman.
8. Tax defaulters.
9. Those having no kitchens and latrines.
10. Those having no jobs but intend to rob properties from people at night times.[16]

Chief Keresi—like other officials who served President Amin's regime—had been carried away by an expanded sense of purpose. For him as for other authorities who served Idi Amin's regime, governmental oversight stretched into areas of life that had never before been subject to regulation.

═══════

Even as administrators like Chief Keresi pursued an ever-expanding company of wrongdoers, the resources with which they worked were radically diminished. The many campaigns that the Amin government launched were not supported by an expansion of budgets, by an increase in staff, or by a renovation of infrastructure. To the contrary. All of the campaigns that the Amin government pursued depended on the uncompensated labor of commoners.

The cost of imported and manufactured goods rose dramatically in Ugandan marketplaces in the latter months of 1973. The causes of price inflation lay largely in the dynamics of the global economy. Poor crop yields in the United States, the Soviet Union, and other major agricultural economies depressed the worldwide supply of agricultural commodities. When the Soviet Union's economic planners began to purchase grain in large quantities there was a worldwide spike in the price of cereals and soybeans.[17] At the outer edge of the world economy, Ugandans found it difficult to keep pace with the global rate of inflation. In October 1973 officials reported that a simple cup of tea purchased in Kampala—priced at 3 shillings 50 cents in 1972—now cost 10 shillings. Primus stoves that had cost 45 shillings in 1972 had doubled in price; while suits of clothes that had cost 700 shillings now cost 1,300.[18]

The rapid rate of inflation made wage employment unprofitable. According to government statistics, the cost of living for low-income workers increased by 531 percent between 1971 and 1977; while the cost of living for high-income groups rose by 234 percent.[19] Wages did not keep pace: the legal minimum wage was increased by a bare 40 percent. Wage-earning employees had little reason to do their jobs.[20] Even a generous cash salary could, within a matter of months, be rendered valueless. The driver of the road grader in Lango was employed in July 1977 at a salary of 505 shillings a month. By January 1978—six months after he signed his contract—he was demanding a raise of 400 shillings, saying that his salary would not allow him to make ends meet.[21] Drivers at the Ministry of Foreign Affairs were similarly incensed about inflation. Senior drivers made 800 shillings a month in July 1977. They demanded an increase of 400 shillings per month, as the value of their cash salaries had evaporated.[22]

Lacking labor, spare parts, and raw materials, Uganda's manufacturing economy ground to a halt. Uganda's sugar farms produced 110,000 tons in 1973. In 1978 farmers produced only 3,000 tons of sugar.[23] In 1971 Uganda produced 1.4 million hoes; in 1978 it produced only 333,000.[24] Factories produced 171,000 tons of cement in 1971; in 1978, they produced only 50,000 tons. These shortfalls made it hard for people to carry out simple transactions. A countrywide shortage of gunny bags, for example, made it difficult for maize buyers in eastern Uganda to collect the crop from farmers, as there was no means to convey it.[25] Building contractors faced shortfalls in the most basic items. In 1975 the contractor responsible for building schools in Lango District was obliged to delay work for several months, as he found it impossible to obtain lumber, door locks, nails, or cement.[26] Purchasing these goods on the black market, the contractor reported, would have bankrupted his company.

The shortages were most severe in the provinces. Semuliki District was created in 1974, when President Amin restructured local government and increased the number of districts from nineteen to thirty-four. A year after the district's creation the treasurer did not have stationery or receipt books.[27] The medical officer did not have rubber stamps to mark meat as suitable for human consumption. The surveyor did not have a vehicle by which to traverse the district's mountainous territory.[28] The organizers of the National Literacy Campaign did not have blackboards or chalk.[29] The prison warders did not have uniforms.[30] No one had an office. Most government officials in Semuliki worked in the community hall, which had been partitioned into tiny cubicles. No one had paper. On several occasions the secretary could not distribute minutes for the monthly meetings of the district's executive committee because paper was not available.[31] In one county the chief had to suspend tax collection.[32] There were no receipt books.

In Semuliki as in most other places the costs of government work were borne by commoners. The machinery of administration only functioned when people sacrificed their time, energy, and money. The district's land committee did not have a vehicle with which to inspect properties that people had applied to occupy. It was applicants' responsibility to rent a vehicle that could transport the committee to the site of the property that he or she wished to obtain.[33] It fell on applicants, too, to ensure that the paperwork moved smoothly through the government bureaucracy. When some applicants complained about the slowness of the land committee's work, officials told them to go to Fort Portal— across a mountain range, over a winding and broken road—to collect maps and the forms for processing.[34]

Semuliki was one of Uganda's most remote districts. At the center of things, too, ordinary people had to sacrifice time and resources to uphold government institutions. President Amin's favorite lakeside retreat— called "Paradise Island," in Lake Victoria—was created and maintained by prisoners, who were marshalled by the dozens to clear brush, bring in sand, and build cottages to accommodate visitors.[35] The costs of sending the Uganda delegation to the 1976 Olympics in Montreal were met through a countrywide fundraising campaign.[36] Each parish was to contribute fifty shillings; each trading center was to contribute one hundred. The tourism industry likewise needed a subsidy from commoners. In 1976 the minister for tourism and wildlife ordered local government authorities to organize fundraising campaigns in their provinces.[37] In Semuliki District teachers hurriedly organized concerts featuring choirs of schoolchildren. Adults were charged a shilling each to attend; children paid fifty cents.[38] Schoolchildren and parents in one of Uganda's most remote localities thereby underwrote the running costs of a government ministry.

Public works projects likewise required subsidies from Ugandan commoners. The "Self Help Projects Decree," adopted in 1975, made it obligatory for every rural person to present themselves at county head-quarters once per month to labor on collective building projects. Anyone avoiding this obligation was liable for a month's imprisonment.[39] Self-help projects were sometimes remarkably ambitious. In Kigezi District local people completed work on fifty-five roads covering 371 miles over the space of one year. The standard was not particularly high. Volunteer work crews lacked tools. There were no lorries to carry crushed stone and murram.[40] There were no pipes for culverts. Drainage must have been a problem. Even so, local officials could rightly boast that local people had "[scored] spectacular achievements" through their communal labor. People in Kasese built a stadium in the center of town on the basis of self-help work.[41] Each county had produced 6,000 blocks for the building's construction.[42]

More than anyone, it was the young whose labor and time subsidized the work of local government. Amin's government created the Uganda Youth Development Organization in 1976. The architects argued that a "child is the property not only of his parents or clan, but is practically owned by the whole community."[43] Younger boys joined the "Uganda Young Pioneers," where they practiced poultry keeping, did handicraft work, and underwent basic military training. Older boys constructed roads, bridges, and schools. To enthusiastic officials it was like a revolution. "The thrust of the youth into the main stream of national life is a phenomenon never before experienced in this country in particular and the whole world in general," wrote an official in western Uganda.[44]

All this earnest ambition could not cover up basic shortfalls in supplies and equipment. The stadium in Kasese—constructed by communal labor—began to collapse within a few months of its completion. The walls were built of wood, and when it rained, they sagged away.[45] Building projects in Semuliki similarly foundered in the absence of equipment and material. By November 1977—three years after the founding of the district—new local government offices had not been built.[46] Workers had assembled heaps of stones at the county and subcounty headquarters, but the district's only tipper had been out of service for months.[47] There was no cement, and neither was there sand with which to erect the walls. Road-building, too, had largely ceased. Although work had begun on a major trunk road in July 1978, the driver of the road grader resigned in October, as his rate of pay was too low to support a living.[48]

As funding dried up, as machinery broke down, and as infrastructure crumbled, civil servants struggled to make up the difference between infrastructural needs and the shortfalls of government provision. In Kasese employees of local government were exhorted to "ask not what your country can do for you, but what you can at all costs do for the good of your country and the welfare of her people."[49] For many civil servants, John F. Kennedy's famous dictum was a sentence of poverty. In Semuliki District local officials were obliged to finance the official celebration of the fifth anniversary of Idi Amin's coup out of their own pockets.[50] It was only one of many instances where they had to sacrifice to make government function.

In 2015 an intrepid doctoral student named Doreen Kembabazi led a project to organize and inventory the archives of the Central Police Station in Kampala.[51] When she and her team started their work it was impossible to get into the room where the archives were stored, for the shelves inside had collapsed, spilling their contents onto the floor and blocking the door. Once the door was opened, the archive revealed a wealth of interesting and incendiary things. One day an intern opened a box and found an explosive device inside. In astonishment the intern picked up the bomb. Fearing it would be detonated if he released it, the police evacuated the building, and the bomb squad removed it—gingerly—from the intern's hands. The cataloguing project was delayed for several weeks while the police swept the room for ordnance.

Like many other government institutions in Amin's Uganda, the police force had to operate with inadequate equipment and limited financial resources. At a time when other police forces were communicating on radio, Uganda's police were transmitting messages in Morse code.[52] The holding cells at the Central Police Station were poorly built and insecure. The police were always short of petroleum to fuel their vehicles. Funding was in short supply: in 1976 the government allocated only half the funds needed to finance the force's budget. The commissioner complained that police dogs were going hungry, as there was no money for their biscuits.[53] By 1977 many police officers were wearing civilian clothes, as the force had not been issued uniforms for years. Housing was in short supply, and many officers were renting private homes outside the police barracks.[54]

These shortfalls undercut policemen's power to pursue criminals and investigate crimes. At the same time, policemen's powers were undermined by the self-interested and violent behavior of men in the Uganda

Army, who often interfered with police investigations. When a British police officer visited Uganda in July 1971, after Amin came to power, he found the police force in a "state of disarray."[55] Several police officers had been killed by soldiers because they had investigated crimes committed by army officers. The force was "leaderless and demoralized," the visitor wrote. Policemen had to be circumspect about investigations that might involve the army. In September 1972 the police recovered the bodies of three Asian men from a swamp near Masaka. There were ropes tied around their necks, and wounds from bullets marked their bodies. Investigators contacted fingerprint experts to identify the victims, but the experts refused to do the work. They had been warned by army officers not to photograph or fingerprint any dead body.[56]

Remarkably, though, government archives show that—even in a time of great danger, even in the absence of money and material—the police were conscientious about their work. They were investigating crimes, collecting evidence, and protecting victims. In the archives of the Central Police Station there are more than 4,000 case files from the 1970s. One exemplary case concerned a young man named Peter Kakooza, a cobbler.[57] On 24 February 1974 he had confronted a thief who had stolen a pair of shoes from him, and the angry thief beat him with a stick. Kakooza came immediately to the police station to report the crime. Two weeks after the incident, a police corporal made his way to Kakooza's market stall to inquire about his case. The cobbler could not be found. Neither could he be found on 21 May, when the policeman again sought him out. The file was closed the following day. I do not know why Kakooza did not pursue his complaint against the thief. The case file demonstrates, though, that in this as in many other instances the police did the work with which they were entrusted.

Foreign diplomats were impressed at the professionalism of Uganda's civil service. In 1970, the year before Amin came to power, the government was the largest employer in the country. The civil service was ethnically balanced and, in the judgment of American diplomats, a "reasonably competent body."[58] According to the head of the Institute of Public Administration, Uganda's twenty district commissioners and 3,000 chiefs had a "strong tradition of a degree of independence from the centre, and of a reasonably equitable approach to the problems of their area, which they had tried hard to maintain."[59] British diplomats agreed. "Perhaps the most surprising aspect of the civil service is that it works as well as it does," remarked a diplomat in December 1972.

The drainage system, electricity and water supplies work; the
Bank of Uganda produces balance sheets; taxes are collected; the
City Council keeps the city clean and carefully tends its numerous decorative flower beds; one can register and license one's car
without having to resort to a bribe; men with pots inspect one's
garden for mosquitoes.[60]

In the early days after the 1971 coup some civil servants saw President
Amin's new regime as an opening for a more rational form of government. "It is important for us to show that we can do this business of running the country better than the politicians," wrote the principal of
Uganda's training college for civil servants.[61] He composed a briefing
paper explaining the reasons for the coup that had brought Idi Amin to
power, listing the tyrannies of the Obote regime—detention without
trial, lack of freedom for political expression, widespread corruption. The
principal ended his paper by quoting Article 15 of the Declaration of
Rights of the State of Virginia: "no free government, or the blessings of
liberty, can be preserved by any people, but by a firm adherence to justice, moderation, temperance, frugality and virtue."[62] It was an unlikely
justification for a government that was—as the principal wrote—engaged
in a violent campaign against its own citizens.

Bureaucrats knew how to tidy things up. Two weeks after Amin came
to power he received a file from a top civil servant. It was full of paperwork that needed his attention: there was a note from the minister of education about the appointment of members of the Senate at Makerere
University; a recommendation about the future of the Miria Obote
Charity Fund; a proposal concerning the President's Polio Fund. In his
cover letter the civil servant who prepared the file coached Idi Amin
through the work, giving him advice on how to handle the different
pieces of business.[63] The bureaucrat was trying to habituate President
Amin into the routines of the bureaucracy. Even the reckless pronounce-
ments of Africa's most mercurial president were subject to the regulatory
oversight of government bureaucrats. In March 1972 an official from
Kampala wrote to district administrators to announce a "research project
on requests from district elders and His Excellency's promises."[64] Everywhere President Amin had met with groups of citizens and made unexpected promises. "All of these requests and promises are now an
important subject of research and analysis," the bureaucrat wrote. Local
authorities were instructed to make cost estimates for the projects that

President Amin had promised to support. The bureaucrats were tying up loose ends and working out plans that could make the president's idiosyncratic and unpredictable decrees into the basis of a coherent policy.

Civil servants were professionally invested in the Amin regime, and throughout the 1970s many of them faithfully did their jobs. But there was much that they simply could not manage. In places where funds were scarce and energy lagged, local officials bridged the gap between the target and reality by cooking up numbers and inventing favorable storylines. The imaginative ability to mask failure was a critically important skill for the overstretched authorities of local government.

The need to demonstrate forward progress was a constant source of tension and anxiety for local officials. In the absence of paper, filing cabinets, and record books it was hard to generate the statistics that drove government-sponsored campaigns. In 1976 Idi Amin made a county-by-county tour of Uganda. Every chief was obliged to prepare a "concise summary" of the past five years of work, outlining "all the development programs achieved, future development plans and problems that the people are facing."[65] It was more than some officials could manage. A county chief in western Uganda, for example, produced a report assuring the president that, since Amin came to power, the "number of children in all schools have doubled." But there were no statistics to prove the claim. Neither were there hard numbers concerning agriculture: the chief waffled on about the loamy soil and the favorable weather, but about crop productivity he could only vaguely talk of "increasing production."[66] It was the best that he could manage.

The paperwork that local authorities produced was sometimes a disguise that covered up a more complicated, less impressive reality. Occasionally—when reading through local government archives—one can see the disguise slip. In September 1976 the governor of Western Province inspected cotton farms in one of the districts under his supervision. Many farmers had registered the acreage of land that they intended to place under cultivation. It was all laid out clearly in the paperwork, but the impressive statistics hid a different reality. When the governor inspected the cotton farms, he found that most farmers had not even begun to prepare the ground for planting. The governor, angry, vowed to return in three weeks, and "during this visit I shall not accept any forms of excuses and alibi."[67] The governor's outrage belied an underlying fact. The paper record documenting the forward progress of Idi Amin's campaigns was sometimes a fake.

Fraudulence was part of local government authorities' work. They needed statistics that could establish the effectiveness of their work. Any numbers would do. The agriculture assistant in Karugutu District, in the distant west, was an enthusiastic writer of reports. In August 1976 he filed a report describing how 87.5 acres of cotton had been planted in his subcounty, with 350 plots cleared and ready for the hoe. The provincial governor had that report in hand when, later that same month, he made an unannounced visit to Karugutu. He measured up the cotton fields and found that a total of ten acres of land had actually been cleared, while only four acres had been planted with cotton.[68] It was a stunning embarrassment for the agriculture assistant, who was accused by his superiors of submitting "lies, inaccurate information, and too much exaggeration" in his reports. Even more embarrassment was heaped upon the hapless agriculture assistant when it came to light that he had composed his August 1976 report while resident at his home, thirty-five miles away from Karugutu.[69] The report was a work of fiction, cooked up by a man who was under pressure to generate hard numbers that signified progress.

I do not know whether the agriculture assistant suffered any consequences for his fraudulence. I imagine he did not. Campaigns need numbers, even inflated numbers, in order to work. Campaigners take abstract and cloudy problems and set numerical, quantifiable goals to address them. They generate the feeling of forward momentum by producing statistics that show progress toward the goal. That is why—even as government officers produced reports that charted the successes of the "Double Production" campaign—the amount of cotton that was actually planted by Ugandan farmers declined markedly over the course of the 1970s.[70] The paperwork that Amin's officials produced did not necessarily record real developments on the ground. It served its own purpose: it was a means by which to make Idi Amin's regime appear to be a "government of action."

At a time when many institutions were poorly resourced, it often fell to citizens to make government function in their favor. Whether out of a sense of duty or a feeling of desperation, ordinary people made serious and sustained efforts to bend the routines of administration to advance their own interests and serve the common good.

In the archives of the High Court of Uganda—which have recently been organized by a team from my university, working with colleagues from Makerere University and the Judiciary of Uganda—there are dozens of cases initiated by injured citizens intent on holding government authorities to account. In a time of great violence in public life, courageous people were opening lawsuits against the violent men who served Amin's regime. In October 1975, for example, Isibosesi Musebi, from Bugisu, in eastern Uganda, brought a civil suit against the attorney general on behalf of his deceased brother.[71] The brother had been arrested by a police corporal, then beaten and shot. Musebi sued for the costs of his brother's funeral and for the loss of income suffered by his family. A second file contains the plea of a man was who arrested and beaten by soldiers of the Uganda Army. He suffered permanent hearing loss in his right ear as a result. He asked for 20,000 shillings in damages.[72] A third plaintiff was injured in her house in Nakawa, outside Kampala, by a stray bullet fired by a police officer.[73] Her arm was paralyzed, and she sued for damages. A fourth file documents the plea of a man who was arrested by his parish chief, tied up, and frog marched to the local government building. During the beating he received his left eye was lacerated, his right hand was twisted and damaged, and his hip was bruised. His injuries made him unable to work.[74]

The lawsuits that these and other injured litigants filed put the High Court in an impossible position. Like other civil servants, the learned justices were subject to the terrifying power of men with guns. The chief justice, Benedicto Kiwanuka, had been pulled from his chambers by Amin's men one afternoon in September 1972. Kiwanuka was murdered in a brutal manner, and his body was mutilated in Amin's presence.[75] This made Chief Justice Kiwanuka's successors exceedingly wary about cases that involved officials of Amin's government.[76] It is not surprising that they equivocated. Most of the civil suits brought by injured litigants against government officials did not receive a hearing. The case files were opened, the plaints were recorded, but the court heard no evidence and made no decisions. It was only in the early 1980s, after Amin's government had been removed from power, that the lawsuits brought by injured litigants began to receive hearings.

Everyone involved in these lawsuits knew that they were on dangerous ground. Isibosesi Musebi waited for a full year after his brother's unfortunate death before filing his suit. Did he wonder about the wisdom of taking Idi Amin's government to court? Did he hesitate, worried about the repercussions for himself and his brother's family?

The remarkable thing is that—even in the face of state-sponsored violence, even at a time when civil institutions were poorly resourced—so many people acted as Mr. Musebi did. They sought to make the government bureaucracy work for them. The "Daily Crime Logbook" at the Central Police Station in Kampala shows that, during the first five months of 1978, 1,029 crimes were reported. In nearly three hundred of these cases complainants physically apprehended suspects and presented them to the police to be taken into custody. An employee of the East African Development Bank brought in a suspect whom he accused of stealing twenty cans of paint from the bank's storeroom.[77] The manager of a hotel in Kampala brought in one of the waiters, whom he accused of stealing six drinking glasses.[78] In several cases angry victims apprehended dangerous criminals. In one instance two men delivered a pair of pickpockets to the police. Both men had been the targets of the pickpockets' attention. They worked together to apprehend the people guilty of the crime.[79]

People had to take matters into their own hands and pursue the criminals who had wronged them. Emboldened by their outrage or burdened by a sense of personal responsibility, Ugandans assumed the duties of the justice system as their own. Out of passion, out of anger, or out of grief, people deputized themselves for public service. Here was a do-it-yourself administration. There was a widened basis for authority—an outsourcing of administrative work—as ordinary people, quite suddenly, felt themselves responsible for the management of public affairs.

In a way that was new in Uganda's politics, President Amin was accessible, available, and (apparently) attentive to the entreaties of ordinary people. He often gave out his telephone number to private citizens. When the British high commissioner called on President Amin, their discussions were repeatedly interrupted by telephone calls from people seeking the president's instruction on trivial matters.[80] As one of Amin's critics put it, Amin "will insist on doing everything himself, therefore he can be in southern Uganda for a farmers meeting in the morning, announce the cancellation of a sports event at lunch time, and be in Jinja for a passing out parade in the afternoon."[81] By the late 1970s President Amin personally held six ministerial portfolios in his cabinet: he was in charge of the Ministries of Health, Foreign Affairs, Defense, Information, Tourism, and Internal Affairs.[82]

Amin placed himself at the center of every question; and many Ugandans, in turn, felt themselves empowered to address the president.

In every local government archive around Uganda there are thick files full of letters addressed to the president. In them people petitioned the president for all manner of things. A girl writes in Luganda for help with school fees. A father asks for money to support his seven children.[83] Everyone, it seemed, felt entitled to an audience with the president. An old man named Yowasi Kiridama wrote in September 1973 asking President Amin to "let me know the day you will be able to see me."[84] Kiridama— who said he was 110 years old—claimed to have fought in the First World War. He complained that local officials had required him to retire from his post as parish chief. As proof of his vigor he vowed to walk the entire distance from his home to the capital—a trip of sixteen days—in order to see the president.

People addressed the president about substantial and weighty matters, too. At regular intervals over the course of the 1970s the government invited unremarkable people to express their views about matters of state. Late in October 1972, for example, the president invited "all Ugandans to come forward to make recommendations on how economic power should be put into the hands of Ugandans."[85] Schoolteachers, civil servants, businessmen, and other groups were to submit memoranda laying out their views. The deadline was less than a week away. It must have been impossible to arrive at a considered view. Nonetheless, a wide range of people composed memoranda. Chemists thought the government should set up rice farms in swamps to increase food production.[86] Prison warders thought the government should nationalize banks, cinemas, and factories.[87] This and many other hastily contrived consultations had little effect on government policy. Nonetheless, occasions like these encouraged some people to embrace a widened sense of responsibility over civic affairs.

One man who appears repeatedly in the archives of the Amin presidency is Tito Bisereko. Bisereko—whose home was in western Uganda— claimed no special knowledge about anything. In his correspondence he usually signed himself as "A Local Farmer." He began writing to Idi Amin in February 1976, when he sent the president a typed missive titled "The World Source of Living Peacefully."[88] In it he congratulated Amin for the "amount you have done to solve the problems with our neighboring countries by means of negotiation in the spirit of African brotherhood." In March 1976 Bisereko apparently made a visit to Kampala to discuss Uganda's borders with government officials. President Amin had made an incendiary speech in which he claimed much of western Kenya as Uganda's possession.[89] The ensuing diplomatic fracas was covered widely in the press, and Kenyans were marching through the streets of Nairobi in protest against Amin's claims. Bisereko saw himself as a mediator. In his report he told President Amin that, because of his deliberations with government officials, "from now onwards our National Map and Border Marks confirm each and every thing with our neighboring countries, that Uganda shall ever stay with her 235,880 square kilometers only."[90] Mr. Bisereko had no expertise in the field of cartography. Neither did he have any standing as a diplomat. None of that stopped him from commenting on the borders of Uganda, or on many other matters.

In November 1976 Bisereko produced his most ambitious comment on government policy: a lengthy report describing his month-long walking tour from the Zaire border in the west to the eastern border with Kenya.[91] He covered an extraordinary amount of ground. In the west he had seen Zairian smugglers buying shirts and beer; in the east he had seen "weak minded" Ugandans buying sugar and batteries at extortionate prices from Kenyan smugglers. He wanted smugglers detained in their villages and deprived of their passports. Bisereko also had ideas about gonorrhea, which was "spreading like bush fire through the country." Treatment for the disease should be free of charge, since obliging people to pay for medicine would antagonize married couples and increase the divorce rate. He thought that the government should keep herders from pasturing their cattle along the verges of roads because cattle "trouble drivers and walkers on the road." He had advice about local problems, too. Bisereko thought that the bar near the hospital in Bundibugyo should be banned from playing dance music. He offered his views about the location of schools in Mubende, about the provision of social services in Kampala, and about resettlement in Bukedi District.

Mr. Bisereko was unusual in the wideness of his travels, but his proprietary view of government work was widely shared. Some people came to see themselves as crusaders, at war with irresponsibility. On 21 September 1973 the city council in Kampala organized a daylong effort to clean up the city's streets. It was part of the "Keep Uganda Clean" campaign, which obliged residents to participate in regularly scheduled cleanups in town centers.[92] People had to bring their own slashers, brooms, rakes, mowers, spades, and hoes. The workers threw wet soil at idlers, shouting, "Why don't you join us? Do you fear to have soil on your hands?" They dragooned taxi drivers into service. One of the leaders of the campaign shouted, "We cannot work to clean our country

while others are enjoying an evening drive."[93] A self-righteousness pervaded campaign work. It justified petty tyranny. In June 1973 a chief in
the west of Uganda inspected a series of houses and found that "most of
the houses were dirty, and some were using grasses and banana leaves to
sleep on," making the houses even filthier.[94] On that morning the chief
removed the possessions of twenty-nine people from their homes and in-
cinerated them in a bonfire. Mattresses, shirts, pillows, blankets, and
mats were destroyed.[95]

Uncredentialed people were stepping forward to take over the management of public life, assuming a proprietary authority over matters in
which they had no particular expertise. One such man was Kasujja David,
who in 1975 addressed a long essay titled "Prostitution and the Economic War" to President Amin. Kasujja argued that "money wasted on
prostitutes is a complete loss—national loss and should have been better
used at the expansion and improvement of our businesses." Prostitutes,
he claimed, were the worst offenders against government price controls:
they bought packs of cigarettes at 2 shillings 60 cents—the government-
approved price—and then hawked them by the stick at 70 cents each;
they bought sugar at the official price, then divided it into small packets
and sold them at a high profit. Moreover, prostitutes led men into crime,
forcing them "to rob, steal or get corrupt as a result of wanting to enter-
tain these girls." Kasujja concluded that prostitutes were the "real real
real enemies of our Uganda of tomorrow economically, educationally
etc." He wanted Amin's government to set up work camps where prostitutes would be interned and "taught to live a decent life by working for a
living."[96]

Mr. Kasujja had no training in the field of public administration. He
did not work on behalf of an academic or cultural institution. In his petition he signed himself as a "self research worker." Like Tito Bisereko, the
"local farmer" who authored long reports about abstract matters of government administration, Kasujja felt authorized to take on the management of public affairs. In Idi Amin's do-it-yourself government, the
relationship between governor and governed was leveled out, and all
kinds of people—from busybodies and nosy parkers to self-appointed
vigilantes—claimed an interest in the management of public life.

Tito Bisereko, Kasujja David, and many other people came to see
themselves as proprietors of the civic theater. At a time when government institutions depended on the voluntary contributions of ordinary
people, busybodies like Bisereko and Kasujja claimed a standing in affairs

of state. They were vested in government work by a regime that was out-sourcing public administration to uncredentialed people. It was a license to adopt an expansive sense of vocation and to claim authority over a wide field.

═══

It was self-sacrifice that made the Amin regime work. Government infra-structures were under-resourced and crumbling, and ordinary people—their expertise, their knowledge, their funds—were called upon to subsidize the work of government. A host of self-nominated, self-important, self-righteous people were empowered to take on administrative work that, in an earlier dispensation, had been the job of trained professionals. Many more were compelled into service by government campaigns. Ugandans were obliged to transform their agriculture, to clean up city streets, to over-haul the economy, to defend their cultural and political sovereignty. By making affairs of state into urgent moral imperatives, the Amin regime made government into a test of resolve.

CHAPTER FIVE

The Economic War

IN 1959 THE TEMPESTUOUS activist Augustine Kamya had organized a boycott against Asian-owned businesses, mobilizing black Ugandans to demand a bigger share of the economy. After he came to power Idi Amin made Kamya president of the National Chamber of Commerce. The newspapers described Kamya as a "Kampala businessman." He used his new office as a platform to advance black people's economic power. "Ugandan businessmen must now close their ranks and struggle to win the economy of this country from the hands of foreigners," he told an audience. He planned to set up depots in every district where African retailers could purchase goods at reasonable costs.[1] He urged Amin's government to relieve African businessmen from paying taxes on imported goods, since Africans were "not taking money out of Uganda as the Asians used to do."[2] In the first months of 1972 Kamya barnstormed around the country, raising financial support for black-run businesses.[3]

On 27 October 1972, Augustine Kamya's body was found in Katalemwa, an unremarkable town about ten miles north of Kampala. Government authorities told an unlikely story concerning his death: they claimed Kamya had been part of a gang robbing a passing Asian motorist.[4] Local people told diplomats a different story: they claimed that Kamya had been murdered in cold blood by soldiers of the Uganda Army.[5]

I do not know why or how Augustine Kamya was murdered. It is clear, however, that his lifelong struggle for economic and political freedom did not align with the dictatorship of Idi Amin. A few months before Kamya's murder President Amin had summarily decreed the expulsion of Uganda's Asian community. More than 50,000 people were given a scant three months to tie up their affairs. Businesses and buildings that Asians had owned were handed over to African proprietors. Amin called it the "War of Economic Independence." Later it was named the "Economic War." It was supposed to be a war of liberation.[6] In a speech announcing the measures, President Amin argued that "the Ugandan Africans have been enslaved economically since the time of the colonialists."[7] They had "suffered for their own country. They have been mistreated in their own country. They have been laughed at by foreigners. The Africans have been regarded by these foreigners as second-class citizens in their own country." The Economic War was meant to "emancipate the Uganda Africans of this republic."

> This is the day of salvation for the Ugandan Africans. This is the day of the redemption of the Ugandan Africans. All Ugandans must wake up, in full and total mobilization, determined and committed to fight this economic war until it is won.

Amin was sure that the Economic War would "go down in history as one of the greatest achievements of this century."

Urban people had led the boycott of 1959–60. Their commitment had been fortified by the black-run newspapers of Kampala, which had made it seem as though people's private consumer choices were freighted with political significance. In 1972 Idi Amin's government appropriated the project of black economic liberation from Augustine Kamya and his colleagues. Government—not the urban crowd—fought Idi Amin's Economic War. The war was won by presidential decree, not by the passions of city people. It was fought by government officials, who reallocated Asian properties and overhauled, all at once, whole sectors of the economy. It was a regulatory war, pursued by authorities who sought to control prices and supervise the economy. In the Economic War, Amin's government claimed for itself a novel role: liberator of economic life. It was the most consequential of the many campaigns that the Amin regime launched.

This chapter is about the management of economic liberation in Amin's Uganda. The Economic War made narrowly financial questions about the conduct of business into thrilling matters of racial liberation. There were a great many scapegoats: first the Asian community, latterly

Africans who would not, or could not, follow the official rules. The pun-ishments were draconian: economic crimes were, after 1975, punishable by death. For people in power, the Economic War was a means of mak-ing austerity, inhumanity, and brutality seem essential, a crucial aspect of their heroic leadership, a necessary part of an epoch-making war of racial liberation.

As with the other campaigns that the Amin government launched, the Economic War had to be fought at a rapid pace. The timeline of policy implementation was dramatically compressed. All at once, the expulsion of Uganda's Asians deprived the country of 50 percent of its chemists, 40 percent of its architects, 50 percent of its chemical engineers, 37 percent of doctors, and 40 percent of its accountants.[8] "One's mind boggles at the thought of the effects of the sudden withdrawal of all Asians from Ugan-dan life," wrote a British diplomat.

> Practically everything one can think of has Asians somewhere in the system—doctors, dentists, lawyers, bankers, traders, cinemas, hotels, artisans. . . . How are black Ugandans to take over for all these people? Are they to draw lots or be detailed off—you and you—take over the greengrocers, you and you, the butchers, next two, the petrol station, and so on?[9]

Many businesses did not survive the sudden withdrawal of Asians' expertise and capital. Most of the mechanics, the accountants, and the managers of the Northern Province Bus Company were Asians. In their absence the company was obliged to close.[10] In Moroto, in Ugan-da's distant north, the rapid withdrawal of Asian capital endangered the town's economy. By 21 August—only two weeks after the expulsion was announced—beans, cornmeal, and other foodstuffs were in short supply in local markets.[11] The authorities reported that Asian shop owners, seeking revenge for the foreclosure of their businesses, were vandalizing the radio sets they had on sale.[12] By September the local banks were short of cash, as Asian businessmen were no longer depositing their money there.[13]

By the end of 1972 the departing Asian community had vacated 5,655 farms, ranches, and estates.[14] The abandoned properties fell under the custodianship of a new committee—the Departed Asians Property

Custodial Board—which quite suddenly became Uganda's biggest land-
lord. The board was responsible for allocating houses and business
premises to deserving African proprietors. Some 233 temples, mosques,
and homes vacated by Asians were handed over to the Muslim Supreme
Council.[15] In Jinja town, long the home to a thriving Asian community,
twenty-one business premises were allocated to employees of local government. Three shops were given to wives of senior civil servants. Nine
premises were allocated to teachers, and five employees of the medical
department were given shops.[16]

All at once, uncredentialed people found themselves responsible for
the management of companies whose business they knew nothing of. In
November 1972 the chair of the Uganda Development Corporation appointed dozens of low-level clerks to manage commercial concerns vacated by departing Asian owners.[17] In this way previously anonymous
civil servants became managing directors of Kawempe Flour and
Groundnuts Mill, Aluminum (U) Ltd., Spunpipes Construction Company, the Hotel Equatorial, and a great many other companies. The
management of the Kakira sugar factory, previously owned by Asian
businessmen, was handed over to African proprietors. The man employed to keep the machinery in order remembered his bewilderment at
the complexity of the job.[18] "Men who had recently had nothing had become rich bosses overnight," recounted one of Uganda's most eminent
historians. "Former cooks in Asian households moved into their former
masters' bedrooms. . . . Even professors and lecturers at Makerere abandoned their ivory towers and joined the great scramble for businesses."[19]

A great many government entities, previously short of space, found a
home in buildings vacated by Indian and Pakistani owners. It was a bo-
nanza. Much of the funding for the 1975 meeting of the Organization of
African Unity in Kampala came from the Departed Asians Property Custodial Board. In Kabale, in southern Uganda, an earnest government culture officer organized a new museum of local culture and history in a
building that had formerly been the Hindu temple, as we will see in
Chapter 9. In Jinja, the local offices of the Ministry of Information and
Broadcasting were housed in the vacated Gymkhana club. The recording
studios for Radio Uganda were located in the Ismaili club.[20] In Semuliki,
a new district created by President Amin in 1974, shops formerly operated by Asian businessmen furnished local authorities with much-needed
office space. The town council moved into one vacant shop; the growers'
cooperative society moved into another; the Forestry Department

moved into a third.²¹ At a time when concrete and mortar were in short supply, abandoned Asian properties helped make up the distance between the ambition of government programs and the reality of shortage, deficits, and breakdown.

To international observers it was a human rights catastrophe. There was a scramble to secure new homes for people rendered stateless by the Amin decree. The United Kingdom accepted the greatest number of exiles—more than 30,000 Ugandans were resettled there. Canada opened its doors to 4,000 expelled Asians; and tiny Costa Rica welcomed a small group of refugees.²² The United States accepted 1,043 Ugandan Asians. They were settled in Spartanburg, South Carolina. Their grocery bills were paid by the Salvation Army, and local churches provided cooking facilities.²³

One among the many people displaced by the Economic War was a man named Aloysius Pinto.²⁴ Pinto's father had settled in Uganda in 1904, and Pinto had been born there in 1919. He had married a Ugandan African woman; they had two children and were active members of a church in Kampala. Pinto assured the minister of internal affairs that "we are grooming [our children] towards being good citizens of Uganda." His impending expulsion would be a disaster for his family. "If one member is to depart all that we have built will crumble," he wrote. It was a moving plea. But the minister was adamant. "We can do nothing more," he wrote in the margins of Pinto's appeal. "He must remove himself out of Uganda."

For some Ugandans all of this was an embarrassment. As the expulsion went into effect a group of petitioners wrote to the authorities, arguing that "we have been pushed back twenty years by the present situation."²⁵ Expelling the country's Asians was in their view inhumane and uncharitable. "If we do not stop all these things we will create more trouble for us by God," they wrote. "God is not blind." The prolific essayist and artist Peter Wankulu—whom we will meet in Chapter 7—was likewise incensed. He wrote to President Amin criticizing the expulsion of the Asian community.²⁶ If the Indians "had not built all of these industries," he asked, "in what condition would our state be?" The expulsion "thwarts our plans for agricultural and industrial development," Wankulu argued. "It is a great harm to the state."

There were a few objections, but not many. The Economic War was a landmark victory in public life, and for many people Idi Amin was a hero. A few days after President Amin announced the expulsion, the distinguished nationalist Ignatius Musazi convened a press conference to "rally behind the General's declaration of Uganda's economic emancipation."[27] He told journalists that Amin's declaration had "relieved us of an almost century old burden that was almost going to break our backs." For Musazi—who had for decades worked to organize Uganda's farmers and laborers—Amin's humble origins were a mark of distinction. "It is no accident that this historical decision should be the handiwork and brainchild not of a son of those special people who claim to be born with two umbilical cords [referring to Uganda's kings], nor that of the men of the Educated Intelligentsia," argued Musazi, "but the first Ugandan leader who has not the slightest claim to high family origin nor academic qualification, the son of a humble peasant." It was "this son of a peasant who has boldly expressed the sentiments of all Ugandans and indeed the Africans, that Africans must not be free only politically but also economically." Musazi called on Ugandans to "rise to this God sent moment," for "if we miss this chance our country will continue in chains for another century."

Ignatius Musazi was by no means a dupe. He had spent his life working for the empowerment of Uganda's workers.[28] Like many other people, he saw in Amin's Economic War a passport to liberation. In the years that followed there were yearly celebrations to mark the anniversary of the expulsion decree. "News of the declaration of the Economic War was estimably greeted by all indigenous Ugandans from all corners of this nation," recounted an official at one such celebration, "but non-Ugandan Asians grieved and others fainted on hearing the news."[29] The Economic War folded Ugandans into a storyline of national redemption. "If the Asians were still here now," speculated a district commissioner three years after the expulsion, "I bet you we would be dying of hunger because they would have sacked our Economy completely." But "now these suckers have gone and I am glad to announce that the only Black-run country of Africa ... is now economically developing at supersonic speed."[30]

Like the many other campaigns that the Amin government launched, the Economic War made Ugandans feel as though they were living in momentous times. That is what a campaign could do: transform the mundane into the extraordinary, make ill-defined social issues into urgent problems demanding rectification. That is how the financial and personal ruin of Ugandan Asians was made to seem meaningful, purposeful, part of a larger struggle.

New and more numerous enemies of Uganda's economic liberation came into view as the 1970s went on. As the government sought to exert control over businesses and distribution networks, a great many Ugandans found themselves named cheaters. The commonplace habits that people had developed to manage an unpredictable economy were categorized, abruptly, as acts of sabotage. In this way ordinary people discovered that they were now enemies of the state.

The government established the State Trading Corporation in September 1972, just as the expulsion of the Asian community was getting under way. It had a legal monopoly over the import and export of commodities. There were fixed prices for goods sold to consumers, and in every district, there were government-appointed "agents" who were responsible for the distribution and sale of commodities. These agents exercised monopoly powers. In Fort Portal there were eight grocers who were authorized by the government to sell commodities, at state-mandated prices.[31] Bundibugyo's leading businessman, Haji Juma, was the government agent for Bata Shoes, the *Voice of Uganda*, fishnets, and textiles. He was also the authorized vendor for the national lottery.[32]

Here, in the conduct of business, was a front line in the war of economic liberation. In August 1972, Amin's government convened a "Conference of Representatives of the People on the Transfer of the Economy into the Hands of Ugandans." President Amin framed the expulsion of Ugandan Asians as one aspect of a longer struggle for self-determination. "We have got to fight for our economic independence as we did for our political independence," he told attendees.

> All Ugandans in all walks of life must work very hard in whatever they are doing for the economic development of our country. . . . The Ugandan importers, wholesalers and retailers must come forward with determination to ensure that goods are available throughout the country for our people. . . . They must exercise self-discipline to a very high degree.[33]

Smooth and professional commercial transactions were proof of Africans' capacity for economic self-government. The "days of bargaining are done," a headline in the *Voice of Uganda* declared. The public expected the "new shopkeeper in their town or village to be dedicated and very hard working," a "man of integrity and honesty."[34] In March 1973—three months after the deadline by which Asians were to depart—an official in Kasese town convened a short course for the town's African retailers. He was full of advice about the conduct of business. Housewives were not suited to running businesses, for "when the customer demands goods, the poor woman is so busy with her own work, with a lost temper [she] tells the customer to wait or go away." It was important that men of business should be "courteous, alert, friendly, and ready to serve." Fixtures and equipment in the shop should be kept clean and tidy, and so should the shop counter, for "the cumulative effect of dirt and smudges on display cases can [harm] the sale's effectiveness."[35] All of this required personal discipline. Success in business means "very hard work, saving every cent," said an official at another training course. "It means denial of oneself's pleasures and leisure. In other words it requires total commitment on the part of the trader to the business."[36]

New procedures were created to superintend the conduct of black-run businesses. Every district was assigned a "trade development officer," whose work it was to inspect the conduct of business in their locality. President Amin himself took an active interest in the matter. In the months following the Asian community's expulsion, he made surprise tours of Kampala's businesses. At every stop he would give directions: he would tell a businessman to change his method of work, rearrange the stock, or keep better records.[37]

All of this made for good press. In the archives of the Uganda Broadcasting Corporation there are hundreds of photographs depicting Abdallah Nasur, the governor of Central Province. Nasur was notorious around Kampala: Canadian diplomats reported that he spent his time "making surprise visits to the various business establishments, finding them in breach of various written or unwritten government regulations, closing their business, and allocating them to new owners."[38] In the photos Nasur is always at the center of the frame, thrusting himself into the lives and livelihoods of Kampala's people. Here he is lecturing fishmongers about the quality of their stock. There he is questioning shopkeepers about the prices of their merchandise. In January 1975, the government newspaper printed an image of Nasur—hands on hips—talking with a shopkeeper at a marketplace.[39] The caption described how people had "flocked to Kampala for a spree," while Captain Nasur inspected the items on sale, setting the prices on the goods and insisting that business be conducted according to government rules.

Abdallah Nasur, governor of Central Province, inspecting a shop, 1975
(Courtesy of the Uganda Broadcasting Corporation)

In this way Nasur's petty bullying was made to look like vigor. In 1977 journalists working with Uganda Television produced a short film documenting the successes of the Economic War. It features an amiable journalist who walks the streets of Kampala, entering the shops and quizzing shopkeepers and customers. He asks a great many leading questions. To a man sitting uncomfortably at a desk, he asks, in Swahili, "What words do you have to say about how well the business is going and to thank Idi Amin?" The man dutifully replies by describing the prosperity that he and other men of business enjoyed under Amin's presidency. In another shop the journalist questions a pair of women arranging shoes on the shelves, asking about the price and about the volume of business. The women—visibly uncomfortable—have to be told to look at the camera. The camera lingers over the merchandise as the journalist enthuses over its quality. "You are very happy?" the journalist asks.

That is what the Economic War looked like in official media. The reality was quite different. There was a yawning disparity between the official price structure and the market value of things. Take the prices for hoes, for example. The State Trading Corporation was supposed to sell a carton of hoes to wholesalers at a price of 152 shillings. The wholesaler

Distribution of hoes in Busoga, eastern Uganda, 1975 (Courtesy of the
Uganda Broadcasting Corporation)

was then supposed to sell the same carton to a retailer at 157 shillings,
making a profit of five shillings; and the retailer was meant to sell the
hoes, individually, to consumers at six shillings each, earning a profit per
carton of nine shillings. The official price structure left retailers with
small returns on their business. On the black market, though, there were
fortunes to be made. Hoes were selling for eighty shillings each in
1976.[40] It is no surprise that government-approved sellers of hoes were
uninterested in selling at the authorized price. In western Uganda local
officials reported that the selling agent for hoes was rarely seen. "Sometimes he appears late in the evening and starts selling in some area for
30 minutes, then goes away," an official complained.[41] The occasions

when hoes were actually put on sale at government prices were landmark events. In the photographic archive there is a series of pictures from eastern Uganda showing jubilant women holding newly purchased hoes aloft, dancing with glee.[42]

For retailers, selling commodities at the state-approved price was folly. In one town the manager of the Bata Shoe store hid the shoes she received from the government distributor, closing the shop on the pretext that the stock was exhausted. She spirited the shoes out of the store and sold them at much higher prices—fifty shillings a pair—on the black market.[43] For her and for many other retailers it did not make sense to sell at the approved prices. When the governor toured the main street in the provincial town of Fort Portal, he found that as many as nineteen shops were entirely empty. The proprietors had deserted the premises, for the official selling prices were so low that it was impossible to make a profit. Even where the official prices were reasonable, shop owners feared investing in merchandise to stock their shops. They worried that the official selling price would be reduced on short notice, causing them dramatic losses. Retailers who operated in the formal retail economy had to seize opportunities when they arose. In Kampala shops would change their stock overnight, selling textiles one day and soap the next.[44]

It was difficult for any business requiring a constant and predictable supply of materials to secure necessary items. The baker in Bundibugyo stopped baking bread in April 1974, finding it impossible to obtain yeast, oil, or salt.[45] Traders in Sebei complained that fabric, blankets, fertilizer, soap, cement, salt, iron sheets, and nails were in short supply. They had to obtain commodities from official wholesalers in Mbale, forty-three miles away over broken roads, and their vehicles were often damaged in transit.[46] Bottled beer was particularly hard to find. In Kasese bar owners waited for months to receive crates of beer from the official supplier. In the absence of beer many proprietors transformed their bars into restaurants, selling illegally brewed liquor on the side.[47]

Producers, like retailers, were aware of the disparity between the mandated price and the market value of things. The authorized purchase prices for agricultural commodities were laughably low. When an official in the northwest went to buy maize from local farmers, they ridiculed him for offering two shillings per kilogram, the legal purchase price.[48] "Instead of selling my maize for Shgs. 2/ a kilo, I would rather pour it off, and I will find out later whether there is a Government in this country or not," said one angry farmer. Another farmer, who had seven hundred bags of maize in his storehouse, said that he would pour it out on the road before he sold it at the official price. He could sell his maize for at least 3 shillings 50 cents a kilo on the black market.

Coffee was the crop where there was the greatest disparity between the official purchase price and the market value.[49] In 1975 a killing frost in Brazil destroyed two-thirds of the country's coffee bushes, undercutting the world's largest exporter of coffee. Ugandans hastened to take advantage. The best coffee-growing area in Uganda is in mountainous Bundibugyo, on the border with Zaire. The most prominent businessmen in Bundibugyo were also the most successful smugglers. Haji Juma, the official selling agent for shoes, newspapers, textiles, and other articles, had wide and enduring connections across the political spectrum. He used government vehicles—a police van, the tsetse fly control truck, the Ministry of Works truck, the Ministry of Community Development truck—to smuggle Ugandan coffee across the border for sale in Zaire. He and his cronies were "receiving *high class treatment* from the Law Keepers here," reported a frustrated official.[50] One estimate has it that between 1975 and 1979 as much as $520 million in coffee was smuggled out of Uganda.[51]

Well-connected men like Haji Juma made fortunes from coffee smuggling. Their riches fueled a short-lived belle époque. A politician from Kenya who visited Kampala in March 1978 thought the city "appeared more orderly and prosperous" than it had in the early 1970s.[52] Hotels were fully booked; there were well-stocked markets for food; and even the smaller shops had a plentiful supply of commodities. He urged British firms to re-invest in Uganda, since the "country was on the brink of a period of stability and expansion." An Australian film crew also visited that year and had the same impression: they reported that shops were full of luxury goods. Prices were astronomical—toilet paper was $2 a roll—but the Australians saw large numbers of people shopping on the high street.[53] The city's business district was in good order: hedges were cut, verges were trimmed, road signs were painted.[54]

At the edges of the coffee boom people had to make do with less. Two days after Christmas 1976 an official in a remote part of western Uganda arrested a man named Simeo Kahindo for selling goods without a license.[55] The man had a wide range of articles to offer. He had six coats, twelve shirts, two blankets, and eight pairs of trousers. He had one bed cover and four sheets. He had three pairs of shoes. He had a radio, a bicycle, and two belts. He had eight tablecloths, five neckties, and two hoes. He had three kilograms of sugar and five kilograms of salt. And he had sixty-four shillings in cash. The official who arrested Kahindo totted all of this merchandise up in numbered columns and dispatched everything, together with Kahindo himself, to the provincial police headquarters.

Judging from the tiny amount of cash he had on hand, it is likely that much of Kahindo's trade was conducted in barter. At a time when the value of cash was uncertain and changeable, Kahindo looked for profits through exchange, by assessing things comparatively, by knowing how the value of goods changed over space and time.[56] It was men like him who actually responded to rural consumers' needs. Here was an arbiter who knew what people needed, who knew how to get hold of important things, and who found ways to convey them into people's hands.

=====

The Amin regime regarded entrepreneurs like Simeo Kahindo as saboteurs. They circumvented the official channels of distribution and flouted the official prices. They created their own measures of value. It was—in officials' eyes—a form of treason.

Early in 1975 President Amin published the "Economic Crimes Decree." It established a military tribunal empowered to punish profiteers, hoarders, and others who acted against the economic interests of the state. The penalty was death by firing squad, or ten years in prison.[57] By April traders charged with selling goods in excess of established government prices were being arrested and executed.[58] In one case—reported in the international media—the tribunal ordered the execution of two dozen men who were found attempting to smuggle five hundred bags of coffee out of the country.[59] Over the months that followed the tribunal's remit expanded: in 1977, for example, Amin announced that anyone who diverted commodities to "unscheduled destinations" would be executed by firing squad. People found stealing from their employers would meet the same punishment.[60]

The targets of the Economic Crimes Tribunal were people without connections: petty traders, market women, people whose financial strategies ran afoul of government edicts. There are a great many photos of them in the archives of the Uganda Broadcasting Corporation. The photographs picture people caught in the act and paraded, together with the evidence of their crime, before the cameras. One series of photos, made in 1978, features a pair of paraffin smugglers who were apprehended

Arrest of "overchargers" in Bulemeezi, 1975 (Courtesy of the Uganda
Broadcasting Corporation)

near the border with Zaire.[61] Officials unloaded hundreds of jerrycans
from the truck and arranged them, end to end, in front of a government
building. They made the smugglers sit atop a carpet of jerrycans while
the photographers took pictures. Another series features a group of several dozen men and women who were tried before the tribunal.[62] They
had been accused of selling retail goods at illegally inflated prices. Officials had them pose alongside bottles of gin, sacks of maize flour, and
other articles that had been impounded during the tribunal's investigations. In the last photo they are shown walking to meet their fate, with
their hands held aloft. Were they walking to their deaths?

In these and other photographs, officials were making the stakes
clear. Here, in physical form, were the moral and economic maladies

with which the Amin regime was at war. This is what usury looked like. That is what hoarding looked like. The photographs made otherwise invisible aspects of economic and social life visible as punishable crimes.

But for me—and, it seems, for the officials in whose hands the fate of the guilty rested—it is the humanity of the accused, not their guilt, that comes through. The most emotionally affecting pictures in the whole of the Uganda Broadcasting Corporation's photographic archive were made at a sitting of the Economic Crimes Tribunal in March 1975.[63] The cameraman took dozens of pictures, most of them close-ups of individuals as they faced the judges. In one photo there is a girl, her arms crossed, staring defiantly at the camera. There is an older man—her father? her lawyer?—standing beside her. In another photo there is a middle-aged woman, wearing a print dress, staring at the ground with tears in her eyes, her hand at her forehead. There is an elderly woman, desperately holding the Bible aloft as she testifies before the tribunal. The photos were made to document the identities of the people who were being judged. What they captured, instead, is their fragility, their emotion, their nervousness, their innocence. They are evidence of the arbitrariness of justice and the cheapness of life.

So far as I can find, only one of these photos was ever seen by the general public. The picture was published on page six of the *Voice of Uganda* in June 1975.[64] It features two men, arms crossed, brows furrowed in consternation as they stood before the Economic Crimes Tribunal. The caption named them as Tindimukira and Yusufu Kawesa. They had been sentenced to death, the newspaper reported, and would soon face a firing squad. Beyond this single photo none of the hundreds of pictures taken by government photographers at the tribunal were ever published.

Was the tribunal an embarrassment? Were its judgments too drastic, too inhumane? Were the image-makers of Idi Amin's Uganda squeamish about the tribunal's draconian powers? Did they sympathize with the people whose lives were destroyed?

Uganda's government archives contain vanishingly little information documenting the tribunal's operations. There is a single file, held in the Kabarole District archive, which contains the correspondence of the government lawyers charged with prosecuting cases before the tribunal. The government attorney in Fort Portal seems to have concocted far-fetched and unlikely reasons for declining to prosecute people who were accused of violating the government's regulations. In August 1978 a man

Unnamed defendant at the Economic Crimes Tribunal, 1975 (Courtesy of the
Uganda Broadcasting Corporation)

named James Batekateka was accused of violating the Economic Crimes
Decree. He had sold a crate of beer at 257 shillings 50 cents, when the
price for beer set by the government was 93 shillings per crate. The state
attorney argued that the official price was unrealistic. He found an obscure and unpublished document where a government official had admitted that the black-market price for beer was far more than 250 shillings
per crate. The attorney concluded that it was "unjust and unfair" to prosecute Mr. Batekateka for violating price controls, since even government
personnel admitted that the official price was unnaturally low.[65] In

another instance a trader was accused of selling sixteen rolls of cotton cloth smuggled from Zaire, but again the state attorney declined to prosecute, reasoning there was no way that the trader—who had bought the cloth from a wholesaler in Uganda—could have known that the cloth had been smuggled into the country.[66]

Dozens of cases like these came before the government attorney in Fort Portal. In every instance the attorney found reason not to prosecute the accused; and in every case the provincial governor—who had to approve the attorney's recommendations—ordered the police to set the accused free. Here, in an outpost on the edges of Idi Amin's government, local authorities seem to have recognized the inhumanity of the political system in which they worked. They looked for means to extricate people from a legal machine that led toward an unjustifiable and inhumane death.

In 1977 a group of petitioners wrote in Swahili to Vice President Mustafa Adrisi to highlight the injustice that the Economic Crimes Decree enabled.[67] The tribunal handed out ridiculously disproportionate sentences for minor infractions, while wealthy and well-connected men walked free. The critics had several examples. "Those who smuggle coffee, trailers full, are left free," they wrote, "while the common man who are caught with only a stick of [plantains] are sentenced to death." They knew of an instance where a high-ranking official embezzled millions of shillings, but a "poor clerk who misplaced a small sum of money was sentenced to life imprisonment." There was a butcher who had been sentenced to life in prison for selling offal at three shillings a kilo, instead of the mandated price, which was 2 shillings 50 cents. There was the shop owner who had received a life sentence for hoarding. He had kept a small bar of soap back from sale. In their view the decree did nothing to deter crime. It was a tool for victimizing the poor.

Many people suffered during the Economic War. Many people were pardoned, too. In July 1975 the minister of justice granted a general amnesty to people convicted by the Economic Crimes Tribunal. People found guilty of smuggling, hoarding, or overcharging were to be released immediately; people who had been sentenced to death were to be released after serving a six-month prison sentence.[68] Altogether 497 people who had been convicted by the tribunal were set at liberty under the amnesty.[69] It was the first of several amnesties granted to people convicted by the tribunal. In March 1976, for instance, President Amin visited Luzira Prison in the company of a crew from Uganda Television to confront seven men who had been sentenced to death. They had been convicted by the tribunal for selling goods on the black market. As the firing squad readied their weapons, President Amin lectured the men about the evils of overcharging, hoarding, and smuggling, and then, in English and Swahili, he commuted their death sentences and set them free.[70] The occasion was carefully staged. In the photographs, Amin lectures the prisoners outside the prison gates, gesturing widely; thereafter the grateful men prostrate themselves before him on the ground.[71] It was one of many occasions when President Amin intervened to restore the liberty of people convicted by the tribunal.[72]

Idi Amin's government was a machine for the creation and prosecution of hitherto nameless crimes. That is how people—unwittingly—became enemies of the state, criminals, bound over on death row. That is how President Amin came to wield power over life and death.

———

The Economic War was an enduring legacy of Idi Amin's regime. Even after Amin was driven from power, the central role of the Departed Asians Property Custodial Board in Uganda's economic life endured. In 1992, more than a decade after Amin's ouster, the board owned 7,829 properties, spread across the country.

In that year Yoweri Museveni's government announced that the property seized from Asian owners was to be restored to them. Officials hoped that returning Asians would "bring in capital and managerial skills to help in speeding up the rehabilitation of industries, agricultural estates and commerce."[73] Asians who wished to reclaim properties could obtain the titles from the board; claimants were obliged to secure the eviction of Ugandan tenants themselves. Making a claim was expensive, and only a wealthy few could manage to make the bureaucracy work in their favor. Today the Departed Asians Property Custodial Board retains custody of several hundred properties. At the time I write—in 2024—the board's leadership is under parliamentary investigation: billions of shillings have been stolen from its accounts, and its managers are accused of handing important buildings over to wealthy, well-connected proprietors.[74]

Among the many wrongs of the 1970s, among the many lives that were disrupted or ended by Amin's regime, it is the expulsion of the Asian community that has been the focus of ongoing efforts at compensation and rectification. It is one of a very few instances where the Museveni government sought to redress the injustices of Uganda's history.

There has been no justice for the thousands of Ugandans who were unwittingly caught up in the machinery of the Economic War. No one has compensated the relatives of Tindimukira and Yusufu Kawesa, the two men who were pictured in the *Voice of Uganda* just prior to their execution for economic crimes in 1975. No one has apologized to the hundreds of innocent, terrified men and women who were photographed, in their last hour, on trial before the Economic Crimes Tribunal.

The Economic War was the Amin government's decade-long campaign to establish its authority over Uganda's unruly economy. A host of people—Asians and Africans alike—found themselves made into enemies of the state. They were scapegoats. Their loss helped to fortify the Amin regime's moral role: guarantor of Uganda's liberty, guardian of its independence.

CHAPTER SIX

Violence and Public Life

THE GOVERNMENT BUILDING IN Lira—a provincial capital in northern Uganda—was sacked and looted in July 1985.[1] Troops serving one of several rival political factions broke into the building, demolishing the doors with axes. They took away office chairs, turned the tables into firewood, and carried off type-writers, duplicating machines, and filing cabinets. They dug into the strong room and removed cash boxes and tax tickets. They destroyed a great many archival files, too, using the papers to kindle their cooking fires. Today, the files that survived the tumult of 1985 are stored in a back room at the government building, piled on metal shelves. There is no logic to their organization. The floorspace is packed full of discarded bureaucratic gear: broken filing cabinets, broken chairs, a decommissioned photocopier, boxes of spiral-bound reports from NGOs. When I visited Lira in 2017 I had to go through the archive file by file, perched on a shelf above the paraphernalia piled up below.

One of the files contains a sheaf of notes made in November 1975 by a police corporal—a man named Olwit—who was investigating a prison warder's illicit affair with a female prisoner.[2] Corporal Olwit filled dozens of pages with notes about the case, writing in a careful, unhurried hand. As I flipped through the file, I was brought up short at page five. There, on the back of the page, is a drawing of an instrument of torture. It is a rack, drawn with careful precision. The drawing was not part of Olwit's report: the corporal had used the page as scrap paper. The person who composed the drawing signed himself as clerk in the office of Lira's chief of prisons. Typed in the upper-right corner of the page are measurements describing the layout of the machine. The struts are to be seven feet long. Once erected, the two sides of the structure are to swing apart to a distance of two feet. At the bottom of the page there are directions about how a prisoner is to be fixed to the rack. The wrists are to be chained to the ringbolts at the top; the legs are to be splayed, with the ankles strapped to bolts at the bottom.

This forbidding document is labeled "Appendix." It had once been part of a manual, copied and distributed for others to use. I can guess at the problems that the author of the manual tried to address. He wished to standardize the practice of torture and create a routine that could be employed across the prison system. By November 1975—when the earnest Corporal Olwit wrote up his report—the torture manual had been made into scrap paper. Did the author make too many copies? Perhaps he overestimated the demand for the publication? Perhaps torturers do not read instruction manuals? Whatever the reason, Corporal Olwit found it lying around as he looked for a bit of paper on which to write.

The senseless brutality of Idi Amin's regime is the overriding theme in international reporting about Uganda in the 1970s. Amnesty International, the International Commission of Jurists, and other international agencies produced damning, sensational, and specific descriptions of state violence.[3] These reports were circulated widely in international media; today they can be found in digital repositories dedicated to the memorialization of atrocity. They are the foundation on which contemporary knowledge about the Amin regime rests, part of a larger infrastructure by which the evils of the twentieth century can be remembered by the people of the world.

In Uganda's archives, by contrast, the violence of the 1970s can be glimpsed only in passing, on stray scraps of paper. Thousands of men and women were tortured and killed by agents of the state, but most of the killing was done out of sight: in military barracks, in the cells of government intelligence agencies, in the faraway north of the country. Bureaucrats did not document it. There are no files documenting the identity of people executed by agents of the state.[4] There is no paperwork laying out the logic of state-sanctioned torture. Archives that might have illuminated the terror of the times were hidden from view. In 1974, a government-run commission of inquiry took evidence from hundreds of witnesses around Uganda. The witnesses spoke fearlessly about the losses they had suffered and about the violence done to their kin.[5] The typed report summarizing the evidence was eight hundred pages long. But the report was never released during Idi Amin's presidency, and today there is no trace of it in the archives of Uganda. The only copy—so far as I know—is a faded photostat held by the United States Institute of Peace.[6]

The historian Semakula Kiwanuka once wrote that it was "difficult for many people outside Uganda to appreciate the extent of the reign of terror which existed in Uganda."[7] This chapter responds to Kiwanuka's challenge by reconstructing the social logic of those terror-filled times. In the later months of 1972 Uganda seemed to be confronting an endlessly growing list of enemies—plotting Asians, scheming Israelis, malevolent Tanzanians. Smugglers, hoarders, and overchargers were said to be undermining Uganda's economic and political independence. Everywhere there was a need for security, vigilance, and discipline. The authority of the military expanded rapidly, as matters that had formerly been regulated by the civil authorities became arenas of combat.

Some people became victims of state-sponsored violence. They found themselves classified as plotters, schemers, or delinquents, as treasonous enemies of the government. They suffered, and some died, as punishment for crimes that had only just been named. Their deaths were exemplary, meant to instruct the public about the threats Uganda faced. Other people suffered a social death. The many campaigns of the 1970s expanded soldiers' authority, making everyone—regardless of breeding, status, wealth, or education—subject to military oversight. For dignified people, soldiers' unnatural, arbitrary power cast the very foundations of social order into doubt. It was their abjection in the hands of boorish, uneducated, unmannered men that aroused indignation, fueled outrage, and made fear part of the fabric of public life.

———

On the morning of 17 September 1972, Radio Uganda broadcast a report announcing that soldiers had invaded Uganda from Tanzania. It was the start of a British plan to overthrow the government, said the broadcaster.[8] About 1,300 men among the invaders were Ugandan exiles based in Tanzania. They expected Uganda's populace to rise in revolt against the Amin government; when it did not, the invasion stalled, crippled by disorganization and division.[9]

The quick defeat of this disorganized incursion did not dampen President Amin's eagerness for retribution. Only a few weeks before,

Amin had launched the Economic War, expelled the Asian community, and placed Uganda on the front lines of the war against colonialism. The desultory invasion seemed to confirm that Uganda was, in fact, at war. In the weeks that followed the army set up roadblocks around Kampala, searching for spies and guerrillas. On 10 February 1973 men condemned for supporting the invasion were led out, wearing hoods, and shot before large crowds.[10] Photographs of these public executions were published the following day in the government newspaper. It was a "real lesson to the people of Uganda to know that involvement in guerilla activities means loss of lives," said a spokesman.[11] Other people died in more anonymous ways. On that awful morning in February an American diplomat saw a pile of six bodies alongside the road; he also witnessed a soldier interrogating a group of three men, who were lying prostrate on the pavement with a gun to their heads.[12]

All of this led the American ambassador in Kampala to conclude that Idi Amin's government was "racist, erratic and unpredictable, brutal, inept, bellicose, irrational, ridiculous and militaristic."[13] Many Ugandans came to share the ambassador's assessment. Two weeks after the public executions of February 1973 the deputy minister of education, Edward Rugumayo, resigned from government. In his resignation letter Rugumayo reminded Amin that "man's mission here on earth (including yours) is to preserve, improve and prolong life. . . . Posterity will judge us by our actions of today."[14] By April that year a great many important people had disappeared from public life. The American ambassador called the turnover in government personnel "staggering." "It is hard to recall anyone whom [Amin] pushed ahead in prominence whom he did not later push aside," he wrote.[15]

In those days the men of the army came to the center of public life. New campaigns were being launched, making previously obscure questions of administration into urgent matters that people mobilized around. Military language furnished the organizational framework for government policy-making, and military discipline seemed essential. In the months following the coup that brought Amin to power, more than 2,000 officers and men from Lango—Milton Obote's home area—had been eliminated from the army. Many of them were killed. In their place recruiters brought in men from West Nile, Amin's home district. The army grew from 9,000 to 12,000 men in the first year of Amin's presidency.[16] In May 1973 President Amin ordered his cabinet ministers to enlist as army cadets. They were obliged to wear their uniforms to cabinet meetings and to drill on parade every morning at six.[17] At the same time the government appointed 728 soldiers to serve as chiefs in local governments around the country.[18] The government newspaper heralded these soldier-chiefs as "men of action and, one must declare, men of discipline."[19]

The growing number of people in military service occasioned serious difficulties with discipline. There was very little training to habituate newly enlisted soldiers with their duties. Four months after the coup that brought Amin to power, ordinary soldiers were—in the assessment of the British military attaché—largely unresponsive to commands from their officers.[20] The "stage has long been reached where officers make requests rather than give commands and no one appears surprised if the recipient either ignores or refuses point blank," reported a diplomat.[21] A Ghanaian diplomat regarded the officer corps as "illiterate and incompetent sycophants, whose chief virtue is their unquestioning loyalty to General Amin."[22] One evening in 1973 the British high commissioner gave a cocktail party in a provincial town. At about 11:00 p.m. Lieutenant-Colonel Moses, the commanding officer of the local army barracks, was called away. When he returned he murmured to one of his colleagues that there was fighting in the barracks. "They are killing each other," he said.[23] An hour passed before the lieutenant-colonel finally took his leave and returned to the barracks. Neither he nor any other member of the officer corps could control the restive young men with guns.

The authorities struggled to find ways to exert leverage over a poorly disciplined army. There were many opportunities, outside the barracks, for opportunistic and self-interested soldiers to pursue. The allocation of properties seized from Asian businessmen was overseen by committees chaired by military men, and more than half of the firms, factories, estates, and houses left by departing Asians passed into the hands of soldiers.[24] The American ambassador was sure that "the army has never had it so good: they have newly acquired houses, cars, shops, stereos, and everything else the Asians could buy."[25] Many soldiers took advantage of their newfound power to enrich themselves. In southwestern Uganda an army sergeant named Katumba spent 9 October—the anniversary of Ugandan independence—in a refugee camp, pressing immigrants from Rwanda for bribes. He ordered local traders to reduce their selling prices; after the prices came down, he purchased their stock and sold it himself on the black market. The angry traders reported that Katumba warded off criticism using "the usual threat that he can use the gun to kill us since he is a military man."[26]

The license that the Amin government gave soldiers to superintend public affairs was, for them, an opportunity to pursue personal vendettas. Four months after the January 1971 coup the minister of internal affairs reported that he was constantly receiving entreaties from panicked civilians about relatives who had been arrested or mistreated by army men.[27] "To me, it appears that the security men are getting out of control," the minister noted. In one district three soldiers arrested a magistrate who had offended them while drinking in a bar. They took him to a police station and beat him severely as he lay face-down on the ground.[28] Another victim was a man named Barekya. He had been detained by an army officer who "took me to his home and gave me eight strokes and whip." It was punishment, the officer said, for an incident—many years before—when Barekya had insulted him in a bar.[29] Amin's soldiers upended relationships, gaining undue advantages solely because of their military credentials. Their status as soldiers allowed them to advance their private interests at other people's expense.

Civil servants were especially endangered by Amin's aggressive soldiers. Their professional obligations collided with soldiers' self-serving efforts to dominate public life. In 1972 the government health officer in Entebbe wrote to the authorities in Kampala for instructions on how to handle dead bodies found floating in Lake Victoria.[30] There were many of them. The municipal authorities ordinarily took the deceased for burial in the Town Council cemetery, but the army men had interfered. On one occasion a group of angry soldiers had appeared at the health officer's door, demanding that he show them where he had buried the body of a recently deceased man. The health officer had exhumed the body, and the soldiers had driven it away. The officer—shaken by this encounter—found it impossible to know how to do his job. Was he to take orders from the angry men with guns? To what powers were he and other civil servants meant to answer?

———

Here was a novel form of authority. Soldiers cut through the social hierarchies of education, profession, and status that organized public life, making everyone bend the knee to their private whims. Impersonators hoping to borrow soldiers' power for themselves became a frequent problem. According to local authorities, these pretenders were relatives or friends of ex-soldiers using discarded uniforms to "harass the public, thus spoiling the good name of the army."[31] The impersonators were end-

An impersonator named Mpazaye wearing a Uganda Army uniform, 1975
(Courtesy of the Uganda Broadcasting Corporation)

lessly creative. In southern Uganda a man named Mpazaye made a considerable profit by wearing the uniform of the Uganda Army and
demanding money from unsuspecting citizens. Mpazaye's acting was so
convincing that—for several years—he managed to avoid paying taxes altogether, blustering his way through encounters with government tax
collectors.[32] Another impersonator—a man named Lazaro Bazirutwabo—
dressed in an army uniform and claimed to be an officer of the
infamous Malire Regiment. Soldierly authority was portable: any unscrupulous person with theatrical talent and the appropriate costume could
borrow it.

Behind these terrifying impersonations lay a real danger. The threat of violence underwrote the unnatural powers of Uganda's soldiery. Amin's soldiers had power over life and death. President Amin granted immunity to any person who acted under government authority "for the purpose of maintaining public order or public security in any part of Uganda."[33] There was no reason to wait for due process. Soldiers exercised their power abruptly, without checks or balances. At ten o'clock one evening someone knocked on the door of a forestry officer's home in southern Uganda.[34] Earlier that evening the official—whose name was Lukyamuzi—had refused to loan the Forestry Department's truck to another government officer. Upon opening his door that evening Mr. Lukyamuzi was surrounded by a group of soldiers who asked him, in Swahili, why he had refused to offer the vehicle for his colleague's use. "I was trying to explain to them the whole situation but they did not want me to talk English and my knowledge for [the Swahili language] was limited," he lamented in a letter of complaint. "Then I became confused." The soldiers bundled Lukyamuzi off to the local prison, where he was stripped of his clothing, watch, and money. He was beaten and locked in a cell for two days, with no food or medical treatment, until he was finally released.

The most notorious men of violence were in the State Research Bureau, the agency responsible for pursuing internal enemies of the government. The bureau was formed shortly after Amin came to power, when his cabinet allocated nine million shillings to create a new intelligence service. The agency's first head promised that he and his colleagues would "avoid nepotism, corruption, and tribalism," along with "wrong reporting on public resulting from personal quarrels."[35] In January 1972, when the first report was sent to President Amin, the unit consisted of fifty-six men.[36] By 1977 the State Research Bureau employed 1,000 people.[37] Its agents earned $350 per day, received free lodging in state-run hotels, and drove in fast Toyotas outfitted with radio equipment. British diplomats thought the State Research Bureau was a menace to good order.

They maintain a constant threat of terror among the general population, particularly in the towns. The units are above the law and are made up of grotesque young men in dark glasses and funny hats, leather jackets and tight jeans. They snatch selected people from their homes in the early hours, and on the streets,

beating up minor offenders before releasing them but, sometimes, battering the dangerous ones to a slow and horrible
death.[38]

The French ambassador—whose residence was located next to the offices of the State Research Bureau—could not sleep at night, because
every evening there was a volley of semiautomatic gunfire. Throughout
the day the diplomats could hear the pained cries of people undergoing
torture. "It is most unpleasant," wrote the ambassador.[39] Autobiographies
written by Ugandans imprisoned in the State Research Bureau building
detail the horrors of the place. One of them is titled *The Dungeons of Nakasero;* another is *Escape from Idi Amin's Slaughterhouse.*[40] They describe
the baroque cruelty with which the bureau's men tortured and murdered
the people held in their custody.

Other government officials administered bloody punishment in a
more mundane manner. Yustasi Mukirane, formerly one of Amin's chiefs,
told me in an interview about the beatings he used to give to wrongdoers.

As chiefs, we would arrest people who had no pit latrines, and as
chiefs, such a case would be solved on the spot. If the householder was found without a pit latrine, then he would be arrested
with his wife and children. Then the man would be separated,
and in the presence of his family, he would be caned six times.[41]

People who failed to weed their cotton properly were likewise subject to
caning, as were people who failed to produce sufficient cotton to meet
local quotas. Mukirane chuckled at the memory of the floggings he had
administered, moving his arm rhythmically in time with the strokes.

For Idi Amin's men corporal punishment was an ordinary aspect of
government work. It was a habit. One morning in June 1973 a man
named Jackson Bifabusha was breakfasting in his home in southern
Uganda when several soldiers appeared and demanded that he produce a
substantial sum of money.[42] When he refused, he was dragged to the road
and beaten on his buttocks until he bled, then stuffed into the boot of a
car and driven to the house of a neighbor, where he was again beaten.
When Bifabusha lost consciousness his tormentors threw mud and water
on his face to revive him. His crime was that he was delinquent in paying
his taxes. Bifabusha was imprisoned for two days, and thousands of shillings were taken from him.

In a former time—under the colonial government—flogging had been an intrinsic part of justice. In the 1920s and 1930s government chiefs flogged people for the smallest infractions. A man who sold adulterated butter, for instance, was punished with fourteen strokes; a man who failed to report the birth of his child was punished with six strokes.[43] By the middle of the twentieth century, though, flogging had largely disappeared from public life. In the wake of the Second World War, colonial officials were appointing Africans to positions that hitherto had been occupied by Britons or Asians.[44] New politics demanded new forms of law enforcement. By 1970, the year before Idi Amin came to power, the Uganda Police could publish a slickly attractive recruiting brochure—full of enticing photographs—to encourage university students to enlist. "The police offer an extremely exciting, varied and most rewarding career," wrote the inspector general.[45] Prison warders were likewise proud of their professionalism.[46] Flogging had largely receded into memory.

That is why so many Ugandans reacted to Idi Amin's soldiers with indignation. Amin's regime elevated uncredentialed, uneducated men to positions of great authority. For many people it was an outrage, a return to the old barbarism, a form of savagery. The weapons that men of the army possessed made everyone—regardless of breeding, status, education, or merit—fearful.

People had to struggle to defend their dignity. There was a constant stream of complaints about soldiers' behavior. People in western Uganda were particularly angry about a soldier named Ojuk, who appeared at the police station in Fort Portal one day and secured the release of a prisoner accused of murder. "We being polite to every one of the Uganda Army personnel does not mean we are [cowards]," wrote a group of complainants.[47] They called Ojuk and his colleagues "beasts or animals," vowing that "we know how to [fight]. We could beat up Ojuk like a child." These indignant petitioners saw soldiers as barbarians. They looked for ways to reinforce their endangered sense of honor.

Women likewise defended their dignity. In 1973 a government chief in southern Uganda—who often carried a whip at his side—paid an unexpected visit to the wife of the local agriculture officer. He asked for food. When the woman explained that she was peeling plantains to cook, the chief replied that "he never wanted food which she was going to cook, but he wanted food of her body."[48] The woman ordered the chief to leave her house. When he offered her fifty shillings, she took up an axe and raised an alarm. The chief was shocked at the force of her rejection and by the profanity of her language: he had "never seen a lady like her in behavior," he said.[49] I do not know what the agriculture officer's angry wife said to the lusty chief that afternoon. But there were a great range of insults available in the vernacular language, and it is plain that the agriculture officer's wife deployed the full vocabulary in her loud protests against the chief's untoward advances.[50]

Occasionally people's indignation and outrage at soldiers' violence could fuel protest against the Amin government. In January 1976 an open letter to President Amin circulated around Kampala.[51] It claimed that "since your rule thousands of people have been killed by you and your military men. Most of the clever educated people have [departed] and you have left only the lower type of people poor and not clever ones." The authors of this letter wrote in English, the language of government bureaucracy. Their complaint was grounded in their conviction that the Amin regime did not honor their credentials or value their expertise. That is how dignified people saw Amin's domineering soldiery: as an affront to their pride, as a danger to the social order.

———

History had different lessons to teach people in northeastern Uganda. In Karamoja, the district on the border with Kenya, government-sponsored violence had—from the early days of British administration—been embedded in the fabric of politics. Karamoja was governed as a military colony. For Karimojong people, Idi Amin's regime, in all its inhumanity, was true to form.

A cultural and agronomic frontier divides the Karamoja plateau from the rest of Uganda. During the dry season cattle herders drove their herds to far distant places, searching for water and luxuriant grass.[52] British administrators regarded these unpredictable movements with anxiety.[53] They sought to confine Karimojong people into an enclave. The only permanently flowing river—the Kanyangareng—was closed to Karimojong herders and given to their neighbors. In the west Teso farmers were given control over grazing land and sources of water, while in the south Karimojong pasture was incorporated into Bagisu and Sebei lands. Under the "Special Regions Ordinance" of 1958, Karamoja became a closed district, making it illegal for any Ugandan from outside the region to enter without government permission. The penalty was a year of imprisonment.[54]

It is not surprising that Karimojong herders, fenced in at every turn, would seek access to pasturage that had been closed to them. During the dry season there were constant confrontations over water, grass, and cattle. British officials called these violent conflicts "cattle raids." In 1960 and '61 there were 157 confrontations pitting Karimojong men against Turkana herders, who lived in northern Kenya. As many as 20,000 cattle were stolen, and 124 Karimojong people, 118 Turkana people, and 51 people of other ethnicities were said to have died.[55] Many of the dead perished at the hands of the militaries of Uganda and Kenya, which made brutish and ineffective efforts to suppress cattle raiding. The violence increased in the months leading up to Uganda's independence. On the very day that other Ugandans were gathering to celebrate the end of British colonial rule—9 October 1962—a raid was mounted by the Karimojong against Turkana people in Kenya. Fifty-one people were killed.[56]

Under the colonial government and, later, under Milton Obote's regime, northeastern Uganda was a laboratory for the practice of military absolutism.[57] There was no effort to cultivate the public's faith in government institutions. British authorities invested very little in infrastructure: when a police officer flew over the district in 1962, he saw only a small handful of roads during four hours of flying.[58] There was a court of law before which cattle raiders were tried, but the usual rules of legal procedure did not apply. Punishments were, in the words of one British official, "severe." Administrators had to make a choice between "preserving the law and preserving the peace."[59] A vanishingly small proportion of people attended school: in 1964 there were fifty-seven primary schools and 5,546 students in the entire district, among a population of around 180,000 people. Only eighteen children—all boys—were attending secondary school in that year.[60] Swahili—the language of the military—was the official language of government in Karamoja. It was not until 1962 that the first grammar of the Karimojong language was published.[61] The Karimojong Bible did not appear until 2011, more than one hundred years after the Bible had been published in the Ganda language.[62]

For African nationalists Karamoja seemed to be out of step with the rest of the country. In 1955 the Uganda National Congress—an early political party—sent out questionnaires to solicit public opinion about its agenda. The party's leaders claimed to have received a million responses. They did not bother to send any copies of the questionnaire to Karamoja.[63] The following year a journalist from one of Buganda's newspapers visited the district. The report he published accused the colonial government of deliberately depriving Karamoja of political advancement.[64] The backwardness of the district, he feared, would allow the British to delay the independence of the whole of Uganda. Two years later the Legislative Council had a lengthy debate over what politicians called "The Karamoja Problem." "Must we wait for Karamoja?" they asked. Politicians worried that the district had been turned into a "human zoo."[65]

Just before Uganda's independence a commission of inquiry was sent to investigate the situation in Karamoja.[66] Its chair was the politician Basil Bataringaya, who later became minister of internal affairs under President Obote. Bataringaya and his colleagues were confounded by the place. They found the Karimojong attitude toward cattle to be "a most complicated theo-socio-psycho-economic hybrid altogether incomprehensible to an outsider." The place was "20 to 50 years behind the rest of Uganda." Bataringaya concluded that there was no reason to insist on the "paraphernalia that go with modern justice." What was needed were "tough and fearless fighter[s]" in administration. He and his colleagues wanted Karamoja to be placed under military rule; they wanted the army deployed to disarm the cattle raiders; and they wanted Karimojong cattle branded to indicate their place of pasturage.

Bataringaya's report reflected the impatience with which Ugandan politicians regarded the northeast. His prescriptions were to be lastingly important in shaping official policy. After Uganda's independence the Obote government recruited a new battalion of the Uganda Rifles and assigned it to police the internal affairs of Karamoja.[67] The region was not governed by elected representatives: instead, an official appointed personally by the president was responsible for the administration of the region. Karamoja was a police state.

For a substantial number of Ugandans, government by armed force—with all of its inhumanity and violence—was not a departure from the norm. For the half century prior to the rise of Idi Amin's regime Karamoja had been governed by soldiers. Once he came to power in Kampala, Amin and his officials adopted the same punitive approach to the region.

The archive of the Uganda Broadcasting Corporation contains a number of photographs taken in Karamoja during Amin's occasional visits. Amin came to Karamoja in August 1972 to launch an agricultural exhibition. He seems to have spent a great deal of time inspecting a single field of cassava. He lingered in front of a stand displaying produce—sorghum, some melons.[68] He also spent considerable time standing before a collection of plows, lined up for his inspection. Someone seems to have dug a furrow in the road directly in front of the police station. Amin's

President Amin at an agricultural show in South Karamoja, August 1972
(Courtesy of the Uganda Broadcasting Corporation)

ministers tripped over it as they viewed the military guard posted outside.[69] At a time when the Amin government was demanding that Ugandans double the production of cotton, someone bundled together a
gunnysack of cotton and attached it to a scale. In the photos Amin is
shown standing next to the display, a bemused expression on his face, as a
local official explains the exhibit to him.[70]

Was that exemplary bale of cotton grown in Karamoja? It is possible,
but unlikely. The tomatoes and watermelon that President Amin handled
may have been imported from outside Karamoja, or possibly they were
the product of an individual farmer's fastidious attention. Neither the
produce nor the cotton could be grown at a large scale in the district.
Farmers generally did not plant the crops: they were too demanding of
water. Neither was the plow in wide use across the district, for plows disrupted the thin layer of topsoil, depriving the dirt of its nutrients. Traditional Karimojong agriculture had relied on periodic burning to resupply
the soil with nitrogen.

It is quite possible that the people who organized the show in August
1972 fabricated evidence of progress. Perhaps they brought in props
from other parts of Uganda—a bale of cotton, some vegetables, some

plows—to make the district's agronomy recognizable. These and other photographs highlight the lengths to which local officials had to go to make Karamoja look like other parts of the country. Where in other districts the Amin regime could marshal commoners to participate in civic affairs, in Karamoja government was largely by fiat. There were no campaigns, no targets to meet, no competitions to generate forward momentum.

The Amin government's preemptory approach to local affairs can be seen in the regime's bloody campaign against the nakedness of the region's men. In Karamoja the absence of clothing was not a cause for embarrassment. It was an assertion of masculine honor, called *adengei*. The term was rooted in the Karimojong term for divinity, *Deng*. It likened nakedness to nobility, a demonstration of courage. In this view clothing was protection for weak and cowardly people.[71] There is a photograph in the Uganda Broadcasting Corporation archive depicting a gathering outside the government headquarters in Moroto in January 1964.[72] Karimojong people had gathered to watch as Prime Minister Obote, his wife Miria Obote, and a collection of attendants from Kampala arrived on the grounds. The men are wearing suits and ties; the women are wearing modest dresses; the policemen are in uniform. In the foreground, a single Karimojong youth stands, his back to the camera. His body is unencumbered by clothing, save for a strap around his neck. The watching youth is curious, no doubt. Was he proud? Was he making a challenge to the visitors? Was his presence, directly in the line of sight of the powerful men from Kampala, meant to highlight their cowardice?

For Ugandans outside Karamoja, nakedness was cause for alarm. It was a hinge on which Ugandans from the populous south contrasted their own civility with the barbarism of the north. Some argued that the nakedness of northerners was a national embarrassment, a stain on Uganda's reputation. One group of activists toured Karamoja in 1963, and during their tour they "saw some parts of this country where people are naked; where people sleep under trees; where people never tasted the modern amenities and where men folk have to steal to live and endure unbelievable experiences."[73] The activists urged Prime Minister Obote to impose collective farming on northerners. They also wanted public libraries built and stocked with newspapers, and they urged that radio sets should be installed in pubs and other public establishments, so that "everybody who does not own a radio could hear news and other educative lectures."

President Obote and entourage arrive in Karamoja, observed
by an insouciant youth, January 1964 (Courtesy of the Uganda
Broadcasting Corporation)

Idi Amin's regime had no time for these or other development projects. Amin regarded Karimojong nakedness as a sign of recalcitrance, a
problem that needed to be solved. "I very strongly urge you to change
your habits of dressing," President Amin told an audience of Karimojong
men in April 1971, since they were "neither in your interest nor in the interest of the Republic."[74] When several hundred Karimojong people
staged a protest over a government edict requiring them to wear clothing, a government magistrate sentenced them to six months in prison.[75] A
few years later soldiers assembled Karimojong people at a public ground
not far from Moroto. President Amin divided the assembled crowd into

two groups: those who wanted to wear clothes and those who would not. His soldiers gunned down those who refused to wear clothing.[76]

It was a massacre, one instance in a long, violent war that the Amin government fought against Karimojong people. Amin's men governed Karamoja as if it were a penal colony. The district commissioner was a civilian named Kabogoza-Musoke. He was a friend of the commander of the army battalion based in Moroto; and he thought of Karamoja as a "paradise where people rub their shoulders irrespective of whether one is from barracks or elsewhere."[77] His sense of humanity did not extend to Karimojong people. He thought the courts of law were too indulgent. Magistrates were insistent on exactitude in legal procedure, and too many guilty men walked free for lack of evidence.[78] Kabogoza-Musoke saw criminal behavior everywhere. The peace meetings that civil servants organized to alleviate tensions between different pastoral groups were, in his view, an insult to the authority of government, for at the meetings "officers are ridiculed, officials translate themselves into a laughing stock." If it was to be effective, the government's power had to be unchallenged. "It is only by a show of force by Government in the whole issue that will save the situation to make the district settle," he argued. Karimojong people had "refused to learn in the normal way, they understand the Army language alone."[79]

In December 1972 President Amin agreed to provide Karimojong militiamen with a supply of automatic weapons to fight off Turkana cattle raiders. He also committed ten helicopters to the district.[80] The weapons accelerated the militarization of conflict. In 1974 local authorities reported that Karimojong cattle raiders were using automatic rifles from Sudan and Somalia. One group of raiders used grenades of Israeli manufacture.[81] There was constant raiding within Karamoja, as different pastoral groups struggled over cattle, grass, and water. An official in one county reported that raiders had targeted his people every night for more than a month.[82] Karimojong raiders made regular forays into neighboring Lango District, too. In one place in Lango the chief reported that his people had faced thirteen raids over the space of eleven months. "Our suffering is unbearable, and the inhabitants are fleeing with their cattle to distant places," he reported.[83]

Caught in an expanding cycle of military violence, people in northeastern Uganda suffered greatly. According to government figures, the population of one of the leading counties in Karamoja declined from 168,007 people in 1969 to 103,700 people in 1979. In this single county,

64,000 people had died, disappeared, or emigrated during the time of Idi Amin's presidency.[84]

=======

It is impossible to count all the people killed by Idi Amin's men. In the absence of reliable records, activists and authors have had to invent outlandish means of reckoning with the numbers. Henry Kyemba—once Idi Amin's personal secretary, later his leading critic—formulated his estimate by counting the number of bodies that boatmen at the Owen Falls Dam recovered daily. Twenty bodies surfaced every day, and so Kyemba estimated that there must have been 40,000 bodies dumped there between 1971 and 1977 (when Kyemba's book was published). Owen Falls was one of three places where the bodies of the dead were deposited; and one needed to account for the crocodiles, which consumed some of the dead before the bodies could surface. Kyemba therefore estimated 150,000 as the total death toll of the Amin regime.[85] Other observers were less specific in their guesswork. Amnesty International placed the figure at 300,000 total dead in a report to the U.S. Senate in 1978. The authors admitted that the numbers could not be verified.[86]

The impulse to count the dead arose out of a need to establish the scale of Idi Amin's violence. That is why so many authors and activists likened 1970s Uganda to Nazi Germany. If Amin was indeed "Hitler in Africa" (as the title of a book published in 1977 described him), if the events of the 1970s could indeed be called a "Uganda Holocaust" (as another book title put it), then Ugandans were entitled to sympathy, recognition, action, and compensation.[87] Enlarging the scale of the violence, in other words, was a way to gather attention in the international arena. For Ugandan dissidents it generated support. For authors it sold books. For relief workers it made philanthropy seem morally essential.

All the attention paid to numbers makes it hard to see the ways in which violence actually happened. Amin's government was not a genocidal machine. The violence of the age arose out of the militarization of otherwise technical questions of government. People living in Karamoja experienced the 1970s as a continuation of a military occupation launched in the early decades of British colonial control. People in the southern and central parts of Uganda found themselves newly subject to the uncontrollable authority of men with guns. Some men and women found themselves named as enemies of the state, as dissidents, guerrillas, or saboteurs. Other people found themselves subject to the arbitrary authority of individual soldiers, who opportunistically used their power to gain advantages in private disputes. Much of the violence of those days arose in moments when soldiers—puffed up by their guns, unaccountable to civil authority—confronted angry, indignant, humiliated civilians.

Amin's regime made enemies of a great many people. That is how government worked: by blaming specific categories of people for previously cloudy and obscure problems. As more and more of social life was targeted by government campaigners, the army came to be the essential framework for administration. That is how military violence came to be an inescapable fact of social life.

CHAPTER SEVEN

The Front Lines

FOLDED IN THE MIDDLE of an otherwise unremarkable file in the archives of Jinja District is a collage, about thirty-five inches long and twenty-five inches wide, titled—in hand-drawn capital letters—"O.A.U. Patriotic Volunteers."[1] At the top are photographs of eminent African leaders, clipped out of newspapers. On the left is a photo of Haile Selassie, founder of the Organization of African Unity; on the right is Kenyan president Jomo Kenyatta. On the bottom corner there is a typewritten essay laying out the governmental structure for a prospective "Union of African States." The first president is to be Ethiopia's emperor, Haile Selassie. Tanzania's president Julius Nyerere is to head the Ministry of Finance, assisted by the president of Togo. Ugandan president Idi Amin will head the Ministry of Communications.

The creator of this collage was Peter Wankulu, a clerk working at a sugar plantation near Jinja. He set aside a corner for a handwritten autobiography. He was born in 1940 in Busoga, to the east of Kampala. His father had served in the army during the Second World War. Wankulu described himself as a servant of the cause: he "makes personal sacrifices by staying in a single room, walks and cycles to his employment to save for these printings, papers and stamps—for Africa." Along the bottom margin is a handwritten directive, surrounded by a black border to make it stand out. "Please, kindly put on notice board, public place, and help to teach the value of unity in Africa," it reads.

This remarkable collage was one of several that Peter Wankulu created in 1974 and 1975, as the Organization of African Unity convened in
Kampala under the chairmanship of Idi Amin. In the years before the
O.A.U. conference Wankulu had composed dozens of circulars, posters,
flyers, and pamphlets that advocated for the formation of a pan-African
government. In the mid-1970s he reworked the archive he'd created. He
clipped apart the letters and pamphlets, combined them with photographs and essays from the government newspaper, and reassembled
them as collages, which he put up on the streets of the city of Kampala.
All of this was financed from his own meager resources and done in
his spare time. None of it was done at the behest of the Organization of
African Unity.

Peter Wankulu was a creative and restless thinker, desperately
searching for media that could command the attention of people in
power. That is why he turned to collage. Collage is the art of reorganizing things.[2] In collage artists create visual relationships between things
that are ordinarily kept apart. They connect people, institutions, and
ideas, making new positions and new possibilities visible. Collage is an
artistic style that is suited to conditions of shortage. In places and times
when paint, clay, and other instruments of artistic creativity are in short
supply, collage artists use bits and pieces that come to hand.

In Wankulu's time Idi Amin's government was making Uganda—a remote, landlocked place, far from the theater of battle—into a frontline
state in the global war against racism and imperialism. A whole host of
liberation wars seemed close at hand, and all at once the distance between
the far away and the immediately local was radically shortened. The world
in which ordinary people lived became an arena where battles of global
consequence were fought. It was, for the Amin regime, a way of claiming a
morally essential role: liberator of Africa's hitherto oppressed people.

For people like Peter Wankulu, life on the front lines was all-consuming.
It inspired extraordinary self-sacrifice. Wankulu's work was motivated by a
sincere commitment to big ideas, by an expansive sense of mission, and by
an enlarged feeling of scale. He was a self-made man, a determined curator of
his own reputation, and the self-identified author of some of the great events
of the age. His cut-and-paste posters help us see how, at a time of economic
austerity and profound violence, some resourceful Ugandans found a wide
and embracing role to play in global politics.

To British diplomats, the coup that brought Idi Amin to power initially seemed to herald a new era of friendly cooperation. Many of the leading figures in Amin's government—cabinet ministers, the police chief, officers in the army—had been trained in Britain. Everyone was impressed by the grandiose funeral of Frederick Muteesa, the late Kabaka of Buganda. One bemused diplomat guessed that "God Save the Queen" was played as often as Uganda's national anthem during the week of Muteesa's funeral.[3] "For the first time in some while we have a Government of a Central African State who is really on our side," wrote a group of British parliamentarians in April 1971.[4]

Even so, it was Israel, not Britain, that played the leading part in the first year of Amin's government.[5] At the rosy dawn of Amin's regime, Israeli diplomats claimed that—as a "small, half-way country"—Israel was "perhaps better able to understand the attitudes of people in developing countries than are experts from highly industrialized lands."[6] During his years as commander of the Uganda Army, General Amin had cultivated a close relationship with the Israeli defense attaché, Colonel Bar-Lev. Amin was in constant touch with Bar-Lev during the 25 January coup, and as the coup unfolded diplomats from other countries congregated at Bar-Lev's house to get up-to-date information.[7] In the months after the coup Israel sent dozens of soldiers to Uganda. They equipped and trained the key units in the security services: the paratrooper unit, the escort unit that guarded key government officials, the Public Service Unit, and others.[8] In June 1971 Amin wrote to Israeli defense minister Moshe Dayan, assuring him that "Uganda under my government will maintain the best possible relations with the State of Israel."[9] Amin visited Israel the following month, where he met with Prime Minister Golda Meir and other politicians. During his state visit Amin promised to locate the Ugandan embassy to Israel in Jerusalem.[10]

For the Israelis all of this required tact and careful diplomacy. They were particularly worried about Amin's brother-in-law, the lawyer Wanume Kibedi, who was minister of foreign affairs. The Israeli ambassador described Kibedi as "remarkably confident in person," and a committed man of the Left.[11] At a meeting in mid-January 1972 Kibedi berated the ambassador, complaining loudly to Amin about Israel's outsized role in Uganda. President Amin reprimanded Kibedi, warning him that he would be jailed if he spoke in such a way again.[12] But Kibedi was not alone in his aversion to Israel. Intelligence sources reported that one of the leading figures at Kibuli Mosque—the country's most consequential Islamic institution—was campaigning against Israel.[13] The man's name was Muhammed Yasin Bira. Bira had studied in Cairo and was married to an Egyptian woman. Together with a delegation of several hundred Ugandan Muslims Bira made a pilgrimage to Mecca in January 1972. There, in front of large crowds, he and his companions criticized the Amin government, arguing that Uganda was complicit in Israel's occupation of Palestinian lands.

Idi Amin made a pilgrimage to Mecca during the same season that Muhammed Yasin Bira made his. Israeli diplomats worried that Amin would be "influenced by the raging hatred for Israel which he will encounter in Mecca."[14] They worked hard to curate and control Amin's pilgrimage. A Ugandan cleric who was sympathetic to Israel—Sheikh Obeid Kamulegeya—traveled to Mecca at Israel's behest. In his company was a delegation of 170 Ugandan Muslims who shared his views. The Israelis paid Kamulegeya's expenses.[15]

I do not know what happened during those days in January 1972, but the evidence suggests that his pilgrimage to Mecca played a key role in shaping President Amin's politics. A week following his return from Saudi Arabia, Amin paid a state visit to Tripoli and signed a joint statement with Libyan leader Muammar Gaddafi. It assured the "Arab people" of Uganda's support in their "struggle against Zionism and imperialism for the liberation of confiscated lands and the right of the Palestinian people to return to their land and homes."[16] Israeli diplomats speculated that Amin had been awed by Gaddafi's charm and charisma, and had signed the statement without understanding its meaning.[17] They were caught by surprise when, in the evening on 23 March 1972, President Amin ordered the expulsion of Israeli diplomats and soldiers from Uganda. Seven hundred people were given four days to leave the country.[18] The Israeli military advisers were rounded up at gunpoint and made to hand over their personal property to Ugandan soldiers.[19] The Israeli embassy was reduced to a staff of four people. In those tumultuous days Amin—in an address on Radio Uganda—summoned "the Israel community" for a hurried meeting in the International Conference Centre. In photographs taken at the occasion five Israeli diplomats sit, arms folded, as Foreign Minister Kibedi lectures at them from a rostrum in the front of the hall.[20] One of them takes notes. There are no handshakes, no smiles. The pictures depict the end of an alliance.

In a press statement Amin described the expulsion as an act of solidarity with oppressed Palestinian people.[21] Gaddafi celebrated the

Israelis' ouster, saying that Uganda had at last "discovered her true African identity." The Libyan leader imagined that—with the Israelis gone—"we shall lead Uganda forward as long as she remains on this newly liberated path."[22] In September that year Amin wrote to Prime Minister Golda Meir, comparing Israel to the white settler colony in Rhodesia. Like the Rhodesians, Israelis had occupied land that was not their own. "Hitler and all German people knew that the Israelis are not people who are working in the interest of the people of the world," Amin wrote. "That is why they burnt the Israelis alive with gas on the soil of Germany."[23]

Pushed by activists like Muhammed Yasin Bira, prodded by Wanume Kibedi and other men of the Left, inspired perhaps by Gaddafi, Idi Amin found a new role to play in global affairs. After his visit to Libya he told Israeli journalists that "Uganda is the centre of Africa, and the centre of its politics."[24] In June—a few months after the expulsion of the Israelis—President Amin made a return trip to Saudi Arabia. According to American observers he was received as a "Muslim prodigal returned to righteousness from the evils of Zionism."[25] By October 1973 Amin could announce that three million Ugandans had volunteered to fight in a military campaign against the state of Israel. Once the Middle East had been liberated, the fighting force would turn its guns against the white minority regimes of southern Africa.[26] In January 1974 he published a book titled *On the Middle East Crisis*. In it he called on all "just and peace loving nations of the world" to support Palestine's liberation with their "fullest and undiluted moral and material support."[27] Amin personally autographed two copies and sent them to Kurt Waldheim, the secretary-general of the United Nations.[28]

That is how Amin found a voice with which to speak to a whole range of matters that—on the face of it—had nothing to do with Uganda. He was particularly interested in American politics. In May 1972—just after the expulsion of the Israelis—Amin called in the American ambassador and delivered a ninety-minute monologue about Vietnam, the Suez Canal, and Okinawa.[29] "We are aware that your multiracial society is not going well," he wrote in a letter to Richard Nixon.

> There are endless racial conflicts. Black people are kept in perpetual economic, political and cultural serfdom. Riots and other rebellions are common in your country. At this moment you are uncomfortably sandwiched in the unfortunate Watergate affair.[30]

The question of Scottish independence was one of his enduring concerns. The "people of Scotland are tired of being exploited by the English," wrote Amin in a telegram to the United Nations. "Scotland was once an independent country, happy, well governed and administered with peace and prosperity"; but under British government "England has thrived on the energies and brains of the Scottish people."[31] In 1975 Amin wrote to the head of the new military government of Ethiopia—then embroiled in a bloody war with the Eritrean Liberation Front—to offer Kampala as a venue for peace talks. Amin urged Ethiopia's leaders to recognize the "right of Eritrea to full independence."[32] In 1976 Amin received a missive from 175 residents of Hawaii, who asked for his help in securing the island's independence from the United States. Journalists reported that Amin was studying the question.[33]

All the cables that President Amin sent to the world's leaders were read out over Radio Uganda, and many were subsequently printed in government newspapers. There were no secret overtures, no private dialogues, no circumspection or politesse or tact. Amin's diplomacy was conducted in the open, and diplomatic communication was itself a media event. In July 1973, for example, Amin sent a cable to Marshal Lon Nol decrying American policy in Cambodia. The American ambassador received a copy of the telegram thirty minutes before the cable was read out on Radio Uganda.[34] When Amin cabled the Queen of England to argue the case for Scotland's independence, he invited the British high commissioner to the Imperial Hotel in Kampala and presented the cable—signed personally—before an audience of journalists.[35]

His overtures in international politics were not usually successful, and Amin often aroused the indignation of governments that he offended. The Ethiopian government, for instance, condemned Amin for making a "deliberate attempt to undermine the sovereignty and territorial integrity of a sister state." It was a shame, they said, "that some people have more time to spare for the affairs of other nations than for their own."[36] The American government likewise took offense at Amin's interest in U.S. foreign policy. When Amin expressed support for the insurgent government of South Vietnam, diplomats of the U.S. State Department took umbrage at the "intemperateness and bias" of Amin's telegram.[37] In a private telephone conversation President Richard Nixon and National Security Adviser Henry Kissinger agreed that Amin was an "ape without education" and a "prehistoric monster."[38]

Was there logic behind President Amin's diplomacy? The American ambassador thought it was a charade, meant to distract the public's attention

from the regime's misgovernment. Every day, he reported, Ugandan newspapers showed Amin receiving delegates from the Soviet Union, Canada,
Liberia, or other places, creating the impression among readers that "all
these potentates take Amin seriously and take trouble to respond to him."
Radio broadcasts likewise created false impressions: they showed "Amin telling Qadafi and Sadat to cool it; telling Palestinians not to worry about Hus-
sein's speech . . . counseling the British to keep hands off Northern Ireland."
When the listener turned off his receiver, the feeling was that "one is living
in a totally unreal situation, for . . . there is no mention of what ought to be
the major story of the day," that is, the desperate condition of Uganda's politics and economy.[39]

The ambassador missed the point. International diplomacy was not
a distraction from the real issues of the time. It was a way of making
Uganda into a frontline state in the global war against racism and imperialism. Amin was leading black Ugandans in a War of Economic Independence. It was a platform on which to claim a wide political role: as
champion of the world's oppressed people. Amin made connections
across the global Left, and an array of crackpots, schemers, and unlikely
revolutionaries passed through Kampala. There was Nguyen Huu Tho,
president of the National Liberation Front of South Vietnam. There was
the deposed Cambodian king Norodom Sihanouk, who came to Kampala shortly after he entered an uneasy alliance with Pol Pot.[40] There
were soldiers-in-training from Zimbabwe. Their leader—Ndabaningi
Sithole—made several visits to Kampala. All of them were marginal revolutionaries, discredited by mainstream nationalist movements. All of
them were figures in Uganda's public life, lavished with attention, the
focus of press reports.

Amin's diplomacy made Kampala into a center of the global Left. In
1974 Amin called for the reorganization of the United Nations. He
wanted the headquarters transferred to Kampala, "which is the heart of
the world between the continents of America, Asia, Australia and the
North and South Poles."[41] He argued that the composition of the
Security Council was a relic of the colonial past, and demanded that African countries be given veto power to match that of their former colonial
rulers.[42] The following year he wrote to the governments of the British
Commonwealth, offering to take over the headship of the organization
from Queen Elizabeth. The collapsing British economy had made Britain unable to maintain its leadership of the Commonwealth, he wrote;
and moreover the "British empire does not now exist following the

complete decolonization of Britain's former overseas territories."[43] As evidence of his fitness to head the Commonwealth, Amin pointed to the "success of my economic revolution in Uganda."

======

The struggle against South Africa's apartheid government was one of the several wars of liberation that Idi Amin claimed to lead. In no other war of liberation were the stakes clearer. For Amin's regime, anti-apartheid organizing was an enduring source of moral and political orientation.

In December 1971—eleven months after coming to power— President Amin wrote to the Organization of African Unity, offering Uganda as a base for the training of an all-African army that could fight against the apartheid regime.[44] The O.A.U.'s defense commission shelved the idea, but Amin was determined to press forward. In January 1972, as he was returning from his consequential pilgrimage in Mecca, Amin offered financial subsidies to several liberation movements in southern Africa. A few weeks later the ambassador of the Ivory Coast visited President Amin to discuss the expulsion of Uganda's Israeli community, which was then under way. During their conversation Amin hammered the table with his first, shouting that black African countries must band together and destroy apartheid South Africa.[45]

Greatly to President Amin's irritation, though, Uganda was far from the theater of conflict, hedged in by the boundaries of intervening states, without a direct route to the sea. There was no means by which Uganda could pursue a military campaign against the apartheid government. In frustration Amin wrote to Sekou Toure, the president of Guinea, complaining that neither Julius Nyerere nor Kenneth Kaunda—presidents of frontline states—would allow Uganda intelligence operatives or soldiers access to Mozambique, Zimbabwe, or Angola, where wars of liberation were being fought. It was a travesty, argued Amin. Nyerere and Kaunda were playing a double game, mouthing their support for anti-apartheid activists while remaining "afraid of military intelligence which is directed toward the real liberation of the remaining colonies in Africa."[46]

The cold facts of geography put Uganda at a distance from the front lines. It must have been a relief when in February 1974 a prominent anti-apartheid activist—Potlako Leballo, leader of the Pan-Africanist Congress—made an official visit to Kampala. Radio Uganda was there to cover the occasion.[47] With the microphones assembled in front of him, Amin told Leballo that he was "trying to see that all OAU states are revolutionary." If every African country would contribute 120 properly trained soldiers, Amin mused, the combined force could crush Ian Smith's racist regime in Rhodesia and thereafter confront the army of apartheid South Africa. Leballo, in turn, congratulated Amin on being "the only one who realized and faced the problem of liberating Africa seriously."

What brought Potlako Leballo to Kampala in February 1974? He was a controversial figure. He'd been made head of the P.A.C. after the organization's founder, Robert Sobukwe, was imprisoned by the South African government. By February 1974 Leballo and his colleagues had been expelled from South Africa, Lesotho, Zambia, and Botswana. He was living in Dar es Salaam, trying desperately to attract financial and logistical support from African governments. A leading newspaper in Johannesburg had called him a "liar, fool, braggart."[48] His contemporaries in the African National Congress thought him a "disruptive adventurist," undermining anti-apartheid solidarity for his private benefit.[49]

In July 1975 President Amin stepped up to the rostrum at the Organization of African Unity summit in Kampala and called for a continental war against apartheid South Africa. He had been elected as the O.A.U. president that very day. Amin asked black African states to join their militaries into an anti-apartheid force, similar to NATO or the Warsaw Pact.[50] "We are totally committed to the liberation of our continent," he told his audience. "If the Whites of Rhodesia and South Africa cannot accept immediate majority rule, then we must get a solution militarily."[51] There was no real prospect for a shooting war against the minority regimes of southern Africa. Neither Tanzania nor Zambia were represented at the Kampala meeting, as they regarded Amin's presidency of the O.A.U. as a travesty. In the absence of military resolve Amin had to invent a stand-in for the real thing. At the conclusion of the meeting Amin brought his distinguished guests to a lakeside retreat—which he called "Cape Town View"—to watch as the Uganda Air Force bombed an unremarkable island located a few kilometers from shore. In the newsreel film made of the occasion the Palestinian leader Yasir Arafat, the president of Somalia, Kenya's vice president, and other dignitaries watch in bemusement as Uganda Air Force jets lay waste to uninhabited forests.[52] It was training, said Amin, for the coming invasion of apartheid South Africa.

Amin's support for the Pan-Africanist Congress was—like his anti-apartheid support—a piece of political theater. By October 1975 a group of around two hundred P.A.C. men were undergoing military training in

Masaka at a Uganda Army barracks. The *Voice of Uganda* carried several stories about it. In early November Amin welcomed Leballo—along with the leaders of two Angolan liberation movements—to his office with the goal of "formulating a strategy to liberate the whole African continent once and for all."[53] A few days later Leballo visited the P.A.C. men at their training ground. He told the press that "the liberators are being trained morally and politically to sacrifice their lives in order to free other millions of our brothers."[54] He made sure to applaud Idi Amin for his work to "eradicate imperialism, racism and Zionism because they are the very root of evil, which is hated by all mankind."

Who were the men who were being trained by the Uganda Army? And what did they learn? They left no trace in the paper records of government. It is the photographic archive that offers a few insights. It seems that the P.A.C. recruits were enlisted without regard to their fitness: some of them are of a distinctly unmilitary physique. They were issued the khaki service uniforms worn by the regular Uganda Army, with berets bearing the Uganda Army crest. Their automatic rifles, outfitted with bayonets, were standard-issue Uganda Army, too. A few of the P.A.C. men carried the ceremonial swords that Uganda Army officers brandished when inspecting the troops, but it is unlikely that the South Africans learned the drill that was a standard part of regular army training. Their training course lasted a bare two weeks. When Potlako Leballo returned to the barracks, a rank of armored personnel carriers piloted by Uganda Army drivers was drawn up for him to inspect. The P.A.C. men did not march or perform any demonstration of military accomplishment. They stood still, behind a line that had been drawn in the dirt, and listened to a speech from Leballo and another from the commanding officer of the Masaka barracks.[55] Were the Ugandan officers who ran the training program nervous about exposing their men to ridicule? Were they afraid that their men, if called upon to march, would stumble or fall?

When they left the barracks at Masaka in late November 1975 the P.A.C. men were almost certainly obliged to return their rifles to the armory, for the weapons were marked with Uganda Army serial numbers, written in white paint on the stock. The berets, the swords, and probably the khaki uniforms likewise had to be returned to Ugandan custody.

For President Amin, the war against apartheid was an enduring source of political momentum. Potlako Leballo came to Uganda on three occasions in 1976. In October 1977 he was again in Kampala, where Amin

Passing-out parade for Pan-Africanist Congress trainees at Masaka, November 1975 (Courtesy of the Uganda Broadcasting Corporation)

offered him a weapon—made, he said, by "revolutionary Ugandans"—that allowed, he claimed, one man to defeat 1,000 to 2,000 opponents. Amin offered to send a mechanized battalion to Rhodesia, and assured his listeners that Ian Smith would soon be a P.O.W. in Kampala.[56] In January 1978 President Amin offered to provide medical training to P.A.C. nurses, who would care for wounded men during the coming guerrilla war. Potlako Leballo was at the time involved in a fratricidal conflict with other P.A.C. leaders: a few weeks before he had ousted the whole high command of the P.A.C. army and expelled several highly trained cadres from the party.[57] Even in the midst of this conflict he found time to bring a group of a dozen women to Kampala, where they spent a pleasant afternoon in

Nurses of the Pan-Africanist Congress greet President Amin, January 1978
(Courtesy of the Uganda Broadcasting Corporation)

Amin's company at the government hotel. In the photographs Leballo presents Amin with a P.A.C. wall calendar; the assembled women shake Amin's hand and sing an anthem for his enjoyment.[58]

Both the weapon built by "revolutionary Ugandans" and the training program for nurses were illusory. The president's offer of medical training caught the secretary-general of the Uganda Red Cross by surprise.[59] The Red Cross had no financial means to support the twelve women during their four-week residence in Uganda; neither did it possess equipment with which to supply their needs. Besides, the Red Cross's leader said, the presidential directive concerning the training program had been "rather abrupt," giving the organizers only five days' notice before the training course was to begin.

That is what Idi Amin's support for the P.A.C. entailed. The training programs offered by Amin's regime were hastily organized, poorly supported, and badly run. Much of the military and humanitarian support that Idi Amin offered was a fiction. But that was not the point. For Amin's regime, being anti-apartheid was a role to play. It was a credential, a potent source of legitimacy. It made his government appear morally essential.

When President Amin attended the Organization of African Unity summit in Addis Ababa, the Uganda government published a 127-page booklet heralding his achievements there.[60] It was reported that, upon his arrival at the venue, he was given a "tumultuous welcome" by a waiting crowd, all of them "competing for a chance to get a glimpse of the man ... in whose hands lie[s] the true salvation of the Black Man." During his speech, President Amin was "interrupted by thunderous applauses of acclamation and cheers, almost word for word, by Heads of State and Government and by everybody else who had a chance to hear it." It was, wrote the reporter,

> very clear that Uganda had emerged as the forefront of a True African State. It was clear that African nationalism had been born again. It was clear that the speech had brought new life to the freedom struggle in Africa. ... The Ugandan leader had given Uganda its rightful place on the map of Africa.

———

What did it mean to live on the forefront of the freedom struggle in Africa? Even in the remotest provinces questions of international importance were never far away. The great and enduring controversies of the age shaped the commonplace locales in which people lived.

In May 1976, the district commissioner in Bundibugyo marked the opening of the district's celebrations of Africa Day by framing local history as a long-term struggle against racism. Under colonial government, he told a crowd,

> we were given second-class citizenship on our own soil. The best jobs, the best places in functions, the best hospitals and the best hotels ... were exclusively for whites. ... There were even very

big posters in red warning Africans and Dogs as out of bounds,
as if an African was equated with a dog.

In fact Bundibugyo—a remote borderland, neighboring Zaire—had
never been home to white settlers. There was no hospital until 1969,
seven years after Uganda's independence. The nearest hotel was in Fort
Portal, dozens of miles away over a broken road. In colonial times Bundibugyo's people had been governed indirectly, by African aristocrats
from the Tooro kingdom, not by white administrators. The local experience of colonial government did not entail overt, exclusionary racism.
That did not make the district commissioner's account less potent. His
speech concluded by contrasting the colonial past with Uganda's bright
future. Under President Amin, he said, Uganda "ranks among the proud
independent states of the world where the indigenous people hold the
destinies of their own nations."[61]

The Amin government brought the struggle against imperialism and
racism close to home, giving Ugandans reason to see themselves as global
actors. In 1972 the Liberation Committee of the Organization of African
Unity launched a fundraising campaign to support the liberation movements of southern Africa. It was an opportunity for Africans to "demonstrate their firm commitment and unflinching dedication to the noble
cause of the valiant and struggling masses in Southern Africa," wrote the
organizers.[62] In Jinja, the town clerk wrote to civic organizations—the
Lions Club, the Rotary Club, the Sunni Muslim community—asking
them to solicit for funds "door to door and shop to shop."[63] In the space
of a week the people of Jinja donated 6,800 shillings.[64] In total, Ugandans
contributed 600,000 shillings (about $85,000) to the O.A.U. Liberation
Committee campaign that year.[65] Even in places that were distant from
the anti-apartheid, anti-racist struggles of the south, Ugandans felt that
there were urgent battles to fight. In 1973 several hundred policemen and
policewomen volunteered to serve in an Africa-wide army meant to
achieve the "Liberation of Africa from Colonialism, Imperialism and Zionism."[66] The police commissioner totted up the volunteers' names and
ranks and sent them to Kampala, ready for mobilization.

All this self-sacrifice was the seedbed for new heroes. For the first
anniversary of the coup that brought him to power Amin created a number of new military honors, including the "Order of the Source of the
Nile," the "Republic of Uganda" medal, and several others. At the anniversary ceremonies some 15,000 people were given a medal.[67] Later that

year Amin hosted as a state visitor the much-bemedaled president of the Central African Republic, Jean-Bédel Bokassa. Within a week Uganda's army had bestowed eight new honors on Amin, including the "State Combat Star," the "Victorious Cross," and the "Efficiency Decoration Medal."[68] In 1977 the Defence Council bestowed a new honor on President Amin. It was called "Conqueror of the British Empire," abbreviated C.B.E.[69]

There were new martyrs, too. On 4 July 1976 a force of Israeli commandos landed at Entebbe airport, shot up the Ugandan military units that were encamped around the terminal, and freed a contingent of Jewish hostages whose airplane had been hijacked by the Palestinian Liberation Organization. More than a hundred officers and men of the Uganda Army were killed in the so-called Entebbe Air Raid, among them the commander of Uganda's air force.[70] All at once, a whole new arena for patriotic sacrifice suddenly opened up. The day after the Israeli raid at Entebbe a man named Abubakar Kibudde wrote to President Amin on behalf of an organization calling itself the "Ex-Soldiers of Toro."[71] He and his colleagues—who claimed to have served in the colonial military—volunteered to join the liberation army that Amin was recruiting to fight against Israel and the white-dominated governments of southern Africa. They asked for a meeting with President Amin, during which they intended to offer

> undaunted and unequivocal support to face the threat posed by imperialists, capitalists and Zionists, whose lust to exploit and enslave the peace loving African World and Arabs must be fought and repulsed completely.

Idealistic men and women thought that the struggles of their time were right before them, demanding action and dedication. Early in 1978 Kibudde and his colleagues again wrote to President Amin to express their jubilation over "all the successes you have achieved and put Uganda to present SHINING STAR and renewed it on the Map of the World."[72] In a separate letter—sent on the same day—they wrote to the officer commanding the army regiment based in Fort Portal, volunteering themselves for military service. They wished to join the Zimbabwe liberation forces, promising to be "brave, honest, faithful, and [to] fight on Land, Sea and Air, as may be directed by the Commander and Chief." There were three volunteers, among them Mr. Kibudde himself.[73]

A great many people volunteered to serve in Idi Amin's wars of liberation. Black Americans were among the most eager to enlist. Impressed by the Economic War and the promise it held out, some Black activists looked upon Idi Amin as a champion for racial and economic justice. In March 1973, Roy Innis, leader of the Congress of Racial Equality, visited Uganda at President Amin's invitation. Innis and his colleagues had been pressing African governments to grant dual citizenship to Black Americans, just as Jewish Americans could earn citizenship from the state of Israel. In an interview Innis had compared Black Americans to prodigal sons, returning to their fathers' mansion.[74] Over the course of their eighteen days in Uganda, President Amin loaned his helicopter to carry them around the country. The C.O.R.E. delegation toured Kigezi District in southern Uganda, where they inspected a cattle farm, and Jinja in eastern Uganda, where they visited a textile factory. In one series of photos Idi Amin awkwardly hugs the members of the C.O.R.E. delegation, one after the other. It is the only place in the photographic archive where Amin is shown embracing another person.[75] Everywhere Innis spoke with enthusiasm about President Amin's accomplishments. He was the "third greatest modern African leader," after Patrice Lumumba and Kwame Nkrumah, Innis told an audience at Makerere University.[76] Part of Innis's poem, published in the government newspaper, reads:

> Before, the life of your people was a complete bore,
> And they were poor, oppressed, exploited and economically sore.
> And you then came and opened new, dynamic economic pages.
> And showered progress on your people in realistic stages.
> In such expert moves that baffled even the great sages,
> your electric personality pronounced the imperialists' doom.
> Your pragmatism has given Ugandans their economic boom.[77]

In May 1973, Innis was back in Uganda. He promised to recruit a contingent of five hundred Black American professors and technicians to serve in Uganda. Amin offered them free passage to Uganda, free housing, and free hospital care for themselves and their families. The American weekly *Jet* predicted that Uganda was soon to become an "African Israel," a model state upheld by the energies and knowledge of Black Americans.[78] Innis announced in early July that an advance party of fifty people was ready to depart.[79] They had been screened and selected by Congress of Racial Equality staff. "General Amin is the key to success and black liberation all over Africa," Innis told a reporter.[80]

Roy Innis (at left in the first row behind the children), Idi Amin (center, next to
Innis), Louis Farrakhan (other side of Amin, wearing a bow tie), and other Black
Americans meeting with the president at State House, August 1975 (Courtesy of
the Uganda Broadcasting Corporation)

The C.O.R.E. volunteers whom Roy Innis recruited were never actually sent to Uganda. President Amin eventually refused their offer of
service.[81] He was wary of their ambition: Innis had promised the volunteers the ownership of businesses and shops formerly possessed by deported Indians and Pakistanis.[82] But all through the 1970s Black activists
continued to make pilgrimages to Kampala. The photographic archives
are full of pictures documenting their visits. In June 1973 the Black Pan-
ther leader Stokely Carmichael toured the country in the company of his
wife Miriam Makeba, the famous South African jazz musician. At every
stop on their tour Makeba performed before large audiences, while during the interval Carmichael expounded on the philosophy of Black liberation. Both Makeba and Carmichael received Ugandan passports from
Idi Amin's hand.[83] In August 1975 Louis Farrakhan, leader of the Nation

of Islam, visited Kampala and met with Amin. In the photographs Farrakhan poses in the company of Amin's children, all of whom are wearing
shirts bearing the president's photograph.[84] In March 1977 there was another delegation from Farrakhan's group, who visited in the company of
reporters from radio station WNJP in New Jersey. A photo depicting
the delegates alongside President Amin was published on the front page
of the *Pittsburgh Courier*, a leading African American newspaper.[85]

   Abubakar Kibudde's "Ex-Soldiers of Toro" had little in common with
the volunteers whom Roy Innis mustered. What they shared was an enthusiasm for Idi Amin's regime, and a resolve to serve it. Even as the violence and dysfunction of Amin's government became ever more obvious,
some patriotic and idealistic people continued to regard Amin as their
champion. For Kibudde and Innis—as for many others—his assertive efforts to confront racial and political injustice were a source of inspiration
and orientation.

                                   ====

British diplomats first heard of Peter Wankulu in 1962, when he wrote to
the High Commission in Kampala on behalf of an organization called
the "All Africa Youth League." His aim was to bring together the continent's youth to create a new United States of Africa.[86] British diplomats
thought he was a crank, "given to issuing manifestos designed to set the
world at rights." In 1963 Wankulu organized a program of lectures and
events in Nairobi. Kenya's newspaper ran a short editorial about his Africa Youth League, calling it "virtually a one-man operation."[87] In 1964
he set off on a walking tour across Uganda. Styling himself a "voluntary
civil servant, Africa Unity Government," Wankulu visited Jinja, Tororo,
Mbale, and Soroti in the east and Gulu, Lira, and Arua in the north.[88] At
every place he visited he gave a public lecture urging his listeners to
"bury tribalism and all those unfounded suspicions and accusations that
have ruined our progress everywhere and join hands to save Africa."

   His early advocacy fortified Wankulu's latter-day career as a self-
professed pioneer of Pan-Africanism. In 1970—the year before Idi Amin
came to power—Wankulu distributed a carbon-copied circular on an extraordinary letterhead. The header, which occupied a third of the page,
consisted of an essay about the history of Pan-Africanism. It began with
Marcus Garvey and the "back to Africa" movement, then moved to
W. E. B. Du Bois. The essay continued by putting Wankulu at the center of
the story. "In the late 1962," it read, "a few young men in Kampala started

the first direct Pan-Africa Youth Movement," paving the way for the foundation of the Organization of African Unity in 1963.[89] Peter Wankulu's letterhead made an unlikely claim: Kampala was where Pan-Africanism had first taken organizational form. His historical role made Wankulu feel entitled to dictate to his contemporaries. In the text of his letter he called on all "professors, teachers, press editors, businessmen, police and army forces, student, women youth organizations and street men" to "forget any differences and form into a UNITED FRONT." That front, he wrote, would be called the African Unity Youth Organization, to be headquartered in Kampala.[90]

A few years later Wankulu had changed his stationery.[91] Perhaps he decided that the older version was too cumbersome? The new version was cleaner and more compact: it featured the names of six "directors," each of whom was responsible for a "Regional HQ." There were offices in Johannesburg, Leopoldville, Accra, Cairo, Nairobi, and Kampala. The director of the Cairo office was named as David Mabunda. In a former time Mabunda had been the secretary-general of Mozambique's nationalist party; in 1963 he was expelled from the party in a dispute over its leadership.[92] He thereafter denounced party president Eduardo Mondlane as an "American tailored leader" and went to live in exile in Cairo.[93] Another of the directors of the "Africa Youth League" was Nelson Rwagasore. As a younger man Rwagasore had worked as a research assistant to a French anthropologist.[94] By the mid-1970s he was living in Stanleyville, in eastern Zaire. It is not clear how Peter Wankulu knew Rwagasore, Mabunda, or any of the other men he identified as directors of his organization. Regardless of their relationship, the names on the letterhead helped generate the impression of a continent-wide reach. So did the return address. The organization's headquarters was listed as "Organization of African Unity Secretariat, Addis Ababa, Ethiopia." But the "Temporary Directing Address" was Wankulu's residence: Nakawa Estate, Port Bell Road—about three miles east of Kampala.

In July 1975, Idi Amin, chairman of the Organization of African Unity, hosted the international body's biannual summit in Kampala. There were 3,000 delegates, including nineteen heads of state. The government purchased sixty-eight new Mercedes cars for the occasion, together with 110 Peugeot 504s and fifty Fiats.[95] Two hundred fifty men were specially trained to chauffeur the distinguished visitors. New carpets and new toilets were installed in the government-run hotel, and staff members were drafted from provincial hotels to serve delegates staying in Kampala. The organizers purchased five red carpets to roll out when important people arrived at the airport.[96] Amin's cabinet reviewed and approved the slogans that were printed on the banners hung throughout the city. "Down with Economic Imperialism!" was one. "Africa Must Be Completely Free of Colonialism!" was another.[97] Most of the expenditure was financed by the Departed Asians Property Custodial Board, the government entity that had taken over the assets of the Pakistani and Indian families who had been expelled from Uganda in 1972.[98]

None of this outpouring of money and material was directed toward Peter Wankulu's organization. In advance of the summit Wankulu wrote to the O.A.U.'s headquarters in Addis Ababa to ask for the gift of a flag and for a supply of posters. He also asked for a copy of the O.A.U. anthem. An O.A.U. official replied with an uninterested letter: there were no spare flags; the posters were out of date; and an O.A.U. anthem had not been agreed.[99] It was, so far as I have found, the only occasion when Peter Wankulu actually received a piece of correspondence from the headquarters of the Organization of African Unity.

Wankulu was a free agent, not a functionary. He could not rely on support from the O.A.U. Neither did he edit a newspaper, or have access to professional printing equipment, binderies, or a broadcasting studio. So far as I can tell he only published one article in a Ugandan newspaper: an earnest editorial in the *Voice of Uganda* in 1972, calling on educated Ugandans to invest in modern, scientific methods of agriculture.[100] Wankulu was locked out of the official media infrastructure. He had to work with the materials he had at hand.

In the 1960s and early 1970s Wankulu had distributed his long, winding essays through the postal system: they were carbon-copied or cyclostyled, folded into envelopes, and mailed to addressees. He must have been frustrated at the constraints of the form. He was limited by his address list, by the price of postage and paper, and—most of all—by the absence of an audience for his manifestos. Wankulu thought of himself as the leader of a vast movement: a circular letter in 1964 was titled "An Appeal to You All"; an essay in 1970 was addressed to the "Whole African Community." But even with all of their grand ambition, Wankulu's essays had to be distributed to recipients with discrete mailing addresses. There was a disjuncture between the wideness of Wankulu's imagined readership and the sharply limited audience his essays could actually reach.

That is why he turned to collage. He composed his first one in 1974. It consists of four pages of A4 paper, held together with pieces of cellophane tape.[101] The poster is headed with a banner displaying the photocopied emblem of the O.A.U. and, in hand-drawn capital letters, "O.A.U. Only" and "Africa Must Unite." On the left side of the poster is a handwritten history of Wankulu's "All Africa Youth League." In the early 1960s, said the essay, Wankulu had "spent most of his hobby [time] in Kampala libraries and noticed the misunderstandings" among the African youth organizations of the time. He therefore

> sat down in his small room at Nakawa Housing Estate KR 43 near Kampala and drafted a 7 year Master Plan based mainly on economics for Africa with the special appeal to all Heads of State and their Govts. *Forget your differences get together into one very strong organization that will save Africa.*

His work, said the essay, had "kindled a fire into PanAfricanism, moved here and there recruiting members and posting the philosophy throughout the continent, and whether it was coincidence or not, what followed was the O.A.U."

Why, in 1974, did the prolific essayist Peter Wankulu suddenly begin to compose collage? He was inspired by the appearance, all at once, of a new audience. In the months leading up to the O.A.U. conference Kampala was gripped in fevered preparations. "We shall be at a test," warned a government minister.[102] Motor drivers were to be "courteous and helpful to visitors." Businessmen and women were to "maintain orderly commerce with courtesy and honesty." "Let us not forget that a lot has been propagated by the imperialist press to try and smear the good image of Uganda," wrote the minister.

> The challenge of demonstrating [our success] will rest with every Ugandan, especially those people who, in one way or another, will come into direct contact with our brothers and sisters from the rest of Africa.

Here—on the streets of Kampala—was an opportunity to address people who had hitherto been out of reach. Wankulu seized the moment in his collages. One of his posters, entitled "Africa of Our Times," featured images of twelve heads of state, each image carefully clipped to the same size, aligned in a row.[103] Every photograph was carefully labeled. Looming above them, in a photograph that was trimmed to a larger size, was

Nzo Ekangaki, the O.A.U.'s secretary-general. The poster made Africa's most prominent leaders look like functionaries of a centralized government, subject to a hierarchy headed by the O.A.U. It was, in pictorial form, a representation of the federated government that Wankulu hoped to achieve in reality. In his collage he could line things up, visualizing a solution to political challenges that were, in fact, hard to sort out. In the technique of collage he could create alignments and relationships between states that were otherwise autonomous.

Another exemplary collage, composed around the same time, was designed to make Wankulu's frustrations with African leadership visible and actionable. The slow pace of unification had long been a theme in his correspondence. In a long epistolary essay he had complained that there had been

> very many meetings on the same subject, that is, African Unity. A lot of money is used and many resolutions are passed, but it seems as though nothing worthy of mention has ever been implemented.[104]

The letter vibrates with the frustrations of its author, with his indignation about the long delays in achieving African unity. But the epistolary form could do little to convey the anger that Wankulu felt. The text flattened out his sentiments and emotions. It miniaturized righteous anger, compressing it within the typewritten page, making it impossible to convey the scale of the problem. It made a big problem hard to see.

That was why Wankulu composed a collage.[105] He wanted to break out of the enclosures of epistolary writing. On the upper-left corner was a photograph of a group of youthful men who had, in 1962, organized a rally in Kampala to advocate for Pan-Africanism. On the upper-right corner was a photo of Kenyan president Jomo Kenyatta, who Wankulu hoped would become president of a new "Union of African States." Between the two photos there was an arrow leading the viewer's eye from left to right, from the righteous idealism of youth to the sobering slowness of Africa's unification. "African Unity—Yes, But When!!" read the handwritten caption beneath Kenyatta's photograph. The collage brought delay itself—as a moral disappointment—into focus. At the bottom of the poster Wankulu addressed the African leaders assembled for the O.A.U. summit, vowing that they must approve the bonds of the [United African States] government and the official historical ceremony to take place in the O.A.U. seat. But wooo! Some of the present leaders seem to be enemies of African Unity and real hypocrites. . . . RESIGN AND GO TO HELL, YOU BASTARDS!

The last line was colored in red pen, in capital letters, and underlined. Wankulu needed a medium in which to make his impatience visible. In collage, he could contrast hope with disappointment, aspiration with frustration, unity with disunity. He could make outrage impossible to miss.

From what materials did Wankulu make his collages? He clipped from his correspondence files, cutting up old essays and other bits of paper and pasting them into his new compositions. On one of his posters Wankulu recopied—in his own hand—a letter that he had received in 1961 from Kwame Nkrumah's personal secretary.[106] It was a demonstration of the longevity of his commitments. In another collage, titled "O.A.U. Patriotic Volunteers," he pasted a long essay about the structure of the "Union of African States." He had originally composed the essay as an epistle; it had been typed, reproduced, and circulated through the post office. In 1975 Wankulu photocopied the document, shrank the text, and inserted photographs around the edges to illustrate the officers responsible for different parts of his imaginary government. Wankulu's collages were organized around set pieces, things clipped from papers he had accumulated over his decade-long career as an activist. These bits of paper had lived independent lives as stand-alone epistles. By placing them in his collages Wankulu was bringing his long struggle into view. He was repurposing his correspondence, making it into evidence of his relationships, his connections, his long travail on behalf of the cause. He was making his private archive into a public record of his long political career.

It was a form of self-promotion. Wankulu used his status to demand attention, respect, and the entitlement that he believed he was owed. In December 1972 Amin's government was hastily allocating thousands of businesses formerly owned by Asians to worthy African applicants. The allocation committee was amused when Peter Wankulu appeared before them, asking to be given the Madhvani Sugar Factory to operate. It was one of Uganda's largest business concerns, with an annual turnover of 600 million shillings. Newsmen reported that committee members were "nearly laughing their heads [off]" at his application. But Wankulu was sincere. As evidence of his competence and his connections he pointed to his long service as an advocate of African unity.[107]

The allocation committee did not give Wankulu the Madhvani Sugar Factory to operate. Neither did he receive respect from Uganda's journalists. In 1973 he visited the offices of the *Voice of Uganda*—the government newspaper—to complain that "credit for founding the Youth League is being stolen from him by confusing and jealous elements in other African countries."[108] As proof of his claim to historical importance Wankulu showed the skeptical reporter a sheaf full of campaign posters and his All Africa Youth League membership card from 1962. The reporter was unimpressed. "Can he be taken seriously?" the reporter asked. "That is for you to answer."

Peter Wankulu had no doubt about the answer to the skeptical journalist's question. His achievements as a leader of pan-African unity—self-curated as they were—were a platform on which to speak. In 1974 he composed a pair of critical letters to President Amin. The first of them, posted in June, was titled "Trying to Restore the Good Name of Uganda." It called on Amin to "allow freedom of the press and personal expression." Wankulu directed Africa's most verbose president to "guard your tongue and see that nothing wrong happens."[109] In December Wankulu sent a further advisory letter to President Amin.[110] "Your Excellency, USE SPECIAL DIPLOMACY AND TACTICS," he wrote. "Control your temper and respect your fellow Heads of State." Wankulu argued that the expulsion of Uganda's Asian community had been a mistake. Uganda's Indians, he argued, were the country's "Industrial Experts"; their absence "thwarts our plans for agricultural and industrial developments." The letter ended by reminding Amin about Wankulu's patriotism. "We only intend to correct your very many mistakes," Wankulu wrote.

> We are a sincere, faithful, frank and fearless group of real patriots, under any difficulties not willing to run away from our country and even if we fear death—no one will live for ever.

At the bottom of the letter were directions to the place where he could be found: either in an office next to Nakawa Bus Stage in Kampala or in Kaliro village in Busoga.

Did Wankulu think he had diplomatic immunity? Did he hope to become a martyr? He was imprisoned by Amin's men on at least one occasion.[111] However he saw himself, Wankulu felt able to criticize Africa's most notorious tyrant. His fearlessness was grounded in the very practical work of self-positioning, on the evidence he created and curated, proof of the constancy of his commitment and the purity of his aims. Through his artistic creativity, he wrenched his private correspondence out of his files and made them into a public record, proof of the hard work he had done, over the course of decades, to build African unity. It was a means by which other people could know of his valorous deeds. It secured his place in history.

———

I met Peter Wankulu one morning in a bar near Kampala.[112] It had not been hard to find him. The address he gave in his brave letters to Idi Amin was still correct, and when one of my colleagues visited his rural home, he found a relative who gave us his telephone number. The morning we met, Mr. Wankulu carried under his arm a file folder full of laminated posters. He told me he was working on his autobiography. On one of his posters there were miniature photographs of Kwame Nkrumah and Haile Selassie. They had been recycled from a poster he had made to mark the 1975 O.A.U. conference in Kampala. A photo of himself as a younger man had likewise been copied from an earlier collage. Wankulu brought two green flags to our meeting, emblazoned with the symbols of the O.A.U. On his lapel he wore a medal given to him by President Museveni on the occasion of Uganda's fiftieth anniversary of independence.

In recent years Peter Wankulu has earned some part of the respect he feels he is owed. In 2000 Uganda's leading newspaper carried a full-page feature headlined "Mzee Wankulu: Forgotten Hero of the OAU?"[113] In it Wankulu describes his self-financed, self-motivated career as an advocate for Pan-Africanism. When he fell ill in 2007, newspaper reporters launched a campaign to call attention to his plight. Press reports described him as a "well known Organization of African Unity veteran, and Pan-African activist."[114] In the years that followed he made statements and wrote editorials about a broad range of issues.[115] In 2016 a civic organization—the "Pan-African Pyramid"—gave Wankulu a "Global Award" in recognition of his long career in advocacy.[116]

In his collages Peter Wankulu created a showcase that transformed his life into a landmark of Africa's political history. Many other people were likewise drawn into the great struggles of the age. Everywhere, even in the mundane affairs of local politics, there were battles to fight.

That is what life on the front lines was like. Some people became partisans of grandiose causes and unlikely projects that were far removed from the affairs of their localities. It was a kind of extraversion. It was also a way of reframing the knotty and violent times, of finding a code by which to live, of gaining a platform on which to speak.

CHAPTER EIGHT

Governing Religion

J OHN MBITI WAS ONE of eastern Africa's most consequential scholars. Born in Kenya, he was both a scholar and an Anglican priest, earning his Ph.D. from Cambridge University in 1963. The next year, in 1964, Mbiti was appointed to a lectureship at Makerere University in Kampala, where he wrote his book *African Religions and Philosophy.*[1] The book set out the framework for a new field of study, showing that African traditional religion—often scorned as superstition—was logical and consistent, and could be productively understood as a coherent theological system. By the time Idi Amin came to power in 1971, Mbiti had risen to become head of the Department of Religious Studies and Philosophy. He was a prominent figure in Uganda's cultural life, an influential and accomplished teacher, and a leading churchman.

In those tumultuous days Amin's regime was drafting Ugandans to serve on the front lines of the global war against racism and imperialism. Officials were inventorying businesses, expelling Asian owners, and assigning properties to black Ugandans. In the eyes of patriotic men and women, culture, like economics, needed to be liberated from outsiders' control. Practices and rituals needed to be classified, purged of foreign influences, and made into possessions of the black majority. That was what Idi Amin's culture war involved. Patriotic curators set out to determine the ownership of cultural properties, distinguishing the native-born from the foreign import.

"African Traditional Religion" was a tool that patriotic curators could use, a framework making it seem as though—their outward diversity notwithstanding—Africans were unified in their devotion to deeply held principles. It made dissent, nonconformity, and oddity appear unnatural and countercultural. In 1973, 1975, and again in 1977 Amin's government banned Pentecostal and evangelical churches. It also banned the Baha'i faith, the Adventist Church, and dozens of other religious denominations. Some of the leaders of banned religious institutions were imprisoned, their property was seized, and their worship was foreclosed. By 1977 the government had consolidated religious life around three bodies: the Anglican Church, the Catholic Church, and the Muslim Supreme Council.

Professor Mbiti never worked for Idi Amin's government. He was not involved in the suppression of dissident religions. He could not control the purposes to which his theological ideas were put. But the ideas he pioneered both shaped and were shaped by the political world. From his study at Makerere, Professor Mbiti helped to make the unification of religious institutions seem both possible and necessary.

═══

In the late 1960s Makerere University was full of creative, politically engaged scholars. At the center of Uganda's literary culture was *Transition* magazine, edited by Rajat Neogy with the assistance of the political scientist Ali Mazrui, the poet Christopher Okigbo, and others. The magazine boasted a continental reach: it published short stories from the South African writer Bessie Head, essays from Wole Soyinka, fiction from Paul Theroux, and philosophy from Okot p'Bitek. Professor Mbiti published two poems in *Transition* during those years. One of them, titled "The Snake Song," went as follows:

> I have neither legs nor arms
> But I walk on my belly
> And I have
> Venom, venom, venom![2]

There is a lovely creativity about this poem. In poetry Mbiti felt free to experiment, to try on authorial voices that were not his own, and to invest unlikely beings with character. It must have been a source of enjoyment at a time when so much work had to be done, for in prose,

Professor Mbiti was engaged in the intensely serious labor of world-building. He published *African Religions and Philosophy* in 1969. The book was composed to fulfill Mbiti's obligations to an academic discipline that was, under his stewardship, coming into view. In his book there was no time for experimentation with literary voice. The book laid out, chapter by chapter, a systematic theology for African traditional religion. Mbiti argued that Africans shared a veneration for the divine, a sacred sensibility, rituals, an awareness of evil, and an account of creation. The book made a powerful argument for the doctrinal and theological coherence of traditional religion.

In his own time Mbiti's account was subject to a scathing criticism from one of his colleagues, the anthropologist and poet Okot p'Bitek.[3] In his book *African Religions in Western Scholarship*, Okot argued that Mbiti and other scholars had forced the dynamics of African religious practice into the foreign categories of Western theology. "The African deities of these books, clothed with the attributes of the Christian God, are, in the main, creations of the students of African religions," he wrote.[4] Mbiti surely knew of Okot's criticism, for Okot's book was discussed in the newspapers.[5] But Mbiti chose to make no public response. The same year that Okot's book was published Mbiti brought out his second book, *Concepts of God in Africa*.[6] The book was based on the premise—as stated by Mbiti—that "there is but One Supreme God." His scholarly work was an aspect of his larger vocation. He was a liberal, building bridges that brought the old religion into a close relationship with Christianity.

In August 1972 Idi Amin announced the expulsion of Uganda's Asian community and launched the Economic War. Quite suddenly, Ugandans found themselves engaged on the front lines of the global struggle against colonialism and racism. There was urgent work to do in the theater of culture. All at once, institutions and practices borrowed from other places had to be freed from foreigners' control.

The call for cultural liberation was widely heard across the African continent in the 1970s. It was the decade of *authenticité*, the ideology of self-assertion propounded by the dictator of Zaire, Mobutu Sese Seko. Zairians adopted new African names to replace European names and discouraged Western clothing in favor of authentically African styles.[7] Mobutu's cultural program attracted interest and support in Uganda. "What is wrong with calling yourself Rubanga, Twenomujuni, Mirembe

etc.?" asked an editorialist in the *Voice of Uganda*.[8] In 1972 the Amin government summarily banned the wearing of miniskirts. At a meeting of
Amin's cabinet the minister of culture and community development
warned that miniskirts had "spread throughout the country very fast to
the extent of threatening or even signaling the extinction of our National
dresses. These dresses are a source of scandal, they encourage crime and
they are not in the interest of our culture."[9] Shortly thereafter the Amin
government prohibited the growing of bushy beards and the wearing of
long hair by men. The government blamed "foreign hippies" for all manner of criminal behavior, including printing counterfeit money, kidnap-
ping, and assassination.[10]

Here was a new front in Uganda's war against imperialism. Yekosofati Engur, the minister of culture and community development, barnstormed through Uganda, making speeches about traditional culture. He
told one audience that Africans were more moral than whites, comparing
the lewd dances of Europe with the staid and decorous conventions of
African dance. Women's fashionable attire had played a key role in
"spoiling our culture," he preached.[11] "We cannot be independent until
we have done away with colonial politics and culture."[12] It was the responsibility of government officials to ensure that the struggle against
colonial culture was fought and won. Shortly after Amin came to power
his government appointed "culture officers" to carry out the work of
preservation in the remote districts. "We cannot afford to watch our
Culture rot or die a gradual death when we ourselves are able people," a
culture officer in the west of the country told an audience.[13] The officers
identified and surveyed historical sites, encouraged and regulated the
publication of African-language literature, and organized concerts where
the traditional arts were performed.

Under government oversight cultural practices were made into routines that could be rehearsed and mastered. Dance, for example, had to
be regimented and standardized. Amin's government revived the Heart
Beat of Africa—Uganda's national dance troupe—and brought fifty dancers to Kampala, where they were trained in a repertoire that was meant
to represent the whole of Uganda: the Otole, Bwola, and Araka-Oraka
dances from Acholi, the Imbalu, Mwaga, and Ifumbo dances from Bugisu, and a great many others besides.[14] In a former time all of these
dance routines had been performed as part of ceremonial or celebratory
occasions. The Imbalu, for instance, was a circumcision ceremony
wherein Gisu boys were made men by their elders. The ceremony was

politically controversial: in the 1950s Gisu leaders had asserted their ownership over their district's leading town by convening an annual Imbalu festival within the town precincts.[15] Once the Imbalu came into the hands of the choreographers of the Heart Beat of Africa troupe, however, all of the political history was stripped away. What was important was the choreography, the steps, and the costumes. That is how the repertoire of traditional dance was established: by making kinetic human movement into a choreographed series of steps to be mastered.

All the work that conservationists did—inspirational as it might have been—was a cover thrown over the real-life men and women who performed, danced, and sang. Government culture officers had to disguise performers' idiosyncratic personalities. They also had to disguise their poverty, their trauma, their needs. In 1972 a troupe of twenty-two Batwa pygmies arrived at the Kigezi District culture show attired in rags and covered in dirt. The culture officer—who was relying on them to dance before a large audience—was horrified. He hastily made his way to a shop, bought several hundred shillings worth of cloth, and had tailors stitch costumes for them.[16] It had to be done in a tremendous hurry, for their performance was the following day.

Through this and many other acts of remediation curators and choreographers cleaned up Uganda's performance traditions and made them into cultural property. Shortly after Amin came to power Uganda Television launched a new program titled *Our Heritage*, which displayed "cultural dances, indigenous handcrafts, indigenous customary ceremonies, traditional music etc." Performers were told to wear "uniform costumes."[17] Over the course of the 1970s culture officers organized seminars to tutor local performers on the elements of Uganda's dance repertoire. At one exemplary seminar the conveners promised to "embrace all aspects of our culture, i.e. drama, music, storytelling, and carving." There were instructors from the Heart Beat of Africa troupe on hand to offer direction.[18]

That is what Idi Amin's war against foreign culture entailed. That is how performance genres became defined, how human creativity was hemmed in by rules and standards. It was also how some people became experts, authorities in their field.

=====

Two weeks after the 1971 coup, Amin's secretary wrote to John Mbiti and other church leaders to ask for their views on a new initiative:

a Department of Religious Affairs, with political and administrative powers over religious organizations. "What field of responsibility would the Ministry or Department cover in relation to religious affairs?" he asked. "Do you seriously think that there is a need for such a Ministry?"[19]

Mbiti was thrilled at the prospect. In six typed pages he laid out a series of justifications for government supervision over religious life.[20] Uganda had known too much religious conflict, Mbiti wrote. The new ministry would reduce conflict between religions through "reconciliation, mediation, or even the use of governmental powers." Moreover it would allow for easier coordination between different service agencies. While universities could enable dialogue in small-scale settings, "the practical meaning of dialogue would best be achieved under governmental initiative, supervision, and encouragement."

The most important part of Professor Mbiti's letter came toward the end, where he set out a theological rationale for the government of religious life. "African traditional life does not have a division between 'secular' and 'sacred,' between what is religious and what is not," he argued. "The division of life into 'religious' and 'secular' compartments was imported into Africa from Europe." Mbiti continued:

> this division has greatly undermined and ignored a basic African philosophy in which the universe and the whole of life are conceived religiously, and in which the spiritual realities and physical realities are only two dimensions of the same basic concept of existence.

He was copying—almost word-for-word—from his book *African Religions and Philosophy.*[21] Europe and America had already paid the price for their secularism: the evidence could be seen in the "rebellion of their young people against authority, tradition, and so on." Professor Mbiti was confident that Amin's government could mend the division between the sacred and the secular. The new Department of Religious Affairs would be

> a concrete symbol and expression of the basic African philosophy which sees the whole of life as a deeply religious experience. In setting up this ministry, Uganda would be reasserting a profoundly African heritage which our colonial past has eclipsed. . . . [It would] be an exciting platform where the religious heritage,

values, commitments and sacrifices of the different religious traditions can be pooled together and better utilized for the good of the nation.

Mbiti saw in Amin's regime a vehicle by which to bring dissension, argument, and debate to an end. Here was an opportunity for unification.

Reverend Mbiti had good reason to be worried about unity. In religion as in politics the violent destruction of the Buganda kingdom had caused many Ganda people to doubt the legitimacy of public institutions, and both Christians and Muslims were deeply divided over their leadership. In the 1960s President Obote's government had set up a new organization—the National Association for the Advancement of Muslims (NAAM)—to lead Uganda's Muslim community. Its leader, Apolo Nekyon, was a convert to Islam and a cousin to President Obote.[22] He sought to sideline Prince Badru Kakungulu, cousin of Kabaka Muteesa II and head of Buganda's Muslims. In October 1970 President Obote put Prince Badru in prison, accusing him of conspiring to overthrow his government.[23] Three months later, after the January 1971 coup, Idi Amin released Prince Badru from prison, and welcomed him back to public life in a ceremony attended by tens of thousands of people.[24] In the weeks that followed Muslims in Buganda organized a series of celebrations heralding Prince Badru's release and demanding that he be made leader of Uganda's Muslims.

Like their Muslim contemporaries, Christians in the Buganda kingdom were keen to oust the men who had come to power with Milton Obote's backing.[25] In 1966, just as the Buganda kingdom was being dissolved, Uganda's Anglican Church had consecrated a new archbishop. Rev. Erica Sabiti was the first African priest to lead the church. His home was Ankole, in southwest Uganda, not in the Buganda kingdom. For Christians from Buganda the elevation of a cultural outsider as their archbishop was a cause for alarm. The Anglican Church—called the Church of Uganda—had been the foundation of Buganda's royalism: the cathedral which sat atop Namirembe hill had been built through the exertions of the kingdom's Anglican aristocrats, and the kingdom's rulers had been consecrated in its precincts.[26] In the view of Ganda patriots, the elevation of Reverend Sabiti was a betrayal of this long and distinguished legacy. "Buganda has been oppressed too much and has suffered so terribly, both politically and now in the Church they helped to build, maintain, and undeniably spread throughout Uganda," wrote a clergyman in a panicked letter.[27] "The other members of our church outside Buganda are slowly but steadily converging on Buganda to swallow it up. This is not the fair reward of our grandparents' sacrifices."

The tensions dividing the Church of Uganda were at the forefront of public life when Idi Amin came to power. On 23 January 1971—two days before the coup that brought Idi Amin to power—the Diocese of Namirembe resolved to secede from the rest of the church.[28] In February 1971, when President Amin organized the funeral of the deceased Kabaka of Buganda, Archbishop Sabiti had to ask for security guards to protect him during the service at the cathedral. He told President Amin that he had received several letters "threatening to fall on me and knock me down and trample me to death."[29] In the months that followed the Luganda press published reports accusing Sabiti of plotting with Milton Obote to turn the Buganda king's palace into an eight-story high rise.[30]

Religious unity was the most pressing issue that Idi Amin had to confront in his first year in power. His government established the Department of Religious Affairs in April 1971. The department's first act was to organize a conference to iron out differences within the Muslim and Christian communities. In the speech that opened the conference President Amin emphasized that "religion must be a source of togetherness."[31] It was the responsibility of leaders in government and in religious institutions to "ensure that all Ugandans are truly united."[32] At the conference Amin established a new organization—the Muslim Supreme Council—to supersede the discredited National Association for the Advancement of Muslims.[33] Divisions among Christians were harder to sort out. Over the ensuing months Amin's government organized, funded, and hosted two additional conferences meant to resolve the divisions in the Church of Uganda. Matters came to a head in the last days of November 1971, when the Diocese of Namirembe announced that it intended to form its own, independent Anglican church.[34] The day following the announcement President Amin called all the Church of Uganda bishops to Kampala. "My sorrow knows no bounds," Amin told the bishops.[35] If the leading diocese in the defunct Buganda kingdom "were allowed to separate, there might be a further break up into small, ineffective units. . . . It could have very harmful and great effects in the unity of this country." Amin accused the bishop of Namirembe—Rev. Dunstan Nsubuga—of "showing utter contempt to me personally and his attitude, and that of his supporters, is close to that of a traitor." He threatened to evict Reverend Nsubuga from Namirembe Cathedral.

Archbishop Erica Sabiti greets President Amin, September 1972
(Courtesy of the Uganda Broadcasting Corporation)

The next day, the bishops of the Church of Uganda resolved their disagreement. Namirembe Cathedral was to be independent of any diocese; both Archbishop Sabiti and Namirembe's diocesan bishop would have their thrones there. Archbishop Sabiti described what had happened in that conference hall as a religious awakening. "Walls of division were collapsing, feelings of hatred, anger and suspicion were being replaced by love and trust, smiles replaced hardness in people's hearts, hands were waved in joy across the hall," he hymned.[36] It was a rosy account of a meeting that had been—by all reports—extraordinarily tense.

That is how Idi Amin's government came to have a vested interest in religious unity.[37] There was a new bureaucracy—the Department of

Religious Affairs—that was empowered to monitor religious organizations and suppress conflict. It was one of several new bodies that worked to regulate and control cultural life.

———

The imposition of order in religious institutions went hand in hand with the persecution of nonconformity. Idiosyncratic churches and charismatic religious bodies were made illegal, and religious life was forcibly consolidated under government supervision.[38]

In May 1972 a man named Paul Kadoma—a Catholic, living in Kampala—wrote to leading churchmen complaining that his wife had "unilaterally decided to break my family."[39] She was under the influence of an Indian religious teacher named Charan Singh, the head of a religious organization called the Radha Soami Satsang Beas, headquartered in northern India.[40] Following Singh's instruction, Mr. Kadoma's wife had become a vegetarian. For Mr. Kadoma it undermined culture itself. "Meat is a staple food here," he wrote, and "eating it is very much serious in my country." Mr. Kadoma had organized a meeting between his wife and a sympathetic Catholic priest, but Singh's disciples had continued to pass "confusing books and teachings" to his wife, and despite the priest's admonitions, she was "more determined than ever before not to eat meat."[41] Moreover, Singh's disciples had threatened to kill him by magic. "I am now living a miserable life with my children while my wife is being paraded everywhere by these people," Mr. Kadoma wrote. He asked the priest to "use your Holy Ghost power to bring back my wife to her senses, so that she comes back to our Catholic Church and forget all about this new religion."

At the end of June 1972 Mr. Kadoma, convinced that his wife was "3/4 mad," wrote to President Amin to ask him to make Singh's religion illegal in Uganda.[42] The "unity, love, respect and freedom of our families have been very much interfered with by confusing agents" of Singh's community, he complained, for "they have no respect for families let alone husbands." Under the influence of drugs, Kadoma claimed, women who joined Singh's disciples "appear to be hypnotized and they become stubborn, unruly, half mad, and disrespectful to whatever the husband might advise." Women who followed Singh would "leave their homes on Sunday in the morning against the wish of the husbands and . . . return home late any time they please." Kadoma insisted that Charan Singh presented a threat to civil and political order. He wanted this "alien

Religious teacher Charan Singh at Entebbe airport, 1964
(Courtesy of the Uganda Broadcasting Corporation)

religion banned before it brings bloodshed and destroys our cherished families beyond repair."

Paul Kadoma was uniquely extravagant in his paranoia about his wife's vegetarianism, but his anxiety was shared by many men and women whose relatives refused to play their part in the performance of family duty. Members of dissident religions disregarded the obligations that custom and tradition imposed on them, challenging husbands' and fathers' control over their time, labor, and loyalty.[43]

I do not know whether Idi Amin read Paul Kadoma's anxious letters. I do know Amin believed that religious division was dangerous. He was perplexed by the divided character of Christian leadership: during his first years in office he had long conversations with Archbishop Sabiti, asking why Christians parceled themselves into small groups.[44] In May 1973 the government outlawed several religious denominations that were said to be disposed against order. Among them were the United Pentecostal Churches, the Jehovah's Witnesses, and the Pentecostal

Assemblies of God.[45] "If you arrange subversion, you will find yourself locked into the guard-room of God," Amin warned.[46] In 1975 the list of banned religious groups was expanded to include the Quakers and several evangelical organizations based in the United States.[47] In 1977 the government banned twenty-seven organizations, among them the Baha'is, the Baptists, the Holy Ghost Church of East Africa, the Dini ya Roho, and the Nomiya Luo Church.[48] Their buildings were seized by the government, and their leaders were forbidden to preach or carry out services. After 1977 the religious field was cleared of competition and placed under the management of the Anglican, Catholic, and Muslim institutions.

All of this was full of violence. The Deliverance Church, for instance, was a noisy charismatic church that met in a red brick building near Makerere University. "The time is drawing nearer and nearer to His second coming and we must compel people to enter the kingdom of God while there is still time," wrote their leader. "Let us paint for them a horrible picture of hell so that we warn them of the danger of rejecting the Lord Jesus."[49] The church's musical ensemble was called the "Explosion Choir." In April 1978 Uganda's vice president, who was passing by, heard the noisy congregation at worship and ordered the church disbanded. Amin's men surrounded the building, shot randomly into the congregation, beat a number of the congregants, and imprisoned two hundred people. They were held in the cells of the notorious State Research Bureau, where they were abused and tortured for two months.[50]

That is what the consolidation of Christian churches involved. The space for idiosyncratic and demonstrative religion was sharply constrained. One afternoon in 1976 a group of argumentative members of the "Isa Messiah" church came before the minister of internal affairs to ask for government recognition.[51] The church—which consisted of about fifty members—had broken away from the Seventh-Day Adventist Church a few months before. At issue was the name of Jesus. The leaders of the "Isa Messiah" group told the minister that the name Yesu Kristo was a fake. They had discovered that the real name of Jesus—Isa Messiah—had been hidden from Africans by European missionaries. The minister had no time for this obscure argument. He lectured the dissident church's leaders about the need for unity. There were

> several religious sects most of which served no purpose at all as
> they were splinter groups from the main religions or exotic beliefs

imported into the country by foreigners who used them to pene-
trate the country and cause confusion among the law abiding citizens. . . . A few main religions were left at liberty to operate in the
country because their objectives were clearly defined.

The minister imposed an official ban on the "Isa Messiah" church, and
ordered its members to join any of the religious groups legally operating
in the country.

There were a great many practical issues to sort out. The banning of
so many churches left many buildings vacant. Local government authorities took custody of these buildings and allocated them to organizations
that could claim them for the public interest. In Bwera, on the border
with Congo, the Seventh-Day Adventists had built an impressive center:
there was a church building, a school, houses for teachers and for the
pastors, and a great amount of equipment. After the Adventist Church
was banned in 1977 the pastor and his family lived in the parish house,
looking after the church buildings and—after dark—convening clandes-
tine religious services in the bush.[52] Matters came to a head in February
1978, when the government chief arrived at the church and gave the pastor fourteen days to vacate the premises. He told the pastor that "his private worship had been reported and was known to the State Research
Bureau and the Intelligence sections."[53] It was a threat. The pastor hastily handed over the keys to the buildings.

For the established churches—the Anglicans in particular—it was an
opportunity for expansion. In the months following the banning of Pentecostal and evangelical churches, Archbishop Sabiti carried on a campaign to persuade their members and their leadership to join the
Anglican Church. "We have the same Bible, the same savior and we are
admitted into his church through baptism by water," he told the bishop
of one of the banned churches. "Why don't we ignore the other small
differences and come together?"[54] Several Protestant organizations did,
in fact, come into the management of the Anglican Church in those
years. For many people it was a cause for celebration. "Christ came to
unite all people of all races, the whole of mankind," wrote a social worker
named Livingston Kiyise. "Is it not high time that we as brothers and
sisters, and all who believe in Christ, should unite in one Christian
church?"[55]

Here was a new license for religious unification. Even as Amin's
regime consolidated dissident churches, the theology of ecumenicism

enjoyed a newfound relevance in Christian life.[56] As John Mbiti argued in 1973, in an essay about Christian divisions, "denominationalism and its proliferation ... are the product of human selfishness and weakness."[57]

═══════

In the archives of the Church of Uganda there is a file full of scraps of paper.[58] On each of them there is a list of names. They are the Anglican Christians who were murdered by Amin's men. Each of the lists is headed with the name of the diocese from which the deceased came. The lists appear to have been jotted down toward the middle of 1979, a few months after Idi Amin's government was overthrown. Were the lists composed as part of an official memorial project? Were they created on the spur of the moment, as a group of Christians talked about loved ones they had lost? Were they an aid for a priest leading a congregation in prayer?

Over the course of the 1970s a great many people died, far more than those listed on the papers in the church archives. The most eminent of the Christian martyrs was Erica Sabiti's successor, Janani Luwum, who had been made archbishop in 1974. In February 1977, Luwum was accused of plotting with exiles in Tanzania to overthrow Idi Amin's government. Early one morning soldiers appeared, unannounced, at the archbishop's residence, forced their way into the building, and searched the premises.[59] They were looking for weapons, which, they claimed, the archbishop was hiding. Luwum and his colleagues responded with a letter condemning Amin and his men for their violence against Uganda's people. "The gun whose muzzle has been pressed against the Archbishop's stomach ... is a gun which is being pointed at every Christian in the Church," the bishops wrote.[60] It was a courageous protest against the inhumanity of Uganda's leaders.

On 16 February Amin's men organized a show trial at the International Conference Centre in Kampala. There, in front of an audience of several thousand soldiers, Vice President Mustafa Adrisi accused Archbishop Luwum of plotting with Uganda's enemies. My colleagues and I have recently digitized the sound recording made by Radio Uganda technicians at the occasion. For several hours a former civil servant read out a memorandum, supposedly written by Milton Obote, detailing his plans to mount an insurgency with the archbishop's help.[61] Standing next to the terrified civil servant was Colonel Isaac Maliyamungu, Amin's most notorious henchman. Maliyamungu's voice can be heard in the

President Amin greets Archbishop Janani Luwum (Courtesy of the Uganda
Broadcasting Corporation)

Radio Uganda recording, occasionally interrupting the speaker to ensure
that every word in the memorandum was read out. At one point the civil
servant fainted. There is a disturbance in the recording, as Amin's men
hurriedly revived the distraught man. At the end of the show trial Vice
President Adrisi came to the microphone. Speaking in Swahili, he asked
the assembled soldiers for their verdict. "Kill him," they shouted. When
Adrisi asked whether anyone voted against the verdict, there were no
dissenters.

That evening Janani Luwum was taken to the headquarters of the
State Research Bureau, where he was tortured and murdered.[62] Accord-

ing to one account Amin himself fired the fatal bullet.[63] The following day a spokesman on Radio Uganda read out an announcement explaining that the archbishop—together with the two cabinet ministers—had been killed in an unfortunate automobile accident.[64] Supposedly, the three men had attempted to overpower their military driver, causing a fatal crash.

The day following the announcement of the archbishop's death someone pinned a note to a tree outside a busy marketplace in eastern Uganda.[65] "Our friends have already died for their faith," the authors wrote. "You should all wake up and fight like men and see to it that you defeat the brigand, the Muslim." The authors called on Uganda's Christians to arm themselves with spears, clubs, and arrows. At midnight on 19 February they were to attack Amin's men. "The Brigand has finished us! Fight like men!" the author urged. Government officials were quick to call for comity between church and state. Two weeks after Archbishop Luwum's murder the district commissioner in one provincial town noted that "the mass had developed fear of attending church services [and instead were] exiling themselves and starting to spread rumours against their motherland." He advised priests of the church to "concentrate on preaching the word of God, pray for peace rather than dangerous weapons."[66] Later that year one of Amin's most autocratic officials spoke before an Anglican audience. "Let the church become instrumental in the development of nations," he said. "Let division be a background to help the government mould people into good citizens."[67]

What did Christians hear in government officials' calls for unity and solidarity? Even in the wake of the archbishop's murder, even at a time when thousands of people were being imprisoned, tortured, and murdered, there were reasons for optimism. Even after the bloody events of February 1977, some high-minded people saw in Amin's regime an opportunity to suppress petty divisions and promote Christian unity.

Eighteen months after the archbishop's murder an Anglican priest in western Uganda opened up a correspondence with a local government official named Cypriano Mutahigwa. Mutahigwa was a person of consequence. In colonial times he had been a member of a committee that promoted literature in the local language; in the 1960s he served Obote's government as a chief. By 1978—when the parish priest wrote to him— he was an assistant district commissioner in the government of Idi Amin. The priest was sure that "all governing authorities were instituted by God," but it seemed to him that Mutahigwa was uniquely determined to "develop the spiritual realm, as this obviously has been a source for your being and all that you have."[68] Mutahigwa responded by laying out a theological justification for government work. If a "Christian society is to be effective in faith" there must be "true and brotherly cooperation" among its leaders, he wrote. God

> offers to us the possibility of bringing about the required significant mutual esteem, respect and love of one another; and thus reproducing Christ's image in society we are leading rather than demonstrating unnecessary separation and disregard. In so doing, we render a valuable spiritual and social health to our country by assisting it to achieve the goals of a perfect society.[69]

I have no reason to think that either Cypriano Mutahigwa or the priest were insincere. Their theological thinking was animated by a feeling of possibility. At a time when—for many people—public life was full of terror and death, Mutahigwa could imagine a "perfect society," where government and church worked in harmonious concord to reproduce Christ's image in the social order. There were no grounds for suspicion, or for resistance, or for division.

That year the Amin government launched a nation-wide campaign to raise funds for the construction of a new high-rise building—called Church House—in Kampala. It was meant to honor the centenary of Anglican missionaries' arrival in Uganda. The government bureaucracy was put in the service of the fundraising campaign, and officials were instructed to collect funds from businesses and civic organizations. Each province was given a financial target to meet. In one province the Uganda Revenue Authority, a dairy farm, an oil company, several tea estates, and the Muslim community made donations.[70] In another place fundraisers encouraged donations by organizing a game of tug-of-war between Anglican clergymen and officials of local government.[71] The culminating event in the fundraising campaign came in September, when representatives of all of these organizations appeared at the Anglican cathedral to present their offerings.

Church House was not actually built during the presidency of Idi Amin. The building—now named Janani Luwum Church House—was completed in 2018 and opened in a public ceremony involving Uganda's prime minister.[72] It is a sixteen-story high-rise, located in the center of the city. The building is a monument to the murdered archbishop. It is

President Amin at a church service, December 1974 (Courtesy of the Uganda
Broadcasting Corporation)

also a memorial to an enduring alliance. The financial beginnings for the
building lie in the months immediately following Archbishop Luwum's
murder, when Idi Amin's government mobilized Ugandans to contribute
toward its construction. The campaign was an apology, meant to allay
the outrage that many Christians felt. It was also a sincere work of theological justification, growing out of the historical alliance between the
Uganda government and the Anglican Church. Even in those dark and
dangerous years, it was possible for some earnest Christians to think that
Idi Amin's government was working toward the perfection of the social
order.

In those vexed days a great many scholars left Uganda, seeking refuge in
other places. John Mbiti remained at his post at Makerere University. In
1971 he published *New Testament Eschatology in an African Background*,
and in the years that followed he brought out several other works: trans-
lations of *African Religions and Philosophy* in French and German; an edi-
tion of the inaugural lecture he gave when he was made professor;
a book about love and marriage; another about prayer and African

religion.[73] The early years of Idi Amin's regime were the most productive period of Mbiti's scholarly career.

In the first months of 1973 Mbiti gave a series of lectures at universities and seminaries in the United States. In none of these lectures did Mbiti speak about Idi Amin, about the campaign against Pentecostals and other evangelical Christians, or about the people who had died at the hands of the Ugandan state. Everywhere he spoke about the happy convergence between Christianity and African tradition. "Christianity and traditional African religion are in accord in many areas," he told an audience in Pittsburgh. "Churches are developing their own sense of independent judgment and control."[74] Early in May he was at the San Francisco Theological Seminary. "Christianity, from ancient orthodox forms to nouveau workshop based on spontaneity and exuberance, is thriving in Africa," he told the audience. African heritage "really prepared the groundwork for the Christian message to be heard and accepted."

This outpouring of theological writing supplied material for a curriculum that Professor Mbiti and other members of the Department of Religious Studies and Philosophy launched. There was a traveling seminar—called the "Seminar on Religion and Culture in Africa"—organized through Makerere's extramural education unit and convened in several provinces around Uganda.[75] The aim, wrote one of the tutors, was to "address itself to the African traditional religious beliefs and practices and their impact on and interactions with Revealed Religions, namely Christianity and Islam." There was a unit on "African Concepts of God," derived from a book that Professor Mbiti had published.[76] There was another unit on "Spirits and the Spirit World in Africa"; and a third on "The Meeting of Christianity with African Religion and Culture." In the places where the seminar was convened government officials shared the platform with Makerere lecturers. There was much on which they could agree. The curriculum was an expansion of the work that Professor Mbiti was doing to define the basic elements of African religion.

In March 1974 the Libyan dictator Muammar Gaddafi made a state visit to Uganda. A crowd of several thousand people greeted him at the airport, and Idi Amin called him the "most revolutionary leader in the world."[77] Over the course of three days Gaddafi spoke before large audiences, calling on Uganda's Muslims to seize the opportunity that was before them. There was "no doubt that God wanted Islam to progress in Uganda because he had chosen a dynamic leader like General Amin to lead the people."[78] "In order to stamp out imperialism," he told an audience of university students, "one had first to stamp out Christianity whose suitcase brought imperialism."[79] At a private meeting Gaddafi asked Amin's Christian cabinet ministers to leave the room, then presented Amin with a written agreement. It was a promissory note, obligating Amin to eliminate Christianity from Uganda. Amin refused to sign. It must have been too much even for President Amin. Later, he told his cabinet ministers about the demand that Gaddafi had made.[80]

Shortly after Gaddafi's departure John Mbiti delivered a sermon before a packed audience at the chapel of Makerere University. It was a refutation of Gaddafi's religious program. "Christianity and Africa have fallen in love with each other, and intend to live in the bonds of a lifelong marriage," he said. "Christianity is here to stay."[81] The sermon was an act of great courage. It made Mbiti into a target of Amin's men. Later that month Professor Mbiti—fearing for his life—left Uganda. By the end of the month he was in California, where he spoke at the University of the Redlands.[82] Thereafter he moved to Geneva and took up the directorship of the Ecumenical Institute of the World Council of Churches. He was to spend the remainder of his life in Switzerland.

The first essay that Professor Mbiti wrote after coming to Geneva was titled "The Future of Christianity in Africa," published in 1978.[83] It was sunnily optimistic. A great many "prophets of doom have spoken about either a complete extinction of Christianity in Africa or a substantial reduction of its presence there," wrote Mbiti. In fact, the religion was growing at a rapid pace—5 percent per year. He attributed this rate of growth to the new liberties of independent Africa, for the end of colonialism had "restored human dignity to African peoples both in secular life and the Church." Mbiti lamented the many divisions among African Christians. But he applauded the growing "spirit of ecumenism." In many places, he noted, churches were being made to unite by African governments, "which will increasingly see denominational differences as working against national unity."

Nowhere in his essay did Mbiti write about the dangers that he had personally faced as one of the leading spokesmen for Uganda's Christianity. He did not write about Janani Luwum, archbishop of Uganda, who had been murdered a year before the essay was published. Neither did he write about the bloody consequences of Amin's campaign to consolidate evangelical churches under the management of the Anglican Church. The African Christianity about which Mbiti wrote was a depoliticized abstraction, disconnected from the real world of conflict and terror.

Forged in the context of Uganda's cultural politics of the 1960s and '70s, "African Traditional Religion" was one of several frameworks that helped the Amin government regiment the cultural field. Through the publications of Professor Mbiti—its leading theologian—African traditional religion made its way into the scholarly canon; today, one can study African traditional religion in the world's leading theological schools. According to one bibliographic database, there are more than a hundred books in publication with the phrase "African Traditional Religion" in the title. Most of them are written by Christian theologians.

How ought we remember John Mbiti? He was one of the architects of the curriculum of multiculturalism. From his lecture hall at Makerere University he documented and analyzed the elements of a distinctively African religious order. Mbiti's view of African religious life—as integrated, whole, and all-embracing—made idiosyncratic and dissident versions of religious practice seem to be a danger to social order. By drawing attention to the unity that existed underneath outward diversity, Professor Mbiti's scholarship unintentionally laid out a theological framework for the Amin regime's coercive program of religious unification.

CHAPTER NINE

Making History

Hⁱˢᵗᵒʳʸ was being made in Idi Amin's Uganda. Everywhere there were wars to fight and campaigns to win, as Ugandans found themselves on the front lines of globally consequential struggles. There was much to document, much to remember, and many heroes to hymn. There was a rapid expansion in the field of collecting and conservation, as forgettable places were redefined, almost overnight, as sacred ground. "Seldom has such a small group of people been given a broader mandate or a more exciting or challenging responsibility," wrote the director of the Department of Antiquities in a report.[1] The government created new institutions to discover, curate, and maintain heritage sites. The Department of Antiquities employed sixteen people at the Kasubi Tombs, nineteen at the tombs of King Kabalega, and six at the remote fort at Patiko.[2] In the provinces, too, district "culture officers" set to work documenting and standardizing the performance traditions of Uganda's people.

One of these patriotic curators was John Tumusiime, an otherwise obscure civil servant who from 1972 to 1976 was the government's culture officer in Kigezi, Uganda's southernmost district. Over the course of four years Tumusiime conceived, financed, organized, and built several institutions that preserved local history. Among them was a museum of local culture, which Tumusiime organized in a Hindu temple abandoned after the Asian expulsion of 1972, and a monument to the end of the First World War, which he erected in a remote and misplaced locality. Neither site was to endure the passage of time: the memorial was wrecked a few years after it was opened, and the museum was closed once the Asian community returned to Uganda. Their impermanence helps us see how much work it takes to make history. Valorous deeds, heroic actions, and meaningful events do not create their own mark. Erosion—of memory, of culture, of landscape and soil—is a constant challenge. Building a memorial is a way to cheat time of its spoils, but it takes maintenance and repair to ensure that sites of importance, once defined, do not decay. And— especially in places like Idi Amin's Uganda, where glass, concrete, and wire were in short supply—it requires human ingenuity, self-sacrifice, and dedication to turn fragile objects into museum pieces.[3]

As patriotic Ugandans pursued Idi Amin's campaigns against real and imagined foes, as sites of historical consequence became more numerous and heroes multiplied, the labor of securing public memory became more urgent and more essential. The preservation work that patriotic conservationists did was rarely acknowledged by people in power. Most often it was entirely unseen. That is how conservation works. The mythology of Idi Amin's government rested on the invisible, uncompensated, and unacknowledged labor of curators.

========

The British officials who governed colonial Uganda were sure that their history—their deeds, their heroes—deserved to be remembered. In March 1935 the chief secretary directed British officials to "mark the more important historical sites in this protectorate before the passage of time has made them unidentifiable."[4] One of the earliest monuments erected in Uganda was at Fort Thruston, in the east. It commemorated the death of two British officers, killed by mutinous Sudanese soldiers. The plaque described how one officer was "treacherously made prisoner and was shot ... on 19 October 1897," while another officer was killed while he "deliberately risked his life in the endeavor to save the English from grave peril and recall the mutineers to their duty."[5] The monument—like the many other monuments that colonial conquistadores created—cast a partisan view of history into stone. It was impossible to see the mutineers' side of the story.

In 1956 the colonial government created a Hotels and Tourism Board to oversee the development of the tourist infrastructure.[6] The history of European conquest was the selling point. An early promotional pamphlet invited tourists to "follow in the steps of the great explorers."

"This is the land of Livingstone's explorations," the pamphlet announced, "the scene—in those not-so-long-ago days—of Stanley's Travels in Darkest Africa."[7] In 1957 the director of public works erected a concrete obelisk, a platform, and a shelter on the west bank of the Nile River. It marked the site of the explorer John Hanning Speke's discovery of the river's headwaters.[8] These and other monuments were meant to build the record of the British civilizing mission into the landscape. When there was a proposal to allow African-run local councils to identify sites of historical importance, British officials demurred. One of them argued:

> This might very well open the door to extremist politicians agitating for the abolition of sites connected with British historical significance. Conversely nationalistic trends being what they are, it might lead to invidious arguments concerning sites of local or pretended historical importance, e.g. the birthplace of some temporarily popular local personality.[9]

Colonial officials insisted that they alone possessed the perspective to measure greatness in history. The concrete legacy of colonialism was a monumental architecture that testified to the heroism of Uganda's British rulers.

After Uganda's independence in 1962, Milton Obote's government had very little material to work with in constructing a national personality. The heroism of colonial conquistadores could not be the foundation for an independent nationalism. Neither could Uganda's antique kingdoms furnish the basis for solidarity. When the Uganda Army sacked the palace of the kingdom of Buganda in May 1966, leaving many of the buildings wrecked, some people saw it as a lost opportunity. A critic wrote to Obote shortly after the Kabaka's palace was destroyed:

> In almost every civilized country, which was formerly ruled by Kings who were later deposed by popular uprisings, royal palaces and all that goes with them were preserved even to now. They are important historical monuments, relics of the past, attracting thousands of tourists every year. They are sources of revenue and a lesson to the generations of the future.[10]

But President Obote had no reason to honor the heritage of kings. His government was at war with the royalists of Buganda. Kingdoms—

whether conceived as political entities or as museum projects—had to be bundled out of sight. In the last months of 1967 the palaces of the kings of western and southern Uganda were seized by the government. The palace of the Tooro kingdom was transformed into an assembly hall and dormitory for a nursing school, while the outbuildings were made into offices. Within a year the grounds were occupied by squatters, who filled the premises with banana trees and other crops.[11]

It was hard to know, in the last years of the 1960s, where history was heading. Whose accomplishments were to be hymned? Whose past was to be celebrated? When the government established a new "Inspectorate for Monuments and Attractive Sites," its mandate was the "preservation of all the existing attractive monuments and other interesting historical pieces."[12] The minister responsible asked local government officials to document previously unrecognized sites which "are known only to the local people." Local officials were mystified about how to proceed. It was not clear, wrote a perplexed district commissioner, whether "places of local interest would actually qualify as being of national interest in Uganda at large."[13] The list that he submitted was full of uncontroversial things: a cave where hyenas used to live; a rock where one of the region's mythical ancestors was said to have buried his wife and son.

There were very few national ancestors to hymn. In the absence of an inspirational past, history was depoliticized. The focus was on foreign visitors. In 1963 the Obote government sent out a delegation to generate global interest in tourism in Uganda. The delegation was led by a British businessman, whose credential for the job was his leadership of the Uganda Cricket Association.[14] The Ministry of Tourism produced a series of Christmas cards and posters that advertised Uganda to tourists and visitors. The posters featured scenes of cultural significance—dancing festivals, circumcision ceremonies—and pictures of natural landscapes.[15] There was nothing about colonialism, war, or politics. Officials expected that the tourist business would "reflect mostly the African culture and personality," and encouraged hotel owners to "concentrate on the African way of life."[16]

As a business strategy the Obote government's depoliticized version of public culture worked admirably. The number of tourists visiting Uganda rose steadily in the late 1960s, from 53,000 in 1968 to 74,000 in 1969.[17] In that year tourism was the third-largest sector in Uganda's foreign exchange economy. In 1970, on the eve of the coup that brought Idi Amin to power, the number of tourists visiting Uganda rose to 78,000, the largest number in history.[18]

In September 1971 President Amin loaded the British high commissioner into his personal helicopter and flew to Kangai, in the northern part of the country, to lay the foundation stones for two monuments. One marked the place where Kabalega, the warrior king of Bunyoro, had been captured by British forces. The other, a few kilometers away, marked the place where Mwanga, the rebellious king of Buganda, had likewise been captured by the British. The two kings had forged an alliance against British conquistadores in the late nineteenth century; their capture had come at the end of a long and bloody military campaign. The two sites were decidedly unimpressive. They lay on either side of a minor road, at a place that had never before been marked. Nonetheless, President Amin was convinced that there were lessons to be learned on this unremarkable terrain. "Contrary to what one might suppose after reading foreign historians, Africans did play an active part in their own history," he said. If Uganda's people "had joined forces then, why could they not work together now?"[19]

Under Amin's presidency a host of previously unnoticed places and unremarkable objects were made into evidence of Ugandans' long struggle against British oppression. In November 1971 the Uganda Museum's curator traveled to Hoima, the capital of the defunct Bunyoro kingdom, where he acquired a large mace with three long metal spikes, together with a spear measuring 55 centimeters in the blade. Both weapons were said to have belonged to the rebellious king Kabalega.[20] The curator also acquired an axe, covered in bark cloth, which had been used to execute criminals in Kabalega's time.[21] In Mparo, near Hoima, local people pointed out a shrub with proliferating branches that was supposed to have been planted by King Kabalega. They reported that Kabalega had sacrificed nine men, nine cows, nine goats, and nine chickens on the occasion when the bush was planted.[22]

What explains this sudden surge of interest in Kabalega and other anti-colonial heroes? Amin's government was positioning Uganda on the front lines of an ongoing war against the colonial powers. In historical remembrance as in other domains there were battles to fight and win. One of the monuments that President Amin inaugurated during his September 1971 tour of northern Uganda marked the place where King Kabalega—fleeing from British forces—had met Chief Daudi Odora of Lango, who gave him support. Amin argued that the monument had uncovered a hitherto forgotten past. It was his government's policy to "start

President Amin lays the foundation stone on a monument marking the capture of Kabaka Mwanga, 1971 (Courtesy of the Uganda Broadcasting Corporation)

a thorough search and study of all meaningful sites in the hope that this will lead to a better understanding of the earlier people of Uganda." The tombs of the ancient kings were to be rebuilt in concrete, and museums would be created at each site.[23]

The Department of Antiquities was established in 1973. The first conservator thought his task was clear: to engage in "rediscovering our cultural heritage."[24] He and his colleagues sought to challenge "the false ideas of cultural superiority" which Europeans had cultivated through their well-stocked museums. The Uganda Museum's curator told a committee that, as the government sought to build an "African personality,"

we need to build integrity, we need Ugandans to respect themselves, and they cannot respect themselves unless they respect
their culture, their history, their past, they know who they
are, what they stand for. This can only be done through the
Museum.[25]

Queens Road renamed Lumumba Avenue, January 1973 (Courtesy of the
Uganda Broadcasting Corporation)

Across Uganda there was a rapid repurposing of geography. Everywhere
there were reminders of the anti-colonial struggle. The unremarkable
shrub in Mparo—apparently planted by King Kabalega—was made into
a site of pilgrimage for visitors. In August 1973 President Amin visited
Mparo in the company of Somalia's vice president. The guests were
shown the spears, shields, and drums that Kabalega had used; then went
to view a "growing tree which was planted in nine human corpses, nine
sheep, and nine goats."[26] In January 1973 workers took down the statue
of King George VI, which had sat in front of the High Court.[27] Later
that year Idi Amin and Zairian president Mobutu Sese Seko renamed
Lake Albert with the name Lake Mobutu Sese Seko. A few days after
that, they likewise renamed Lake Edward, christening it Lake Idi Amin
Dada.[28] In January 1977, on the anniversary of his coming to power,
Amin laid the foundation stone for a new monument. It was to be two
hundred feet high, built in honor of Uganda's fallen heroes.[29]

History had never been so urgent. There was a pressing need for inspirational people, styles, sites, and objects, for a distinctive historical repertoire
to name and celebrate. The Department of Antiquities hastily brought out a

book titled *Kabalega and the History of Uganda* for its newly established "Uganda's Famous Men" series. According to the publisher, the book portrayed Kabalega as he "fell victim to forces of colonialism and imperialism and not as a rebellious and barbaric King as he had been labeled by the British colonialists."[30] Neither this book nor other books in the series were based on primary historical research. The authors drew material from already published texts and rushed them into print. That was what was needed: short, inspirational texts that could furnish a new narrative about Uganda's history.

In Kampala, the curator of the Uganda Museum began, for the first time, to collect newspapers. In the acquisitions catalogue he made a point of transcribing the contents of each of the newspapers he acquired, writing down the headlines, and listing the chief events mentioned in the issue. Item H71.04/13, for instance, is an issue of the *Uganda Argus* newspaper acquired a few weeks following the coup that brought Amin to power. The catalogue entry describes the newspaper in this way:

> The front page shows the Minister of Education, Mr. A.K. Mayanja, pictured at the Uganda Teachers Association. On the right, the cabinet of the military meeting at State House, Entebbe. Below: Major General Idi Amin signing the visitors' book after the church service conducted by the dean of Namirembe, Rev. Mukasa. At the back page left, the military head of state of the Republic of Uganda, Major General Idi Amin, touring the site of the OAU Hotel and conference hall buildings which were under construction in Kampala.[31]

The curator was making the newspaper—an ephemeral, disposable thing—into an artifact testifying to events of great consequence. There were a great many things that needed to be collected, for all around, history was being made. Curators scrambled to ensure that consequential things would not be lost. In the early 1970s the curator at the Uganda Museum—a young man named Charles Ssekintu—acquired dozens of articles that seem to have been junk. In August 1971 he bought a grinding stone—one of ten that were for sale—along a roadside in Kokolumbo village.[32] The following day he acquired two pieces of iron slag from an old smelting site in Buganda.[33] In 1972 Ssekintu bought twenty-nine articles from a boy named Bebwa. The collection included a used cooking pot, a used beer pot, a wooden basket mended with pieces of aluminum, and a toy bicycle.[34] All of these things appear to have been trash, unworthy of inclusion in the museum's collections. But for Mr. Ssekintu even the smallest and most incidental things were evidence of the changing tides of history. Item E.73.17, for example, consists of seven tin candles, which the curator purchased from a market. The curator explained in the acquisitions catalogue that the candles were "widely used in Uganda before the use of the hand lamp and electricity later on." In fact, tin candles were, and still are, in wide use in Uganda, but in Mr. Ssekintu's eyes times were changing. His acquisitions strategy reflects a sincere sense that historical preservation was necessary at a time of dramatic technological and political change.

Here was a form of curatorship that was animated by a feeling of momentum. All the campaigns that the Amin government launched generated their own enemies, their own urgency, and their own artifacts. Perhaps the most haunting artifact that the Uganda Museum acquired in those years is item E75.13, which came into the collections on 31 August 1975. It is a "magical bottle," containing small bits of wood bound up with two green nylon strings. In the catalogue the curator wrote that he had acquired the object from the "Abandoned Property Committee," which had found it in a "Ugandan big man's sleeping room." He called it an "amulet," and examined it under a microscope to see how the bundles of bark had been inserted into the bottle. The more interesting question has to do with the "big man" whose medicine this bottle was. There were a great many abandoned properties in Idi Amin's Uganda, for whole populations of people were summarily obliged to flee their homes. Was the man one of the thousands of Ugandans of Indian or Pakistani descent who were expelled by presidential decree in 1972? Their abandoned property was made into assets of the state, to be distributed to African owners. Was the man one of the thousands of Ugandans who were murdered by the brutal agents of the State Research Bureau? It is impossible to know what the man hoped for in the use of the amulet. Was it potency? Protection?

Item E75.13 was one of many things—businesses, houses, pets, vehicles, family—that were left behind by the men and women who fled Uganda. Someone had once held it close, trusting in its power to protect and enable, until its owner—finding himself a target—had hastily departed his home. Like many of the other objects held in the Uganda Museum, item E75.13 became a museum piece at the end of a violent history of disruption. It is a leftover, a thing that bears the imprint of a human life violently expunged from the body politic.

———

The things that preservationists sought to conserve—historical land-marks, regalia, cultural practices, trees, land—had been living other lives. It was not always easy for preservationists to pull historical places and things away from those who had other purposes for them.

Katasiha Fort was one of several earthworks constructed in the 1890s, during Britain's bloody conquest of the kingdom of Bunyoro. When an official from Kampala visited the site in 1965, he found that a farmer named Kyomya was cultivating the fort's central square.[35] There was—as yet—no legislation in place to establish the fort, or any other site, as a national monument. A bargain was duly struck: Kyomya agreed to cultivate the land inside the fort, while the trenches that ran along the perimeter of the old fort were to be kept free of cultivation. There the matter rested until 1974, when the district's culture officer wrote to Mr. Kyomya warning him not to cultivate the land at Katasiha.[36] Kyomya replied with a tart and pointed letter. "The land I am cultivating has been legally possessed, cultivated and recultivated by my grandfather, father and myself since 1927," he wrote.[37] The following week the subcounty chief visited the site and found that Mr. Kyomya had a certificate of occupancy for the land on which the fort was located.[38]

The preservationist's interests—to set aside, to separate, to conserve—were always in competition with the interests of other users. In 1974, the conservator of antiquities angrily noted that the burial mound of Suna II—one of Buganda's kings—had become the site of a building project, as a householder had erected a structure on the premises. The monument at Fort Thruston—the site of a famous mutiny—had been demolished, and the memorial plaques had been wrenched off.[39] In 1975, the conservator erected a wire fence around the Muganzirwazza earthwork, a fortification constructed by Buganda's rulers in the late nineteenth century. Within a few weeks, the new fence had been compromised by playful children, who made a game of swinging on the wires, causing them to bend and break.[40]

Monuments are never in a solid state. Even the most solid and impressive monument needs attention. Natural forces—the growing of trees, the erosion of soil, the drying of mortar—continually undermine the monument, making it crack, list, and eventually disappear. Maintenance is a vital requirement for any monumental architecture. In Idi Amin's Uganda the tools and equipment needed for maintenance were always in short supply. Culture officers—like other officials in Amin's government—had to work in conditions of shortage and austerity. Creativity and ingenuity were needed to maintain sites of culture.

There are dozens of tombs in western Uganda where the rulers of the ancient kingdom of Bunyoro are buried. All of them survived the tumultuous 1970s because of the constant labor and attention of ordinary people. In January 1972 the impressive tomb of King Duhaga was overgrown with weeds and brush. The headmaster of the local school had to marshal his students and spend a week clearing the site.[41] The culture officer in Bunyoro was overwhelmed by the maintenance work that was needed. One site—a cave with seven compartments—was overgrown with bushes, and inside it there were snakes and other dangerous creatures. The official wanted the fire brigade to clear and maintain the site.[42] Some officials suggested that the government build concrete monuments for each of the region's tombs.[43] It was a noble suggestion, but concrete was scarce. When Tito Winyi—the deposed king of Bunyoro—died in 1972, the burial committee hoped to put up a permanent structure, in rock and concrete, to mark the site of his tomb. But money was short. By the end of the year Winyi's clansmen had erected a tomb made of wood and thatch, far cheaper than concrete.[44]

Even the site at Mparo—where the famous bush planted by King Kabalega grew—was maintained by the efforts of commoners. The tomb of Kabalega's female relatives, which was located on the site, was derelict by 1975, and the regalia were being eaten by termites. The conservator of antiquities removed the regalia from the tomb and stored it in an office.[45] There were plans to build the tomb in concrete, at a cost of 60,000 shillings. In the end government allocated a bare 1,000 shillings to the project.[46] When the reed fence collapsed in heavy winds, an official from Kampala ordered the subcounty chief to marshal a working squad within two days to make repairs.[47] Each parish was to produce three hundred bundles of reeds, one hundred poles, and one hundred bundles of thatch. The government did not pay for the materials or the labor.

In Idi Amin's Uganda as everywhere else, permanence was always an illusion. Monuments and museums are always in process, needing maintenance and upkeep.[48] But even in the face of decay and erosion, the idea of the museum—a place where historically important things could be stored, inviolate, against loss and decay—furnished patriotic Ugandans with an aspiration, a program to pursue. Even in places where a physical brick-and-mortar building was absent, preservationists acted in anticipation of a time when the accoutrements of the old order would be safely museumized. "Traditional furniture and weapons are very scarcely used merely in very Remote homes," wrote a young woman named Theresa

Akech in 1978.[49] She was the government culture officer in Bunyoro District. She did not speak the local language, and she found it hard to "get the confidence of the local people." Even so, Akech felt empowered to create an inventory—several pages long—of the "Ancient Traditional Dress and Tools of the Banyoro." Akech was identifying things that needed to be saved, describing their condition, planning for their preservation. Like the many people who served on the front lines of Idi Amin's culture war, Theresa Akech saw herself as a curator.

That is how heroes were made in Idi Amin's Uganda: through routine acts of repair and maintenance. That is also how cultures were preserved. Unremarkable people—their labor, their time, their treasure—were called upon to maintain national myths. Some people acted out of a sincere sense of devotion, their imaginations fired by the requirements of the time. Other people were compelled to take part. Whether out of a sense of patriotic enthusiasm or out of an intimidated resignation, it was commoners who fabricated the materials with which the Amin government fought its war against cultural imperialism.

Like other culture workers in Amin's Uganda, John Tumusiime strove to ensure that the fragile substance of history would not be lost. From where did he get his sense of purpose? Tumusiime's files—held in the recently renovated archives of the Kabale District government—bulge with paperwork about faraway things. The largest amount of external material came from the organizers of FESTAC II, the Second Black and African Festival of Arts and Culture, which originally was meant to take place in Lagos in January 1975, then was postponed to 1977.[50] The planning documents generated by the festival's organizers were duplicated in Kampala and distributed to Uganda's far-flung culture officers. They are interleafed throughout Tumusiime's papers. The file titled "Festivals and Competitions" contains the earliest documents from the FESTAC II planning committee in Lagos, inserted back-to-back with paperwork concerning the "Kigezi Cultural Festival" that Tumusiime organized.

FESTAC II offered Amin's government resources by which to reform and superintend the creation of culture. Nigeria promised to fund five hundred artists and performers from eastern Africa, and each participating country established a working committee to identify individuals and objects that were to be sent to Lagos. An extraordinary amount of work was involved in preparing Uganda's contribution. There were sub-

President Amin with a statue made in his likeness, July 1975 (Courtesy of the
Uganda Broadcasting Corporation)

committees responsible for organizing exhibitions on tattoos, cosmetics,
leatherwork, woodworking, and art. There was a committee to identify
dances to be performed in Lagos; and another to select theatrical works
to be staged. Uganda did not contribute to the exhibition concerning
"modern dressing," since miniskirts and wigs had been banned by presidential decree. But there was an embroidery subcommittee.[51] The music
subcommittee spent hours debating the question "What is the real difference between traditional music and Western music?" The meeting
minutes, unsurprisingly, report that "no final and satisfying conclusion
was reached" to that debate.[52]

     In faraway Kigezi, John Tumusiime was as an active participant in all
of this activity. The chair of the national pottery committee visited
Kigezi in 1974, collecting two pots for display in Lagos. The following
year Tumusiime sent four additional pots to Kampala for inclusion in
FESTAC II. There was a small one, traditionally used for washing; a
large one, used for storing butter; and a curved one, used for feminine
hygiene. He was careful to note the vernacular names for each of the
pots.[53] He was likewise helpful to the committee preparing the list of
Ugandan celebrities to be profiled in Lagos. First on Tumusiime's list
was Makobore, ruler of the ancient kingdom of Rujumbura. The king of

old was "kind, liberal and just. He helped all in need and punished wrongdoers," wrote Tumusiime. "He was gifted and knew how to rule."[54] There was no evidence offered to support these characterizations. Tumusiime's description of the magnanimous Makobore was written to conform to the expectations of audiences in Kampala and Lagos.

Tumusiime had grown up in Kigezi, and in his youth he had trained for the priesthood. Shortly after his ordination he had an inappropriate relationship with a house girl, and thereafter he abandoned his priestly vocation and retrained as a civil servant.[55] As the district's culture officer he brought to his work all the enthusiasm and commitment of a religious calling. The first report he filed vibrated with ideas and energy.[56] He had organized committees in each of the district's subcounties, through which elders and citizens could "assist and advise . . . on how best [to] preserve, promote, and develop the Culture of the people in this District." There was a new society of blacksmiths, dedicated to making traditional knives and spears. There was a committee working on local history and folklore. There were, he said, twenty-six dance troupes. Tumusiime welcomed the Amin government's decision to ban miniskirts for Ugandan women, claiming that

> short dresses were a contradiction of people's culture . . . because traditionally a woman had to dress completely and even her ankles were not to be seen. So this good move restored the moral and culture of the people.

Tumusiime felt empowered—by virtue of his position—to speak as an authority on a wide range of matters. He lamented the unpopularity of traditional food, for the "educated class tend to be interested in foreign dishes like Italian soup, HOT DOG etc." By early July, only three weeks after his arrival in the district, Tumusiime was busily organizing a fashion show, with "traditional dressing of all four ethnic groups in Kigezi." There would be no Italian soup or hot dogs. Neither would there be miniskirts. The central part of the show featured a "traditional homestead," to be built of reeds, poles, and grass thatch.[57] Later that month he prepared an inventory of the dancing traditions of Kigezi and Ankole Districts.[58] The report began with "Kikiga" dance, the tradition of the "Bakiga tribes." The dance was said to vary in instrumentation and melody in different parts of the region, but "what is in common is that it is danced by jumping and hitting the ground very hard with one's feet." He lectured the district's leading dance troupe about the need to perfect their steps, and announced that he was planning to go on tour, teaching dancing troupes a "new style that can be used in our culture."[59]

The work that Mr. Tumusiime did to define traditional culture was conducted in a time of economic crisis. There were constant shortfalls of funding, infrastructure, and material. Tumusiime's office had no furniture. There was no stationery, and even the paper on which his reports were printed had been borrowed from other offices.[60] The culture festival in 1976—which Tumusiime organized—was nearly scuppered due to lack of transport. Two days before the festival was to begin, Tumusiime was writing to Kigezi's district commissioner asking for the use of a vehicle that could carry "people, handicrafts, traditional dishes and brews from the subcounties" to the site.[61] It was hard to find the resources— petroleum, transportation, accommodation, attire—necessary for the occasions where traditional culture could be performed.

Ambitious culture workers like John Tumusiime had to contend with the constraints of a collapsing infrastructure. They had to make personal sacrifices to make culture and history memorable.

———

John Tumusiime launched a great many improbable projects. Here I focus on two. In the first example, Tumusiime managed to build a memorial to the end of World War I in an unlikely and inappropriate place; in the second, he founded a museum to local culture in a building that had formerly been a Hindu temple. Both projects were grounded in fictitious or inflated accounts of the past. Both projects depended on Tumusiime himself—his energy, his entrepreneurship, his time.

In November 1972 President Amin celebrated Remembrance Day—a British holiday commemorating the end of the First World War—at Kisoro, in Kigezi District. Twelve cabinet ministers and most of the diplomatic corps were in attendance. Amin appeared at the hotel in Kabale town the night before the ceremony, and he, his ministers, and a few diplomats danced to the music of an army band until 3:30 a.m. Early the next morning, after a few hours of sleep, they made the trip by helicopter to Kisoro. At 11:00 a.m. the audience sang "Oh God, Our Help in Ages Past" as a flag was lowered and wreaths were laid.[62] In his speech Amin told the audience that the last battle of World War I had been fought there. Indicating a derelict stone monument, Amin claimed that it marked the place where the last shots of the war had been fired. In fact, the derelict monument commemorated a different event: it marked the

President Amin lays a wreath at a monument marking the end of
World War I, Kisoro, southern Uganda, November 1972 (Courtesy of
the Uganda Broadcasting Corporation)

place where, in 1909, a company of Sikh soldiers commanded by a British major had repulsed a group of German troops marching north from
Rwanda.[63] But by 1972 the plaque had fallen off the stone. It was there, a
lieu de mémoire waiting for an assignment.

John Tumusiime was present at the ceremony that morning. For him
President Amin's offhand comment was the starting place for a project of
historical commemoration. A few days after the ceremonies he wrote to
the conservator of antiquities:

> After World War I had ended, and even trities [*sic*] to end the
> war signed, the British Legion and the German Battalion contin-
> ued fighting on this place. So the last blood to be shed in this
> war and the last shot to be fired was done on this place two years
> after the end of the war. . . . This was due to the lack of Commu-
> nication for the Forces here never knew that the war had ended.
> Even today one can see big pits where Soldiers used to take
> cover during the fighting.[64]

Tumusiime was right about the unevenness of the war's end date. The German army in East Africa had, in fact, continued to fight for several weeks after the signing of the armistice of 11 November 1918. But that army was in North Rhodesia—contemporary Zambia—not in Uganda, when the war ended. The last shots of the war had been fired several thousand miles to the south of the monument in Kisoro. Idi Amin's reconstruction of events was inaccurate. But John Tumusiime had no reason to be concerned with accuracy. He asked the conservator of antiquities for funding to erect a "traditional house" on the site, "so that the place is given its full splendour."

There followed a long negotiation over the logistics of building the traditional house. As it turned out, traditional building routines were difficult to organize. By April 1973 a porter had been hired, the site had been demarcated, and the memorial had been established in Ugandan law, but the bamboo poles had not been found. The nearest bamboo forest was five miles away. A lorry was needed to move the poles to Kisoro.[65] By April 1974 the four workers who had been employed to build the traditional house were on strike, demanding payment before they would commence work.[66] By October of that year the frame had finally been erected, and Tumusiime reported that it was "beautiful." It was unroofed, for the thatching grass needed to cover the building was located five miles away.[67] In May 1975 Tumusiime reported that thatching grass had been cut on four separate occasions, but it had not been moved to the site because there was no transportation. In consequence the grass had rotted.[68] In December 1975 Tumusiime asked the authorities to force local people to carry the grass to the memorial site, for the bamboo frame was decaying because of its exposure to the rain. By April 1976 the thatching was, finally, under way. The work was done by local residents as part of the communal labor in which they were forced to engage. It took three months to finish the job.[69]

Very few people ever saw Tumusiime's memorial to the end of the First World War. In 1974 there were sixty visitors; in 1975 there were six; in 1978 there were twenty-one.[70] In 1979, during the Tanzanian invasion that toppled Amin's government, the monument was damaged by gunfire. The bamboo house was demolished, and the caretaker brought the metal plaque to the subcounty chief's headquarters for safekeeping.[71] By 1980, the year following Amin's overthrow, farmers were cultivating the plot on which the monument sat. In 1986, when the government of Yoweri Museveni came to power, it fell to a new culture officer to write to the Kampala authorities for funding to rebuild the monument. His appeal began with a familiar claim: "after the First World War the British and the German battalion continued fighting at this place, so that the last shot to be fired took place two years after the war had ended," he wrote. He was copying from the petition that his predecessor, John Tumusiime, had composed fifteen years before.[72]

As the history of the monument that Tumusiime built suggests, sites of memory are actively made, not simply preserved. Narratives that make memorials meaningful can be borrowed, plagiarized, and pinned onto sites that actually have nothing to do with their purported meaning. What I want to stress here, though, is this: conservation is hard work. There is labor involved in the making of myths. It needs concrete, wire, bamboo, thatch, and sweat. All heritage work takes maintenance. No monument—however grandiose it might be—can be sustained without ongoing work.

That brings me to a second project that Tumusiime pursued: the Kigezi District Museum. Here, as with the ill-fated monument, he had to exert himself to make history memorable. The district's "Culture Committee" passed a resolution calling for the building of a museum in 1973. The aim, wrote Tumusiime, was to "collect our traditional ornaments, the early black smithing, some sculptures and other ancient and traditional skills."[73] The town council agreed to allocate a building on 14/15 Ruchiro Road to house the new museum. The building had formerly been a Hindu temple, seized by the Departed Asians Property Custodial Board after the expulsion of Uganda's Indian community. In 1976, when Tumusiime developed a plan for the rehabilitation of 14/15 Ruchiro Road, he estimated that it would take sixty tons of cement to rebuild the structure's floor.[74] He planned to put a craft shop on the right side of the museum, a lecture hall near the front, and a showcase at the center in which a diorama was to be positioned. By 1977, when a new culture officer took over Kigezi District, the building was in disarray: it had been looted twice in the previous year. Thieves had taken away thirty-six windowpanes, two padlocks, one office desk, and all of the boards that had lined the showcases.[75] The watchman, who was supposed to protect the property, had absconded from duty, as he had not been paid for eight months.

The museum was finally opened to the public in July 1978. It was an impressive occasion: two dance troupes entertained the guests, and the minister for culture and community development cut the ribbon.[76] But in 1980—after the fall of the Amin government—the new culture officer reported that the lock for the main door was broken. The photographs displayed in the museum's halls had faded with time, and the paint needed renewing.[77] He had to use his own money to repair the lock. There were 6,614 visitors in the first half of 1982. The culture officer pointed out the urgent need for a latrine to accommodate the many people visiting the place.[78] By 1990, the museum was derelict. The caretaker reported that the place "smells of urine and feces is found outside the building." Thirty windowpanes were missing. Ants had invaded the displays, consuming several of the exhibits. The roof leaked and needed repair. The signpost had fallen down. Children made a habit of playing on the grounds, while nearby householders grazed their cattle on the premises.[79] In 2007 the museum was permanently closed, as Indians returning to Uganda repossessed the building and refounded their temple.

—————

I met John Tumusiime's daughter on a Sunday morning in August 2017. A mutual friend introduced us following an early-morning service at the Anglican cathedral in Kabale. She was the youngest of Tumusiime's several children, born in the early 1980s, only a few years before he died. There were tears in her eyes as I told her about the monument Tumusiime had built, about the museum he had founded, and about his work with dancers, musicians, and blacksmiths. Later I sent her copies of the archival documents on which this chapter is based. On that Sunday morning, though, I did not know what to say. In many ways John Tumusiime was a failure. Seen in a certain light, his work on behalf of a murderous dictator might even be considered malignant.

FESTAC II took place in Lagos in January and February 1977. More than 17,000 artists, dancers, and intellectuals participated. At their final rehearsal before departing for Nigeria the Uganda delegation marched before President Amin, wearing traditional feathered costumes. Photographs show the men and women standing stiffly in ranks, as if on parade, as Amin walks between their ranks. He exhorted the performers to behave with discipline, since "everyone knows that they come from a revolutionary country."[80] The delegation brought a collection of wooden carvings and an array of articles crafted from bamboo to Lagos. Journalists who inspected the pavilion were most impressed with the embroidery, which featured exciting patterns they thought "likely to stun visitors."[81] Professor John Mbiti, the distinguished theologian who had

President Amin reviews dancers departing for the Second Black and African
Festival of Arts and Culture, January 1977 (Courtesy of the Uganda
Broadcasting Corporation)

done so much to define African traditional religion, gave a lecture and
contributed to a souvenir book commemorating the festival.[82] The Heart
Beat of Africa dance troupe performed at the National Theatre, at
Tafawa Balewa Square, and at the national stadium in Lagos.[83] When the
Ugandan delegation returned from Nigeria in February 1977, President
Amin organized a state luncheon for them. The jamboree in Lagos, he
said, had "set in motion a new wave of cultural awareness throughout the
continent."[84] Every African "should from now on try and have a greater
cultural awareness in their everyday life."

The great Nigerian intellectual Wole Soyinka thought the whole
thing was a farce. "Our people were offered a narrowed-down, reduc-

tionist aspect of culture in a gargantuan orgy of ill-organized spectacles," he wrote. Soyinka decried what he called "Culture with a capital C," which was "pronounced into being by a Ministry of Culture." The FESTAC II convocation had taken rich and complicated artistic traditions and relegated them to "token, or symbolic, expositions, starved of funds and given scant coverage even in the media."[85]

What did John Tumusiime make of all of this? It is impossible to say. In April 1976 he was transferred from Kigezi to another district.[86] He left many projects unfinished. I do not know whether any of the pots that he sent to Kampala were placed on display in the impressive stall in Lagos. His organizational and curatorial work was never publicly acknowledged. That is how curatorship works: it renders itself invisible, making the art and the performance appear, finished, before an audience.

John Tumusiime invested himself in two heritage institutions—a monument and a museum—that are now lost to posterity. From a preservationist's point of view these projects were failures. For us, however, the story of Tumusiime's failures lets us see how transitory sites of memory are. The infrastructure of heritage conservation in Idi Amin's Uganda was shaped by shortage: by the absence of petrol to fuel vehicles, by shortages of glass and concrete, by deficits in the government payroll. All of these shortfalls made the work of repair and maintenance more difficult and vexing, more demanding of human ingenuity. That is why John Tumusiime's career as Kigezi's culture officer is worth studying. He was not particularly successful in his work, and neither did the institutions he built outlast his tenure in office. Nonetheless, his work helps us see how essential human creativity, persistence, and dedication are in the maintenance of national myths.

CHAPTER TEN

Living Off the Grid
The Rwenzururu Kingdom

B Y THE LATE 1970s there were large groups of Ugandan exiles living in Nairobi, Dar es Salaam, and London. Many of them were
pursuing far-fetched schemes for Idi Amin's overthrow. Foreign
governments received a constant stream of pamphlets and letters decrying the violence of Amin's government and soliciting support
for his ouster. None of these exile groups were particularly effective. A
British diplomat described Uganda's exiles in this way:

> Some are idealistic, mostly somewhat impractical, wanting
> somebody else to fight their battles for them. Some are primarily
> concerned with their own interests, searching for funds or schol-
> arships. A few are outright confidence tricksters, and some are
> probably agent provocateurs.[1]

Some of these exile groups were to play a leading role in the political life
of Uganda after the fall of Amin's government in 1979. In history books
and in autobiographies they have made themselves the heroes of the liberation struggle.[2]

Within Uganda's borders, though, there was only one organization
that sustained military and political resistance to Amin's government.
That was the Rwenzururu kingdom, located in the mountainous border
between Uganda and Zaire. Founded in 1962, Rwenzururu partisans

fought for twenty years to secure their independence. The kingdom was the first and most effective form of government for thousands of western Uganda's people. During an epoch of austerity, institutional dysfunction, and widespread political violence, Rwenzururu's institutions commanded loyalty. On the margins, in a remote and inaccessible place, here was a kind of freedom.

How did a group of poorly equipped mountaineers create and sustain a rebellion against the tyranny of Idi Amin? This chapter focuses on the modest, slow-moving media infrastructure that upheld Rwenzururu's patriotism. Rwenzururu's leaders encouraged people to listen critically to President Amin's radio broadcasts. They would not be drawn into the campaigns that the Amin government launched. They created and nurtured an information infrastructure that demystified official propaganda, circumvented the power of Amin's media machinery, and set Amin's campaigns at a distance. Rwenzururu brokers led their people to see themselves as defenders of a specific identity, a community defined by the historical experience of oppression. They named their own heroes, founded their own memorials, and created their own archive. In so doing, they made themselves free.

=====

Western Uganda's mountain people have a long experience in the art of not being governed.[3] The summits of the Rwenzori massif—which lie along the border between Uganda and Zaire—rise to 5,000 meters, 3,650 meters above the plains to the east and 4,250 meters above the Semliki valley to the west. "No one who has not explored the Ruwenzori Mountains can have any conception of the difficult nature of the country," wrote a colonial official in 1921.

> In climbing one often has to use both hands and feet and the tracks are quite impossible for ordinary porters. There are huge gorges and crevices with almost precipitous sides and the torrents rushing down from the snows, moreover the natives, who clamber around like monkeys, can observe all movements of anyone approaching them. Almost every track is an ideal spot for an ambush and the natives (if they chose to do so) could roll huge boulders down the mountains and inflict considerable damage on the attacking force.[4]

Like the soldiers of colonial times, the soldiers of independent Uganda had to climb the mountains on foot. "The barefooted [mountaineer] can scale the mountain with amazing speed when pursued by security forces," wrote a Ugandan official in 1964. It was "rather expecting too much of a soldier equipped with heavy boots, rifles, ammunition, woolen clothing and rations to chase and arrest a [mountaineer] on the mountain."[5] The mountains themselves were an encouragement for a separate political identity, placing the mountain's people at a geographical and political distance from the administrators of the lowlands.

In colonial times the Tooro kingdom, a lowland society of cattle-keepers, had attempted to rule the mountains on behalf of the British colonial state. Tooro's aristocrats were confident in the superiority of their civilization. They were unwilling, or unable, to see the Konzo and Amba people who lived in the mountains as possessors of unique, credible ways of life. "Though it appears that there exist differences between" Tooro, Amba, and Konzo people, "the [Tooro] Government has never at any time shown differences between them," wrote the kingdom's prime minister.[6] He claimed that the Konzo people had come to western Uganda's mountains in the seventeenth century, and "right from the beginning of their arrival . . . all of them accepted readily Toro rule, paying homage to the [king] of Toro." When census takers working for the Uganda government counted the region's people, they identified a mere 123 Konzo and 395 Amba people living in the Tooro kingdom. They managed to count 190,272 Tooro people.[7]

In reality, the kingdom was not a culturally homogeneous polity. Activists from among the mountains' Konzo minority founded the Bakonzo Life History Research Society in the early 1950s. Their objective, according to the society's constitution, was to "instill patriotism among the Konzo people and have them unite together."[8] The society's moving spirit was Isaya Mukirane, a primary school teacher who had worked as a research assistant to a visiting British journalist. With Mukirane at the helm, researchers fanned out across the mountains, carrying duplicated forms with historical questions.[9] Their research led Konzo partisans to regard themselves as inheritors of a long history of struggle. In the late 1910s mountaineers had raised a revolt against the government of Tooro. Led by three heroes, the rebels had driven away their chiefs and caused "considerable unrest."[10] One of the rebels was at large for three years; when he was finally captured in January 1921 he was subjected to a public trial and summarily executed.[11] In the later twentieth century, the memory of these events served to guide the political thought of the mountain's patriots. Here were martyrs on whose behalf activists could harbor a sense of grievance.

The first mention of the term "Rwenzururu" in Uganda's public life came in January 1962, when Isaya Mukirane composed a memorandum to the committee that was responsible for drafting the new constitution of the kingdom of Tooro. He asked that minority groups—Konzo and Amba people—be mentioned explicitly in the constitution; and he asked that the kingdom's administrative jobs, including the prime ministership, be open to people of any ethnicity.[12] The return address that Mukirane gave on this seminal document was:

Kasulenge
Bundibugyo
Rwenzururu

Rwenzururu did not as yet exist as an identifiable location on the map, but Mukirane and his colleagues were acting as though it did. In the postal system, if not yet in actuality, Mukirane and his colleagues were coming to identify themselves as residents of a distinctive, separate place.

For oppressed mountaineers "Rwenzururu" was a passport to freedom. By the end of March 1962 officials reported that virtually everyone in the mountains agreed that they should secede from the Tooro kingdom. In August partisans burned two buildings containing the tombs of Tooro's kings.[13] In a parish near Mukirane's home angry partisans burned down the chief's house, the police station, and the assembly hall. The following day a crowd of 2,000 people assaulted the county chief, beating him and his attendants.[14] A month later a party of men shouting "Rwenzururu!" chased off builders constructing a road that linked the highlands to the Tooro kingdom's capital in Fort Portal.[15] By December 1962 the Tooro kingdom's government in the mountains had collapsed, as the officials sought refuge in the lowlands. Most of the schools in the highlands were closed, as the teachers had fled.[16] Milton Obote's new government declared a state of emergency and deployed the Uganda Army. Over the course of three months the police arrested 653 people accused of working for Rwenzururu.[17]

There were very few pitched battles. Rwenzururu's struggle for independence was largely fought through acts of defiance. A government chief described the situation in this way:

People use obscene language in addressing the [parish] chiefs, which is against our customary law. They thoroughly despise us and tell us to pack and follow our Mukama [the Tooro king]. . . . They have neither the respect nor the decency to abstain from abusing chiefs in the road in the presence of other people. During the night these people stand on the hills and they shout abuses at chiefs and tell them to quit.[18]

When the chief visited a village to collect taxes, not a single person would agree to take tax assessment forms from his hand. All around the place was the echoing sound of whistles, as Rwenzururu partisans warned others of the chief's presence.

By June 1963 Isaya Mukirane was calling himself "king" of Rwenzururu.[19] He and his supporters established ministries of finance and education, immigration, internal affairs, and health for their nascent government.[20] According to Ugandan officials there was a "complete hierarchy of chiefs" to govern the affairs of Rwenzururu's people. There was also a comprehensive legal system.[21] Magistrates appointed by Rwenzururu were passing judgments and imposing fines on litigants. They passed death sentences on the worst offenders.[22] There was an annual poll tax; taxpayers were issued typed receipts, stamped with an official stamp. Litigants stayed away from Uganda government courts, and by the end of 1963 an official could report that the Uganda government court in the heart of the mountains was "virtually defunct": the magistrate heard only twenty-five cases that year, as compared with 730 in the year before.[23]

Officials of the Uganda government were confounded at Rwenzururu's newly formed regime. Ministers in Milton Obote's cabinet agreed that "there is no doubt whatever that the Rwenzururu administration has been for some time extremely effective in the mountain areas."[24] There was a "full organization of chiefs, a considerable number of so-called ministers, an assembly of representatives," with a court system, schools, prisons, and a military. The legal code—while it was unwritten—was nonetheless "extremely effective." The "regime is accepted by the people who live in the area . . . because they have no alternative but to do so," wrote a cabinet minister. "This fact is an embarrassment to the Central Government."

Rwenzururu's supporters were rolling back the bureaucracies and routines that formed the architecture of the Ugandan state. When

Isaya Mukirane (seated, center) and his son, Charles Wesley Mumbere (standing next to him), pose in front of the Rwenzururu flag, 1962 (Courtesy family of Tom Stacey)

Obote's government organized a national census in 1969, Rwenzururu's leaders warned that people who agreed to be counted would be killed.[25] A few weeks later the kingdom's prime minister wrote to Kampala with a list of organizations that he wanted the Uganda government to withdraw from Rwenzururu's territory. Among them were the National Ugandan Youth Organization, the National Trading Corporation, and the Agriculture Department.[26] Rwenzururu was "no longer part of either Uganda or Congo Republic governments," the prime minister wrote. It was "now an independent sovereign state."

People, like organizations, had to be pushed out of Rwenzururu. In the early months of 1963 Rwenzururu's leaders threatened to kill the chiefs of the Tooro kingdom living in the mountains. The terrified chiefs came down from the mountains and took shelter at government buildings in the lowlands.[27] Critics of Mukirane's movement were placed under house arrest by Rwenzururu's leaders. At the height of the Rwenzururu war government officials estimated that 5,000 people had fled the high-lands and were living, as refugees, in the lowlands.[28]

From the start, the kingdom's leaders looked for ways to align their struggle with other Ugandans' campaigns for cultural and political inde-pendence. They were particularly impressed with Buganda's struggle for self-government. In May 1966 the prime minister of Rwenzururu wrote an open letter meant to "help and comfort the Baganda in the kingdom of Bu-ganda."[29] Milton Obote's army had assaulted Buganda's palace, driving the Kabaka into an unhappy exile. Rwenzururu's leaders expressed "their heart feelings for this sad news for such an embarrassing situation." Rwenzururu did not have an army that could fight for Buganda, but they could make their kingdom a safe haven: the prime minister instructed "all Rwenzur-uru" to "get together and let us help the Baganda." Buganda's struggle against Obote's tyranny was their own. "You Obote, a Langi, ex-Uganda Republican Government: you are given this letter cursing you from the Kingdom of Rwenzururu and Buganda," wrote the insurgents' prime min-ister. He ended the letter by referring to Romans 13, verses 1 through 4. "The powers that be are ordained by God," it read. The prime minister ar-gued that Obote was "not respecting the God of Rwenzururu and Buganda kingdom governments. You are determined to demolish all of them."

In the archives of Kabarole District there is a printed flyer produced by Obote's administration.[30] It was a piece of propaganda, one of many leaflets that the Obote government distributed to convince mountaineers of the folly of rebellion. A Rwenzururu censor defaced almost every part of the leaflet. With a ballpoint pen he crossed out the government coat of arms on the top of the page, and wrote "It is cursed" next to it. He stamped the flyer with a Rwenzururu seal on the upper corner, crossed out the smiling portrait of Milton Obote, and inked out the president's eyes. Over the photo he wrote, "Mr. Obote, our enemy, go to Lango your home area." He likewise crossed out an article promising schools, hospitals, and other development projects. In the margins he wrote, "The friendship is not known by Rwenzururu kingdom."

Rwenzururu partisans were pushing away infrastructures and media that connected the mountains with the Ugandan republic. Communities of people had to be rearranged. Loyalties had to be clarified. Outsiders had to be purged. It was all a way of building a political community that was, in some way, free.[31]

Isaya Mukirane—schoolteacher, homespun historian, king—died in September 1966, a few months after Milton Obote crushed the kingdom of Buganda. In other parts of Uganda populist political movements faded from view during the late 1960s, as the Obote government consolidated its power. The Rwenzururu movement was to thrive during the political tumult. Immediately after Mukirane's death a delegation from Rwenzururu visited the lowlands, asking a surprised schoolteacher for help in securing the chemicals necessary to embalm the dead king's body.[32] Rwenzururu's minister of justice led the delegation. In an interview he told me that they had hoped to create a mausoleum, where partisans could view the preserved body of their dead king.[33] The funeral of Mukirane was held on 23 October.[34] The son of the dead king, Charles Wesley Mumbere, was a teenager. The kingdom's prime minister therefore became regent until, in 1971, Charles Wesley reached a mature age.

The vigor with which Rwenzururu administrators conducted government business increased in the 1970s, as the bureaucratic dysfunction of Idi Amin's regime became more pronounced. At a time when shortages made it difficult for Ugandan civil servants to transact even the most basic administrative tasks, Rwenzururu's leaders could count on their people's financial and political support. In one county Rwenzururu loyalists built a new administrative headquarters, consisting of a house for the county chief, a dormitory for policemen, and a prison cell. All of the new buildings were roofed with thatch.[35] There was a schedule on which Rwenzururu tax collectors appeared in local markets: at Kyanya market they came on Thursdays; at Maliba market Saturday was tax day; at Katoke it was Friday.[36] At a time when the Amin government struggled to place officials in permanent posts, Rwenzururu's Public Service Commission regularly updated staff assignments and filled vacancies, even in the lowest levels of administration.[37]

Early in 1973 police intelligence sent the minister of internal affairs an assessment of Rwenzururu's strength.[38] In two of the counties that Rwenzururu claimed the insurgents had about 270 men under arms. Most of them were teenagers. They were armed with knives, bows and arrows, and slingshots. Very few possessed firearms. Rwenzururu security forces were smartly turned out: the army wore black uniforms with ropes as lanyards, while the police wore rough khaki uniforms with crossed belts. At a time when Uganda's army was at war with its people, Rwenzururu's soldiery could rely on widespread support: messages and reports from the insurgents' leaders were entrusted to anyone, including women and children, who willingly carried Rwenzururu correspondence up and down the mountains. By 1977 the rebels were said to be manufacturing homemade guns in the mountains. Police intelligence estimated that they possessed around thirty rifles of different calibers.[39]

Officials of the Amin government considered Rwenzururu's bureaucrats to be "thieves [who are] using force day and night." "Even though they are calling themselves Government," Amin's officials wrote, "we know we have only got one Government."[40] In fact it was the rebel bureaucrats—not the officials of the Amin government—who commanded local people's loyalties. On one occasion a government chief and his police escort encountered a force of 150 men, clad in Rwenzururu uniforms and "marching very threateningly in Army style." The Rwenzururu force attacked the chief and his companions and did not retreat in the face of rifle fire. For the whole of the pitched battle that followed, women and children from the surrounding villages stood on the hillsides, cheering the Rwenzururu men on and urging them to fight with courage.[41]

It was not only military force that inspired the kingdom's patriotism. Rwenzururu's architects aimed to build a separate culture, too. Shortly after the kingdom's foundation Rwenzururu partisans wrote to the Anglican archbishop, demanding that the church use the Konzo language, not the Tooro language, in liturgy and in prayers.[42] By 1971 the kingdom was appointing its own clergymen. At a public meeting King Charles Wesley read out a fifty-eight-page statement, ordering church leaders to send their collections to a newly formed Ministry of Religious Affairs.[43] By 1976 Rwenzururu partisans were demanding that couples who wished to marry obtain a license from the kingdom's registrars. On one occasion Rwenzururu partisans appeared at a church to confirm that the bridegroom had obtained the necessary certificate. The wedding went forward when he produced the required paperwork, but the Rwenzururu men arrested four teenagers attired in bell-bottomed trousers, citing their crime as "wearing awful clothing that were against Rwenzururu customs."[44]

Grounded in the patriotism of its people, Rwenzururu could command allegiance. Here was an effective administration that could convert local people's support and energy into visible progress. At a time when—for many Ugandans—the dictatorial government in Kampala was increasingly malign, here was a homeland for which men and women would willingly fight and die.

Rwenzururu soldiers confront a visiting journalist, 1962 (Courtesy family of Tom Stacey)

For Rwenzururu patriots Idi Amin's radio station was a prison cell. It stifled their ambitions, silenced their voices, and made the authority of Uganda's government seem to be above dispute. Throughout the history of their rebellion partisans made constant efforts to find media that could circumvent the broadcasting power of Uganda's media.

When a British journalist visited Isaya Mukirane at his mountaintop capital in 1963, he found him, rapt and focused, listening to radio broadcasts beamed from Kampala.[45] He and other Rwenzururu leaders were outraged at what they heard. "You are merciless to the People whom you are betraying and destroying without even a broadcast," wrote a Rwenzururu official in a letter to Uganda's government. The radio reports masked the brutality of Uganda's armed forces and allowed officials to avoid being "ashamed in Africa."[46] Rwenzururu listeners' outrage was amplified in the 1970s, after Idi Amin came to power. President Amin's "[blind] misdeeds and benighted provisions [are] radioed and promulgated, extentioned, and diffused via information and broadcasting," complained the kingdom's prime minister.[47] Their exclusion from the airwaves was a constant source of irritation for Rwenzururu partisans. It was "astonishing," the king told President Amin, that the views of their opponents were "broadcasted on Radio Uganda—while the true and reasonable documents of news from Rwenzururu reach you and they are not broadcasted."[48]

The postal system—like the radio service—seemed to be conspiring against Rwenzururu's leaders. They were sure that unscrupulous clerks were opening Rwenzururu's correspondence and destroying it. "A lot of letters from the Rwenzururu Government are often addressed to you," wrote the king in a letter to world leaders, but "most of them are opened and caught by the East African Posts and Telecommunications staff then thrown away."[49] That was "why you don't get Rwenzururu ideas and sufferings." A great many people had cause to complain about the efficiency of the post office during the years of Idi Amin's presidency. But Rwenzururu's leaders felt that they were uniquely targeted for censorship. Rwenzururu's king told Kenyan president Jomo Kenyatta that "we always call and inform the O.A.U. General Secretary ... to confirm a quickest assistance to Rwenzururians." Notwithstanding their efforts, "all our letters [that] reach East African Post and Telecommunications are nefariously funneled into baskets."[50]

The ordinary means of communication were closed to them. Rwenzururu's officials circumvented the official machinery by placing their correspondence in the custody of the people. There were a great number of delivery routes. In one instance Rwenzururu agents tacked three undated letters to trees in the neighborhood around Bundibugyo. The letters threatened the people of the town with death if they cooperated with the Uganda government.[51] In another instance Rwenzururu supporters left copies of a pamphlet authored by their prime minister lying around the bus terminal in Kasese town.[52] It took weeks or sometimes months for letters composed in the mountain heights to reach their intended audience. One letter, addressed to fishermen living in a village on the edge of Lake Edward, was dated 25 February. It was found lying on a pathway near the village on 22 April.[53]

Here was a delivery system that was deliberate and slow.[54] Rwenzururu's correspondence rested on an apparatus that was unprofessional, winding, and unplanned. That was the point. Letters composed by Rwenzururu's leaders passed through many hands as they made their way to their recipients. One exemplary letter, composed by the kingdom's

Isaya Mukirane writing (Courtesy family of Tom Stacey)

prime minister in 1967, illuminates the idiosyncrasy of Rwenzururu's postal communication.[55] It was addressed to the following:

Secretary General, Organization of African Unity
Addis Ababa, Africa

The Hon'able U Thant, General Secretary
United Nations Organization, New York, America

The Chairman
World Human Rights Council

The European
United Nations

The following were copied on the letter:

The Chairman, Uganda National Assembly
The Foreign Countries
The Uganda Information Newspapers
The United Nations Military
The Liberation Special Committee
The World Information Newspapers
The Rwenzururu Kingdom Government Officials

There were no postbox numbers or street addresses. Neither were there postcodes. Rwenzururu leaders were sending their letters out like a farmer sowing his seed. Yolamu Mulima, the kingdom's prime minister in the 1970s, told me that Rwenzururu's leaders used to rely on students to deliver their correspondence to Kampala. They presumed that their missives—however indiscriminate in their address, however slow their mode of delivery—would find their destination, whether through the help of knowledgeable travelers or through the public-spiritedness of strangers. The delivery of correspondence rested on the connections, commitments, and itineraries of ordinary people, who were—by happenstance or by appointment—made into delivery agents.

Rwenzururu's leaders would not accept the machinery of the Ugandan state as the container in which their community was to exist. They were constantly searching for bigger frameworks in which to place their emergent state. Isaya Mukirane first wrote to United Nations secretary-general U Thant in November 1962, asking for "protection against the Uganda disturbers government which has failed to protect us properly."[56] A year later Mukirane asked for a contingent of United Nations peacekeepers, who would support the "weaponless Rwenzururu Kingdom military" against the Uganda government.[57] None of these petitions received a reply. So, in 1968, the kingdom's leaders organized a delegation to personally present their case to the United Nations in New York. The group traveled by car to Rwanda, intending to fly from Kigali to New York. They had with them several files full of letters.[58] The Rwandan police intercepted the delegates in Kigali. When the police searched them, they found they had tens of thousands of Uganda shillings in their luggage.[59] The money had been collected, over the course of months, from thousands of donors in the mountains.

Rwenzururu's partisans were trying to draw international diplomats into their local affairs. It was an enduring strategy. In 1971 Charles Wesley—newly installed as king of Rwenzururu—wrote to Jomo Kenyatta, then head of the East African Community. The king urged Kenyatta not to "neglect the Rwenzururuians as dead persons, vagrants, chimpanzees and foolish people who cannot form a government."[60] A year later, in 1972, King Charles wrote to the United Nations and the Organization of African Unity, asking the organizations' leaders to come to a meeting in Kampala, where "high powered ministers" of Rwenzururu could "distribute their sufferings openly face to face."[61]

The archives of the United Nations are located in an unmarked, anonymous office building in New York City. The files about Uganda are voluminous, full of details about the technical work that United Nations agencies did. Nowhere in the whole of the archive are there petitions from Rwenzururu. If U Thant, Kurt Waldheim, and their colleagues did receive correspondence from Rwenzururu secessionists, then the files were destroyed. In fact, there are scarcely any documents produced by the hundreds of dissident and separatist organizations who petitioned the United Nations in the 1950s, '60s, and '70s. Out of the tens of thousands of pages that must have been sent to the United Nations, the archivists seem to have kept only one file, numbered S-0974-025-4. The file is titled "Courageous Nuts." It contains, among other things, bits of correspondence from the "Head of State, Republic of South Moluccas," who laid claim to part of Indonesia. The United Nations had no interest in advancing the cause of these and other separatists. Today, it has little reason for preserving their memory.

The same is true for other diplomatic archives. The British National Archives holds no correspondence from Rwenzururu's leaders. Neither does the Library and Archives of Canada, or the Israeli State Archives. In the archives of the U.S. State Department there is a single document from Rwenzururu's avid petitioners. It was received by the American embassy in Kampala in 1970. The ambassador was surprised to receive the letter: he and other diplomats had thought Rwenzururu was abating. It was, he remarked, an "obscure African struggle."[62]

The energy with which Rwenzururu's leaders pursued international diplomats was not met with attention, support, or even acknowledgment. Why, then, did those leaders keep writing? It was because their audience was not in New York, Ottawa, Geneva, London, or Nairobi. Their audience was in Bwera, Muhokya, and Kasese—Ugandan localities whose people Rwenzururu claimed to lead. All of their letters were copied to Rwenzururu audiences: to "Rwenzururu Citizens," to "Rwenzururu Kingdom Government Offices," or to the "Rwenzururu Government Officials and Authoritatives." Once the movement's leaders had composed their letters by hand, secretaries would type them out on one of several machines that the rebels maintained.[63] Dozens of copies of every letter were circulated around the mountains of western Uganda. Rwenzururu chiefs regularly convened public meetings attended by hundreds of people, where they read out letters that they had received from the kingdom's leaders.[64] Many of Rwenzururu's supporters had never seen Isaya Mukirane or Charles Wesley Mumbere in person, but they knew them through a media infrastructure that made their leaders' correspondence—ostensibly composed for a few recipients—into open letters.

Rwenzururu leaders invited partisans to question Idi Amin's logic and listen with a critical ear to his radio broadcasts. It was a practice that fed political dissidence. In May 1972, for instance, Radio Uganda broadcast a report concerning a group of petitioners who had approached President Amin, asking him to create a new district government at Kasese, a town at the core of Rwenzururu's domain. Upon hearing the report the prime minister of Rwenzururu typed out a lengthy circular letter reminding partisans about their political vocation. The proposal for a new district, he urged, was a plot to "put you into a trap and throw [you] in a ditch [out] of which you will never come."

> I wish to remind and advise you, Rwenzururu citizens, that you should respect yourselves and remember that as people who are within their own land you have the responsibility of constructing a proper Rwenzururu. Since 1830 our great grandfathers have never ceased to fight for our power, and in reality for the peace of the people of Rwenzururu. ... We also are fighting for the same cause.[65]

Here was a narrative that ran against the government's media, communicated in an infrastructure that worked outside the official channels. It challenged Idi Amin's government, encouraging critical listenership.

Rwenzururu's media infrastructure was decidedly low-tech. The Amin government had invested in powerful new medium-wave broadcasting towers to expand the national radio network and amplify the president's dictates. Rwenzururu's leaders relied on the attention and dedication of its people to convey their messages from the center. They were always looking for ways to expand the impact of the modest media with which they worked, to reach other senses and convey wider sentiments. In February 1972 police manning a road barrier in the lowlands stopped and searched a Rwenzururu emissary named Alifonse Mazimora.[66] In his possession were two photographs of Charles Wesley Mumbere, newly installed as king of Rwenzururu. In one of them the king wears a suit and stands outside a house with mudded walls. In his right hand he carries a flag, and in his left there is a briefcase. On the back a Rwenzururu propagandist wrote:

> A nephew, Charles M. Wesley, son of Isaya Mukirane. Now who is 20 years of age. In his suit, Charles is with a national flag.

The other photo shows the king in a military uniform, with polished shoes, puttees, and a tie. On the back side is written:

> Our C in C, Charles M. Wesley, son of Mukirane, pictured taking the salute. Together with him there is a national flag and a national spear. Charles is pictured while he is wearing his commander in chief's uniform. Wesley is now 20 years old.

The photos were among a collection of typed Rwenzururu documents that Mazimora had in his possession. Like the public letters the Rwenzururu leaders composed, the photographs were meant to be handed around at public assemblies and grasped by faithful patriots. Their purpose was to deepen people's attachment to their leader, making him seem like a relative, not a potentate. They were meant to inspire people's affection for their king.

———

The most remarkable of the open letters that Rwenzururu's leaders composed were drafted in the early 1970s, when Isaya Mukirane's son and successor, Charles Wesley, conducted a one-sided correspondence with Idi Amin.

King Charles wrote to Uganda's president for the first time in May 1971, four months after the coup that had brought Amin to power.[67] In the letter—typed and carbon-copied to the United Nations, the Organization of African Unity, and the editors of *Newsweek* and other publications—the

king congratulated President Amin and exulted in the overthrow of Rwenzururu's longtime nemesis, Milton Obote. Obote had seen himself as a
"Worldly God," wrote King Charles. He "thought that he is immortal and
he never think [*sic*] that there will be another man behind him." It was possible—in these early days of innocence—for King Charles to describe Idi
Amin as a liberator. "I know that you were sent by God so that his people
should have the complete liberty and settle their disputes between each
other," he wrote. The king was particularly impressed with the funeral of
the deceased Kabaka of Buganda, which the Amin government had orches-
trated. It was in his view "a marvel and sensible action to all Ugandans."

The king's pleasure with Amin's rise to power did not last long. Early
in 1973 President Amin announced over Radio Uganda that he intended
to give the people of the mountains their own district. In reply, King
Charles insisted—in capital letters—that "RWENZURURU IS AN INDEPEN-
DENT NATION. . . . . WE MUST NOT WELCOME A DISTRICT." King Charles argued that Rwenzururu's people deserved freedom from Uganda's heavy
hand.

> President, you must not be as the imperialists and colonialists
> who always want to milk, mistreat and rule over the entire Africa
> which is not their [land]. You and I are the sons of Africa, what's
> why you must consider the Rwenzururuians who are suffering
> just for the sake of their freedom and authority seized from
> them.[68]

A month later, in March 1973, Idi Amin called on Rwenzururu's partisans
to lay down their weapons, in return for which they would be given amnesty.[69] King Charles saw it as an affront to his kingdom's sovereignty. It
was a parting of the ways. King Charles had previously asked President
Amin to regard Rwenzururu's people as fellow freedom-fighters. Now he
adopted a defiant stance. "You are restricted and strongly prescribed on
your republican provisions and from taking intervention into Rwenzururu kingdom government affairs," the king told the president, again
using capital letters at the start of his letter.[70] Rwenzururu had "no time
to waste in supplicating before Uganda Government because Uganda
Government has no power to grant peace to Rwenzururians, merely God
himself—who created our country." He went on at considerable length,
laying out the case for an independent Rwenzururu. Rwenzururu's
people were

well known as the true inhabitants of their country, who have taken a long run in military confrontation and have taken 143 years on restoration to power—peace and traditional cultures of our country. Obviously, foreign invaders like you have tried to take our estates—but have failed completely.

The text was a word-for-word repetition of letters that Rwenzururu's leaders had composed in the 1960s. It was a liturgy, a catechism, reminding readers and listeners of the essential elements of their struggle. Did the crowds that gathered in the mountains recite the key phrases together, as the letter was read out for them by a Rwenzururu official? The formula would have been familiar from the history lessons that Isaya Mukirane and his fellow researchers had given them.

Having reminded Rwenzururu listeners of their purpose, King Wesley was keen to undermine Idi Amin's political claim: to be at the vanguard of African struggles against racism and apartheid. The Amin government was dragooning Ugandans into service as frontline warriors in the theater of international conflict. King Charles argued that Amin was an oppressor, not a liberator.

You are going to command and send Barbarians army and air force, then startle and hunt to death Rwenzururians ... and expel them off their country disturbing them [just as] Europeans are still disturbing Africans in African countries, e.g. Rhodesia, Angola, Musabique [*sic*], South Africa, and Guinea Bissau, who have done no errors in Africa as a whole, except that they were fighting for their liberty in Africa.[71]

The king was turning the tables on the Amin government. The Ugandan war against Rwenzururu, he argued, was like Ian Smith's campaign against black Zimbabweans, or the apartheid state's war against South Africa's black nationalists. It was an assault on an independent people's way of life. King Charles promised to resist Amin's aggression.

We shall have to stand firmly in control and manumition [*sic*] of our motherland with our few weapons of massive annihilation, for God's power and his deliverance we shall have ambushed and tumbled them in a total defeatism and triumph their reactionary Forces [*sic*].

It was a fortification for wavering souls, a reminder of shared purpose, a call for solidity and commitment. It was also an exposé, meant to highlight the hypocrisy of Amin's claims to continental leadership.

The king returned to this theme a few months later, in May 1973, when he renewed his correspondence with Uganda's president. Here again the king showed Idi Amin to be on the wrong side of history. As the king wrote, Israeli fighter jets had just shot down a Libyan airliner, killing 108 of its 113 passengers, and Israeli commandos had raided Beirut, killing three leaders of the Palestine Liberation Organization. King Charles was aware of these and other instances of Israeli aggression. He argued that President Amin was, like the Israelis, "pending to react such insensitive, disaster and absurdity exploiters [sic]."⁷² King Charles argued that Uganda's government was no different than Israel's. Amin's bloody aggression endangered the lives of the innocent. In this as in his other correspondence King Charles buttressed the courage of Rwenzururu partisans.

> Although Uganda Army and Air Forces come to capitulate on land and in the Air with Air-Bombing-Crafts and Army equipments, we shall not surrender, threat and leave our Mother-land Rwenzururu. Our Heavenly God in heaven will conceal us into extremity Caves where no one can see and your Army will be straying and off our sight, and all Rwenzururuian Mountain Spirituals and God's Host with shape [sic] swords will fight, repel totally and cool off your Arrogant Army.

Life off the grid, the king told his listeners, was a life of independence and freedom. The very geography of their mountainous home set them beyond the reach of Idi Amin's government, making it impossible for Uganda's military, or its technology, to subdue them.

There is a final letter to Idi Amin, sent by Yolamu Mulima, the kingdom's prime minister, in April 1973. Mulima's missive was a comprehensive indictment of the Amin regime, contrasting the promises Amin had made with the realities of dictatorship and misgovernment. Amin, wrote the prime minister, had "predicated and radioed" the following:

> 1. That the elucidation of Dada [Amin's nickname] meant the Redeemer of Mankind who would solve problems of the Sufferers and Secure them from Slavery, Colonial rules and Draconian Legislations.

2. That you were sent by God to manumit the Innocent People from serious heroic initial potential attacks and slaughter.

3. That one of the Major undertakings why you Expelled Obote regime ... was to terminate and solve our longstanding [disputes] and problems that [afflicted] Rwenzururians within a hundred forty three years struggle Anti-Foreign invaders. . . .

6. That you would crush burglary, Swindling, Murderers, Robberies, and other corrupted elements as inclined by Eighteen reasons submitted by the Uganda Army that prescribed the downfall of Obote.[73]

All of these promises had signaled a dramatic change in Uganda's politics. All of them were lies. It had become clear, wrote the prime minister, that "you are revising the same plot by [the Tooro kingdom], the invaders who hanged and killed our Brave innocent posterities in 1919."

I interviewed Yolamu Mulima on two occasions.[74] As a younger man he had helped Isaya Mukirane conduct the research of the Bakonzo Life History Society. In the 1970s the society's research findings were kept in typed, hard-covered files, locked in a wooden box. As prime minister he had the only key to the box. On occasion he would remove the box's contents and dry the papers in the sun, as they became damp in the mountains' mist. They were the originals. But there were copies dispersed throughout the mountains. In every Rwenzururu chief's office there were files of historical papers, memoranda, and research notes. Rwenzururu's archive was dispersed, held in the hands of the generality of its partisan supporters. It was a way of ensuring that the historical record would not be lost to posterity.

One curator of Rwenzururu's dispersed national archive was Francisco Mubiru, a Rwenzururu leader who lived in Busaru, on the western side of the Rwenzori mountains. When the police arrested him he was found to possess sixty-two documents.[75] There were several typed judgments issued by Rwenzururu courts. There was a list of people who had paid taxes to the kingdom. There was a letter from Rwenzururu soldiers asking for payment for their work. There was a letter from a father, complaining that his son had been beaten by Rwenzururu men. There was a copy of a Rwenzururu cabinet minute concerning the appointment of a county chief. For the Uganda government authorities all of this was evidence of criminality: they typed up an inventory of the archive and used it to indict Mr. Mubiru as an agent of an illegal organization. For

Mubiru and for many other partisans the archive was a critical resource, a tool of administration, a record of sacrifice and heroism.

The Rwenzururu kingdom did not have a radio station. It did not have the correct postal addresses of the many eminent people addressed in its petitions. It did not have an arsenal full of modern weaponry.[76] Amin's government was master of the airwaves, and its military power far outstripped Rwenzururu's meager armaments. But Rwenzururu could rely on the memories of its people. The lessons of history—clarified out of the research done in the 1950s—taught Rwenzururu's people to see themselves as engaged in an ongoing struggle against oppression. In their archives they had stored a record of their campaign against the dictatorial governments of Milton Obote and Idi Amin. Here was material they could use to highlight the hypocrisies of Uganda's leaders, condemn their failures to fulfill their promises, and expose their posturing, their self-interest, and their brutality.

—————

The Rwenzururu kingdom was to outlast the presidency of Idi Amin. As I detail in the following chapter, the army of Tanzania invaded Uganda in the last months of 1978, driving Amin's soldiers northward in disarray. Rwenzururu partisans collected several truckloads full of weapons and ammunition from Amin's defeated and demoralized men.[77] By May 1980 Rwenzururu partisans were fully in command of Kasese town. They were so confident in their position that the mother of King Charles came down from the mountains for a celebratory fête. Everywhere she was celebrated, and, according to her critics, "anyone who did not adore her was kicked."[78]

Two weeks after Amin's ouster King Charles Wesley wrote to the president of Uganda's newly formed government, offering "many congratulations to you to defend the lives of Ugandans who have been thrown into the endless hole." Amin's regime had been a catalogue of woe: Amin had used his "gloomy power of Dictatorship in my nation Rwenzururu . . . in sending his barbarian troops entering the borders of my nation Rwenzururu using brutal malicious actions." For the insurgent king Amin's overthrow was an opportunity to recast Rwenzururu's relationship with the government in Kampala. King Charles proposed a détente: "I humbly invite you that you should rule your country, Uganda, while you are recognizing Rwenzururu as an independent nation which is no longer under the domination of Uganda," he proposed.

The proposal was by no means new: Rwenzururu's leaders had been claiming their independence since the early 1960s. But by the 1980s King Charles was in a position of strength. The new Ugandan government—desperate to exert some sort of control over local affairs—gave Rwenzururu's king the final word in the composition of a new government for Kasese.[79] The king chose Blasio Maate as the new district commissioner. Maate's credentials were impeccable: an early member of the Bakonzo Life History Research Society, he had spent four months in a government prison, convicted as a Rwenzururu partisan.[80] The commander of the kingdom's army was to be the district's chief of police.[81] In September 1980 King Charles appointed a cohort of new councilors for the district: twenty-seven men, all of them Rwenzururu partisans.[82]

There followed a "mini-Marshall plan," organized by the Ugandan government for the benefit of the region's people.[83] Rwenzururu's partisans demanded that, in recognition of their long service, they should receive pensions from Uganda's government. They asked for free education for their children, an exemption from taxes, and shops for ex-partisans.[84] They demanded that the names of the streets in Kasese be changed to honor Rwenzururu's heroes.[85] All of these demands reflected a serious conviction. Standing in the wreckage of the Amin regime, Rwenzururu's partisans could see themselves as Ugandan patriots, whose struggle against tyranny entitled them to enjoy recognition and honor from other Ugandans. The Ugandan government agreed to cover the kingdom's debt, which totaled 2.5 million shillings.[86] It also agreed to wipe the slate clean of illegality. Partisans were not held liable for the acts of violence they had committed over the course of their struggle.[87]

There were more than 20,000 people gathered on the day in August 1982 when Charles Wesley Mumbere, king of Rwenzururu, came down from the mountains and declared that the war was at an end. His speech, which lasted for over two hours, began with a history lesson. "Before the British set foot in Uganda," the king said, "the [Konzo] were a separate people from the then Toro kingdom."[88] He described the deaths of the ancient heroes, hanged by the British for their refusal to bend the knee to colonial government. Even now, said the king, the memory of the mountains' martyrs "evokes not only a feeling of deep anguish and suffering but also a feeling of patriotism and a belief in the eventual victory for justice." The king ended his speech by reflecting on the lessons of the past. When it came time to write the history of Rwenzururu, said the king, he hoped that historians would "seriously take into account our social and political interests and respect our cultural identity."

It was a victory, but it was also a capitulation. To become Ugandans, King Charles and his colleagues were obliged to compress their political ambitions to fit within the boundaries of the Ugandan state. The office equipment that had formerly upheld Rwenzururu's dissident media was re-located, carried down from the heights and installed in the offices of Kas-ese District. There were four typewriters and one duplicating machine.[89] A committee was created—the "Kasese District Elders Committee"—with the king, twenty-eight years old, as the district's "Chief Elder." The com-mittee's membership consisted of the most prominent members of the Rwenzururu movement.[90] Soon after their installation the elders commit-tee had a long discussion concerning the "dignity of the elders," resolving to "look for ways of making the chiefs and the masses realize the impor-tance and the role of the elders in the district."[91] Their discomfiture reflected their distance from real, substantive authority.

That is how—in the aftermath of Amin's fall—government in western Uganda was rebuilt. The combative activists of the mountains were made into gentlemen, into elders. Their expansive and innovative political proj-ect was compressed into a culture. Their instruments of organization and community building were made into traditions. The mechanisms of the heritage industry were a means of transforming their political struggle into a distant memory, their patriotic fury into nostalgia, and their freedom into citizenship within the Republic of Uganda.[92]

CHAPTER ELEVEN

Liberating Uganda?

IDI AMIN'S REGIME INVENTED enemies, launched campaigns, put Ugandans on the front lines, and made history. The end came more quickly than anyone expected.

On the morning of 30 October 1978, thousands of Uganda Army troops crossed into northwest Tanzania and occupied the Kagera Salient, an area of 710 square miles.[1] A spokesman boasted that the invasion had been accomplished at "supersonic speed," in a mere twenty-five minutes.[2] Ugandan soldiers killed as many as 1,500 Tanzanian civilians, leaving their bodies to rot in the sun.[3] Amin toured the region in the company of cameramen from Uganda Television, posing in front of a Tanzanian bank building and exhorting his soldiers to prepare for a counterattack from Uganda's enemies.[4] Tanzania's president, Julius Nyerere, called Amin a "modern day Hitler," and the Tanzanian government newspaper warned that "we are not going to give up one inch of our territory to the buffoon to satisfy his ego."[5] Amin was unmoved by this or other warnings. Two sons were born to President Amin in November 1978. One, borne by his senior wife, he named "Kagera River," after the river that had demarcated the border between Uganda and Tanzania. The other, birthed by his youngest wife, he named "Kyaka," the name of the region his army had captured.[6]

It took two months for the Tanzanians to organize their army. In January 1979 they pushed through the contested region, crossed the international border, and invaded Uganda. In their company were militias composed of Ugandan exiles. Amin's army put up an incompetent defense. The tank drivers were apparently incapacitated with alcohol and drugs, their machines lacked spare parts and ammunition, and—according to the Tanzanians—they had prostitutes with them in the cockpits.[7] The Tanzanians made rapid progress: Masaka, a major town west of Kampala, fell to Tanzanian troops on 24 February; the following day Mbarara, leading town of the south, also fell.[8] Libyan ruler Muammar Gaddafi sent a force of soldiers to Amin's aid, but by early April much of the Uganda Army had dissolved. The Libyans were left to defend Kampala by themselves.[9] On 11 April 1979 the victorious Tanzanians and their Ugandan allies marched into Uganda's capital.[10] Idi Amin fled to Libya, and from there to Saudi Arabia, where he lived until his death in 2003.

The rapid collapse of Amin's regime caught Ugandan officials off guard. Alex Owor, governor of Western Province, had been an enthusiastic advocate of the many campaigns that Idi Amin had launched. He had paraded around his province, demanding discipline and exactitude. Governor Owor found it hard to comprehend the threat the invading Tanzanians posed. At a meeting early in February 1979 he warned that "saboteurs had entered Uganda from Tanzania." He ordered the police to guard the province's banks day and night, and fretted that there was no fence around his official residence.[11] In early March, after Masaka and Mbarara fell to Tanzanian troops, Owor warned against the "unwarranted panic which has caused many people to abandon their homes."[12] By late March the Tanzanian army was just outside Kampala, and there were thousands of refugees spilling into Owor's province. At a security meeting Governor Owor said nothing about the war. Instead, he lamented the moral condition of the young. There were "rumour mongers and law breakers" lounging about in the province's towns. He ordered the police to clean up the city streets and resettle urban idlers on government-run farms.[13]

Owor had spent the 1970s pursuing scapegoats that Idi Amin's government had imagined. In 1979, facing an enemy that was very real, he carried on his campaign against spectral threats. He fought the wars of his time, not the war that had, quite suddenly, come upon him.

Some people did answer the call to duty. As the Tanzanians closed in on Kampala, Amin's cabinet ministers called on ex-servicemen to rejoin the Uganda Army.[14] A considerable number of people enlisted to defend Amin's regime. One hundred twenty men from Jinja signed up for military service in those last days of March 1979. All of them could produce receipts showing that they had faithfully paid taxes over the course of several years. Most of them had Christian baptismal names.[15] Were they press-ganged into the ranks? Or did they feel themselves led, as patriots, to defend Amin's government?

Many people were caught unawares by Amin's downfall. There was little time for organizing or planning. Ugandan exiles in Nairobi, Dar es Salaam, or London had spent the 1970s composing damning exposés about Idi Amin's regime and planning unlikely schemes to oust him. In March 1979 the Tanzanian government convened a meeting to coordinate the exile groups.[16] The twenty groups that assembled represented contradictory interests. There was the Uganda People's Congress, the party of Milton Obote's defunct government. There was the Uganda Action Group, based in London, led by the ex-diplomat Paulo Muwanga. There was the Front for National Salvation, based in Dar es Salaam and led by a young radical named Yoweri Museveni. The delegates spent the first day arguing over credentials, and some of them nearly came to blows.[17] The exiles could agree that they would "never again allow a foreigner to rule us."[18] About the agenda of their government-in-waiting they had little to say.

The organization that emerged out of that contentious conference was called the Uganda National Liberation Front, known as the UNLF.[19] On 13 April, two days after Kampala fell to the Tanzanians, the leader of the UNLF was inaugurated as president of the Republic of Uganda. President Yusufu Lule was a university academic, not a political figure. He did not know the names of many of the people who served on the governing council.[20] A diplomat compared him to a "one-armed man with no experience hired as a head juggler for a bankrupt circus."[21] All of the accoutrements of his office had to be conjured up. On the day of President Lule's inauguration there were no chairs for dignitaries, as looters had stripped government offices bare. The Tanzanian colonel who organized the event acquired furniture by stopping looters on the street and requisitioning the chairs they were carrying.[22] There was no telephone or telegraph linking Kampala with Nairobi or London. Prices for basic commodities were skyrocketing: a British diplomat estimated that the rate of inflation was at 700 percent.[23] The Tanzanian troops were hard to control. The hotel in the city center was full of soldiers shooting wildly into the ceilings.[24]

The remarkable thing is that, even in those most challenging times, the UNLF government made serious attempts to engage Ugandans in discussion about the past and future of their country. President Lule's first official act was to ask the assembly gathered for his inauguration to pray for "those who have died at the hands of Idi Amin."[25] The campaigns that the Amin government had launched were at an end. For a brief time, in 1979 and early 1980, the urgent tempo of politics slowed. A census was made to name and number the Ugandans who had died fighting against Idi Amin's regime. The government collected the names of widows and orphans bereaved by Amin's soldiers.[26] Godfrey Binaisa, who replaced Professor Lule as president in June 1979, announced that the building of the State Research Bureau, where so many people had been tortured and murdered, was to be turned into a national museum of atrocities. It would "teach the future generations the effects of dictatorial rule." Binaisa also vowed to turn Namanve Forest, where the bodies of the dead had been dumped, into a national cemetery.[27] In November he opened a war heroes monument in northern Uganda. It honored two men who had been executed by Idi Amin's soldiers in 1973.[28]

A reckoning with Uganda's bloody past seemed to be at hand. Candidates wishing to sit on the newly established National Consultative Council were obliged to fill in a form prepared by the UNLF authorities. It asked candidates to address a series of difficult questions about the future of Uganda. "What do you think should be the best method for handling Amin's State Research [Bureau] and other Amin agents?" was one question. In the newly catalogued files of the Uganda National Archives there are several thick files containing candidates' responses. One candidate wanted retribution: "reduce them to the level they reduced the level to. Those who shed blood should have theirs shed."[29] Another wanted them tried in court. "Do we have laws in Uganda? Do we have a High Court?" he asked. "If the answers are yes, then take them to court; if the answers are no, then keep them in custody until law is established."[30] A third wanted Amin's loyalists dispersed and resettled in remote places. Their villages should be seized by the state, the candidate advised, and made into universities.[31]

In some places residents earnestly discussed how local affairs ought to be run. In Fort Portal an assembly put together a list of selling prices that they hoped retailers would follow: bananas should be fifteen shillings a bunch; fish should be four shillings each; eggs should be one shilling each.[32] Another assembly wrote to the UNLF government with a systematic list of reforms. They wanted the army to be shrunk and the number of barracks to be reduced. They insisted that soldiers should be required to take written and oral examinations in English. They wanted schools to offer civics classes "in order to foster a deeper sense of national unity and consciousness in our youngsters and adults alike."[33] The assembly concluded the memorandum by asking that a monument to Julius Nyerere be built in Kampala; and in every provincial town a major street should be named after the Tanzanian president.

That was the world that earnest people conceived in the wake of Idi Amin's ouster. It is a tragedy that, for all their ambition, the idealistic men of the UNLF were unable to take control over the men with guns.[34] In Jinja, capital of the east, the invading Tanzanian army had been greeted by joyous, singing crowds as it marched down the town's high street, driving Idi Amin's disorganized troops before them. Three months after Amin's overthrow, though, local authorities reported that there was "now a general feeling of hatred for soldiers by the public."[35] Tanzanian soldiers were visiting the town's factories and demanding goods at absurdly low prices. If their overtures were refused, they threatened murder.[36] The residents of one subcounty set up a roadblock to deter thieves. When a soldier was stopped at the roadblock, he and his fellows attacked the nearby village, destroying forty houses and killing several people.[37]

Royalists of the defunct kingdom of Buganda were convinced that the UNLF government was working against their interests. "The joy of liberation has been shattered. Instability prevails. The future is gloomy. Your bloody socialistic ideas will never work in Uganda," wrote a group calling itself the "Lusty Ugandan Organization."[38] "Tanzania is controlling Uganda as its colony," wrote another organization, claiming that 150 Ugandans were dying daily in Tanzanians' hands.[39] By the middle of 1979 the British high commissioner in Kampala was receiving a "steady stream" of letters from critics of the UNLF government. One such petition came from a group calling itself the "Buganda Elders," who wrote to Queen Elizabeth as follows:

> Many thousands of Baganda have been killed and other thousands of Baganda are going to be killed. What UNLF wants is all Baganda to be scattered all over the world, homeless and have no state, only the Baganda to be slaves of the communist countries. ... It is your duty as Head of Commonwealth Countries to start arming the Baganda with sophisticated modern weapons.[40]

An activist wrote to Prime Minister Margaret Thatcher arguing that the British government "still has the right to defend Buganda Kingdom and intervene into this unhuman and murder regime which is supported by arrogant and megalomaniac President Nyerere." He was sure that Thatcher's Conservatives would "preserve the democratical [*sic*] agreements made between Buganda Kingdom and Her Majesty's Government" in 1900.[41] Standing at the end of a long and violent history of dispossession, Ganda royalists hoped to re-activate the bonds that had once structured their colonial relationship with Britain. At a time of dramatic upset their advocacy was decidedly antique. They hoped for a protectorate.

In December 1980 the UNLF organized a national election to choose a new government. The infrastructure was almost entirely borrowed from elsewhere. Uganda had not held a general election in twenty years. In September—three months before the election—the electoral commission wrote to foreign governments asking for 50 duplicating machines, 200 typewriters, 10,000 duplicating stencils, 15,000 ballot boxes, 15,000 padlocks, 250 calculators, and 12,000 lanterns.[42] They also needed one hundred Land Rovers to transport election materials. The apparatus for Uganda's 1980 election had to be hastily ferried in from London on a fleet of transport planes organized by the U.S. Air Force.[43]

The election in 1980 imposed weighty burdens on everyone involved.[44] Canadian diplomats were sure that a "free and fair election is impossible," and hoped only that the vote would be a "small step in the direction of stability."[45] There were not enough lamps to illuminate polling stations, so in many constituencies the counting of votes had to be done in the twilight hours or delayed until the following morning.[46] In the northwest there was ongoing violence between Amin loyalists and UNLF troops. Officials managed to register just a few dozen people prior to the election.[47] In Kasese, the town at the center of the Rwenzururu rebellion, Rwenzururu activists insisted that voters should support Milton Obote's party, the Uganda People's Congress. They barred candidates from other parties from the ballot.[48] In Gulu, in the north, there were so many voters that election officials ran out of ballot papers by 11:00 a.m.[49] There were serious accusations of malpractice. The leaders of the Uganda Patriotic Movement called the elections "one of the greatest farces in electoral history."[50]

The government that came to power after this bitterly contested election was led by Milton Obote, the man whom Idi Amin had ousted in 1971. Obote had spent the 1970s living in exile, writing bitter letters about the iniquities of Amin's regime. On the day he was sworn in—for the second time—as president, Obote promised a "new future" for Uganda.[51] In a speech over Radio Uganda he decried the "murder, terror, and ignorant economic policies practiced by the murderous regime" of Idi Amin. His new regime promised "peace and tranquility" to Uganda: curfews were to be lifted, roadblocks were to be removed, and soldiers were to be back in their barracks.[52]

It was a beguiling picture of a regime that was, from the start, on the way to collapse. In February 1981 a militia led by Yoweri Museveni began a guerrilla war against Obote's government. There followed—in the words of one of Uganda's leading historians—"four and one-half years of brute violence."[53] Museveni's insurgents vowed to "use any method at our disposal to uproot the Milton Obote dictatorship."[54] In March 1982 they made an attack on an army barracks near the center of Kampala, killing two soldiers. In response Obote's army went on a rampage. One hundred civilians living in the vicinity of the barracks were killed. People gathered for the Ash Wednesday mass at the Catholic cathedral were arrested by Obote's men. They were never seen again.[55] People living in Luweero, where Museveni's guerrillas were based, were rounded up by Obote's soldiers and held in detention camps. United Nations observers reported that thousands of women and children interned in the camps were poorly fed and lacked medical care.[56] An Amnesty International report revealed that, under President Obote, "the killing of unarmed civilians by the army has again become widespread."[57] The Catholic and Anglican bishops, together with the head of the Muslim community, issued a statement decrying the "groanings, tears, sighs and pains of the people of Uganda."[58] "The Uganda you lead is bleeding to death," they told President Obote. "It needs a Good Samaritan to give it first aid and healing."

———

In January 1986, Yoweri Museveni's militia—called the National Resistance Army—won its long war against the Uganda government, marched into Kampala, and founded a new order.

Museveni was not the Good Samaritan for whom religious leaders had hoped. He and his people were revolutionaries.[59] "In the annals of history, no language can be too harsh an indictment" of Milton Obote and Idi Amin, wrote Museveni and his colleagues. Two decades of bad government had loosened the moorings of civilization itself. "Our society is demoralized, disillusioned and in disarray. The future of the nation's coming generations is bleak and irretrievable," wrote Museveni's party.[60] He and his colleagues promised to make a clean break with the past. The new government set up representative bodies—called "resistance councils"—to govern Uganda's localities. "Who is a member of a Resistance Council?" asked an official in Kasese District. He was

> the model of the new man. . . . He is the individual who has moved beyond the classical solution to human problems. . . . It is thus necessary that this individual member be completely disencumbered of a shameful past. He must be free to think and to act, he must have great strength of soul and character, he must be exemplary in his talent, his zeal, in performance of his duties, in his behavior.[61]

History was a burden, a source of shame. Everything had to be started anew.

There were a great many things that had to be bundled out of sight after the fall of Idi Amin. The building of the State Research Bureau, Amin's intelligence service, had been opened to the public on 14 April 1979, three days after the Tanzanian military seized Kampala. The journalists who entered the building found the brutalized bodies of dozens of prisoners—executed by S.R.B. warders—lying on the pavement outside the building. There were thirty bodies in the basement cells. There was a great amount of paperwork, too; it was ankle deep in the hallways. There were detailed reports on government officers, with "reliability ratings" estimating the person's loyalty to Amin.[62] There were thousands of identity cards collected from people who had died at the hands of Amin's men. For several days relatives and friends of deceased people filled the corridors, going through the papers in search of evidence and information about their loved ones. On Easter Sunday one man, formerly a detainee, led a tour of the building.[63] In his company were forty Christians, the men dressed in suits and the women in bright dresses. The remains of the dead had been taken away, but the documents were still there, piled up in the corners of the building. There were bloody footprints on the floor.

For a few days Ugandans conducted the most consequential kind of historical research. By the end of the month, all of that had been closed down. The authorities packed up the papers and removed them from the building. The curators at the Uganda Museum tell me that, one afternoon late in April, government officials arrived at the door with bundles of files from the S.R.B. building. The papers were locked in a basement room at the museum; a few months later, officials came and took them away. It is not clear whether the records were subsequently destroyed or hidden in some other place. In recent years a great many government archives have been organized and opened for research, but the archives of the S.R.B. have never again come into view.

The building of the State Research Bureau was similarly locked away. President Binaisa had planned on turning the building into a museum, but he was removed from office before this project could come to fruition. When Milton Obote returned to power the State Research Bureau was reestablished. In the early 1980s the building was again a site of torture and murder.[64] Today, under Yoweri Museveni's government, the State Research Bureau building has been made into the headquarters of the Internal Security Organization, a counterintelligence agency. It sits behind a high wall, enclosed within the security perimeter of one of the president's official residences. It has been closed to public view since April 1979.

Other places that might have encouraged deliberation over the legacies of Idi Amin's rule have likewise been placed out of bounds. In Amin's time the Nile Hotel was both an important place of public meetings and the scene of awful violence.[65] Diplomatic receptions and concerts took place on its grounds, while dissidents were interrogated, tortured, and murdered in the basement rooms. One day in February 1977 the archbishop of Uganda, Janani Luwum, was brought to the hotel, subjected to a sham trial, and pronounced guilty of conspiring against the state. Today the hotel has been renamed and made into a luxury resort. In 2005, during a renovation project, workers uncovered the remains of three people buried in the basement.[66] There is no memorial to the people who died in the building, and neither is there room for mourning or reflection. No one other than paying guests is allowed on the grounds.

Museveni's government has compressed the space for historical remembrance, depriving people of opportunities and occasions around which to deliberate over a painful history. Institutions that are meant to curate public memory are dramatically underprovisioned. In 2011 a powerful government minister proposed to erect a new, 222-meter-high skyscraper on the land where the Uganda Museum sits. Designed by London-based architects, the "Kampala Tower" was to be the tallest building in Africa. The schematic drawings show a massive building, illuminated by floodlights, towering over the city. It was to have over 100,000 square meters of office space, suitable for up to 12,500 people.[67] The Uganda Museum was to occupy a single floor, directly above the shopping arcade. That proposal was shelved thanks to an effective pressure campaign to "Save the Uganda Museum." Nonetheless, the museum remains in a precarious position. The exhibitions have scarcely changed since the time they were laid out in the 1950s and early 1960s. In Uganda's national museum there are no displays about Idi Amin's government, or about Milton Obote's regime, or about the violence and injustice of colonial rule.

In the absence of infrastructure it has been desperately hard for the victims of Amin's regime to find their voice. There is a website—titled "Atrocities of Amin"—whose organizer has collected information about hundreds of murders committed by the Amin government.[68] There is a small collection of autobiographies composed by men who were imprisoned and tortured by Amin's men.[69] There is a correspondingly small body of hagiographical literature about the sufferings of eminent Christian people.[70] In Uganda today there is no victims' group for people who suffered during Amin's regime. There are no infrastructures for therapy, no programs of public healing.

Martyrdom is central to Uganda's Christianity—but about the dead of the 1970s the Ugandan church says almost nothing.[71] There is only Janani Luwum, archbishop of the Church of Uganda, who was famously murdered by Amin's men. He has been canonized by the worldwide Anglican communion, and in recent years the date of his death has been marked in Uganda with a public holiday. Beyond Reverend Luwum there are no martyrs. Tens of thousands of men and women died at the hands of Idi Amin's government, but the meaning of their deaths, the larger cause for which they died, remains cloudy. Their sufferings were intense and real, but it is not clear that they served a larger purpose.

=======

In 2015 archivists uncovered a very large collection of photographic negatives in a storeroom at the Uganda Broadcasting Corporation headquarters in Kampala. There were more than 70,000 medium-format negatives, all of them carefully labeled, filed in glassine envelopes, and lined up in the drawers of an unremarkable filing cabinet.[72] This profuse collection of pictures was the archive of the Photographic Unit in the Ministry of Information. Most of them were made in the 1970s, during Idi Amin's presidency.

In 2018 my colleagues and I launched a project to inventory and digitize the negatives. We soon found that the UBC archive had been very carefully edited. Pictures that show President Amin in an uncompliment-ary light—sneezing, chewing with his mouth open, picking his nose—are nowhere to be found. Those negatives must have been destroyed as soon as they came out of the chemical bath. There was a further round of editing once the negatives were labeled and placed in envelopes. In the whole of the archive, there are almost no photographs of dead people. Government photographers had been present in 1973, when a dozen persons accused of conspiring against Amin were executed before watching crowds. Photos of these events had been published in the government newspaper.[73] As the 1970s went along, however, Amin's image-makers came to regard public displays of state violence as an em-barrassment. They went back over the photo archive, removing packets full of negatives that had been developed, numbered, and inventoried. The 70,000 pictures that the censors left behind survived because they were uncontroversial. They made no one nervous. They reflect a kind of consensus as to what Uganda's posterity ought to see. There is almost nothing in the photographic archive that directly illuminates the human costs of the time.

The most mournful pictures in the whole collection were made in March 1979.[74] The occasion was the burial of the infant son of Brigadier Isaac Maliyamungu. Mourners cluster around a graveside in the shadow of Namirembe Cathedral. There is a tiny coffin. Maliyamungu stands in the midst of his relatives, eyes downcast, hands clasped. Beside him is his wife, in tears. He does not look at the camera: he is distracted, dis-traught, sad. Maliyamungu was the most infamous servant of Idi Amin's regime, known widely for the creativity with which he killed people: by disemboweling them, by dismembering them, by driving over them with a tank. The photographs of the funeral were taken in the waning months of Amin's government. Maliyamungu had been the commanding officer of the garrison at Masaka. On 24 February—a few weeks before the child's funeral—Masaka had been attacked by the invading Tanzanian army, and Maliyamungu's soldiers had retreated in disarray.[75] After the battle Maliyamungu had wandered in the bush, disoriented, in hiding, before finally making his way to Kampala. Had he come directly from the battle to attend the funeral? His hair is uncombed; his uniform is rumpled.

A few days after these photographs were taken, Tanzanian soldiers marched into Kampala, and Amin's dictatorship came to an end. Isaac Maliyamungu fled to the Congo, and five years later he died.[76]

Burial of the infant son of Brigadier General Isaac Maliyamungu, Namirembe Cathedral, Kampala, March 1979 (Courtesy of the Uganda Broadcasting Corporation)

Out of the hundreds of thousands of people who mourned in those years, it is Isaac Maliyamungu whose grief appears as a subject in the archive. For most people there were no funerals. The dead were buried in haste, often in anonymous places. It was not a time for public displays of grief. In any case, government photographers were not tasked with taking pictures of the dead, and archivists were intent on cleaning up Idi Amin's image. They destroyed any photos where death was visible. It is the biggest absence in an archive that is full of absences, misrepresentations, and fallacies.

In 2019 I worked with colleagues and curators to stage a special exhibition at the Uganda Museum titled *The Unseen Archive of Idi Amin*.[77] It
was the first time that any public institution in Uganda had attempted to
create a memorial to the Amin years. We lined the walls of the hall with
the photographs that Amin's cameramen had made. There was a twenty-
minute documentary film, derived from footage we had digitized from
the UBC's cinema archive. We broadcast Idi Amin's radio addresses
through loudspeakers arranged throughout the space. More than 8,000
people visited *The Unseen Archive of Idi Amin* during the eight months it
was on show in Kampala. The opening ceremony was broadcast, live, on
national television, and so were the three panels that we organized to
promote public engagement with the exhibition. Newspapers in Uganda,
Kenya, Britain, Lithuania, the Netherlands, and the United States carried stories about the exhibit. The headlines heralded the exhibition as a
new beginning. "Ugandans Begin to Confront Blood-Soaked History of
the Idi Amin Years," announced the *Sunday Times*.[78]

There was much that remained invisible and hard to see. The awful
fact of political violence had been expunged from the photographic archive by the editorial work that Amin's image-makers had done. We had to
create visual prosthetics that could illuminate the violence of the times.[79]
At the opening of the exhibition we placed a timeline, juxtaposing photographs of grandiose state occasions with pictures of Ugandans who had
been murdered by Amin's men. None of the dead men and women were
shown in their final hour: the pictures had been made in the 1960s, when
they were young and rising figures in Uganda's public life. In our timeline
we repurposed these uplifting, youthful photographs, making them into
mementos of the many unjust deaths of the 1970s. In another part of the
exhibition we filled a wall with photos of the innocent men and women
who had been brought up before the Economic Crimes Tribunal in 1975.
The photographs highlighted the youthful innocence of the convicted
men and women. They were meant as an indictment of the awful logic of
the Economic War. At the time the exhibition opened we put together a
discussion panel titled "Victims of Amin," where the children of eminent
Ugandans murdered by the regime could tell their stories. In these and
other ways we tried to make the experience of people who suffered or died
under Amin's dictatorship visible.

It could never be enough. In 2020 we installed the exhibition in two
provincial cities: Soroti, in eastern Uganda; and Arua, near Idi Amin's
hometown in the northwest. As we organized the exhibition in Arua we

approached the relatives of Michael Ondoga, asking them to take part in a public discussion around the opening of the show. Ondoga, the minister of foreign affairs in Amin's time, had been murdered by agents of the state one morning in March 1974. As he dropped his daughters off at a primary school in Kampala, Amin's men apprehended him, beat him, and bundled him into the trunk of a sedan. The following day his mutilated and disfigured body was found floating in the Nile River.[80] We asked Ondoga's relatives to talk about their experiences under Amin's government. They refused our request. If they were to be involved in a public discussion about the 1970s, they said, Idi Amin's relatives would need to come to them to ask for forgiveness. There could be no dispassionate discussion until the horrific injustice of their relative's death had been resolved.

━━━━━

The exhibition at the Uganda Museum could not reconcile Ugandans with the traumas of the past. Neither will this book. There is no evidence here for prosecutors to work with. I have not exposed the hidden evils of the Amin regime. Violence and terror—the major theme in so many Ugandans' experience of the 1970s—have not been my subject. In a study that is about a time and place in which so many people suffered, I have not indicted the guilty.

This book has been about things that most everyone knew. I've written about infrastructures—museums, monuments, radio, churches, bureaucracies—that guided public life, imparting meaning and direction to the times. Radio Uganda was a broadcast medium, not a secret organization. It acted as a prosthetic arm of the authorities in Kampala, a vehicle by which officials in the capital could address, hail, identify, cajole, and motivate people in the provinces. It was the medium of record, a loudspeaker that commanded citizens' attention and pushed them to act. Some people learned—through a hard process of habituation—how to draw back, listen critically, and reframe the exhortations that came over the airwaves. The most critical listeners of Radio Uganda were the Rwenzururu secessionists of western Uganda, whose independent kingdom was upheld by the independence of their media. For the majority of Ugandans, though, Radio Uganda was inescapable. It set the pace of things, imparting a tempo to public life.

Many people were drawn into the drama of their times. The urgency of the moment shaped people's vocations. Tito Bisereko—who called himself "a local farmer"—traveled the length and breadth of the country, making on-the-spot assessments of government policies. Sergeant William Baker, chief in a remote and inaccessible locality, filed breathless reports describing his emphatic successes in implementing government policy. A great many people felt themselves deputized by the Amin government to root out criminality. All these people were of humble station. They were not at the center of power. Nonetheless, they felt empowered to assume political and administrative roles that had hitherto been closed to them. That is what the times required.

Filled with a campaigning sense of purpose, patriotic Ugandans extended themselves to fill in gaps and make up for shortfalls in funding and infrastructure. Peter Wankulu—self-made founder of Pan-Africanism—created collages from recycled bits of paper, stitching a grandiose vision out of humble things. John Tumusiime, who labored in a remote province as a humble culture officer, built a monument that commemorated the end of the First World War, using his meager resources to make Idi Amin's invented version of history seem real. These men made something from nothing. The skills they wielded were widely shared by Uganda's patriotic activists. They had to paper over gaps in government infrastructure. The skills of the collage artist—scavenging, repurposing—were the techniques by which patriotic people made government effective. At a time when essential commodities were in short supply, the creativity and artistry of committed people were essential to the maintenance of public institutions.

Many people came to see themselves as proprietors of public life and curators of public culture. All over Uganda committed people were selecting, organizing, inventorying, and conserving assets. At the university and in government policy African traditional religion was being newly defined and clarified by committed scholars like John Mbiti. Musical traditions and dance routines were being standardized and professionalized. History was being renovated, and patriotic curators of the Department of Antiquities and the Uganda Museum named and celebrated a whole host of new heroes. Ugandans had never before been able to see and measure their national purpose with such clarity. Everywhere there were inventories, lists, routines, and salvage plans, as Ugandans worked out means by which to protect the fragile and forgettable things that were essentially theirs.

Proprietorship is a form of property management. The patriotic campaigners of Idi Amin's Uganda thought it urgently necessary to identify and liberate properties that were under the illegitimate control of outsiders. Some people found themselves on the wrong side of history. A great many properties were vacated under Amin's dictatorship. A great many lives were disrupted or lost. Most famously, the Asian community was summarily expelled in August 1972. People who had lived for generations in Uganda were given a scant three months to tie up their affairs and find new homes. They were one among many communities that were suddenly disentitled, deprived of property and life. The Israelis were expelled from Uganda in March 1972. Their embassy was handed over to the Palestine Liberation Organization. In 1973, 1975, and again in 1977 government outlawed religious organizations that were thought to be inimical to good order. In this way the private property of religious and cultural minorities came under the management of the majority.

Other people found themselves the target of campaigners' attention because their style, their language, their sexuality, or their ethnicity set them at odds with the newly empowered majority. Karimojong people were obliged to attire themselves after the fashion of Amin's government, and those who refused were massacred. Women who wore miniskirts or wigs, or men who had long hair and beards, were imprisoned and tried in government courts. Smugglers, overchargers, hoarders, and other people who violated the official rules about economic conduct were likewise brought before the courts, and some of them were executed. That is how people became victims of state violence. Behaviors, aptitudes, styles, identities, and practices that had formerly been ordinary and uncontroversial were, quite suddenly, made to seem like traitorous deeds.

It is not—as is so often said—that the violence of Idi Amin's time was senseless. I have argued here that violence made too much sense. Driven forward by the tides of history, acting with the urgency the times seemed to demand, Idi Amin's principled campaigners felt empowered to persecute and punish enemies of the public. The disentitlement and dispossession of minorities went hand-in-hand with the populist campaign to assert black Ugandans' exclusive ownership over civil society, the economy, and culture. Under Idi Amin the outrage and passion of the majority became the fuel on which politics worked.

As I write, the politics of my own time and place—the United States in the 2020s—seems to be converging with Uganda's politics of the 1970s. Then as now, new media sources empower demagogues and shape people's passions. In the 1970s Idi Amin's addresses on Radio Uganda cut through the routines of government bureaucracy, engaging Ugandans directly in public affairs and imparting an urgency to hitherto uncontroversial administrative tasks. In today's America, Twitter (now X) offers demagogues a means to inflate their followers' petty grievances and incite their ire. On social media, Donald Trump, Jair Bolsonaro, and other media-savvy populists can sideline experts and speak directly to their people. In the 1970s Idi Amin enlisted black Ugandans to battle against cultural and racial minorities who dominated the economy and public life. The "War of Economic Liberation," like other campaigns, was meant to free the property of the black majority from the control of foreigners and outsiders. Today—in France, the United States, and elsewhere—an ascendant right wing encourages aggrieved people to regard themselves as a majority, dispossessed of their inheritance by greedy immigrants. Donald Trump came to power in 2016 promising to "take our country back"; as I write, he proposes to deport between 15 million and 20 million people from the United States. In the 1970s Idi Amin encouraged Ugandans to regard themselves as frontline soldiers, engaged in a globally consequential war against colonialism and other evils. Vigilantes answered the call, and all over the country people campaigned to liberate their culture, their economy, and their property from outsiders' ownership. In the United States a right-wing group called "Stop the Steal" organized a rally in Washington, D.C., on 6 January 2021, the day the presidential election was to be certified by Congress. President Trump warned them that "if you don't fight like hell, you're not going to have a country anymore."[81] Later that morning 2,500 rioters rampaged through the U.S. Capitol. They very nearly brought democratic government to an end.

The idea that "we"—whomever we might be—are entitled to control the infrastructure of public life is at once a motivation for self-sacrifice and a charter for demagoguery. It could make some people into busybodies, inserting themselves into the management of state institutions. It could make other people into patriots, committed to defending their people's culture and upholding their community's way of life. It could also feed violent campaigns to repossess a stolen inheritance, to reclaim properties that ought, by right, to belong to the majority.

The Amin regime brought the great struggles of the day home to Uganda. It was a kind of translocation. Some people invested their lives in pursuing projects that were far away, distant from their time and place, impossible to achieve. Others fought wars that were very close to home. They came to see that their contemporaries were enemies, traitors, delinquents, deserving scorn, correction, or punishment. Their conviction could inspire self-sacrifice, dedication, commitment. It could also make them vigilantes, empowered to take justice into their own hands.

That is the place where the patriot and the demagogue are together born.

Notes

Introduction

1. International Commission of Jurists, "Violations of Human Rights and the Rule of Law in Uganda" (Geneva, May 1974).
2. "Report of the Commission of Inquiry into the Disappearances of People in Uganda Since 25 January 1971" (Entebbe: Government Printer, 1975), discussed in Alicia Decker, *In Idi Amin's Shadow: Women, Gender, and Militarism in Uganda* (Athens: Ohio University Press, 2014).
3. Kabale DA Comm. Dev. 17, "Festivals and Competition" file: Eli Kyeyune, report of the Visual Arts Committee, February 1975.
4. Kabale DA Comm. Dev. 17, "Festivals and Competition" file: Visual Arts Sub-Committee meeting, 30 December 1974.
5. Kabale DA Comm. Dev. 17, "Festivals and Competition" file: Visual Arts Sub-Committee meeting, 8 January 1975.
6. Thomas Melady and Margaret Melady, *Idi Amin Dada: Hitler in Africa* (Kansas City, Mo.: Sheed Andrews and McMeel, 1977); David Gwyn, *Idi Amin: Death-Light of Africa* (London: Little, Brown, 1977); Dan Wooding and Ray Barnett, *Uganda Holocaust* (London: Pickering and Inglis, 1980).
7. Trevor Donald, *Confessions of Idi Amin: The Horrifying, Explosive Exposé of Africa's Most Evil Man* (London: W. H. Allen, 1978).
8. "Twiggy Most Beautiful," *Tampa Bay Times* (1 February 1977).
9. John Allen, *History's Villains: Idi Amin* (Farmington Hills, Mich.: Thompson Gale, 2004).
10. "A Painter of Great Talent," *Daily Nation* (12 July 1966).
11. Hilary Ng'weno, "Letter from Nairobi," *African Arts* 1 (2) (1968), 66–69.
12. "East African Artists' Work Shown in N.Y.," *Reporter Dispatch* (24 October 1969).
13. "1970 Prizewinners," *African Arts* 4 (2) (Winter 1971), 8–17.
14. "Paintings of the Uhuru Era," *Daily Nation* (28 August 1969).

15. Eli Kyeyune, "Symbols of Cultural Revolution," *Voice of Uganda* (7 February 1973).

16. BNA FCO 141/18363: Research Section, "Apollo Milton Obote," 13 August 1958.

17. "Uganda Army Coup Fails," *The Observer* (28 May 1972); LAC RG 25 11446 20-UGDA-1-4 pt. 6: Nairobi to Sec. of State for External Affairs, 25 March 1974; "Coup Fails in Uganda," *Miami Herald* (25 March 1974); "Uganda Chief Ambush Target," *Clarion-Ledger* (27 February 1975); "Uganda's Amin Survives Assassination Attempt," *Los Angeles Times* (11 June 1976); "Many Reported Killed in Ugandan Purge," *St. Louis Dispatch* (1 February 1977).

18. "Uganda's Amin Living on Borrowed Time," *Calgary Herald* (19 March 1975).

19. Henry Kyemba, *State of Blood: The Inside Story of Idi Amin* (New York: Ace, 1977).

20. Semakula Kiwanuka, *Amin and the Tragedy of Uganda* (Munich: Weltforum Verlag, 1979), 197.

21. Samwiri Karugire, *The Roots of Instability in Uganda* (Kampala: Fountain, 1988).

22. Mahmood Mamdani, *Imperialism and Fascism in Uganda* (Trenton, N.J.: Africa World Press, 1984), 2; Phares Mutibwa, *Uganda Since Independence: A Story of Unfulfilled Hopes* (London: Hurst, 1992), xi.

23. Will Kaberuka, *The Political Economy of Uganda, 1890–1979: A Case Study of Colonialism and Underdevelopment* (New York: Vantage, 1990).

24. "Visitors to Uganda Get Currency Rules," *Daily Nation* (1 June 1987).

25. A. B. K. Kasozi, *The Social Origins of Violence in Uganda, 1964–1985* (Montreal and Kingston: McGill-Queens University Press, 1994), 5.

26. Kiwanuka, *Amin*, 198; Mamdani, *Imperialism*, 2.

27. BDA box 530, file with no cover: B. B. Oluka, Secretary, Commission of Enquiry, 22 July 1986.

28. "Tribunal Sets Sights on Amin," *The Guardian* (13 December 1986).

29. Commission of Inquiry into Violations of Human Rights, *Report of the Commission of Inquiry into Violations of Human Rights: Verbatim Record of Proceedings* (Kampala: The Commission, 1995), ix.

30. Joanna R. Quinn, "Constraints: The Un-Doing of the Uganda Truth Commission," *Human Rights Quarterly* 26 (2) (May 2004), 401–27.

31. "Rights Commission Records in Owino," *The Star* (31 August 1988).

32. I have digitized the report and the evidence; these materials can be found at https://derekrpeterson.com/archive-materials/.

33. LDA "Amnesty Statute, General" file: "A Statute to Provide for an Amnesty for Persons Involved in Acts of a War Like Nature," 30 June 1987.

34. Richard Reid, *A History of Modern Uganda* (Cambridge: Cambridge University Press, 2017), 66.

35. Mark Leopold, *Idi Amin: The Story of Africa's Icon of Evil* (New Haven, Conn.: Yale University Press, 2020).

36. Christopher Sembuya, *The Other Side of Idi Amin* (Kampala: Sest Holdings, 2009); Jaffar Amin and Margaret Akulia, *Idi Amin: Hero or Villain?* (Kampala: Millennium Global, 2010).

37. Jason Schultz, "Supporting Capacity Building for Archives in Africa: Initiatives of the Cooperative Africana Materials Project Since 1995," *African Research and Documentation* 121 (2013), 3–12; Edgar C. Taylor, Ashley B. Rockenbach, and Natalie Bond, "Archives and the Past: Cataloguing and Digitisation in Uganda's Archives," in *African Studies in the Digital Age: Disconnects?*, ed. Terry Barringer and Marion Wallace (Leiden: Brill, 2014), 163–78.

38. Available at https://derekrpeterson.com/wp-content/uploads/2021/09/high-court-of-uganda-archive-catalgue.pdf.

39. The inventories can be found at https://derekrpeterson.com/archive-work/.

40. Kasese DA file with no cover: D.C. Rwenzori to all members, Rwenzori District Team, 21 January 1975.

41. BDA box 508, "Cotton" file: D.A.O. Semuliki to Agriculture Assistant, Karugutu, 30 August 1976.

42. Kasese DA "Research Projects and Archives" file: A. Luziraa to provincial governors, 20 January 1977.

43. J. M. Akita, "Development of the National Archives and the National Documentation Centre" (Paris: UNESCO, 1979).

44. Kabale DA JLOS 23, "Reports on Guerrilla Activities and Smuggling" file: Saza chief Rukiga to O.C. Police Kabale, 12 February 1973.

45. BDA box 516, file with no cover: P.C. for Forests to D.C. Semuliki, 9 July 1975.

46. BDA box 516, file with no cover: District Forest Officer, monthly report for August 1977, 28 September 1977.

47. Daniel Goldhagen, *Hitler's Willing Executioners: Ordinary Germans and the Holocaust* (New York: Vintage, 1996).

48. Thomas Healy, *Soul City: Race, Equality, and the Lost Dream of an American Utopia* (New York: Metropolitan, 2021).

49. Cedric J. Robinson, *On Racial Capitalism, Black Internationalism, and Cultures of Resistance* (New York: Pluto, 2019).

50. Antina von Schnitzler, *Democracy's Infrastructure: Techno-Politics and Protest After Apartheid* (Princeton, N.J.: Princeton University Press, 2016).

51. The scholarship concerning the history and anthropology of radio broadcasting in Africa includes—among other works—Harri Englund, *Human Rights and African Airwaves: Mediating Equality on the Chichewa Radio* (Bloomington: Indiana University Press, 2011); Harri Englund, *Gogo Breeze: Zambia's Radio Elder and the Voices of Free Speech* (Chicago: University of Chicago Press, 2018); Brian Larkin, *Signal and Noise: Media, Infrastructure, and Urban Culture in Nigeria* (Durham, N.C.: Duke University Press,

2008); Marissa Moorman, *Powerful Frequencies: Radio, State Power, and the Cold War in Angola, 1931–2002* (Athens: Ohio University Press, 2019); and Liz Gunner, *Radio Soundings: South Africa and the Black Modern* (Cambridge: Cambridge University Press, 2019). For Uganda, see Florence Brisset-Foucault's *Talkative Polity: Radio, Domination, and Citizenship in Uganda* (Athens: Ohio University Press, 2019).

52. See Emma Park, "Infrastructural Attachments: Technologies, Mobility, and the Tensions of Home in Colonial and Postcolonial Kenya" (Ph.D. thesis, University of Michigan, 2017). See also Emma Park, "'Human ATMs': M-Pesa and the Expropriation of Affective Work in Safaricom's Kenya," *Africa: The Journal of the International African Institute* 90 (5) (Nov. 2020), 914–33.

53. Nelson Kasfir, *The Shrinking Political Arena: Participation and Ethnicity in African Politics, with a Case Study of Uganda* (Berkeley: University of California Press, 1976).

Chapter 1. A Nervous State

1. See Nancy Rose Hunt, *A Nervous State: Violence, Remedies, and Reverie in Colonial Congo* (Durham, N.C.: Duke University Press, 2015).

2. A. W. Southall and P. C. W. Gutkind, *Townsmen in the Making: Kampala and Its Suburbs* (Kampala: East African Institute of Social Research, 1957), 22.

3. Southall and Gutkind, *Townsmen*, 36.

4. SOAS Christian Aid archive CA/A/7: Inter-Church Aid, "Kampala's Need," n.d. (but 1960).

5. BNA FCO 141/6640: Chief Secretary, "Paper on the Uganda National Movement and Its Successor Organizations," 24 October 1959.

6. BNA FCO 141/18426: Uganda monthly intelligence report, April 1960.

7. BNA FCO 141/6640: Chief Secretary, "Paper on the Uganda National Movement and Its Successor Organizations," 24 October 1959.

8. USNA RG 59 CDF 1960–63 1707/745s.00/1–161: Van Oss to State Department, 18 January 1961.

9. BNA FCO 141/18165: Background information for the Privy Council Commission, 29 December 1961.

10. USNA RG 59 CDF 1960–63 1707/745s.00/1–161: Van Oss to State Department, 18 January 1961.

11. "Bakabaka Bambalidde Muzinge," *Uganda Post* 105 (21 March 1960).

12. UNA OP (Confidential) 15/S.09436: Governor, notes on a discussion with the Kabaka, 11 August 1959.

13. Derek R. Peterson, Emma Hunter, and Stephanie Newell, eds., *African Print Cultures: Newspapers and Their Publics in Modern Africa* (Ann Arbor: University of Michigan Press, 2016).

14. "Even the Young Are Nationalists," *Uganda Empya* (19 May 1959).

15. "Rule Breakers Leave Their CGI Sheets Behind," *Obugagga* (12 May 1959).

16. BNA FCO 141/6640: Chief Secretary, "Paper on the Uganda National Movement and Its Successor Organizations," 24 October 1959.

17. "Apology to the U.N.M.," *Uganda Empya* (30 April 1959).

18. USNA RG 84 Consulate General, Kampala, General Records, 1956–61 1/350.1: Hooper to State Department, 9 May 1959. Thanks to Edgar Taylor for calling my attention to this article.

19. BNA CO 822/1845: Crawford to Colonial Secretary, 5 May 1959.

20. BNA CO 822/1845: Binaisa to Stonehouse, 2 May 1959.

21. BNA FCO 141/18367: Chief Secretary to Resident, n.d. (but August 1959).

22. USNA RG 84 Uganda Kampala Embassy, Classified General Records, 1956–63 1/360.11: Hooper to State Department, 9 December 1958.

23. UNA OP (Confidential) 38/C.8336: H.E. the Governor's speech to Legislative Council, 24 April 1956.

24. BNA FCO 141/18233: Buganda Resident, file note, 10 March 1961.

25. MUL AR/BUG/5B/1: S. K. Masembe Kabali and John Bakka, "Kabaka Yekka," n.d.

26. USNA RG 59 CDF 1960–63 1707/745s.00/10–160: "Termination of British Protection," n.d. (but September 1960).

27. USNA RG 59 CDF 1960–63 1707/745s.00/10–160: London Embassy to State Department, 21 October 1960.

28. USNA RG 59 CDF 1960–63 1707/745s.00/10–160: Van Oss to State Department, 25 October 1960.

29. BNA FCO 141/18238: Criminal Investigation Department report on Omwoyo gw'Egwanga, 10 December 1960.

30. BNA FCO 141/18238: The Buganda Defence Force, Constitution and Roles, 19 October 1960.

31. BNA FCO 141/18238: Buganda Resident to P.S. for Security, 21 October 1960.

32. BNA FCO 141/18238: D. Le Poidevin to P.S. for Security, 10 November 1960.

33. Reported in USNA RG 59 CDF 1960–63 1707/745s.00/10–160: Van Oss to State Department, 26 October 1960.

34. BNA FCO 141/18363: Special Branch, Lango, to Commissioner of Police, 7 December 1960.

35. BNA FCO 141/18238: Commissioner of Police to P.S., Security and External Relations, 26 November 1960.

36. BNA FCO 141/18239: Buganda daily situation report, 31 December 1960.

37. USNA RG 59 CDF 1960–63 1707/745s.00/1–161: Mem. Con., Harold Funk and J. Zake, 1 January 1961.

38. BNA FCO 141/18239: Buganda daily situation report, 4 January 1961.

39. BNA FCO 141/18239: Extracts from the vernacular press, 16 January 1961.

40. BNA FCO 141/18239: British Embassy, Athens, to Foreign Office, London, 24 February 1961.

41. RH Mss. Afr. S. 2114: Interview with Richard Stone, 25 February 1971.

42. BNA FCO 141/18239: File note, 24 February 1961.
43. BNA FCO 141/18357: "Lukiiko Notice," n.d.
44. USNA RG 59 CDF 1960–63 1707/745s.00/1–560: Hooper to State Department, 23 June 1960.
45. USNA RG 59 CDF 1960–63 1707/745s.00/10–160: Van Oss to State Department, 17 November 1960.
46. USNA RG 59 CDF 1960–63 1707/745s.00/1–560: Van Oss to State Department, 25 August 1960.
47. USNA RG 59 CDF 1960–63 1707/745s.00/1–161: Van Oss to State Department, 17 March 1961.
48. UNA Elections 3/ L.155/3: List for Buganda, n.d. (but March 1961).
49. Kiwanuka's political biography is given in Jonathon Earle and J. J. Carney, *Contesting Catholics: Benedicto Kiwanuka and the Birth of Postcolonial Uganda* (Rochester, N.Y.: James Currey, 2021).
50. BNA FCO 141/18239: Political Intelligence and Security meeting, 28 April 1961.
51. MUL AR/BUG/5B/4: Nnaganga Nnamuzisa to governor, n.d. (but 1961).
52. MUL AR/BUG/5/4: "The King Kills the Small Red Ants," n.d. (but 1962).
53. BNA FCO 141/18392: Special Branch to P.S. Security and External Relations, 27 June 1961.
54. UNA OP (Confidential) 44/CGLO 20: Senior Assistant Resident Masaka to Buganda Resident, 19 June 1961.
55. BNA FCO 141/18392: Special Branch to Buganda Resident, 20 June 1961.
56. BNA FCO 141/18392: Special Branch to P.S. Security and External Relations, 18 November 1961; see I. R. Hancock, "Patriotism and Neo-Traditionalism in Buganda: The Kabaka Yekka Movement, 1962–62," *Journal of African History* 11 (3) (1970), 423–24.
57. MUL AR/BUG/5B/2: Kiirya Kalikwani to chairman, Kabaka Yekka, 20 December 1963.
58. USNA RG 59 CDF 1960–63 1707/745S.00/1–560: State Department to Kampala, 24 February 1960.
59. USNA RG 59 CDF 1960–63 1707/745S.00/1–560: Hooper to State Department, 5 February 1960.
60. Described in Muteesa II, Kabaka of Buganda, *Desecration of My Kingdom* (London: Constable, 1967), 160–61.
61. BNA FCO 141/18392: Special Branch to Deputy Governor, 12 April 1962.
62. BNA FCO 141/18363: Special Branch to P.S., S.E.R., 28 December 1957.
63. BNA FCO 141/18363: Research Section, "Apollo Milton Obote," 13 August 1958.
64. BNA FCO 141/18363: D.C. Lango to Chief Secretary, 14 May 1958.
65. *Uganda Post* (27 July 1960), summarized in JDA 117/INF 2/2 pt. 7: Summaries of the local press, 6078.
66. UNA Elections 2/L.119 vol. II: D.C. Teso to Supervisor of Elections, 8 May 1962.

67. UNA Elections 2/L.119 vol. II: D.C. West Nile to Supervisor of Elections, 24 May 1962.
68. UNA Elections 2/L.119 vol. II: Town Clerk, Kampala, to Supervisor of Elections, 15 May 1962.
69. UNA Elections 2/L.119 vol. II: Elections Officer, Lango, to Supervisor of Elections, 12 May 1962.
70. UNA Elections 1/L.105: File note for Council of Ministers, 9 January 1962.
71. BNA FCO 141/18392: Record of a meeting between the Deputy Acting Governor and Kabaka Yekka, 9 March 1962.
72. UNA OP (Confidential) 16/C.10698/1: Solicitor General to Clerk of the National Assembly, 20 August 1962.
73. Bodleian Library Mss. Afr. S. 2117: James Barber, "The Uganda Cabinet, 1962."
74. CoU 1 Abp 51/4: Obote to Bishop Sabiti, 20 September 1962.
75. MUL AR J 3/3: Notes for the first press conference, n.d.
76. MUL AR J 3/6: Souvenir Program, n.d. (but October 1962).
77. "Kamya Yesowodeyyo," *Uganda Eyogera* 15512 (21 December 1962).
78. UNA MoIA S.9564: Special Branch to Permanent Secretary, Ministry of Internal Affairs, 14 January 1963.
79. UNA MoIA S.9564: Press release, Ministry of Justice, 1 February 1963.
80. UNA OP (Confidential) 99/PM: Buganda: Central Government meeting with Kabaka's Government, 16 January 1963.
81. Described in Shane Doyle, *Crisis and Decline in Bunyoro: Population and Environment in Western Uganda, 1860–1955* (Athens: Ohio University Press, 2006).
82. Derek R. Peterson, "Violence and Political Advocacy in the Lost Counties, Western Uganda," *International Journal of African Historical Studies* 48 (1) (2015), 179–99.
83. UNA OP (Confidential) 26/P.M. 1: Lost Counties.
84. UNA OP (Confidential) 15/S.10482: E. Norris to Obote, 16 November 1964.
85. UNA OP (Confidential) 100/P.M. 15: Handwritten file note, no author, n.d.
86. UNA OP (Confidential) 45/PMC/C.48: "Nantabulirwa" to Kabaka, n.d.
87. Virika 952, "Kingdom to Tooro" file: "Milton Obote," "This is my secret plan of ruling Uganda," n.d. (received 23 September 1964); UNA OP (Confidential) 99/PM/Buganda: "Obote," "This is my secret plan . . .," n.d.; CoU 1 Abp 157/11: "Obote," "This is my secret plan . . .," n.d.
88. "Omusaija ono Alina Plan Yino," n.d. (but late 1964).
89. UNA OP (Confidential) 81/C.9: Speech by the Prime Minister, 3 March 1966.
90. BNA DO 213/176: British High Commission, Kampala to Foreign and Colonial Office, 15 April 1966.

91. UNA OP (Confidential) 45/PMC/C.48: S. Musajatimbwa Kigye, Chairman of the Bataka, to Milton Obote, 26 April 1966.

92. BNA DO 213/186: British High Commission to Commonwealth Relations Office, 23 May 1966.

93. BNA DO 213/186: Conversation between A. E. W. Chilvers and the British High Commissioner, 24 May 1966.

94. RH D. S. Henderson papers: Notes on 25 May 1966.

95. RH D. S. Henderson papers: Notes on 3 June 1966.

96. BNA DO 213/35: British High Commission, Bujumbura, to Foreign Office, 22 June 1966. The episode is narrated in Kabaka of Buganda, *Desecration*, Ch. 1.

97. BNA DO 213/186: High Commission to Secretary of State for the Colonies, 22 July 1966.

98. BNA DO 213/186: British High Commission to Commonwealth Relations Office, 2 June 1966.

99. RH Mss. Perham 528, file 4: J. de V. Allen to Margery Perham, 3 June 1966.

100. USNA RG 59 Central Foreign Policy files, 1967–69 2559/POL 15-5: Stebbins to State Department, 1 October 1967.

101. LDA file with no cover: D.C. Lango to Ben Otim, Lango District Administration, 19 September 1967.

102. Kabale DA JLOS 1, "Kigezi District Intelligence and Security Reports" file: Intelligence and Security Report for the month ending 30 September 1967.

103. Kabarole DA 386/2: P.S. Ministry of Regional Administrations to D.C. Toro, 25 September 1967.

104. BNA FCO 31/470: David White, British High Commission, to Purcell, 19 December 1969.

105. "Uganda: Four African Presidents Attend Ruling ??? Congress Opening" (18 December 1969), *Reuters Screen Ocean*, record ID: 265225, at https://reuters.screenocean.com/record/265225.

106. USNA RG 59 Central Foreign Policy Files, 1967–69 2559/POL 15-1: Nalle to State Department, 20 December 1969.

107. USNA SNF 1970–73 2644/POL 15-1: Kampala to State Department, 5 January 1970.

108. USNA SNF 1970–73 2644/POL 15-1: Kampala to State Department, 13 March 1970.

109. USNA SNF 1970–73 2644/POL 15-1: Kampala to State Department, 13 March 1970.

110. UNA OP (Confidential) 74/S.6190/16: Mpigi Division Intelligence Summary, 1 June to 9 July 1966.

111. UNA MoIA 275/S.10574: Special Branch to P.S. Ministry of Internal Affairs, 17 May 1966.

112. ISA MFA-Political-ooomeqv: "The War Signal has been Sounded," 9 November 1966.

113. ISA MFA-Political-ooomeqv: "Uganda Security Council," n.d. (but 1966).
114. ISA MFA-Political-ooomeqv: "The Secret Council, Buganda" to Milton Obote, n.d. (but 1966).
115. USNA RG 59 Central Foreign Policy Files, 1967–69 2560/POL 29: Kampala to State Department, 14 March 1967.
116. USNA RG 59 Central Foreign Policy Files, 1967–69 2560/POL 29: Kampala to State Department, 24 February 1968.
117. ISA MFA-Political-ooomeqv: "Uganda Security Council," n.d. (but 1966).
118. USNA RG 59 Central Foreign Police Files, 1967–69 2560/POL 17: Secret Council to Milton Obote, 29 August 1968, enclosed in Kampala Embassy to State Department, 14 September 1968.
119. BNA FCO 31/716: British High Commission Kampala to East Africa Department, 25 June 1970.
120. Kabale DA JLOS 1, "Kigezi Security and Intelligence Reports" file: Kigezi District Intelligence Report, 30 April 1967.
121. ISA MFA-Political-ooomeqv: "The War Signal has Sounded," 9 November 1966.
122. "Lango Master Plan," *The People* (5 March 1971).
123. USNA RG 59 Central Foreign Policy Files, 1967–69 2558/POL 12 Uganda: Director of Intelligence and Research to Secretary of State, 20 August 1968.
124. USNA RG 59 Central Foreign Policy Files, 1967–69 2560/POL 23-7: Kampala to State Department, 10 August 1968.
125. UNA OP (Confidential) 26/CR 901/68: K.Y. Activities in the Mbale area, 9 April 1969.
126. Kabarole DA 102, "Toro Intelligence Reports, 1968–71" file: D.C. Toro to Principal Private Secretary to the President, 28 September 1970.
127. ISA Mfa-IsraliMissionUganda-ooosoep: *Uganda Argus*, 3 July 1964.
128. UNA OP (Confidential)100/012: Security Committee of the Cabinet, 2 March 1967.
129. USNA RG 59 SNF 1970–73 2644/POL 15-1 1/1/70: Kampala Embassy to State Department, 3 August 1970.
130. See Sam Makinda, "Leadership in Africa: A Contextual Survey," in Alamin Mazrui and Willy Mutunga, eds., *Debating the African Condition: Governance and Leadership* (Trenton, N.J.: Africa World Press, 2003), 7–8.
131. Akena Adoko, *Uganda Crisis* (Kampala: Consolidated Printers Ltd., n.d. [1967]), 12.
132. Adoko, *Uganda Crisis*, 16–17.
133. As noted by American diplomats. USNA RG 59 Central Foreign Policy Files, 1967–69 2558/POL 12: Stebbins to State Department, 22 June 1968.
134. Akena Adoko, *From Obote to Obote* (New Delhi: Vikas, 1983), 86.
135. Picho Ali, "Ideological Commitment and the Judiciary," *Transition* 36 (1968), 47–49; Ali, "The 1967 Republican Constitution of Uganda,"

Transition 34 (December 1967), 11–18; USNA RG 59 Central Foreign Policy Files, 1967–69 2558/POL 2: Kampala to State Department, 31 March 1968.

136. USNA RG 59 Central Foreign Policy files, 1967–69 2558/POL 12: Memorandum of Conversation, 17 April 1969; Kampala to State Department, 12 April 1969.

137. Adoko, *From Obote to Obote*, 87.

138. UNA OP (Confidential) 99/PM: Buganda: Permanent Secretary to Prime Minister, 14 September 1964.

139. Kabale DA JLOS 1, "Kigezi Security and Intelligence Reports" file: Kigezi Intelligence and Security Report for the month ending 30 September 1967.

140. UNA OP (Confidential) 87/SC/PC/3: F. Kalimuzo to G. Murphy, Chair, Commission of Inquiry, 28 October 1971.

141. Editorial, *The Democrat* (3) (June 1969), in USNA RG 59 Central Foreign Policy Files, 1967–69 2559/POL 12.

142. UNA OP (Confidential) 74/S.6190/16: A. R. Kalisa to Permanent Secretary to the Cabinet, 10 November 1966.

143. UNA OP (Confidential) 26/CR 901/68: Silver Abraham to N&E, 10 April 1968.

144. UNA OP 11/17, titled "Mr. Akena-Adoko, Chief General Service Officer."

145. UNA OP 11/17: B. W. Bato to Permanent Secretary, Minister of Internal Affairs, 18 September 1968.

146. Henry Kyemba, *State of Blood: The Inside Story of Idi Amin* (New York: Ace, 1977), 31.

147. USNA RG 59 Central Foreign Policy Files, 1967–69 2559/POL 12: Kampala to State Department, 9 September 1969.

148. UNA OP (Confidential) 40/002: Democratic Party Headquarters, Press Statement, 8 March 1969; Charge Sheet, Benedicto Kiwanuka and Paulo Semogerere versus Uganda, 6 September 1969.

149. UNA OP (Confidential) 18/S.10904: Tillett, Commander, Uganda Rifles, "Expansion of Uganda Rifles," 1 June 1963.

150. The course of events is described in Timothy Parsons, *The 1964 Army Mutinies and the Making of Modern East Africa* (Westport, Conn.: Praeger, 2003), 116–17 and 124–25; and in Ami Omara-Otunnu, *Politics and the Military in Uganda, 1890–1985* (Basingstoke, Hampshire: Macmillan, 1987), Ch. 4.

151. UNA OP (Confidential) 43/001: Cabinet meeting, 27 January 1964.

152. UNA OP (Confidential) 43/001: Cabinet meeting, 24 January 1964.

153. UNA OP (Confidential) 43/001: Cabinet meeting, 16 September 1964.

154. Ably shown in Mark Leopold, *Idi Amin: The Story of Africa's Icon of Evil* (New Haven, Conn.: Yale University Press, 2021), Ch. 1.

155. UBC sound reel 013: President Amin at saza headquarters, 29 October 1971.

156. BNA DO 213/50: G. Griffith, file note, 27 January 1964.

157. UNA OP (Confidential) 18/S.10904: S. Semakula, Regional Fisheries Officer, to Administrator, Fort Portal, 19 March 1964.

158. Bodleian Library Mss. Afr. S. 2195: L. W. Taylor, "Alleged Misconduct by Soldiers of the Uganda Army," 8 December 1964; see UNA OP (Confidential) 18/S.10904: Basil Bataringaya to Minister of Internal Affairs, 6 April 1964.

159. Kabarole DA 102, "Toro District Intelligence Reports" file: Toro District Intelligence Report, 29 June 1964.

160. BNA DO 213/50: Le Tocq to Norman, 24 March 1964.

161. UNA OP (Confidential) 18/S.10904: P.S. Ministry of Internal Affairs to Commander, Uganda Army, 10 April 1964.

162. UNA OP (Confidential) 18/S.10904: Davies to Commander, Uganda Rifles, 16 April 1964.

163. UNA MoIA S.2164/IV vol. I: Wilson Oryema to P.S., Ministry of Internal Affairs, 2 July 1965.

164. UNA OP (Confidential) 31/014: Commander Uganda Army to members of the Defence Council, 25 October 1965.

165. USNA RG 59 Central Foreign Policy files, 1967–69 2559/15-1: Stebbins to State Department, 1 February 1967.

166. Bodleian Library D. S. Henderson papers, notes on 25 May 1966.

167. Interview with Henry Kyemba, Bugembe, Jinja, 26 May 2019; Kyemba, *State of Blood*, 26.

168. UNA OP (Confidential) 100/003: Major General Idi Amin Dada, "Speech at the End of Exercise Macho Mingi at Masaka," 1 September 1968.

169. UNA OP (Confidential) 100/002: Idi Amin, "Report by the Commander, Uganda Army and Air Force," n.d. (but 1968).

170. BNA FCO 31/489: Defence Advisor to Minister of Defence, 17 June 1969.

171. UNA OP (Confidential) 100/002: Idi Amin, "Report by the Commander, Uganda Army and Air Force," n.d. (but January 1968).

172. BNA FCO 31/489: Crawford, Defence Advisor, to Minister of Defence, 25 February 1969.

173. BNA FCO 31/489: Defence Advisor to Minister of Defence, 17 April 1969.

174. "Armed Forces for All Ugandans—Dr. Obote," *Daily Nation* (25 February 1969).

175. UNA MoIA 279/S.10788: Security Committee of cabinet, 18 July 1969.

176. UNA MoIA S.90: Senior Superintendent of Police to P.S., Ministry of Internal Affairs, 2 October 1968.

177. UNA MoIA S.90: Inspector General of Police to P.S., Ministry of Internal Affairs, 21 September 1968.

178. UNA MoIA S.90 vol. IV: Meeting of representatives of the Ministries of Defence and Internal Affairs, 14 August 1970.

179. UNA MoIA S.90 vol. IV: Idi Amin, Commander of the Uganda Armed Forces, to Ministry of Defence, 11 March 1970.
180. BNA FCO 31/1023: British High Commission, Kampala, to Foreign and Commonwealth Office, 25 January 1971.
181. "Ugandans Hail Army Coup," *Daily Nation* (26 January 1971).

Chapter 2. The Second Republic

1. USNA RG 59 2645/POL 23-9: Kampala to State Department, 26 January 1971.
2. JDA ADM ALG 26/7: "Why We Took Over Power," n.d. (but 1971).
3. "Lango Master Plan," *The People* (5 March 1971).
4. Government of the Republic of Uganda, *The Birth of the Second Republic of Uganda* (Entebbe: Government Printer, 1971).
5. UNA OP (Confidential) 1/004: "Comment by H.E. the President Gen. Idi Amin Dada on Obote's letter," n.d. (but 1977).
6. BNA FCO 31/1019: British High Commission to East Africa Department, 29 January 1971.
7. USNA RG 59 2644/POL 15-1, 1/1/71: Kampala to State Department, 5 February 1971.
8. UNA OP (Confidential) 84/1977: Meeting of cabinet, 13 May 1971.
9. UBC photo archive, 3054-2a-026.
10. UBC photo archive, 3069-2a-009.
11. Asaph Mureria, "Dancing in the Streets," *Daily Nation* (26 January 1971).
12. BNA FCO 31/1020: S. Galabuzi, F. Mpanga, and others to Prime Minister, 31 January 1971.
13. UNA OP (Confidential) 78/CM/14: M. Davies to Nkambo Mugerwa, 8 February 1971.
14. "The Bloody Facts of Uganda Coup," *Times of Zambia* (10 February 1971).
15. USNA RG 59 SNF 1970–73 2643/POL 1/1/70: Kampala to State Department, 25 March 1971.
16. LDA 523, file with no cover: Y. Mungoma, D.C. Lango, to Idi Amin, 2 February 1971.
17. LDA 609, "Speeches, Policy Statements" file: Memorandum to Idi Amin from the Elders of the People of Lango District, 21 March 1971.
18. UBC photo archive, 3073-2-014.
19. UBC photo archive, 3073-2-007.
20. BNA FCO 31/1074: R.J. Owen to Lord Boyd, 4 March 1971.
21. BNA FCO 31/475: Wenban-Smith to East Africa Department, 2 December 1969.
22. BNA FCO 31/1075: Joseph Serubyale to Chairman, Ministerial Committee for the Return of the Kabaka's Body, 24 February 1971.
23. UNA Ministry of Health 55/MIS/45: Ministry of Health, "Arrangements for Efficient Provision of 1st Aid and Medical Services," 31 March 1971.

24. USNA RG 59 2644/POL 15-1 1/1/71: Kampala to State Department, 9 April 1971.
25. LAC RG 25 8794 20-1-2-UGDA vol. 3: High Commissioner to Ottawa, 7 April 1971.
26. USNA RG 59 2644/POL 15-1 1/1/71: Kampala to State Department, 9 April 1971.
27. LAC RG 25 8794 20-1-2-UGDA vol. 3: High Commissioner to Ottawa, 7 April 1971.
28. USNA RG 59 2644/POL 15-1 1/1/71: Nalle to State Department, 28 May 1971.
29. Henry Lubega, "The Return and Burial of Kabaka Mutesa's Remains," *Monitor* (28 March 2015).
30. USNA RG 59 2643/POL 6, 1/1/70: Kampala to State Department, 20 March 1971.
31. Kabale DA ADM 46, "Intelligence Reports" file: D.C. Mubende to Henry Kyemba, P.S. to the President, 23 March 1971.
32. BNA FCO 31/1074: Redshaw, British High Commission, to East Africa Department, 16 March 1971.
33. LDA 523, file with no cover: D.C. Lango to P.S., Ministry of Internal Affairs, 15 June 1971.
34. LDA 609, "Speeches, Policy Statements" file: Memorandum to Idi Amin from the Elders of the People of Lango District, 21 March 1971.
35. USNA RG 59 SNF 1970–73 2645/POL 23-9: Dar es Salaam embassy to State Department, 8 April 1971.
36. UNA MoIA 189/S.90 vol. V: Obite Gama to Oboth Ofumbi, 4 June 1971.
37. Iain Grahame, *Amin and Uganda: A Personal Memoir* (London: Granada, 1980), 114.
38. LAC RG 25 8794 20-1-2-UGDA vol. 3: High Commissioner to Ottawa, 12 August 1971; "Baganda Urged by Amin Not to Think on Tribal Lines," *Daily Nation* (6 August 1971).
39. USNA RG 59 SNF 1970–73 2644/POL 15-1 1/1/71: Ferguson to State Department, 12 August 1971.
40. UBC "Radio Uganda, Archives Library" index.
41. USNA RG 59 SNF 1970–73 2645/POL 18, 1/1/70: Nalle to State Department, 26 August 1971.
42. USNA RG 59 SNF 1970–73 2644/POL 15-1 1/1/71: Kampala to State Department, 26 August 1971.
43. USNA RG 59 SNF 1970–73 2643/POL 13-2, 1/70: Ferguson to State Department, 16 September 1971.
44. UNA OP (Confidential) 78/CM/14: M. Davies, "Security Threats," 23 February 1971.
45. "Buganda Elders Warned," *Uganda Argus* 5211 (1 October 1971).
46. BNA FCO 31/1018: Redshaw to East Africa Department, 8 October 1971.
47. "President to Tour Buganda," *Uganda Argus* 5226 (16 October 1971).

48. LAC RG 25 8996 20-UGDA-1-4 pt. 4: Amin, speech on the ninth anniversary of Ugandan independence, 9 October 1971.

49. LAC RG 25 8996 20-UGDA-1-4 pt. 4: Canadian High Commissioner to Ottawa, 22 October 1971.

50. UNA OP (Confidential) 84/1977: Suspension of Political Activities Decree, n.d.; USNA RG 59 SNF 1970–73 2643/POL 1/1/70: Kampala to State Department, 12 August 1971.

51. UNA MoIA 275 S.10574: Special Branch to P.S., Ministry of Internal Affairs, 15 November 1971.

52. BNA FCO 31/1234: H. Evans to East Africa Department, 4 January 1972.

53. BNA FCO 31/1950: British High Commission to East Africa Department, 20 March 1975.

54. BNA FCO 31/1950: Mulengera Lubwana to Idi Amin, 30 October 1975.

55. BNA FCO 31/1950: Hennessy to Evans, 25 February 1975,

56. BNA FCO 31/1584: E. Mukasa et al. to Sec. General of the British Commonwealth, 26 May 1973.

57. BNA FCO 31/2671: Longrigg, East Africa Department, to Rosling, 13 February 1979.

58. Jinja DA ADM ALG 26/7: A.D.C. touring report, Buzaya county, 13 to 17 March 1972.

59. Kabarole DA 1219/1: D.C. South Bunyoro to Mr. Besisira, 19 March 1975.

60. BDA 515, "Compensation" file: Land Reform Decree, 1975.

61. UNA OP (Confidential) 31/06: Minister of Mineral and Water Resources, cabinet memo 130.

62. *Voice of Uganda* 1 (789) (6 June 1975), p. 6.

63. Laban Mukidi Aboki Nyakaana, "Agriculture Development Planning and Policy in Uganda" (Ph.D. dissertation, University of East Africa, June 1970).

64. Kabarole DA 1191/4: Villagers of Kanyandahi-Kiiko to Provincial Governor, 4 May 1977.

65. Kabarole DA 1191/4: Provincial Executive Secretary to Provincial Governor, 3 June 1977.

66. Kabarole DA 483/2: Secretary Toro Land Board to Provincial Executive Secretary, Toro, 28 January 1975.

67. Kabarole DA 483/2: Paulo Murwa, Kibiite, to D.C. Toro, 26 May 1976.

68. BDA 522, file with no cover: Semuliki District Land Committee meeting, 6 February 1976.

69. LAC RG 25 8794 20-1-2-UGDA vol. 9: African Affairs Division to Nairobi, 28 October 1974.

70. Bagaya had come to a different view by the time she published her autobiography. Elizabeth Nyabongo, *Elizabeth of Toro: The Odyssey of an African Princess* (New York: Simon and Schuster, 1989).

71. SOAS MS 380513 1/6: J. Kazairwe to Idi Amin, 3 May 1971.

72. JDA ADM Central 4/1: P.S., Ministry of Provincial Administration, to all Provincial Governors, 5 January 1978.

73. Kabarole DA 437/1: North Kigezi District Team, 12 July 1977.

74. "Karwemera: A Walking Encyclopedia on the Bakiga," *Daily Monitor* (16 March 2015).

75. Kabale DA ADM 46, "Intelligence Reports" file: District Intelligence Committee report, 2 January 1971.

76. Kabale DA ADM 46, "Intelligence Reports" file: Intelligence Committee meeting, 7 April 1971.

77. UNA OP (Confidential) 91/8: Intelligence Unit, President's Office, 30 January 1972.

78. Kabale DA ADM 46, "Intelligence Reports" file: Malinga to Minister of Public Service and Local Administrations, 28 July 1972.

79. Festo Karwemera, interview with Derek Peterson and Rev. John Basingwire, 27 June 2004.

80. Kabale DA NW/CM 11, "Recording by the Radio Uganda van" file: Programme items selected and prepared for recording in Kigezi District, 28 July 1971.

81. Kabale DA Comm. 21, "Language and Literature Committee" file: Minutes of the District Language and Literature Committee, 4 August 1971.

82. Kabale DA ADM 5, "Kigezi District Annual Reports" file: Department of Culture, Annual report, 15 January 1975.

83. Kabale DA Public Works 23, "Public Libraries" file: Minutes of the Kabale Library fundraising committee, 26 October 1977.

Chapter 3. The Transistor Revolution

1. UBC "Old Files, 1950 to 65, Ministry of Information" box, file 15: Humphreys, "Magnetic Recording Tapes, Revised Control Procedure," n.d. (but 1969).

2. UBC tape 71/021: "President's Closing Speech at Religious Conference at Conference Hall," 6 June 1971.

3. UBC "Old Files, 1950 to 65" box, file 23: Humphreys, Sound Broadcasting Development Scheme, 7 April 1965.

4. "Improve our Radio," *Uganda Argus* 5229, 18 October 1971.

5. UBC "Old Files, 1966–1970" box, unnumbered file: Humphreys, "Project no. 13-15-03: Links to Medium Wave Transmitters," n.d. (but 1969).

6. UNA CSO 62/11,507: M. F. Hill, Memorandum on the broadcasting service arranged by the Kenya Information Office, 11 February 1941.

7. UNA CSO 62/11,507: Information Officer, Kampala, to Chief Secretary, 12 July 1941.

8. UNA CSO 62/11,507: Information Officer, Kampala, to Commissioner on Special Duty, n.d. (but 1945).

9. JDA Info. 5/16: D.C. Busoga to Kyabazinga, 21 March 1958.

10. Kabale DA ADM 15, "Public Relations" file: Department of Information, monthly report for March 1954.

11. Uganda Protectorate, *Report of the Committee of Enquiry into the Organization, Policy, and Operation of the Government's Information Services* (Entebbe: Government Printer, 1958).

12. JDA Info 2/15: Community Development Officer, Busoga, to District Commissioner, 25 April 1956.

13. UNA Mbale DA 6/MBL 15/2: Conference of provincial commissioners, June 1957.

14. *Ndimugezi* (16 Sept. 1955), summarized in JDA Info. 7/11: Summary of the local press, no. 1055.

15. JDA Info 35, "UBS Programmes" file: "Details of Programmes for the Week Ending 18 November 1960."

16. Derek R. Peterson, *Ethnic Patriotism and the East African Revival: A History of Dissent* (Cambridge: Cambridge University Press, 2012), Ch. 1; Christine Obbo, *African Women: Their Struggle for Independence* (London: Zed, 1980).

17. Kabale DA NW/CM 11, "Recording by Radio Uganda van" file: Kigezi District, "Proposed items for recording by the Radio Uganda van," 3 November 1970.

18. See Harri Englund, *Gogo Breeze: Zambia's Radio Elder and the Voices of Free Speech* (Chicago: University of Chicago Press, 2018).

19. UBC "1974–1989" box, file 9: P. M. Nsibirwa to G. R. Katongole, 25 May 1966.

20. UNA MoIA 189/S.288: P. M. Nsibirwa to Alex Ojera, 26 July 1966.

21. UBC "Old Files, 1974–89" box, "Commercial Programmes Production" file: Benjamin Kizito and others to head, Luganda Programmes, 16 November 1968.

22. Uganda Parliamentary Debates, vol. 13: Apolo Nekyon, Minister of Information, Broadcasting and Tourism, 25 June 1963; see Apolo Nsibambi, "Language Policy in Uganda: An Investigation into Costs," *African Affairs* 70 (278) (Jan. 1971), 62–71.

23. UBC "Old Files, 1966–1970" box, file 4: Sound Broadcasting Expansion Scheme, Medium Wave Project, n.d. (but September 1965).

24. UBC "Old Files, 1950 to 65" box, file 23: Humphreys, "Sound Broadcasting Development Scheme," 7 April 1965.

25. UBC "Old Files, 1966–1970" box, "Development, 1969/70" file: Humphreys, "Project No. 13-15-03," n.d. (but 1969).

26. LDA 517, file with no cover: County Chief Dokolo to D.C. Lango, 10 January 1974; County chief Oyam to D.C. Lango, 18 January 1974.

27. UBC "1972–1973" box, file 10: Raphael Kangye to Chief Engineer, 19 April 1972.

28. UBC "1972–1973" box, file 10: Lucy Apaco to Chief Engineer, n.d. (but April 1972).

29. UBC "1972–1973" box, file 10: Abraham Michael to Chief Engineer, 7 April 1972.

30. UBC "1972–1973" box, file 10: Cyril Ondebo to Chief Engineer, 30 May 1972.

31. UBC "1972–1973" box, file 10: James Uyana, St. Edward's Bukooli, to Chief Engineer, 18 May 1972.

32. UBC "1972–1973" box, file 10: Roland Dilmetz to Chief Engineer, 21 June 1972.

33. UBC "1972–1973" box, file 10: G. Johansen to Chief Engineer, 2 July 1972.

34. UBC "1972–1973" box, file 17: Ralph Perry to Radio Uganda, 11 December 1971.

35. Cabinet paper on "Radio Uganda," enclosed in FCO 31/1062: High Commission to East Africa Department, 28 September 1971.

36. UNA Mbale DA 15/2: "Contribution of the Ministry of Information and Broadcasting," 5 November 1973.

37. UBC "1972–1973" box, file 5: Agreement between Brown Boveri and Co. and the Government of Uganda, 15 February 1974.

38. UBC "1972–1973" box, file 5: Katende to Director of Engineering, 9 January 1974.

39. *A Guide to the External Service of the Uganda Broadcasting Corporation* (Kampala: Uganda Press Trust, n.d.).

40. "Swahili and French for Closer Ties with Our Brothers," *Uganda Argus* 5255 (21 November 1971).

41. UNA OP 9/1: Minutes of the 37th meeting of the Cabinet, 9 November 1971.

42. "Press Freedom Is Not a License to Mislead," *Uganda Argus* 5249, 15 November 1971.

43. "Uganda Bans Imperialist Newspapers," *Voice of Uganda* 1 (472) (10 June 1974).

44. See Emma Park, "Infrastructural Attachments: Technologies, Mobility, and the Tensions of Home in Colonial and Postcolonial Kenya" (Ph.D. dissertation, University of Michigan, 2017). See also Brian Larkin, *Signal and Noise* (Durham, N.C.: Duke University Press, 2008), Ch. 2.

45. JDA Info 5/16: Acting Town Clerk to Chief Broadcasting Engineer, Kampala, 14 May 1956.

46. E.g., the *Greeley Daily Tribune*, 4 September 1964; the *Marion Star* (Marion, Ohio), 14 October 1964; and the *Ithaca Journal*, 2 October 1964.

47. UBC Central Control Room logbook, 12 January to 26 February 1966, entry for 14 February 1966.

48. UBC Central Control Room logbook, 29 January to 1 April 1967, entry for 8 February 1967.

49. UBC Central Control Room logbook, 13 April 1971–, entry for 12 June 1971.

50. UBC Transmission Report logbook, 3 September 1965 to 21 March 1965, entry for 4 September 1965.

51. UBC Transmission Report logbook, 3 September 1965 to 21 March 1966, entry for 15 October 1965.

52. UBC Engineering logbook, 13 April 1971–, entry for 9 June 1971.

53. UBC Engineering logbook, 13 April 1971–, entry for 19 April 1971.

54. UBC Engineering logbook, 13 April 1971–, entry for 18 May 1971.

55. UBC Engineering logbook, 13 April 1971–, entry for 10 May 1971.

56. UBC "1974–1989" box, file 9: Assistant Controller of Programmes to Controller of Programmes, 8 August 1975.

57. UBC "1974–1989" box, file 39: Cosmas Warugaba, "Some of the Failures in Transmission Emanating from Unreliable Transport at U.B.C.," 21 May 1978.

58. JDA Info. 1/20: Secretary for Administration to all District Commissioners, 19 March 1971.

59. Kabarole DA 270/3: Provincial Information Officer, Western, to P.S. Ministry of Information and Broadcasting, 12 March 1975.

60. LDA 517, file with no cover: G. Obwona, report for April 1971, 5 May 1971.

61. LDA 517, file with no cover: G. Obwona, report for December 1971, 10 January 1972.

62. LDA 517, file with no cover: G. Obwona, report for March 1973, 6 April 1973.

63. LDA 517, file with no cover: G. Obwona, report for April 1973, 7 May 1973.

64. UBC "1972–73" box, file 10: E. Ssemambo to Chief Engineer, 7 April 1872.

65. UBC "1972–73" box, file 10: Lawrence Obonyo-Pata to Chief Engineer, 18 April 1972.

66. Kabarole DA 271/1: Address of the Three Directors to Members of the District Team and Planning Committee, North Busoga, 6 June 1974.

67. UBC "1972–73" box, file 10: William Ocen, Aber P7 school, to Chief Engineer, n.d. (but 1972).

68. BNA FCO 31/1950: Mulengera Lubwana to Idi Amin, 30 October 1975.

69. JDA 117/TRD 1: Trade Development Officer, Jinja District to all government agents, 3 April 1978.

70. UBC "Old files, 1966–1970" box, file 22: Charles Mpanga, untitled seminar paper, 9 April 1973.

71. UBC "Old files, 1966–1970" box, file 22: Cosmas Warugaba, "The Transcription Service as a Foreign Service," 1973.

72. "National Language, New Flag Being Considered," *Voice of Uganda* 1 (139) (15 May 1973).

73. "Broadcasts in Rwamba," *Voice of Uganda* (17 March 1973).

74. "National Language, New Flag."

75. A. R. Khadiagala, editorial letter, *Voice of Uganda* (30 March 1973).

76. David Gwyn, *Idi Amin: Death-Light of Africa* (London: Little, Brown, 1977), 71.
77. Lira DA 517, file with no cover: G. Obwona to P.S., Ministry of Information, 2 September 1972.
78. BNA FCO 31/1234: Kampala home service, 29 August 1972.
79. Kabale DA ADM 50, "Circulars—Secretary General's Office" file: Kigezi District Administrator to all county chiefs, 30 August 1972.
80. "Decree Bans Women's Wigs and Trousers," *Voice of Uganda* 1 (365) (5 February 1974).
81. Editorial letter, C. Kakembo, *Voice of Uganda* 1 (384) (27 February 1974).
82. Doreen Kembabazi, "The State of Morality: Sexual, Reproductive and Sartorial Politics in Idi Amin's Uganda" (Ph.D. dissertation, University of Michigan, 2020); Alicia Decker, *In Idi Amin's Shadow: Women, Gender, and Militarism in Uganda* (Athens: Ohio University Press, 2014), Ch. 3.
83. JDA ADM ALG 1/12: County chief Butembe to all gombolola chiefs, 17 May 1973.
84. JDA ADM ALG 1/12: County chief Butembe to D.C. Busoga, 17 May 1973.
85. Kabale DA NW/CM 11, "Story" file: "Education Announcement," 2 January 1975.
86. Kabale DA NW/CM 11, "Story" file: D.C.'s announcement, 8 January 1975.
87. BDA 513, "Celebrations, Ministry of Information" file: William Baker to Information Officer, Semuliki, 13 July 1976.
88. BDA 518, "Information Services—General" file: Baker to Information Officer, Semuliki, 30 December 1974.
89. BDA 513, "Celebrations, Ministry of Information" file: Baker to Information Officer, Semuliki, 26 April 1977.
90. BDA 518, "Information Services—General" file: Baker to Information Officer, Semuliki, 4 October 1974.
91. BDA 514, "Cooperatives" file: William Baker to D.C. Semuliki, 7 March 1977.
92. UBC "1974–1989" box, file 22: Minutes of a meeting for the Radio Uganda jubilee, 9 February 1979.

Chapter 4. A Government of Action

1. Ministry of Information and Broadcasting, *The First 366 Days* (Entebbe: Government Printer, 1972), i–ii.
2. "Rwenzururu Rebels Given Amnesty," *Voice of Uganda* 1 (77) (3 March 1973).
3. Kasese DA, "Boma" file: Regional Agriculture Officer to all saza chiefs, 15 March 1971.

4. LDA 517, "Cotton Bulletins" file: "Native Agriculture for the Year Ended 31 September 1971."

5. Kabarole DA 733/3: Department of Agriculture, "Double Crop Production Campaign Report," 9–13 April 1973.

6. See Allen Isaacman, *Cotton Is the Mother of Poverty* (Portsmouth, N.H.: Heinemann, 1996), and Michiel de Haas, "Rural Livelihoods and Agricultural Commercialization in Colonial Uganda" (Ph.D. dissertation, Wageningen University, 2017).

7. Kasese DA, file with no cover: President of Uganda, "Nine Point Plan to Farmers to Double the Production of Cotton and Produce More Money for Themselves and the Country," n.d. (but 1974).

8. Kasese DA, "Information and Publicity" file: No author, "Announcement," 27 August 1975.

9. Kasese DA, file with no cover: D.C. Toro to members of the District Cotton Judging Competition, 4 January 1973.

10. Kabarole DA 733/3: Department of Agriculture, "Double Production Crop Campaign Report," Busongora, 9–13 April 1973.

11. Kabarole DA 733/3: Secretary, Toro District Productivity Committee, "Double Production Campaign, 1973," 9–13 April 1973.

12. Kasese DA, "Bukonjo meetings" file: County team meeting, 18 May 1978.

13. BDA 516, file with no cover: "Tree Planting Programme by All Ugandans, Summary for Western Province," 1979.

14. Kasese DA, "Circulars from D.C. Kasese" file: Report of the Honourable Governor, Mr. Alex Owor's tour of Rwenzori District, July 1978.

15. LDA 517, file with no cover: Mohammed Ohamungo to District Information Officer, 9 July 1973.

16. Kabarole DA 402/1: County chief Kibaale to Governor, Western Province, 22 April 1975.

17. Nikos Alexandratos, "Food Price Surges: Possible Causes, Past Experience, and Longer Term Relevance," *Population and Development Review* 34 (4) (Dec. 2008), 663–97.

18. Kabarole DA 629/1: D.C. West Buganda to P.S. Ministry of Provincial Administration, 12 October 1973.

19. Jan Jørgensen, *Uganda: A Modern History* (New York: St. Martin's, 1981), 298.

20. LAC RG 25 12623 20-Uganda-1-4 pt. 7: Nairobi to Undersecretary of State for External Affairs, 12 September 1978.

21. LDA box 576, "Population Census" file: Grader operator, Works Department, to Treasurer, East Lango District Administration, 3 January 1978.

22. UNA OP (Confidential) 30/4: The Drivers, Minister of Foreign Affairs, to Secretary, Special Grading Committee, 22 July 1977.

23. LAC RG 25 14495 20-Uganda pt. 4: CARE Uganda, "Socio-Economic Background of Uganda, 1970–1982."

24. Jørgensen, *Uganda*, 296.

25. JDA Comm. Dev. 9/25: Meeting to discuss the distribution of maize, 1 October 1976.

26. LDA 523, file with no cover: John Sempa and Brothers to Works Supervisor, Lango, 14 January 1975.

27. BDA 507, "Furniture" file: Treasurer, Semuliki District, to Provincial Executive Secretary, April 1975.

28. BDA 513, "Planning" file: District Team meeting, Semuliki, 26 July 1977.

29. BDA 513, "Planning" file: District Team meeting, Semuliki, 18 December 1974.

30. BDA 502, "Visiting Justice" file: County chief Bwamba to D.C. Semuliki, 8 August 1975.

31. BDA 513, "Planning" file: District Team meetings, Semuliki, 22 April 1976 and 29 June 1976.

32. BDA 531, "Misc. 3" file: Subcounty chief Harugale to county chief Bwamba, 19 August 1974.

33. BDA 522, file with no cover: Semuliki District Land Committee, minutes, 28 November 1977.

34. BDA 522, file with no cover: Semuliki District Land Committee, minutes, 29 November 1978.

35. UNA MoIA 145/C.11230/1 vol. I: Minister of Internal Affairs to Commissioner of Prisons, 11 February 1976.

36. LDA 592, "Commonwealth Games Appeal" file: D.C. East Lango to all county chiefs, 9 June 1976.

37. Kabale DA NW/CM box 11, "Broadcasting, Information" file: Ministry of Tourism to all governors, 21 September 1976.

38. BDA 523, "National Parks and Tourism" file: District Education Officer to all head teachers, 11 October 1976.

39. Kabarole DA 1195/3: Self Help Projects Decree, 28 July 1975.

40. Kabale DA ADM 10, "Department Annual Reports" file: Department of Community Development, annual report, 1973.

41. Kasese DA, file with no cover: Minutes of Rwenzori District Team meeting, 19 April 1978.

42. Kasese DA, file with no cover: Minutes of Rwenzori District Team meeting, 21 June 1978.

43. Kasese DA, "Department of Youth" file: "Programme of Activities for the Development of Youths," 27 July 1976.

44. Kasese DA, "Annual Reports" file: Youth Section, Rwenzori District, Annual Report for 1977, 9 January 1978.

45. Kasese DA, file with no cover: Minutes of Rwenzori District Team meeting, 6 September 1978.

46. Kabarole DA 303/1: Treasurer, Semuliki District, to Senior Road Inspector, 24 November 1977.

47. Kabarole DA 303/1: Treasurer, Semuliki District, to D.C., 16 January 1978.

48. BDA 521, "Rural Development" file: Assistant Supervisor of Works to D.C. Semuliki, 22 March 1979.
49. Kasese DA, "Reports, District Team Correspondence" file: Communication from the chair, n.d. (but 1974).
50. BDA 513, "Planning" file: District Team meeting, Semuliki, 19 January 1976.
51. Doreen Kembabazi's work can be read in "The State of Morality: Sexual, Reproductive and Sartorial Politics in Idi Amin's Uganda" (Ph.D. dissertation, University of Michigan, 2020).
52. BNA FCO 31/1369: "The Uganda Police," March 1972.
53. UNA MoIA S.15573/3: Commissioner of Police to P.S., Ministry of Internal Affairs, 21 October 1976.
54. UNA MoIA S.15573/3: Ali Towilli, Head of the Public Safety Unit, to P.S. Ministry of Internal Affairs, 4 February 1977.
55. Michael Macoun, *Wrong Place, Right Time: Policing the End of Empire* (London: Radcliffe, 1996), 86.
56. UNA MoIA 245/S.9062: Regional Police Commander, Masaka, to Commissioner of Police, 20 September 1972.
57. CPS "Daily Crime Bulletin, 1 Jan.–10 May 1978" file: Report for 9 May 1978. Seen courtesy of Doreen Kembabazi.
58. USNA RG 59 SNF 1970–73 2645/POL 15-2 1/1/70: Kampala to State Department, 18 May 1970.
59. BNA FCO 31/1234: M. Davies to Macoun, Overseas Police Advisor, n.d. (but August 1972).
60. BNA FCO 31/1234: John Stewart, British High Commission, to Wallace, East Africa Department, 1 December 1972.
61. UNA OP (new deposit) 78/CM/14: M. Davies to M. Galagher, 11 March 1971.
62. UNA OP (new deposit) 78/CM/14: M. Davies to Nkambo Mugwera, 8 February 1971.
63. UNA OP (new deposit) 78/CM/4/1: Personal Private Secretary to Pres. Amin, 12 March 1971.
64. Kabale DA Comm. 20, "National Research Council" file: Secretary for Research to D.C. Kigezi, 16 March 1972; JDA ADM 3/14: Secretary for Research to D.C. Jinja, 16 March 1972.
65. JDA ADM ALG 20/26: P.P.S., Office of the President, to all county chiefs, Jinja District, 18 May 1976.
66. Kabarole DA 983/3: County chief Butebe to D.C. Toro, 8 June 1976.
67. Kabarole DA 628/2: Governor Western Province to D.C. Rwenzori, 8 September 1976.
68. BDA 508, "Cotton" file: District Agriculture Officer Semuliki to Agriculture Assistant, Karugutu, 30 August 1976.
69. BDA 508, "Cotton" file: Agriculture Assistant Karugutu to District Agriculture Officer, Semuliki, 4 September 1976.

70. In Western Province the amount of cotton planted in 1976–77 amounted to 15,363 hectares, down from 32,486 hectares in 1975–76. Kasese DA, "Annual Reports: Provinces" file: Dept. of Agriculture, Western Province, Annual Report for 1976.

71. UNA High Court CL 006/010: Isibosesi Musebi v. A.G., 1975.

72. UNA High Court CL 033/067: Nansani Anonya v. A.G., 1974.

73. UNA High Court CL 015/035: Christine Nansamba v. A.G., 1976.

74. UNA High Court CL 073/001: Francis Waniala v. Bugisu Local Government, 1976.

75. USNA RG 59 SNF 1970–73 2646/POL 29 1/1/70: Kampala to State Department, 1973.

76. Samuel Wambuzi, *The Odyssey of a Judicial Career in Precarious Times: My Trials and Triumphs as a Three-Time Chief Justice of Uganda* (Aberdeen: Cross House, 2014).

77. CPS "Daily Crime Bulletin" file, 7 May 1978.

78. CPS "Daily Crime Bulletin" file, 2 May 1978 and 30 April 1978.

79. CPS "Daily Crime Bulletin" file, 5 January 1978.

80. BNA FCO 31/1234: Slater to East Africa Department, 7 March 1972.

81. BNA FCO 31/1234: Joyce Mpanga to Ronald Owen, reported in Boyd to East Africa Department, 5 October 1972.

82. LAC RG 25 12623 20-Uganda-1-4 pt. 7: High Commission, Nairobi, to Undersecretary of State for External Affairs, 12 September 1978.

83. UNA OP (Confidential) 53/5: Halyeti Loda Namubanza to Amin, 15 December 1971; J. K. Zziwe to Amin, 20 January 1972; Sebastiane Mweebe to Amin, 19 January 1972.

84. JDA ADM Complaints 11/19: Yowasi Kiridama to Idi Amin, 6 September 1973.

85. UNA MoIA 191/S.1452/2: Commissioner of Prisons to regional prison commanders, 27 October 1972.

86. UNA MoIA 191/S.1452/2: Chief Government Chemist to P.S., Ministry of Defence, 6 November 1972.

87. UNA MoIA 191/S.1452/2: Commissioner of Prisons to Minister of Defence, 20 November 1972.

88. Kabarole DA 402/1: Tito Bisereko to Idi Amin, 23 February 1976.

89. Al-Hajji Field Marshall Dr. Idi Amin Dada, *The Shaping of Modern Uganda* (Kampala: Government of Uganda, 1976).

90. Kabarole DA 463/2: Tito Bisereko to President Amin, 19 March 1976.

91. Kabarole DA 102/2: Tito Bisereko to Idi Amin, 26 November 1976.

92. See Alicia Decker, "Idi Amin's Dirty War: Subversion, Sabotage, and the Battle to Keep Uganda Clean, 1971–1979," *International Journal of African Historical Studies* 43 (3) (2010), 489–513.

93. "Kampala Excels in Keep Uganda Clean," *Voice of Uganda* 1 (251) (22 September 1973).

94. Kabarole DA 401/1: Statement of Jimmy Oredo, n.d. (but mid-1973).

95. Kabarole DA 401/1: County chief Burahya to Administrative Secretary, Toro, 4 July 1973.
96. UNA MoH 55/MIS/53: Kasujja David, "Prostitution and the Economic War," 2 April 1975.

Chapter 5. The Economic War

1. "Advice to Ugandan Traders," *Uganda Argus* 5217 (13 October 1971).
2. "Scrap These Deposits—Chamber," *Uganda Argus* 5273 (13 December 1971).
3. Kabale DA ADM 46, "Intelligence Reports" file: Kigezi District intelligence committee meeting, 7 February 1972.
4. "Politician Died After Being Shot by Ugandan Security Forces," *Daily Nation* (30 November 1972).
5. USNA RG 59 SNF 1970–73 2645/POL 23 1/1/70: Kampala to State Department, 27 October 1972.
6. Mahmood Mamdani, *Imperialism and Fascism in Uganda* (Trenton, N.J.: Africa World Press, 1984), 38–39.
7. UNA Mbale DA 23/MBL 11/7: "Message to the Nation on British Citizens of Asian Origin," 12–13 August 1972.
8. BNA FCO 31/1363: British High Commission to Ministry of Defence, 29 August 1972.
9. BNA FCO 31/1363: Defence Advisor, British High Commission to Ministry of Defence, 8 August 1972.
10. LDA 626, "Intelligence, Civil Disturbances" file: Northern Province Bus Company to Secretary, Transport Licensing Board, 16 August 1972.
11. UNA Moroto DA 14/S/INT 8: District Intelligence Committee meeting, 21 August 1972.
12. UNA Moroto DA 14/S/INT 8: D.C. South Karamoja to Assistant D.C.s, 23 August 1972.
13. UNA Moroto DA 14/S/INT 8: D.C. South Karamoja to P.S., Office of the President, 20 Sept. 1972.
14. Jan Jørgensen, *Uganda: A Modern History* (New York: St. Martin's, 1981), 288.
15. UNA Moroto DA 15/C/TRD 1/1: General Idi Amin to Minister of Mineral and Water Resources, 27 September 1973.
16. JDA 117/TRD 1: Administration Department, list of shops allocated, 1973.
17. UNA MoIA 233/S.8140/1: S. Nyanzi to J. M. Kanakulya, Marketing Services Division, U.D.C., 23 November 1972.
18. Interview: Augustine Osuman, Soroti town, 30 January 2020.
19. Phares Mutibwa, *Uganda Since Independence: A Story of Unfulfilled Hopes* (London: Hurst, 1992), 115–16.
20. JDA ADM Central 4/11: Eastern Province, minutes, 27 March 1974.

21. BDA 503, "Motor and Other Vehicles" file: District Administrator to P.S. Office of the President, 5 June 1987.

22. LAC RG 25 8887 20-UGDA-1-3 pt. 4: Canadian Embassy to Ottawa, 5 October 1972.

23. Gerald Ford Presidential Library, Edward Hutchinson papers box 88: Memo from Teymuraz Bagration, Executive Secretary, Tolstoy Foundation, 5 March 1973.

24. UNA MoIA 255/S.7452: Aloysius Pinto to Charles Oboth Ofumbi, 24 October 1972.

25. JDA ADM Complaints 8/17: Ugandans to D.C. Busoga, 20 September 1972.

26. JDA Comm. Dev. 8/11: Peter Wankulu to H.E. General Idi Amin Dada, 30 December 1974.

27. UNA MoIA 280/S.10810: I.K. Musazi, "Press Conference," n.d. (but 11 August 1972).

28. Musazi's political biography is given in Jonathon Earle, *Colonial Buganda and the End of Empire: Political Thought and Historical Imagination in Africa* (Cambridge: Cambridge University Press, 2017), Ch. 1.

29. JDA Comm. Dev. 10/15: I. A. Akorya, speech on the twelfth anniversary of Ugandan independence, October 1974.

30. BDA 513, "Celebrations, Ministry of Information" file: "D.C.'s Speech on the Occasion of the Visit of the Minister of Commerce," 21 October 1975.

31. Kabarole DA 629/1: D.C. Toro to all county chiefs, 19 September 1973.

32. BDA 509, "Trade and Commerce" file: Trade Development Section, Bundibugyo, to P.S., Ministry of Commerce and Industry, 4 August 1974.

33. UNA Mbale DA 23/MBL 11/7: Speech by H.E. the President, 29 August 1972.

34. "Days of Bargaining Are Gone," *Voice of Uganda* 1 (7) (9 December 1972).

35. Kasese DA, "Staff Meetings and Traders Meetings" file: Meeting for Kasese traders, 15 March 1973.

36. Kasese DA, "Staff Meetings and Traders Meetings" file: Senior Assistant Secretary, Ministry of Commerce and Industry, 4 October 1973.

37. BNA FCO 31/1586: British High Commissioner to F.C.O., 23 January 1973.

38. LAC RG 25 11446 20-UGDA-1-4 pt. 6: Nairobi to Secretary of State for External Affairs, 4 April 1975.

39. *Voice of Uganda* 1 (658) (15 January 1975). The picture is UBC photo archive, 4440a-05-009.

40. Kabarole DA 463/2: Charles Turyatemba et al. to D.C. Toro, 4 March 1976.

41. Kasese DA, "Busongora County: District Team file": Rwenzori District Team meeting, 4 March 1976.

42. UBC photo archive, packet 4565.

43. JDA ADM Complaints 4/4: People of Jinja Town to Managing Director, Bata Shoes, 15 July 1976.

44. BDA 509, "Trade and Commerce" file: Trade Development Section, Ministry of Commerce, Kampala, to P.C.C., Kampala, 14 April 1976.
45. BDA 512, "Trade and commerce" file: D.C. Semuliki to Sales Manager, Uganda Millers, 2 April 1974.
46. JDA T&I 14/25: Traders' memorandum to the President, 28 April 1973.
47. Kasese DA "Busongora County: District Team" file: Rwenzori District Team meeting, 24 February 1977.
48. Kabarole DA 628/2: Marketing supervisor, North Bunyoro, to Managing Director, Producing Marketing Board, 29 May 1978.
49. See Godfrey Asiimwe, "From Monopoly Marketing to Coffee Magendo: Responses to Police Recklessness and Extraction in Uganda, 1971–79," *Journal of Eastern African Studies* 7 (1) (2013), 104–24.
50. Kabarole DA 628/1: Thomas Arube, Cooperative Officer, Bwamba, to Assistant Administrator, 19 February 1978.
51. Jørgensen, *Uganda*, 299; Arne Bigsten and Steven Kayizzi-Mugerwa, *Crisis, Adjustment, and Growth in Uganda: A Study of Adaptation in an African Economy* (London: Macmillan, 1999), 28–29.
52. BNA FCO 31/2387: Blundell to Secretary of State for African Affairs, 2 April 1978.
53. BNA FCO 31/2388: British High Commission, Nairobi, to East Africa Department, 19 May 1978.
54. BNA FCO 31/2145: M. K. Evans, "Dealing with Amin," 7 February 1977.
55. BDA box 501, "Uganda Police, 1974" file: Samuel Baker to Deputy Police Commander, Semuliki, 27 December 1976.
56. See Kevin Donovan, "Magendo: Arbitrage and Ambiguity on an East African Frontier," *Cultural Anthropology* 36 (1) (2021), 110–37.
57. "Death for Hoarders and Price Pushers," *Voice of Uganda* 1 (656) (13 January 1975).
58. LAC RG 25 11446 20-UGDA-1-4 pt. 6: Nairobi High Commission to Secretary of State for External Affairs, 4 April 1975.
59. "African Nations Escalate War on Coffee Smugglers," *Burlington Free Press* (7 April 1977).
60. "Stick to Set Routes or Die, Says Amin," *Daily Nation* (21 January 1977).
61. UBC photo archive, packet 6533.
62. UBC photo archive, packet 4450.
63. UBC photo archive, packets 4708a 1-4 and 4708b 1-2.
64. *Voice of Uganda* 1 (796) (25 June 1975).
65. Kabarole DA 39/1: Nasaba, Resident State Attorney, to Provincial Governor, 15 August 1978.
66. Kabarole DA 39/1: Peter Nyamutaale Amooti, Pupil State Attorney, to Provincial C.I.D. officer, 11 December 1978.
67. UNA MoIA 265/S.10156/2: Abataka ba Wobulenzi to Mustafa Adrisi, 17 June 1977.

68. UNA MoIA 265/S.10156/2: G. Lule, Ministry of Justice, to Director of Public Prosecutions, 8 July 1975.

69. UNA MoIA 265/S.10156/2: "Economic Crimes Tribunal Decree Suspects Detained in Police Custody," 3 July 1975.

70. "Amin Announces He's Coming to Olympics," *Vancouver Sun* (16 March 1976).

71. UBC photo archive, packet 5191: "H.E. Releases Prisoners in Luzira," 11 March 1976.

72. E.g., "Amin Lifts More Death Sentences," *Daily Nation* (7 April 1975); "Amin Reprieves Seven from Death," *Daily Nation* (3 December 1976); "Kenyan Trader Released from Ugandan Prison," *Daily Nation* (1 April 1978).

73. LDA 506, "Departed Asians Property Custodial Board" file: Joseph Kintu, "Statement on the Repossession of Properties by Asian Former Owners," April 1992.

74. "MPs Dig into Departed Asian Properties Saga," *Monitor* (8 May 2021).

Chapter 6. Violence and Public Life

1. LDA box with no label, "Office Organizations" file: Administrative Secretary, Lira District, to P.S., Ministry of Local Government, 6 January 1986.

2. LDA box 641, "Central Government Court" file: Chief of Askaris, East Lango, to Sergeant, Irega Askaris Station, 25 November 1975.

3. International Commission of Jurists, *Violations of Human Rights and the Rule of Law in Uganda* (Geneva, May 1974), at https://www.icj.org/wp-content/uploads/2013/06/Uganda-violations-of-human-rights-thematic-report-1974-eng.pdf; Amnesty International, *Human Rights Violations in Uganda* (London, 1978), at https://www.amnesty.org/download/Documents/204000/afr590071978en.pdf.

4. Kristen Weld, *Paper Cadavers: The Archives of Dictatorship in Guatemala* (Durham: Duke University Press, 2014).

5. Alicia Decker uses the report to good effect in her book *In Idi Amin's Shadow: Women, Gender, and Militarism in Uganda* (Athens: Ohio University Press, 2014).

6. "Truth Commission: Commission of Inquiry into the Disappearances of People in Uganda Since 25 January 1971," United States Institute of Peace, June 30, 1974; https://www.usip.org/publications/1974/06/truth-commission-uganda-74, accessed 23 July 2019.

7. Semakula Kiwanuka, *Amin and the Tragedy of Uganda* (London: Weltforum Verlag, 1979), 99.

8. BNA FCO 31/1330: Kampala to Foreign and Commonwealth Office, 17 September 1972.

9. USNA RG 59 SNF 1970–73 2646/POL 23-9 4-21-72: Kampala to State Department, 21 September 1972. The invasion is described in Yoweri

Museveni, *Sowing the Mustard Seed: The Struggle for Freedom and Democracy in Uganda* (London: Macmillan, 1997).

10. BNA FCO 31/1583: British High Commission to East Africa Department, 13 February 1973.

11. *Voice of Uganda* (12 February 1973).

12. USNA RG 59 SNF 1970–73 2645/POL 23 1/1/70: Keeley to State Department, 25 February 1973.

13. USNA RG 59 SNF 1970–73 2643/POL 1/1/70: Melady to State Department, 2 January 1973.

14. "Amin Regroups as More Quit," *Guardian* (25 February 1973).

15. USNA RG 59 SNF 1970–73 2643/POL 1/1/70: Kampala to State Department, 18 August 1973.

16. USNA RG 59 SNF 1970–73 2643/POL 1/1/70: Kampala to State Department, 25 March 1971; Holger Bernt Hansen, "Uganda in the 1970s: A Decade of Paradoxes and Ambiguities," *Journal of Eastern African Studies* 7 (1) (2013), 83–103.

17. BNA FCO 31/1584: British High Commission to East Africa Department, 8 May 1973.

18. Jan Jørgensen, *Uganda: A Modern History* (New York: St. Martin's, 1981), 308.

19. "Soldier Chiefs Must Be Efficient," *Voice of Uganda* 1 (7 May 1973).

20. USNA RG 59 SNF 1970–73 2645/POL 23-9 2/5/71: Kampala to State Department, 8 May 1971.

21. BNA FCO 31/1363: "Uganda Armed Forces as of 21 August 1972."

22. LAC RG 25 10849 20-UGDA-1-3 vol. 6: High Commissioner to Ottawa, 4 June 1975.

23. BNA FCO 31/1584: J. Stewart, memo, 2 April 1973.

24. Jørgensen, *Uganda*, 288–89.

25. USNA RG 59 SNF 1970–73 2643/POL 1/1/70: Kampala to State Department, 18 August 1973.

26. Kabale DA ADM 18, "Complaints, Rukiga County" file: People of Bukinda/Kamwezi subcounties to Provincial Governor, 20 December 1975.

27. UNA MoIA S.90 vol. V: Obitre Gama to Oboth Ofumbi, 4 May 1971.

28. UNA MoIA 189/S.90 vol. V: Administrative Secretary, Sebei District, to P.S. Office of the President, 19 March 1971.

29. Kabale DA ADM 18, "Complaints, Rukiga County" file: Barekya and three others to D.C. Kigezi, 19 August 1971.

30. UNA MoH 37/GCB 7: Medical Officer for Health, Entebbe, to P.S., Ministry of Health, 3 March 1972.

31. UNA JDA JLOS 56/33: Busoga Provincial Governor to P.S., Ministry of Internal Affairs, 14 September 1978.

32. Kabale DA ADM 1, "Kigezi, General Complaints" file: P. Ruceribuga to saza chief Rubanda, 4 May 1975.

33. Quoted in Hansen, "Uganda," 91.

34. Kabale DA ADM 46, "Intelligence Reports" file: F. M. Lukyamuzi to Commissioner for Lands and Surveys, 3 May 1971.

35. UNA Office of the President (new series) 91/8: A. Nassar to Chief of Defence Staff, 7 February 1972.

36. UNA Office of the President (new series) 91/8: Intelligence Unit, President's Office, 30 January 1972.

37. LAC RG 25 11446 20-UGDA-1-4 pt. 6: Nairobi to Sec. of State for External Affairs, 19 July 1977.

38. BNA FCO 31/1586: High Commission Kampala, "Learn to Love Big Dada," 28 February 1973.

39. BNA FCO 31/2148: A. Glasby, French Embassy, to East Africa Department, 12 February 1977.

40. WodOkello Lawoko, *The Dungeons of Nakasero: A True and Painful Experience* (Stockholm: Förtarres Bokmaskin, 2005); Wycliffe Kato, *Escape from Idi Amin's Slaughterhouse* (London: Quartet, 1989).

41. Interview with Yustasi Mukirane, Bwera, 3 June 2010.

42. Kabale DA ADM 52, "Complaints, Kinkiizi County" file: Jackson Bisabusha to D.C. Kigezi, 6 June 1973.

43. Derek R. Peterson, *Ethnic Patriotism and the East African Revival: A History of Dissent* (Cambridge: Cambridge University Press, 2012), 66.

44. Kabarole DA 452/3: Chief Secretary, circular letter, 26 September 1951.

45. *Careers in the Uganda Police* (Entebbe: Government Printers, 1970).

46. Kate Bruce-Lockhart, *Carceral Afterlives: Prisons, Detention, and Punishment in Postcolonial Uganda* (Athens: Ohio University Press, 2022).

47. Kabarole DA 1043/2: "Your Faithful Citizens and Residents of Toro" to Governor Western Province, 6 August 1974.

48. Kabale DA ADM 52, "Complaints, Kinkiizi county" file: Agriculture Officer, Tea Section to D.C. Kigezi, 15 December 1973.

49. C. Taylor, *Runyankore-Rukiga-English Dictionary* (Kampala: Fountain, 1998 [1959]).

50. May Edel, *The Chiga of Uganda* (New Brunswick, N.J.: Transaction, 1996), 33.

51. BNA FCO 31/1950: Unknown author to Idi Amin, 16 January 1976.

52. N. Dyson-Hudson, "The Present Position of the Karamojong: A Preliminary General Survey with Recommendations" (Entebbe: Government of Uganda, 1958).

53. Mahmood Mamdani, "The Colonial Roots of Famine in North-East Uganda," *Review of African Political Economy* 25 (Sept.–Dec. 1982), 66–73.

54. UNA Moroto DA 5/C NAF II vol. III: "Special Regions Ordinance," 1958.

55. BNA FCO 31/2145: Research Department, Africa Section, to Hunt, 30 March 1977.

56. UNA Moroto DA 14/C INT 1/D 1: D.C. Karamoja to P.S., Ministry of Internal Affairs, 16 October 1962.

57. J. P. Barber, "The Karamoja District of Uganda: A Pastoral People Under Colonial Rule," *Journal of African History* 3 (1) (1962), 111–24.

58. UNA MoIA 136/C.8712/2: Superintendent CID to Senior Superintendent, 22 February 1962.

59. BNA FCO 141/18330: D.C. Karamoja, comment on Relationships Commission report, 27 July 1961.

60. UNA Moroto DA 18/Edu 4: Ministry of Education Karamoja District, annual report for 1964.

61. UNA Moroto DA 18/Edu 4: Fr. V. Pellegrini to D.C. Karamoja, 15 June 1962.

62. "Karimojong Now Have a Mother Tongue Bible," *New Vision* (27 April 2011).

63. BNA FCO 141/18103: Uganda monthly intelligence appreciation, 16 May 1955.

64. *Uganda Eyogera*, 13 March 1956, summarized in JDA Information 6/20: Summaries of the local press #1275.

65. "The Karamoja Problem," *Uganda Argus* (24 September 1958).

66. BNA FCO 141/18330: Basil Bataringaya, chair, Karimojong Security Committee, to governor, 3 November 1961.

67. UNA OP (Confidential) 45/PM: 1963: Cabinet memorandum, Minister of Internal Affairs, "Security in Karamoja," 6 July 1963.

68. UBC photo archive, 3321-2-024.

69. UBC photo archive, 3321-1-015.

70. UBC photo archive, 3321-2-018.

71. My thanks to Dr. Quincy Amoah for explicating the Karimojong concept *adengei*.

72. UBC photo archive, 2144-5-043.

73. UNA OP (Confidential) 45/PMC/C.48: Uganda Bawejjere Association to Prime Minister Obote, 15 July 1963.

74. "Karamojong Are Advised to Dress Up Like Others," *Uganda Argus* (10 April 1971).

75. "'We Stay Naked' Rioters Jailed," *Daily Nation* (21 July 1971).

76. Mustafa Mirzeler and Crawford Young, "Pastoral Politics in the Northeast Periphery in Uganda," *Journal of Modern African Studies* 38 (3) (Sept. 2000), 416.

77. "Growing Tribute to Kabogoza Musoke," *Voice of Uganda* (12 June 1973).

78. UNA Moroto 5/C/NAF 8: C. Kabogoza-Musoke to P.S., Ministry of Defence, 27 November 1972.

79. UNA Moroto 5/C/NAF 8: C. Kabogoza-Musoke, briefing paper, 28 February 1973.

80. UNA Moroto 5/C/NAF 8: Minutes of the meeting held on Tuesday, 12 December 1972.

81. UNA Moroto 14/S/INT 1/2: Provincial Security meeting, 4 July 1974.

82. UNA Moroto 5/C/NAF 8: Assistant D.C. Bokora County to D.C. Central Karamoja, 7 March 1975.

83. LDA 522, "Cattle raiders and civil disturbances" file: Jago Olilim to D.C. West Lango, 29 November 1974.

84. UNA Moroto 09/C/CST 1: Assistant D.C. Bokora County to D.C. Moroto, 12 Sept. 1979.

85. Henry Kyemba, *State of Blood* (New York: Ace, 1977), 59.

86. Amnesty International, "Human Rights Violations in Uganda" (London, June 1978), at https://www.amnesty.org/download/Documents/204000/afr590071978en.pdf.

87. Thomas Melady and Margaret Melady, *Idi Amin Dada: Hitler in Africa* (Kansas City, Mo.: Sheed Andrews and McMeel, 1977); Dan Wooding and Ray Barnett, *Uganda Holocaust* (London: Pickering and Inglis, 1980).

Chapter 7. The Front Lines

1. JDA Community Development 8/11: Peter Wankulu, "O.A.U. Patriotic Volunteers," n.d.

2. Gwen Raaberg, "Beyond Fragmentation: Collage as a Feminist Strategy in the Arts," *Mosaic: An Interdisciplinary Critical Journal* 31 (3) (September 1998), 153–71.

3. USNA RG 59 SNF 1970–73 2644/POL 15-1 1/1/71: Kampala to State Department, 9 April 1971.

4. BNA FCO 31/1075: Members of Parliament to Foreign Secretary, 13 April 1971.

5. For the larger context, see Zach Levey, "Israel's Strategy in Africa, 1961–67," *International Journal of Middle East Studies* 36 (2004), 71–87.

6. Government of Israel, Ministry of Foreign Affairs, "General Idi Amin's Visit Strengthens Uganda-Israel Ties," in USNA RG 59 SNF 1970–73 2643/POL 7 1/1/71.

7. BNA FCO 31/1024: Lt. Col. Crawford to Foreign and Commonwealth Office, 29 January 1971.

8. BNA FCO 31/1043: R. Slater to H. Smedley, 25 May 1971; UNA MoIA 137/C.9352/5: Obitre Gama to Ministry of Finance, 17 February 1972.

9. ISA PMO-PrimeMinisterBureau-000vb9p: Idi Amin to Moshe Dayan, 17 June 1971.

10. USNA RG 59 SNF 1970–73 2643/POL 7 1/1/71: Zurhellen in Tel Aviv to State Department, 25 August 1971.

11. ISA MFA-Political-0002lql: O. Ofri to Chief of the Mossad, 26 February 1971.

12. ISA PMO-PrimeMinisterBureau-000w3rw: Kampala embassy to Ministry of Foreign Affairs, 17 January 1972.

13. ISA MFA-Political-0007y50: Kampala embassy to Ministry of Foreign Affairs, 20 January 1972.

14. ISA MFA-Political-0007y50: Arye Oded to Uganda Embassy, 26 January 1972.

15. ISA MFA-Political-0007y50: Sheikh Kamulegeya, receipt, 1 January 1972.

16. ISA PMO-PrimeMinisterBureau-000w3rw: Kampala embassy to Ministry of Foreign Affairs, 15 February 1972.

17. ISA PMO-PrimeMinisterBureau-000w3rw: Kampala embassy to Ministry of Foreign Affairs, 15 February 1972.

18. BNA FCO 31/1363L Defence Advisor, British High Commission, to Minister of Defence, 28 March 1972.

19. USNA RG 59 SNF 1970–73 2644/POL 15-1 1/7/72: State Department to Kampala, 21 April 1972.

20. UBC photo archive packet 100240.

21. ISA PMO-PrimeMinisterBureau-000wlob: Press statement by H.E. the President of Uganda, n.d. (but 23 March 1972).

22. BNA FCO 31/1351: British High Commission Tripoli, 27 March 1972.

23. UN Perez de Cuellar papers, S-0907-0010-01: Idi Amin to Secretary General, 11 September 1972.

24. ISA PMO-PrimeMinisterBureau-000w3rw: Kampala embassy to Ministry of Foreign Affairs, 17 February 1972.

25. USNA RG 59 SNF 1970–73 2643/POL 7 1/1/71; Kampala to State Department, 27 June 1972.

26. USNA RG 59 SNF 1970–73 2645/POL 17 1/1/70: Kampala to State Department, 15 October 1973.

27. Idi Amin, _On the Middle East Crisis_ (Kampala: Government of Uganda, January 1974).

28. UN Kurt Waldheim papers, S-0904-0071-11: Kinene to Kurt Waldheim, 15 February 1974.

29. LAC RG 25 8996 20-UGDA-1-4 pt. 4: High Commissioner Nairobi to Ottawa, 25 May 1972.

30. "Another telegram from President Amin to President Nixon," Wikileaks cable: 1973STATE090723_b, dated 11 May 1973, at https://wikileaks.org/plusd/cables/1973STATE090723_b.html.

31. UN Kurt Waldheim papers, S-0904-0071-11: Kinene to Waldheim, 3 January 1975.

32. UN Perez de Cuellar papers, S-0907-0010-01: Amin to Taferi Bante, Chair of the Provisional Ethiopian government, n.d. (but February 1975).

33. "Be Our King, Hawaii Asks Dr Amin," _Voice of Uganda_ 1 (1250) (7 December 1976).

34. Uganda Kampala, "Telegram from President Amin to President Lon Nol," Wikileaks cable: 1973KAMPAL02146_b, dated 3 July 1973, https://wikileaks.org/plusd/cables/1973KAMPAL02146_b.html.

35. "General Presents Scottish Case," _Voice of Uganda_ 1 (645) (31 December 1974).

36. LAC RG 25 10849 20-UGDA-1-3 vol. 6: Canada embassy, Addis Ababa to Ottawa, 29 November 1974.

37. USNA RG 59 SNF 1970–73 2644/POL 15-1: State Department to Kampala, 26 December 1972.
38. Conversation 154-7, 24 September 1972, 11:37–11:52 a.m., Richard Nixon and Henry Kissinger, at http://nixontapes.org/hak/154-007.mp3.
39. USNA RG 59 SNF 1970–73 2644/POL 15-1: Melady to State Department, 8 February 1973.
40. "Prince Norodom Sihanouk Arrives Today," *Voice of Uganda* 1 (936) (5 December 1975).
41. UN Kurt Waldheim papers, S-0904-0040-04: Idi Amin to President of Algeria, 2 November 1974.
42. UNA MoIA 186/S.44 vol. II: Handing Over Report to the Thirteenth Session of the Assembly of the O.A.U., 2–5 July 1976.
43. LAC RG 25 11495 23-1-Uganda pt. 1: Commonwealth Secretary General, circular to Heads of Government, 11 April 1975.
44. "President of Uganda Switching: Position Now More Militant," *Miami Herald* (22 January 1972).
45. LAC RG 25 8886 20-UGDA-1-3 pt. 1: Canadian High Commissioner, Addis Ababa, to High Commissioner, Nairobi, 30 March 1972.
46. Kampala Home Service report, 18 July 1974.
47. Kampala Home Service report, 14 February 1974.
48. The *Sunday Express* (31 March 1963), quoted in Kwandiwe Kondlo, *In the Twilight of the Revolution: The Pan Africanist Congress of Azania (South Africa)* (Basel: Basler Afrika Bibliographien, 2009), 127.
49. Quoted in Kondlo, *In the Twilight of the Revolution*, 127.
50. "Uganda's Idi Amin Urges Black War Against Apartheid Nation," *Kitsap Sun* (19 July 1975).
51. "Africa Must Be Free, Says Amin," *Daily Nation* (29 July 1975).
52. "Uganda: Mock Attack on 'Cape Town' Island Marks the End of OAU Summit Conference" (2 August 1975), *Reuters Screen Ocean*, record ID: 355216, at https://reuters.screenocean.com/record/355216.
53. "Field Marshall Confers with Pan Africanist Congress Leader," *Voice of Uganda* (1 November 1975).
54. "Leballo Says No Dialogue with Racist Regimes," *Voice of Uganda* (3 November 1975).
55. UBC photo archive, 4993-005.
56. "Amin's Secret Weapon Can Take On 2,000, He Claims," *The Guardian* (12 October 1977).
57. Kondlo, *In the Twilight of the Revolution*, 139–40.
58. UBC photo archive, 5962.
59. UNA MoH 35/ECT 27: Secretary General, Uganda Red Cross, to P.S. Ministry of Health, 11 Jan. 1978.
60. UNA OP (new series) 96/30: "His Excellent the President of Uganda, General Idi Amin Dada's Contribution to the O.A.U. 10th Summit, Addis Ababa, May 1973."

61. BDA box 513, "Planning" file: D.C. Semuliki, "A short welcome speech for the occasion of Africa Day," 25 May 1976.

62. JDA ADM (Foreign Affairs) 1/30: 20th Regular Session of the O.A.U. Liberation Committee, 15–22 May 1972.

63. JDA ADM (Foreign Affairs) 1/30: Town Clerk, Jinja, circular letter, 4 May 1972.

64. JDA ADM (Foreign Affairs) 1/30: O.A.U. Liberation Fund committee meeting, 10 May 1972.

65. LAC RG 25 8996 20-UGDA-1-4 pt. 4: High Commissioner Nairobi to Ottawa, 25 May 1972.

66. UNA MoIA 153/C.9352/13: Commissioner of Police to Minister of Internal Affairs, 16 October 1973.

67. BNA FCO 31/1363: Defence Advisor to Ministry of Defence, 1 February 1972.

68. BNA FCO 31/1363: Defence Advisor to Ministry of Defence, 29 September 1972.

69. "Conqueror of the British Empire," *Voice of Uganda* 2 (154) (29 June 1977).

70. Gerald Ford Presidential Library, National Security Advisor papers, Uganda file: Reuters report, 6 July 1976.

71. Kabarole DA box 1043 file 2: Abubakar Kibudde to Idi Amin, 5 July 1976.

72. Kabarole DA box 283, "Military Affairs, General" file: Abubakar Kibudde to Idi Amin, 15 January 1978.

73. Kabarole DA box 283, "Military Affairs, General" file: Abubakar Kibudde to Commanding Officer, Mountains of the Moon regiment, 15 January 1978.

74. "Immigration Plan of Roy Innis," *Daily Nation* (19 July 1971).

75. UBC photo archive, 3493-4: C.O.R.E. delegations, March 1973.

76. "75 Years of Makerere," *Sunday Monitor* (22 March 1998).

77. "Amin, US Activist Attempt to Resettle Black Americans in Uganda," *Sunday Monitor* (7 February 2021).

78. "Back to Mother Africa," *Daily Nation* (29 May 1973).

79. LAC RG 25 10849 20-UGDA 1-3 vol. 6: High Commission Nairobi to Ottawa, 5 July 1973.

80. "50 U.S. Blacks Scheduled to Go to Uganda's Aid," *Orlando Sentinel* (9 July 1973).

81. "CORE's Uganda Plan Delayed by Idi Amin," *Jet* (19 July 1973), 24.

82. LAC RG 25 10849 20-UGDA-1-3 pt. 6: Canadian High Commissioner Nairobi to Ottawa, 5 July 1973.

83. BNA FCO 31/1584: Stewart to East Africa Department, 3 July 1973.

84. UBC photo archive, packet 4867: Black Americans meet H.E. at State House, 11 August 1975.

85. *Pittsburg Courier* (14 May 1977).

86. BNA FCO 31/1773: Information Research Department to British High Commission, 18 July 1974.

87. "Africa Youth League," *Daily Nation* (4 December 1963).

88. HDA 389/3: "African Unity Youth Organization," 17 August 1964.

89. JDA Comm. Dev. 8/11: Peter Wankulu to "The Whole African Community," 28 February 1970.

90. JDA Comm. Dev. 8/11: Peter Wankulu to "The Whole African Community," 28 February 1970.

91. JDA Comm. Dev. 8/11: Wankulu to D.C. Jinja, 11 December 1974.

92. Walter Opello, "Pluralism and Elite Conflict in an Independence Movement: FRELIMO in the 1960s," *Journal of Southern African Studies* 2 (1) (Oct. 1975), 66–82.

93. David Mabunda, "Press Communiqué," 22 August 1963, at http://www. aluka.org.proxy.lib.umich.edu/stable/pdf/10.5555/al.sff.document. chilco285. My thanks to Anne Pitcher and Benedito Machava for their help in identifying David Mabunda.

94. Helen Codere, "Field Work in Rwanda, 1959–1960," in *Women in the Field: Anthropological Experiences*, ed. Peggy Golde (Berkeley: University of California Press, 1986), 156.

95. BNA FCO 31/1966: British High Commission to East Africa Department, 17 February 1975.

96. UNA MoIA 103/C.44/1 vol. II: Committee for the preparation of the O.A.U. summit, 8 May 1975.

97. UNA MoIA 103/C.44/1 vol. II: Minutes of the cabinet meeting on the O.A.U. summit, 18 October 1974.

98. UNA OP (Confidential) 95/CRA/57: "First meeting of the committee of officials preparing for the O.A.U. summit conference in Kampala," 28 October 1974.

99. JDA Comm. Dev. 8/11: S. Mungai, Assistant Chief of Protocol, to Peter Wankulu, 6 January 1975.

100. Peter Wankulu, editorial letter, *Voice of Uganda* (2 December 1972).

101. JDA Comm. Dev. 10/5: "O.A.U. Only, Africa Must Unite," n.d. (but 1974).

102. UNA Moroto DA 12/SCW 7/4: Speech by Hon. Etiang, Minister of State, Office of the President, July 1975.

103. JDA Comm. Dev. 8/11: "Africa Of Our Times," n.d. (but 1974).

104. JDA Comm. Dev. 8/11: Peter Wankulu and others to chair, O.A.U. Council of Ministers, 12 April 1974.

105. JDA Comm. Dev. 8/11: "O.A.U. Only, Africa Must Unite," n.d. (but 1974).

106. JDA Comm. Dev. 8/11: "O.A.U. Only, Africa Must Unite," n.d. (but 1974).

107. "Head Is the Qualification," *Voice of Uganda* (21 December 1972).

108. "Tracking Down the Man Who 'Initiated' the OAU," *Voice of Uganda* (31 March 1972).

109. BNA FCO 31/1773: Wankulu to Idi Amin, enclosure in British High Commission to East Africa Department, 1 July 1974.

110. JDA Comm. Dev. 8/11: Wankulu to Idi Amin, 30 December 1974.

111. UNA MoIA C.44/1 vol. III: Director of Intelligence, Special Branch, to P.S. Ministry of Internal Affairs, 9 July 1976.

112. Interview with Peter Wankulu, Kamwokya, Kampala, 8 August 2018.
113. "Mzee Wankulu: Forgotten Hero of the OAU?" *The Monitor* (20 April 2000).
114. "O.A.U. Veteran Ails, Cries for Financial Help," *New Vision* (14 July 2007), at http://allafrica.com/stories/200707160363.html, accessed 1 May 2024.
115. "Museveni's Former Teacher on Overstaying in Power," *The Observer* (12 August 2012), at http://www.observer.ug/news-headlines/20331-musevenis-former-teacher-on-overstaying-in-power, accessed 13 October 2017.
116. "Mutebile, Olara Utunu Scoop Awards at 2016 Pan-African Pyramid Global Awards," *Chimp Reports* (30 August 2016), at http://chimpreports.com/entertainment/mutebile-olara-otunu-scoop-awards-at-2016-pan-african-pyramid-global-awards/, accessed 13 October 2017.

Chapter 8. Governing Religion

1. John Mbiti, *African Religions and Philosophy* (London: Heinemann, 1969). Mbiti's biography is given in Jacob Olupona, "A Biographical Sketch," in *Religious Plurality in Africa: Essays in Honour of John S. Mbiti*, ed. Olupona and Sulayman S. Nyang (Berlin: de Gruyter, 1993), 1–10.
2. John Mbiti, "The Snake Song," *Transition* 27 (1966), 49.
3. Okot p'Bitek, *African Religions in Western Scholarship* (Kampala: East African Literature Bureau, 1970).
4. Latter-day criticism has largely followed Okot's lead. See Rosalind Shaw, "The Invention of 'African Traditional Religion,'" in *Religion* 20 (1990), 339–53; Paul Landau, "'Religion' and Christian Conversion in African History: A New Model," *The Journal of Religious History* 23 (1) (Feb. 1999), 8–30; and Derek R. Peterson and Darren Walhof, eds., *The Invention of Religion: Rethinking Belief in Politics and History* (New Brunswick, N.J.: Rutgers University Press, 2002).
5. Christopher Mulema, "The Gospel According to Africa," *Daily Nation* (28 May 1971).
6. John Mbiti, *Concepts of God in Africa* (London: SPCK, 1970).
7. See among other works Kenneth Adelman, "The Recourse to Authenticity and Negritude in Zaire," *Journal of Modern African Studies* 13 (1) (1975), 134–39; and Sarah Van Beurden, *Authentically African: Arts and the Transnational Politics of Congolese Culture* (Athens: Ohio University Press, 2015).
8. Editorial letter, *Voice of Uganda* 1 (3) (5 December 1972).
9. UNA OP (Confidential) 31/06: Cabinet memorandum 119, "Mini Dresses," 1 June 1971.
10. BNA FCO 31/1234: Hyde, High Commission, to East Africa Department, 7 July 1972.
11. LDA box 609, "Speeches, Policy Statements" file: Speeches made by the Minister during a Tour of Teso, 13 to 15 September 1972.

12. "Our Identity Depends on Culture," *Uganda Argus* 5267 (2 December 1971).

13. Kasese DA "Boma" file: Culture officer, Toro, to county chiefs, 19 March 1971.

14. Kabale DA Comm. Dev. 21, "Culture Activities" file: E. Galabuzi-Mukasa, national coordinator, to all culture officers, 16 August 1974.

15. Pamela Khanakwa, "Reinventing Imbalu and Forcible Circumcision: Gisu Political Identity and the Fight for Mbale in Late Colonial Uganda," *Journal of African History* 59 (3) (2018), 357–79.

16. Kabale DA Comm. Dev. 17, "Festivals and Competition" file: John Tumusi-ime to P.S., Ministry of Culture and Community Development, 20 October 1972.

17. Kasese DA "Boma" file: Culture Officer, Toro and Bunyoro, to all county chiefs, 14 October 1971.

18. BDA box 521, "Rural Development" file: Culture Office, Toro, Rwenzori and Semuliki, to P.S., Ministry of Culture and Community Development, 20 April 1978.

19. CoU ABP 42/4: J. Okodoi to the archbishop, Church of Uganda, 12 February 1971.

20. CoU ABP 42/4: John Mbiti to J. Okodoi, 17 February 1971.

21. Mbiti, *African Religions*, 3–4.

22. USNA RG 59 Central Foreign Policy Files 1967-69 2558/POL 12: Kampala to State Department, 5 February 1967.

23. BNA FCO 31/712: British High Commission to East Africa Department, 30 October 1970.

24. BNA FCO 31/1019: British High Commission to East Africa Department, 29 January 1971.

25. Akiiki B. Mujaju, "The Political Crisis of Church Institutions in Uganda," *African Affairs* 75 (298) (Jan. 1976), 67–85.

26. Neil Kodesh, "Renovating Tradition: The Discourse of Succession in Colonial Buganda," *The International Journal of African Historical Studies* 34 (3) (2001), 511–41.

27. CoU ABP V General file 43/1: Rev. A.M. Kasozi to Amin, 30 September 1971.

28. BNA FCO 31/1066: High Commissioner to East Africa Department, 17 June 1971.

29. CoU ABP 42/4: Sabiti to P.S., Office of the President, 19 March 1971.

30. UNA OP (Confidential) 22/SRA 22: *Ddobozi lya Uganda* 31 (140) (31 August 1971), "Giving Commands to Arrest the Religious Leaders of Namirembe."

31. CoU PS II 91/1: Speech by H.E. President Amin on the occasion of meeting the leaders of the Church of Uganda, 26 April 1971.

32. CoU PS II 75/3: Conference of Religious Leaders, Speech by H.E. the President, 19 May 1971.

33. Joseph Kasule, *Islam in Uganda: The Muslim Minority, Nationalism, and Political Power* (London: Boydell and Brewer, 2022).
34. CoU ABP V General File 43/1: E. Kamya, E. Sendiwala and others to Archbishop Sabiti, 17 November 1971.
35. CoU ABP V General File 43/1: Address of H.E. the President of Uganda to the Bishops of the Church of Uganda, 26 November 1971.
36. CoU ABP V General File 43/1: Sabiti, circular letter, 3 December 1971.
37. See Ali Mazrui, "The Sacred and the Secular in East African Politics," *Cahiers d'Études Africaines* 13 (53) (1973), 664–81.
38. See M. Louise Pirouet, "Religion in Uganda under Idi Amin," *Journal of Religion in Africa* 11 (1) (1980), 13–29.
39. CoU ABP General File 59/2: P. Kadoma to Mr. Charan Singh, 22 May 1972.
40. The website of Radha Soami Satsang Beas is at www.rssb.org, accessed 18 March 2020.
41. CoU ABP General File 59/3: Kadoma to Rev. John, Makindye, Kampala, 5 June 1972.
42. CoU ABP General File 59/3: Paul Kadoma to Idi Amin, 27 June 1972.
43. An argument developed in Derek R. Peterson, *Ethnic Patriotism and the East African Revival: A History of Dissent* (Cambridge: Cambridge University Press, 2012).
44. CoU ABP V General file 69/5: Sabiti to Mr. S. Mungoma, 19 September 1973.
45. Kabarole DA 382/2: Minister of Internal Affairs, Penal (Unlawful Societies) Order, 31 May 1973.
46. "State Supreme Council Formed," *Voice of Uganda* (26 June 1973).
47. Kabarole DA 382/4: Unlawful Society Declaration order, 21 February 1975.
48. Kabarole DA 382/3: D.C. Toro to all county chiefs, 18 October 1977.
49. CoU ABP General File 69/5: Stephen Mungoma, "The Challenge of the Year," n.d. (but 1975).
50. Dan Wooding and Ray Barnett, *Uganda Holocaust: They Faced Amin's Terror Machine Undaunted* (London: Pickering and Inglis, 1972), 23–32.
51. UNA MoIA 238/S.8358: Meeting to settle matters relating to the Isa Messiah Church and the Seventh-Day Adventists in Busoga, n.d. (but December 1976).
52. Kabarole DA 382/2: Y. Musane to D.C. Rwenzori, 16 August 1978.
53. Kabarole DA 382/2: Y. Mukirane to D.C. Rwenzori, 27 June 1978.
54. CoU ABP V General file 69/5: Sabiti to Rev. Edward Ssebowa, 13 September 1973.
55. UNA OP 6/16: Livingstone Kiyise, Department of Community Development, to Idi Amin, n.d.
56. J. J. Carney, "The Politics of Ecumenism in Uganda, 1962–1986," *Church History* 86 (3) (Sept. 2017), 765–95.

57. Mbiti, "Diversity, Divisions and Denominationalism," in *Kenya Churches Handbook: The Development of Kenyan Christianity*, ed. David Barrett et al. (Kisumu: Evangel, 1973), 144–52.

58. The file is CoU ABP General file 27/2.

59. Described in BNA FCO 31/2148: Luwum, "Report of a very serious incident," 5 February 1977.

60. BNA FCO 31/2148: Janani Luwum, Festo Kivengere, Dunstan Nsubuga, and others to Idi Amin, 10 February 1977.

61. "Obote's Plan Exposed," *Voice of Uganda* 2 (41) (17 February 1977).

62. These events are described in Margaret Ford, *Even Unto Death: The Story of Uganda Martyr Janani Luwum* (Elgin, Ill.: David Cook, 1978); Emmanuel Kalenzi Twesigye, "Church and State Conflicts in Uganda: President Idi Amin Kills the Anglican Archbishop," in *Religion, Conflict, and Democracy in Modern Africa*, ed. Samuel K. Elolia (Eugene, Ore.: Pickwick, 2012), 151–99; Zac Niringiye, *The Church in the World: A Historical-Ecclesiological Study of the Church of Uganda* (Carlisle: Langham Partnership, 2016), Ch. 5; and Kevin Ward, "Archbishop Janani Luwum: The Dilemmas of Loyalty, Opposition and Witness in Amin's Uganda," in *Christianity and the African Imagination*, ed. David Maxwell and Ingrid Lawrie (Leiden: Brill, 2002), 199–224.

63. Don Wooding and Ray Barnett, *Uganda Holocaust* (London: Pickering and Inglis, 1980), 101–2.

64. Wooding and Barnett, *Uganda Holocaust*, 102; "Oryema, Ofumbi, Luwum Dead," *Voice of Uganda* 2 (41) (17 February 1977).

65. UNA OP 2/S.2814: D.C. Bukedi to Provincial Governor, Eastern, 21 February 1977.

66. Kabarole DA 382/2: Juma Aiga, address to religious leaders, 28 February 1977.

67. Kabarole DA 382/2: Alex Owour, speech on the centenary of the Church of Uganda, 30 June 1977.

68. Kabarole DA 382/3: Parish priest Humura to A.D.C. Kyaka District, 12 September 1978.

69. Kabarole DA 382/3: Cypriano Mutahigwa to parish priest, Humura, 25 October 1978.

70. Kabarole DA 382/2: Governor Western Province, list of contributors toward the construction of Church House, 17 August 1978.

71. BDA box 513, "Celebrations, Ministry of Information" file: D.C. Semuliki to Heads of Department, 23 May 1978.

72. "Church House Handed Over to Ntagali," *New Vision* (14 June 2018).

73. John Mbiti, *New Testament Eschatology in an African Background* (New York: Oxford University Press, 1971); Mbiti, *Love and Marriage in Africa* (London: Longman, 1973); Mbiti, "Death and the Hereafter in the Light of Christianity and African Religion: An Inaugural Lecture" (Kampala: Department of Religious Studies and Philosophy, 1974); Mbiti, *The Prayers of African Religion* (London: SPCK, 1975).

74. "Christian Faith Gains in Africa with Freedom," *Pittsburgh Press* (22 March 1973).
75. Kabarole DA 382/2: P. Wangola, Resident Tutor, Makerere University, to Governor Western Province, 22 April 1974.
76. Mbiti, *Concepts of God in Africa*.
77. "Red Carpet Welcome for Libyan Leader," *Voice of Uganda* 1 (388) (4 March 1974).
78. "Libyan Leader Ends Historic Visit," *Voice of Uganda* 1 (390) (6 March 1974).
79. Will Kaberuka, *The Political Economy of Uganda, 1890–1975: A Case Study of Colonialism and Underdevelopment* (New York: Vantage, 1990), 276.
80. LAC RG 25 10849 20-UGDA-1-3 vol. 6: High Commissioner to Ottawa, 4 June 1975.
81. Ford, *Even Unto Death*, 65–66.
82. "U of R Culture Week Starts with Speech Today," *San Bernardino County Sun* (28 March 1974).
83. John Mbiti, "The Future of Christianity in Africa," *CrossCurrents* 28 (4) (Winter 1978–79), 387–94.

Chapter 9. Making History

1. Kabale DA Public Works 23, "Monuments" file: Department of Antiquities Monthly Report, January 1975.
2. Kabale DA Public Works 23, "Monuments" file: Department of Antiquities Annual Report for 1975.
3. Jeffery K. Smith, *The Museum Effect: How Museums, Libraries, and Cultural Institutions Educate and Civilize Society* (London: Rowman and Littlefield, 2014); Derek R. Peterson, Kodzo Gavua, and Ciraj Rassool, eds., *The Politics of Heritage in Africa: Economies, Histories, and Infrastructures* (Cambridge: Cambridge University Press, 2015).
4. Kabarole DA 507/1: Chief Secretary, Entebbe, circular to Provincial Commissioners, 23 March 1935.
5. JDA Comm. Dev. 12/11: D.C. Jinja to P.C. Eastern, 13 August 1952.
6. UNA CSO 100/17701: Development Council, "Tourism," n.d. (but 1955). See Joseph Ouma, *Evolution of Tourism in East Africa (1900–2000)* (Nairobi: East African Literature Bureau, 1970).
7. UNA CSO 64/11861/I: Undated flyer (but 1950).
8. UNA OP (Confidential) 85/C.43/107/01: Director of Public Works, "Speke Memorial," 17 January 1957.
9. Kabale DA Public Works 27, "Monuments" file: P.C. Western Province to P.S., Ministry of Local Government, 28 August 1958.
10. BNA DO 213/237: J. Kiggundu to Obote, 17 July 1966.
11. Kabarole DA 386/2: Rwambarare to Administrative Secretary, Tooro, 12 September 1968.

12. Kabarole DA 1230/4: P.S., Ministry of Information, Broadcasting and Tourism, 12 May 1965.
13. JDA Comm. Dev. 8/8: D.C. Busoga to P.S., Ministry of Information, Broadcasting and Tourism, 18 September 1965.
14. LAC RG 25 5238 7116-DT-40: Wilson to Hake, 31 January 1963.
15. Kabale DA Public Works 26, "Historical Monuments" file: P.S. for Tourism to all District Commissioners and culture officers, 7 August 1968.
16. Kabale DA Public Works 26, "Historical Monuments" file: Principal, Institute of Public Administration to D.C. Kigezi, 19 October 1970.
17. LDA box 517, file with no cover: Hon. A. Ojera, Minister of Information, Broadcasting and Tourism, 8 August 1970.
18. BNA FCO 31/1049: Minister of Finance, Budget Speech, 17 June 1971.
19. BNA FCO 31/1018: Slater, British High Commission, to East African Department, 5 October 1971.
20. Uganda Museum, Ethnography catalogue, items E.71/60 and E.71/61/1–2.
21. Uganda Museum, Ethnography catalogue, item E.71/65.
22. Kabale DA Public Works 23, "Monuments" file: Department of Antiquities Monthly Report, September 1974.
23. "New Move to Retain History," *Uganda Argus* 5211 (1 October 1971).
24. Kabale DA Public Works 26, "Historical Monuments" file: P. Wamala, "Operation of the Department of Antiquities," n.d. (but 1973).
25. UNA OP (Confidential) 31/11: Oral evidence by the Ministry of Culture and Community Development, 29 November 1973.
26. "Bunyoro People Urged to Toil," *Voice of Uganda* (24 August 1973).
27. "At Last It's Pulled Down," *Voice of Uganda* 1 (40) (19 January 1973).
28. "Authenticity Triumphs over Colonialism," *Voice of Uganda* 1 (193) (17 July 1973).
29. "Amin Issues Medals on Sixth Anniversary," *Wisconsin State Journal* (29 January 1977).
30. Kabale DA Public Works 23, "Monuments" file: Department of Antiquities, annual report for 1975.
31. UM "Natural History, Archaeology" catalogue, object H71.04/13.
32. UM "Ethnography, 1970–" catalogue, item 14076.
33. UM "Ethnography, 1970–" catalogue, item 14077.
34. UM "Ethnography, 1970–" catalogue, items E.72/06 to 35.
35. HDA 273/1: P.S. Ministry of Culture and Community Development to D.C. Bunyoro, 3 February 1967.
36. HDA 1026/3: Culture Officer Bunyoro to Augustine Kyomya, 12 July 1974.
37. HDA 1026/3: A. Kyomya to Culture Officer, Bunyoro, 12 July 1974.
38. HDA 1026/3: Gombolola chief Busisi to saza chief Bughaya, 23 July 1974.
39. Kabale DA Public Works 23, "Monuments" file: Antiquities monthly report, October 1974.
40. Kabale DA Public Works 23, "Monuments" file: Conservator of Antiquities, monthly report for April 1975.

41. HDA 273/1: Alexandra Nomukyeya to Administrative Secretary, Bunyoro, 21 July 1972.

42. HDA 273/1: Michael Kaheru, Culture Officer, to Administrative Secretary, Bunyoro, 8 September 1972.

43. HDA 273/1: Administrative Secretary Bunyoro to P.S., Local Administration Division, 16 March 1971.

44. HDA 273/1: Culture Officer Bunyoro to D.C. Bunyoro, 28 November 1972.

45. Kabale DA Public Works 23, "Monuments" file: Conservator of Antiquities, monthly report, April 1975.

46. HDA 1026/3: Conservator of Antiquities to Minister of Culture and Community Development, 8 August 1974.

47. HDA 1026/3: Sam Byagira to muluka chief Butima, 24 April 1975.

48. Ray Silverman, ed., *Museum as Process: Translating Local and Global Knowledges* (London: Routledge, 2014).

49. HDA 400/1: Akech Theresa, "The Ancient Traditional Dress and Tools of the Banyoro," October 1978.

50. See the Chimurenga Collective, *FESTAC '77* (London: Afterall, 2019), and Andrew Apter, *The Pan-African Nation: Oil and the Spectacle of Culture in Nigeria* (Chicago: University of Chicago Press, 2005).

51. Kabale DA Comm. Dev. 21, "Cultural Activities" file: Mrs. Dungu to all Community Development Assistants, 2 April 1974.

52. Kabale DA Comm. Dev. 17, "Festivals and Competition" file: Uganda National Steering Committee meeting, 6 December 1974.

53. Kabale DA Comm. Dev. 17, "Festivals and Competition" file: Tumusiime to Chair, Pottery Subcommittee, 17 November 1975.

54. Kabale DA Comm. Dev. 17, "Festivals and Competition" file: Tumusiime to Principal Culture Officer, 26 January 1974.

55. Interview with Rev. John Basingwire, Kampala, 23 February 2020.

56. Kabale DA ADM 7 "Annual Reports" file: Department of Culture annual report, 1972.

57. Kabale DA Comm. Dev. 17, "Museums" file: Tumusiime to D.C. Kigezi, 7 July 1972.

58. Kabale DA Comm. Dev. 20, "Dances" file: "Brief Note on Filming in Ankole and Kigezi Districts," n.d. (but 1972).

59. Kabale DA Comm. Dev. 20, "Dances" file: Minutes of the Standing Committee of Ndorwa Cultural Committee, 4 November 1972.

60. Kabale DA ADM 5 "Kigezi District Annual Reports" file: J. Tumusiime, Department of Culture, North and South Kigezi, Annual Report for 1974.

61. Kabale DA Comm. Dev. 17, "Festivals and Competition" file: Tumusiime to D.C. South Kigezi, 29 June 1976.

62. BNA FCO 31/1234: Harry Brind to East Africa Department, 13 November 1972.

63. BNA FCO 31/1363: Defence Advisor to Ministry of Defence, 4 December 1972.
64. Kabale DA Public Works 23, "Monuments" file: J. Tumusiime to Conservator of Antiquities, 16 November 1972.
65. Kabale DA Public Works 23, "Monuments" file: J. Tumusiime to Conservator of Antiquities, 9 April 1973.
66. Kabale DA Public Works 23, "Monuments" file: Subcounty chief Nyakabande to Culture Officer, 4 April 1974.
67. Kabale DA Public Works 23, "Monuments" file: Tumusiime to Conservator of Antiquities, 29 October 1974.
68. Kabale DA Public Works 23, "Monuments" file: Tumusiime to Conservator of Antiquities, 6 May 1975.
69. Kabale DA Public Works 23, "Monuments" file: Community Development Assistant to Culture Officer, 14 April 1976.
70. Kabale DA Public Works 23, "Monuments" file: Sinumvaybo John to Culture Officer, 24 January 1985.
71. Kabale DA Public Works 23, "Monuments" file: Subcounty chief Nyakabande to Culture Officer, Kabale, 3 October 1980.
72. Kabale DA Public Works 23, "Monuments" file: E. Baryayebwa, Culture Officer, Kabale to Magistrate, Kisoro, 31 July 1986.
73. Kabale DA Public Works 24, "Kigezi District Museum" file: Tumusiime to Curator, Uganda Museum, 20 April 1973.
74. Kabale DA Public Works 24, "Kigezi District Museum" file: Tumusiime to P.S., Ministry of Culture and Community Development, 18 February 1976.
75. Kabale DA Public Works 24, "Kigezi District Museum" file: James Ssebaduka to Acting Chief Conservator, Antiquities, 17 August 1977.
76. Kabale DA Community Development 17, "Museums" file: John Tiina-Kagundu to county chief, Ndorwa, 3 July 1978.
77. Kabale DA Community Development 17, "Museums" file: H. Baryayebwa to Curator, Uganda Museum, 6 November 1980.
78. Kabale DA Comm. Dev. 17, "Museums" file: Baryayebwa to Curator, Uganda Museum, 22 Feb. 1982.
79. Kabale DA Comm. Dev. 17, "Museums" file: Caretaker, Kabale Museum, to Culture Officer, Kabale, 18 June 1990.
80. "Marshall Watches Final Rehearsal," *Voice of Uganda* (14 January 1977).
81. "Stall in Lagos Is a Wonder," *Voice of Uganda* 2 (23) (27 January 1977).
82. "Festac '77," *Daily Nation* (16 December 1977).
83. Publicity Division, International Secretariat, *FESTAC '77 General Programme* (Lagos: Supercolour Productions, 1977).
84. "Well Done, Cultural Envoys," *Voice of Uganda* 2 (35) (8 February 1977).
85. Wole Soyinka, "Twice Bitten: The Fate of Africa's Culture Producers," *PMLA* 105 (1) (Jan. 1990), 110–20.
86. Kabale DA Public Works 24, "Kigezi District Museum" file: Tumusiime to Curator, Kabale Museum, n.d. (but April 1976).

Chapter 10. Living Off the Grid

1. BNA FCO 31/2675: British High Commission Nairobi to East Africa Department, 7 March 1979.

2. Among others: Y. K. Museveni, *Sowing the Mustard Seed: The Struggle for Freedom and Democracy in Uganda* (London: Macmillan, 1997); Ondoga ori Amaza, *Museveni's Long March from Guerilla to Statesman* (Kampala: Fountain Publishers, 1998); Matthew Rukikaire, *70 Years a Witness: From Colonialism to Resistance and Beyond* (Kampala: Dominant Seven, 2019).

3. James C. Scott, *The Art of Not Being Governed: An Anarchist History of Uplands Southeast Asia* (New Haven, Conn.: Yale University Press, 2009).

4. Kabale DA ADM 86, "Native Affairs, Belgian Congo, 1921" file: P.C. Western to D.C. Kigezi, 5 January 1921.

5. Kabarole DA 753/1: A.D.C. to D.C. Toro, 2 November 1964.

6. UNA OP (Confidential) 28/DG S.270: Samson Rusoke, statement, 11 September 1962.

7. Kabarole DA 482/1: PC Western Province to Chief Secretary, 7 October 1932.

8. George Kahigwa papers: Constitution, Bakonzo Life History Research, central office, 12 January 1959.

9. Interview with Yolamu Mulima, Kasese town, 11 September 2007.

10. UNA A 46/887: Monthly report for November 1919.

11. UNA A 46/1093: Western Province Annual Report, 1921.

12. George Kahigwa papers: Isaya Mukirane to Toro Constitutional Special Committee, 12 January 1962.

13. Kabarole DA 103/1: Telegram to Sec. Inpol., 5 September 1962.

14. UNA OP (Confidential) 28/DG S.270: Security situation in Toro District, 29 August 1962.

15. Kabarole DA 103/1: F. Kyamiza, "Explanation Regarding the Damage of Bubukwanga Gombolola," n.d.

16. Kabarole DA 104/2: District Education Officer to PC, 14 December 1962.

17. Kabarole DA 400/1: Toro District Intelligence Report, 5 March 1963.

18. Kabarole DA 104/2: Y. Mukirane to Administrator, Bwamba, 15 May 1963.

19. Kabarole DA 116/1: Isaya Muirane to Kawamara and Mupalya, 8 June 1963.

20. Kabarole DA 103/1: Fenehasi Bwambale, case file, October 1965.

21. UNA OP (Confidential) 27/N/A: Note by Mr. Pasteur, 6 September 1965.

22. Kabarole DA 1010/1: Mujungu to D.C. Toro, 20 June 1965.

23. Kabarole DA 104/2: No author, "Courts in Bwamba and Busongora" file, n.d. (but 1963).

24. Minister of Regional Administrations, Cabinet Memorandum no. 217 of 1966: "Administration of Bamba/Bakonjo Areas of Toro." Seen courtesy of Tom Stacey.

25. Kabarole DA 989/1: Special Branch, Toro to D.C. Toro, 13 August 1969.

26. Kabarole DA 111/2: Mukirania Samwiri to Milton Obote, 24 May 1969.

27. Kabarole DA 97/1: Chief of Karambi to county chief, Busongora, 9 April 1963.

28. Kabarole DA 104/1: Assistant D.C. Toro, "Banyabindi and Banyagwaki," n.d. (but 1964).

29. UNA MoIA 259/S.9866 vol. VIII: Samwiri Mukirane to "The Baganda Gentlemen," 30 May 1966.

30. Kabarole DA 116/2: Newssheet, Ministry of Regional Administrations, Kampala, 6 December 1965.

31. The history of Rwenzururu in the 1960s is discussed in Martin Doornbos, *The Rwenzururu Movement in Uganda: Struggling for Recognition* (London: Routledge, 2017); David Ngendo Tshimba, "Transgressing Buyira: An Historical Inquiry into Violence Astride a Congo-Uganda Border" (Ph.D. dissertation, Makerere University, 2020); Evarist Ngabirano, "Beyond Ethnic Patriotism: A Comparative Study of Toro and Kigezi Districts in Uganda" (Ph.D. dissertation, Makerere University, 2020); and Yahya Sseremba, *The State and the Puzzle of Ethnicity: Rethinking Mass Violence in Uganda's Rwenzori Region* (Kampala: Makerere Institute for Social Research, 2021).

32. Lazaro Makoma, "The Genesis of the Rwenzururu Freedom Movement" (1 January 1994). Manuscript in the possession of the author.

33. Interview with Eriya Ngobi, Rwimi, Bunyangabu, 8 June 2010.

34. Kabarole DA 117/1: Makumbi ASP to Gen. Pol., 28 September 1966.

35. Kabarole DA 99/2: Gombolola chief Kilembe to D.C. Fort Portal, 4 September 1971.

36. Kabarole DA 99/2: Y. Muliwabyo to police, 27 October 1972.

37. Kabarole DA 99/2: Y. Bwambale to Ministry of Natural Resources, 11 June 1973.

38. UNA MoIA 259/S.9865 vol. IX: Special Branch to Minister of Internal Affairs, 11 April 1973.

39. UNA MoIA 259/S.9866: Special Branch to Vice President, 2 August 1977.

40. Kabarole DA 99/2: Y. Muliwabyo to police, 27 October 1972.

41. Kabarole DA 989/1: Assistant D.C. Toro to D.C. Toro, 18 December 1969.

42. CoU 1 Apb 50/4: Ministry of Churches, Rwenzururu Kingdom Government, to Bishop of Namirembe, 14 July 1965.

43. UNA MoIA 215/S.6190/3: Provincial Intelligence Meeting, 3 May 1976.

44. UNA MoIA 215 S.6190/3: Rwenzori District Intelligence Report, 27 August 1976.

45. Tom Stacey, *Summons to Rwenzori* (London: Secker and Warburg, 1965), 90.

46. Kabarole DA 98/1: Nziabake Yoweri to Milton Obote, 20 September 1967.

47. Kabarole DA 99/2: Yolamu Mulima to Idi Amin, 30 April 1973.

48. Kabarole DA 99/2: Charles Mumbere to Idi Amin, 27 April 1972.

49. Kabarole DA 99/2: Charles Mumbere to Secretary General, Organization of African Unity, and Secretary General, United Nations, 19 May 1972.

50. Kabarole DA 99/2: Charles Mumbere to Jomo Kenyatta, 22 December 1971.
51. Kabarole DA 117/1: Situation Report, 29 April 1967.
52. Kabarole DA 400/1: Toro Intelligence and Security Committee meeting, 29 October 1970.
53. Kabarole DA 400/1: Toro District Intelligence Reports, 3 May 1967.
54. See Isabel Hofmeyr, *Ghandi's Printing Press* (Cambridge, Mass.: Harvard University Press, 2013).
55. Kabarole DA 98/1: Samwiri Mukirania to Secretary General, Organization of African Unity et al., 1 September 1967.
56. Stacey, *Summons*, 83.
57. Kabarole DA 97/1: Isaya Mukirane to U Thant, 15 January 1964.
58. Interview with Yoweri Nziabake, Kasese town, 17 June 2010.
59. Kabarole DA 400/1: Toro District Intelligence Report, 28 June 1968.
60. Kabarole DA 99/2: Charles Wesley to Jomo Kenyatta, 22 December 1971.
61. Kabarole DA 99/2: Charles Mumbere to Secretary General, Organization of African Unity, and Secretary General, United Nations, 19 May 1972.
62. USNA RG 59 SNF 1970–73 2643/POL 7 1/1/70: Ferguson to State Department, 21 September 1970.
63. Interview with James Murumba Kwirabosa, Kisonko, Bundibugyo, 12 June 2010.
64. See, e.g., Kabarole DA 400/1: Toro District Intelligence Report, 4 April 1967.
65. Kabarole DA 99/2: Yolamu Mulima to "All Rwenzururuians," 9 June 1972.
66. UNA MoIA 259/S.9865 vol. IX: Special Branch to P.S., Ministry of Internal Affairs, 24 March 1972.
67. Kabarole DA 99/2: Charles Wesley Irema-Ngoma to Idi Amin, 10 May 1971.
68. UNA MoIA 259/S.9865 vol. IX: Charles Wesley, King Irema-Ngoma and C in C, Rwenzururu Kingdom, to Idi Amin, 11 February 1973.
69. "Rwenzururu Rebels Given Amnesty," *Voice of Uganda* 1 (77) (3 March 1973).
70. Kabarole DA 99/2: Charles Wesley Mumbere to Idi Amin, 8 March 1973.
71. Kabarole DA 99/2: Charles Wesley Mumbere to Idi Amin, 8 March 1973.
72. Kabarole DA 99/2: Charles Wesley Mumbere to Idi Amin, 10 May 1973.
73. Kabarole DA 104/2: Yolamu Mulima to Idi Amin, 30 April 1973.
74. Interview with Yolamu Mulima, Kasese town, 19 November 2007 and 29 May 2010.
75. UNA MoIA 259/S.9866/2: List of documents found with Francisco Mubiru, n.d. (but October 1964).
76. Interview with Eriya Ngobi, Rwimi, Bunyangabu, 8 June 2010.
77. Amos Kambere, *Celebrating Literacy in the Rwenzori Region* (Victoria, British Columbia: Trafford, 2010), 65.

78. Kasese DA, file with no cover: Meeting on the security situation in Bunyangabu county, 3 May 1980.
79. Interview with Charles Wesley Mumbere, Kasese town, 4 June 2010.
80. Blasio Maate papers: 1964 diary, entry for 16 January.
81. Kasese DA, file with no cover: Joint committee meeting, 11 May 1980.
82. Kasese DA, file with no cover: Charles Mumbere to Chairman of the Military Commission, Kampala, 25 September 1980.
83. Kasese DA, "District Team and Planning Meeting" file: District Team and Planning meeting, 15 June 1983.
84. Kasese DA, "Luyira Language" file: Rwenzururu United Kingdom Government Cabinet affairs, 1 August 1982.
85. Kasese DA, "District Team and Planning Meeting" file: Meeting of the District Team, Elders, and District Council, 18 August 1981.
86. Kasese DA, file with no cover: Yeremiya Rukara to D.C. Kasese, 25 February 1983.
87. Kasese DA, file with no label: Yeremiya Rukara to Magistrates Grade 1, Kasese, 13 February 1984.
88. Cosmas Mukonzo papers: "Irema Ngoma Hands Over His Power to the UPC Government," n.d.
89. Kasese DA, file with no cover: Administrative Secretary, Kasese, to P.S., Ministry of Local Government, 4 February 1983.
90. Kasese DA, "Miscellaneous" file: Administrative Secretary, Kasese, to P.S., Office of the President, 17 May 1984.
91. Kasese DA, "Elders Meetings" file: District Elders meeting, 8 May 1984.
92. See Derek R. Peterson, "A History of the Heritage Economy in Yoweri Museveni's Uganda," *Journal of Eastern African Studies* 10 (4) (2016), 789–806.

Chapter 11. Liberating Uganda?

1. Bernard Rwehururu, *Cross to the Gun: The Fall of Idi Amin and the Uganda Army* (Kampala: Netmedia, 2008), Ch. 16; George Roberts, "The Uganda-Tanzania War, the Fall of Idi Amin, and the Failure of African Diplomacy, 1978–79," *Journal of Eastern African Studies* 8 (4) (2014), 692–709.
2. "Uganda Says Enemy Area Now Annexed," *Evening Sun* (1 November 1978).
3. Tony Avirgan and Martha Honey, *War in Uganda: The Legacy of Idi Amin* (London: Zed, 1982), 61–62.
4. "Uganda: Government Film, Found in Kampala, Shows Former President Idi Amin Feted by His Troops in Early Stages of Conflict Against Tanzania" (17 April 1979), *Reuters Screen Ocean*, record ID: 1052940, at https://reuters.screenocean.com/record/1052940.
5. "Tanzania Vows to Hit Amin," *Billings Gazette* (3 November 1978).
6. "Marines Pull Out," *Nation* (10 November 1978).

7. BNA FCO 31/2672: Roy Harding to Peter, 23 March 1979.

8. Avirgan and Honey, *War in Uganda*, Ch. 4.

9. BNA FCO 31/2675: East Africa Department to Robson, 3 April 1979.

10. See Charles Thomas, "Uganda-Tanzania War," *Oxford Research Encyclopedia of African History* (28 January 2022), https://doi.org/10.1093/acrefore/9780190277734.013.1040.

11. Kabarole DA 455/2: Emergency Provincial Security meeting, 5 February 1979.

12. Kasese DA, file with no cover: "Address given by the Provincial Governor to Members of the Rwenzori District Team and Planning Committee," 9 March 1979.

13. Kabarole DA 455/2: Provincial Security Committee meeting, 21 March 1979.

14. Kabarole DA 1043/2: Minister of Provincial Administration to all provincial governors, 22 February 1979.

15. JDA JLOS 65/16: Gombolola chief Kakira to D.C. Jinja, 28 March 1979.

16. BNA FCO 31/2673: M. Bryan to Rosling, 18 April 1979.

17. Avirgan and Honey, *War in Uganda*, 110–19; BNA FCO 31/2673: M. Bryan to Rosling, 18 April 1979.

18. UN Waldheim papers, S-0904-0083-01: Uganda Unity Conference, Moshi, 23 to 25 March 1979.

19. Cherry Gertzel, "Uganda After Amin: The Continuing Search for Leadership and Control," *African Affairs* 79 (317) (Oct. 1980), 461–89; Jimmy T. Tindigarukayo, "Uganda, 1979–85: Leadership in Transition," *Journal of Modern African Studies* 26 (4) (Dec. 1988), 607–22.

20. BNA FCO 31/2672: Hincliffe to East Africa Department, 29 March 1979; Avirgan and Honey, *War in Uganda*, 118.

21. LAC RG 25 12623 20-Uganda-1-4 pt. 7: Nairobi High Commission to Undersecretary of State for External Affairs, 21 June 1979.

22. Avirgan and Honey, *War in Uganda*, 152.

23. BNA FCO 3/2676: Rosling to Private Secretary, 18 April 1979.

24. BNA FCO 3/2676: D. le Breton to Robson, East Africa Department, 18 April 1979.

25. "New Government Installed in Uganda," *Boston Globe* (15 April 1979).

26. LDA box 599, "Vital Statistics" file: D.C. Lira to all county chiefs, 27 October 1979.

27. "Amin's State Research Bureau to Become Atrocities Museum," *Los Angeles Times* (18 December 1979).

28. "Uganda: President Godfrey Binaisa Attends Rally Commemorating Start of Anti-Amin Offensive" (7 November 1979), *Reuters Screen Ocean*, record ID: 1054151, at https://reuters.screenocean.com/record/1054151.

29. UNA OP 3/8: Tibabiganya Merlon, application for candidature to the NCC, 13 September 1979.

30. UNA OP 12/6: Jerry Mbanga, application for candidature in the NCC, 16 September 1979.

31. UNA OP 12/6: Fred Kumbajeegire, application for candidature in the NCC, 22 September 1979.

32. Kabarole DA 487/1: "A List of Proposed Prices Initiated by the Public," 10 May 1979.

33. Kabarole DA 487/1: Memorandum of the Fort Portal Forum to the NCC, Kampala," n.d. (but 1979).

34. See Gertzel, "Uganda After Amin," 461–89.

35. JDA JLOS 56/33: D.C. Jinja to P.S., Ministry of Local Administrations, 28 August 1979.

36. JDA JLOS 56/33: Minutes of Busoga District Security Committee, 6 July 1979.

37. JDA JLOS 56/33: D.C. Jinja to P.S., Ministry of Local Administrations, 28 August 1979; JDA ADM Complaints 3/5: ADC Jinja to P.S., Minister of Internal Affairs, 14 August 1979.

38. UNA MoIA 192/S.2292: Lusty Ugandan Organization to Milton Obote, 10 July 1979.

39. BNA FCO 31/2673: S. Kaasabbuda to all Heads of States, 9 November 1979.

40. BNA FCO 31/2673: Buganda Elders to Queen of England, 21 September 1979.

41. BNA FCO 31/2673: Archbishop Rev. Irienos Magimbi to Margaret Thatcher, n.d. (but August 1979).

42. LAC RG 25 8731 20-Uganda-19 vol. 1: Canadian High Commission, Nairobi to Ottawa, 3 Sept. 1980.

43. LAC RG 25 8731 20-Uganda-19 vol. 2: Otema Allimadi to Canadian High Commission, Nairobi, 12 November 1980.

44. For which, see Justin Willis, Gabrielle Lynch, and Nic Cheeseman, "'A Valid Electoral Exercise?' Uganda's 1980 Elections and the Observers' Dilemma," *Comparative Studies in Society and History* 59 (1) (2017), 211–38.

45. LAC RG 25 8731 20-Uganda-19 vol. 1: Canadian High Commissioner, Nairobi to Ottawa, 6 October 1980.

46. LAC RG 25 8731 20-Uganda-19 vol. 2: Chair, Electoral Commission, to Paulo Muwanga, 5 December 1980.

47. LAC RG 25 8731 20-Uganda-19 vol. 2: Report by Wainwright and Campbell on nominations in Arua, n.d. (but Dec. 1980).

48. LAC RG 25 8731 20-Uganda-19 vol. 2: Report on visit to Kasese District, 9 December 1980.

49. "Shortage of Ballot Papers Prolongs Poll," *The Guardian* (11 December 1980).

50. LAC RG 25 16028 20-Uganda-1-4 pt. 9: National Resistance Movement, "The Political Crisis in Uganda," 1981.

51. "New Uganda President Sworn In," *Miami Herald* (16 December 1980).

52. BDA box 530, file with no cover: An address to the nation by President Dr. Milton Obote, 6 March 1981.

53. Abu Kasozi, *The Social Origins of Violence in Uganda, 1964–1985* (Montreal: McGill-Queen's University Press, 1994), Ch. 7.

54. "Gunmen in Uganda Attack Obote Offices," *Baltimore Sun* (26 March 1981).

55. LAC RG 25 16028 20-Uganda-1-4 pt. 9: Paulo Ssemogerere to President Obote, 9 March 1982.

56. UN Perez de Cuellar papers, S-1024-0087-06: A. Farah, "Allegations of Inhumane Conditions in Uganda," 21 June 1983. See Abigail Meert, "Suffering, Consent, and Coercion in Uganda: The Luwero War, 1981–1986," *International Journal of African Historical Studies* 53 (3) (2020), 389–412.

57. LAC RG 25 11446 20-UGDA-1-4 pt. 6: Amnesty International, "Human Rights Violations in Uganda," 1 July 1982.

58. SOAS Liberation box 15: Dunstan Nsubuga, Sylvanus Wani, Cardinal Nsubuga and Kassim Mulumba, "Memorandum of Uganda's Religious Leaders," n.d. (but 1984).

59. Derek R. Peterson, "A History of the Heritage Economy in Yoweri Museveni's Uganda," *Journal of Eastern African Studies* 10 (4) (2016), 789–806.

60. SOAS Liberation box 15: National Resistance Movement, "Toward a Free and Democratic Uganda" (Kampala, n.d. [but 1982]).

61. Kasese DA "District Council minutes, political" file: Office of the Resistance Council, Kasese District, "Good Message to All, Kasese District," n.d.

62. Andrew Torchia, "Idi Amin Leaves His Bloody Signature," *Sheboygan Press* (14 April 1979).

63. John Darnton, "Uganda: Out of the Nightmare," *The Age* (18 April 1979).

64. "Obote Claimed Holding Foes," *Press and Sun-Bulletin* (13 March 1981).

65. Ryan Lenora Brown, "In Luxury Hotel, a Window into Uganda's Bid to Forget Its Troubled Past," *Christian Science Monitor* (19 February 2016).

66. "Skulls Dug Out at Nile Hotel," *The Monitor* (1 June 2005).

67. David McManus, "Kampala Tower Uganda: Skyscraper Building Africa" (16 January 2012), *e-architect*, at https://www.e-architect.co.uk/africa/kampala-tower-uganda, accessed 8 August 2019.

68. Conrad Nkutu, "Idi Amin Was a Murderer, His Sons Are Sugarcoating the Truth" (31 December 2020), *Atrocities of Amin* (blog), at http://atrocities-of-amin.blogspot.com, accessed 10 March 2023.

69. WodOkello Lawoko, *The Dungeons of Nakasero: A True and Painful Experience* (Stockholm: Förtarres Bokmaskin, 2005); Wycliffe Kato, *Escape from Idi Amin's Slaughterhouse* (New York: Quartet, 1989).

70. Edward Muhima, *Triumph of Faith: Uganda's Experience Under Idi Amin* (Kampala: Fountain, 2017); Festo Kivengere, *I Love Idi Amin: The Story of Triumph Under Fire* (Old Tappan, N.J.: Revell, 1977).

71. Ronald Kassimir, "Complex Martyrs: Symbols of Catholic Church Formation and Political Differentiation in Uganda," *African Affairs* 90 (360) (1991), 357–82.

72. Derek R. Peterson and Richard Vokes, *The Unseen Archive of Idi Amin: Photographs from the Uganda Broadcasting Corporation* (Munich: Prestel, 2021).

73. *Voice of Uganda* (12 February 1973).

74. UBC photo archive, packet 6525.

75. Felix Ocen, "Rise of Maliyamungu from Gatekeeper to Amin's Right-Hand Man," *The Monitor,* 11 August 2019.

76. "Amin's Former Top Aide Dies of Food Poisoning," *Daily Nation* (11 February 1984).

77. Discussed in Derek R. Peterson, Richard Vokes, Nelson Abiti, and Edgar Taylor, "The Unseen Archive of Idi Amin: Making History in a Tight Corner," *Comparative Studies in Society and History* 63 (1) (2021), 5–40.

78. "Ugandans Begin to Confront Blood-Soaked History of the Idi Amin Years," *Sunday Times* (11 August 2019).

79. My colleagues and I discuss the organization of the exhibition in Peterson et al., "The Unseen Archive of Idi Amin."

80. LAC RG 25 11446 20-UGDA-1-4 pt. 6: Nairobi to Secretary of State for External Affairs, 9 April 1974.

81. Aaron Blake, "What Trump Said Before His Supporters Stormed the Capitol, Annotated," *Washington Post* (11 January 2021), at https://www.washingtonpost.com/politics/interactive/2021/annotated-trump-speech-jan-6-capitol/.

Bibliography

Archives in Uganda

Central Police Station Archive (CPS)

This collection was put in order in 2015 and 2016 by a team from the University of Michigan and Makerere University led by Dr. Doreen Kembabazi. A handwritten inventory was created at that time. I consulted the following files:

Daily Crime Bulletin, 1 January 1978 to 10 May 1978
Loose notes concerning Peter Kakooza, Yahya Ssenyondo, and others, 1974

Kabale District Archives (Kabale DA)

This archive was organized and inventoried in 2013 by a team from the University of Michigan and Kabale University. It is presently kept at the Kabale District administration building on Makanga Hill. I consulted the following deposits:

Administration
Community Development
Justice, Law and Order
Miscellaneous
News and Communications
Public Works
Trade and Industry

Kabarole District Archive (Kabarole DA)

This archive was formerly kept in the attic of the old government building outside Fort Portal. In 2009 a team from the University of Michigan and Mountains of the Moon University relocated the collection, and it is now held in the library of MMU's campus at Lake Saaka. The collection was digitized in 2011 and 2012. I went through the following deposits.

Judiciary
Administration
Files concerning the Rwenzururu Movement
Education
Information
Religion
Local Government
Labour
Miscellaneous

Jinja District Archive (JDA)

This collection was formerly held in the basement of the Jinja District administration buildings. In 2015 a team from the University of Michigan and Busoga University put the collection in order and created an inventory. The collection was recently moved to Kampala and taken into the custody of the Uganda National Records Centre and Archives, where it is open for research. I consulted the following deposits:

Administration
Community Development
Justice, Law, Security and Order
Land
Miscellaneous
Public Works
Trade and Industry

George Kahigwa Papers

These papers relate to the history of the Bakonzo Life History Research Society. They were in the possession of the late George Kahigwa, who kindly allowed me to view them.

Kasese District Archive (Kasese DA)

I went through this collection in 2010 and 2011. At that time the files were kept in a disordered manner, and there was no finding aid. I have been told that the records officer subsequently sorted the archive and destroyed a number of files, in accordance with the standing orders of the Ministry of Public Service. Among the files I consulted are the following:

Kilembe Cooperative Savings and Loan Society
Instructions from Headquarters
Staff Meetings and Traders Meetings
Boma file
Research Projects and archives
Visits and Tours
Meetings: Busongora county
Bukonjo meetings
Circulars from DC Kasese
County meetings
Miscellaneous
Dept. of Youth
Uganda-Zaire joint border meetings
Busongora County: District Team file
Annual Reports: provinces
Loss or Damage of Government Properties
Traditional Medicine and Healers
District Council minutes, Political
Kitholu subcounty
District Team and Planning committee
Luyira Language
Rwenzururu Central Office
Cultural and Information Services Management Committee
Elders' Meetings

Bundibugyo District Archive (BDA)

This archive is held in a storage room at the district government headquarters. There is a handwritten finding aid, and the files are boxed and well-kept. Among the files I examined are the following:

Box 501   Uganda Police, 1974–
           Rwenzururu Freedom Fighters Association (Bush War Veterans)
           Currency
Box 503   Agriculture: Coffee General
           Celebrations, General
Box 505   Ministry Headquarters
Box 508   Cotton
Box 509   Trade and Commerce

Box 510	Marriages, general
Box 511	Bakonzo-Baamba Secession Movement, 1983–
Box 512	Supply of Hoes
Box 513	Celebrations, Ministry of Information Planning
Box 515	Dispensaries and Maternity Centres
		Bwamba County Reports
Box 516	Social Welfare Policy
Box 518	Information Services, General
Box 521	Rural Development
Box 522	Postal Services
		Politics, Bundibugyo
Box 531	Trading Centers
Box 553	Moslem Supreme Council
Box 557	District Council Minutes

Hoima District Archive (HDA)

This archive was formerly kept in a mechanic's shed behind the local government buildings in Hoima town. In 2014 a team from Mountains of the Moon University worked with local government to relocate the archive to Fort Portal, where it was cleaned, organized, boxed and catalogued. The paper archive was subsequently returned to Hoima, where it is in the hands of the district records officer; a digital version is held at MMU in Fort Portal. I went through the following deposits:

Administration
Finance
Public Works
Education
Labor
Miscellaneous
Medical
Judicial and Court Affairs
Visitors
Information and Communications
Trade and Commerce
Social and Community Welfare
Native Affairs
Police

Lira District Archive (LDA)

This archive is kept at the local government headquarters in Lira town. There is no inventory or catalogue, but the files are kept in boxes, and for some boxes there is a handwritten list describing the contents. A great many of the files are damaged. Among the files I went through were the following:

Box 506	Native Courts
	Departed Asians Property Custodial Board, Premises
	Magistrate's court of Lango: Policy and report
Box 509	Radio and Television Station—Uganda Broadcasting Service
Box 517	Cotton Bulletins
Box 521	Visit of the President, Vice President and others
Box 522	Cattle Raiders and Civil Disturbance
Box 557	Amnesty Statute: General
Box 568	U.P.C.: Uganda People's Congress
Box 592	Political Parties General
	Lango Transport and General Workers Union
Box 597	Complaints and Enquiries
Box 609	Speeches, Policy Statements
Box 619	Religious Bodies including Missionaries
Box 626	Intelligence: Civil Disturbances
Box 628	Telegraph and Wireless

Uganda National Records Centre and Archives (UNA)

The Uganda National Archives was formerly kept in a series of basement rooms in Entebbe. In 2011 and 2012 a team from the University of Michigan and Makerere University worked with archives staff to organize and inventory the collection. The collection was moved to Kampala in 2016 and placed in a new building. Since that time the archives staff has been acquiring and cataloguing archives from central government ministries and from local district governments. I have gone through the following deposits:

Elections
Chief Secretary's Office (CSO)
Kotido District archive
Mbale District archive
Ministry of Education and Sports
Ministry of Internal Affairs (MoIA)
Ministry of Health (MoH)
Moroto District archive
Office of the President, Confidential files (OP Confidential)
Office of the President (OP)
Office of the President, new deposit (OP new deposit)
Secretariat
Secretariat "Topical"

High Court Archive

The archive of Uganda's High Court was formerly kept in the basement of the grand court building in the center of Kampala. There was no catalogue; older case files and administrative files were piled without logic on wooden shelves. In 2017 a team from the University of Michigan led by Dr. Sauda Nabukenya worked with the Judiciary of Uganda to put the collection in order, place it in boxes, and create a catalogue. The collection consists of around 70,000 files. In 2020 the archive was transferred to the building of the Uganda National Records Centre and Archives, where it can be accessed by the public. I consulted several criminal and civil case files that were created in the 1970s.

Makerere University Library (MUL)

The following materials were consulted:

ARCHIVES

AR BUG: Buganda Government archive
AR J3:   Jacobs papers

NEWSPAPERS

Mwebembezi, 1964 to 1975
Obugagga, 1956 to 1961
Omukulembeze, 1963 to 1975
Munnakampala, 1960 to 1965
Uganda Argus, 1962 to 1972
Uganda Empya, 1953 to 1957
Uganda Eyogera, 1953 to 1963
Uganda Post, 1955 to 1960
Voice of Uganda, 1972 to 1979

Church of Uganda archives (CoU)

This collection is kept on the campus of Uganda Christian University in Mukono. I went through the following collections:

02 Bp: Bishop's papers
1 Abp: Archbishop's papers
CMS: Church Missionary Society papers

Catholic Diocese of Fort Portal archive (Virika)

This collection is kept in Virika, outside Fort Portal town, in the cathedral offices. In 2018 a team from Mountains of the Moon University worked with the University of Notre Dame to digitize the collection. I made particular use of the following files:

Box 260 Bible Society of Uganda
Box 276 Dioceses Kasese
Box 952 Kingdom of Tooro

Uganda Broadcasting Corporation archive (UBC)

The photographic, cinema, and archival collections of the Uganda Broadcasting Corporation are kept at the corporation's headquarters in Nile Avenue in Kampala. There are hundreds of radio reels, thousands of photographic stills, dozens of cinema films, and several boxes of archival papers. In 2017 the University of Michigan and the University of Western Australia opened up a collaboration with the UBC to digitize the photographic stills. More recently we have worked together to digitize the corporation's sound recordings and cinema films. The paper archive—which consists of files concerning the operations of Radio Uganda, the Uganda Broadcasting Service, and Uganda Television in the 1950s through the 1980s—is not organized, and there is no catalogue, but the material is boxed. I consulted the following boxes:

1974 and 1941
Old Files, 1950 to 65, Ministry of Information
Old Files, 1950 to 65
Old Files, 1966–1970
Old Files, 1974–89
1972–1973

Uganda Museum Archive (UM)

The following materials were consulted:

Ethnography acquisitions catalogue, 1948 to 1959
Ethnography acquisitions catalogue, 1958 to 1964
Ethnography acquisitions catalogue, 1970s
Natural History, Archaeology catalogue, 1953–57
Script for exhibition: Tribal Hall
Visitors Book, 1958–84

Blasio Maate Papers

This collection consists of diaries and notes composed by Maate, formerly the district commissioner of Rwenzori District. I went through the material at the invitation of David Nguru, Maate's son.

Mengo Court Archive

In 2018 a team of University of Michigan students worked with staff of the Judiciary of Uganda to inventory the archives of the Mengo Court, which was the highest appeals court in the Buganda Kingdom legal system. The work was led by Dr. Sauda Nabukenya. The papers were junked after 1966, when the kingdom was abolished by Milton Obote's government, and the files had been kept in a disordered manner in a basement storeroom at the court building. They have now been put in order and transferred to the Uganda National Records Centre and Archives in Kampala. I consulted a number of case files from the 1950s and '60s.

Archives in the United Kingdom
British National Archives (BNA)

The following deposits were consulted:

FCO 141 Records of former colonial administrations: migrated archives
CO 822   Colonial Office: East Africa: Original Correspondence
DO 213   Commonwealth Relations Office: East Africa Departments: Registered Files, East Africa
FCO 31   Foreign and Commonwealth Office: East Africa Department: Registered Files

School of Oriental and African Studies (SOAS)

The following deposits were consulted:

CA   Christian Aid
MS 380513 Aidan Southall papers
Liberation   Movement for Colonial Freedom (renamed Liberation in 1970)
PP MS 46   Andrew Hake papers
MCF   Movement for Colonial Freedom
PP MS 38   Melvin Perlman papers

Bodleian Libraries, Oxford

The following deposits were consulted:

Mss. Afr. S. 807   Michael Macoun, diary
Mss. Afr. S. 1565   Fulford-Williams papers
Mss. Afr. S. 1846   Mark Barrington-Ward interview
Mss. Afr. S. 2114   Richard Stone interview
Mss. Afr. S. 2117   James Barber papers
Mss. 5452/1   D.S. Henderson papers
Mss. Perham   Margery Perham papers
Mss. Afr. S. 2195   Taylor papers

Tom Stacey Papers

The papers and photographs of the late journalist Tom Stacey were generously shown to me at his home in Clementi House, London.

Royal Commonwealth Society Archive, University of Cambridge

The following deposits were consulted:

Michael Lee
Jane Bell
Dulcie Barron

Archives in the United States
Gerald Ford Presidential Library, Ann Arbor, Michigan

The following deposits were consulted:

Edward Hutchinson papers
National Security Advisor papers

United States National Archive (USNA), College Park, Maryland

The following deposits were consulted:

RG 59   Central Decimal Files, 1960–63
RG 59   Central Foreign Policy Files, 1967–69
RG 59   Subject Numeric Files, 1970–73
RG 84   Uganda Kampala Embassy, Classified General Records, 1956–63
RG 84   Consulate General, Kampala, General Records, 1956–61

United Nations Archive (UN), New York

The following deposits were consulted:

Perez de Cuellar papers
Kurt Waldheim papers

Archives in the State of Israel

Israel State Archives, Jerusalem (ISA)

The following deposits were consulted:

ISA-MFA   Ministry of Foreign Affairs
ISA-PMO   Prime Minister's Office

Archives in Canada

Library and Archives of Canada, Ottawa (LAC)

The following deposits were consulted:

RG 25   Ministry of Foreign Affairs

Interviews

A disparate collection of interviews upholds this book. I conducted an extensive program of interviews focused on the history of the insurgent Rwenzururu movement. These interviews were conducted in the homes of Rwenzururu patriots in the mountains of Kasese and Bundibugyo districts. They were organized and enabled by Mr. Ezron Muhumuza, who translated from Lukonzo or Luamba into English for my benefit. Separately I conducted on-camera interviews in Kampala with elderly men and women who were involved in the politics of Uganda's independence in 1962. My colleague Dr. David Ngendo-Tshimba and I folded these interviews into a documentary film titled *Uganda at 60: A Film of National Independence*, which we screened at the Uganda Museum in 2022, as part of a historical exhibition marking the sixtieth anniversary of Uganda's independence.

In 2019 and 2020 Richard Vokes, Nelson Abiti, Edgar Taylor, and I organized a photographic exhibition titled *The Unseen Archive of Idi Amin*, which featured newly uncovered images from the archive of the Uganda Broadcasting Corporation. We put together discussion panels to mark the opening of the exhibition in Kampala, Arua, and Soroti. These panels—which were televised by the Uganda Broadcasting Corporation and other channels—featured prominent Ugandans who were involved in the public life of the Amin regime. Separately I conducted private discussions with individuals who attended the exhibition. Interviews in Arua were conducted with family members of Amin, men and women who served in Amin's household, and ex-soldiers of the Uganda Army. Most interviewees in Arua preferred to speak in Swahili. Interviews in Soroti were conducted in English.

Televised Panel Discussions

Aggrey Awori, Al-Hajj Nsereko Abdul, Dick Kasolo, and Elly Rwakoma, moderated by Tony Owana, Uganda Museum, Kampala, 19 May 2019

Deah Amin and other family members of Idi Amin, moderated by Nelson Abiti, Arua Social Centre, West Nile, 14 February 2020

Phoebe Luwum and Sarah Bananuka, moderated by Gyagenda Semakula, Uganda Museum, Kampala, 22 May 2019

Prof. Edward Rugumayo and Henry Kyemba, moderated by Maurice Mugisha, Uganda Museum, Kampala, 18 May 2019

Interviews in and Around Kampala

Prof. Syed Abidi, 20 January 2020
Rev. John Basingwire, 23 February 2020
Moses and Alleni Kaheru, 5 June 2022
Esther Kalimuzo, 4 June 2022
Rhoda Kalema, 3 June 2022
Joyce Mpanga, 24 August 2022
Miria Obote, 4 June 2022
Dr. Charles Olweny, 27 May 2022
Peter Wankulu, 8 August 2018

Interviews in Eastern Uganda

Francis Akello, Soroti town, 30 January 2020
Henry Kyemba, Bugembe, Jinja, 26 May 2019
Augustine Osuman, Soroti town, 30 January 2020

Interviews in Arua, West Nile

Maskini Adua, 14 February 2020
Jaffar Amin, 14 February 2020

Canon Isaac Jaffer Anguyo, 22 February 2020
General (ret.) Yusuf Gowon, 13 February 2020
Corporal (ret.) Mohammed Kassim, 22 February 2020
Owin Kwach, 22 February 2020
Sgt. Major (ret.) Kokola Mawa, 16 February 2020
Sgt. (ret.) Khalfan Mije, 16 February 2020
Maj. (ret.) Andrew Yekka, 17 February 2020

Interviews in Western and Southern Uganda

Festo Karwemera, Rugarama, Kabale, Kigezi, 27 June 2004
Josephat Kule, Bwera, Kasese, 13 September 2007
James Murumba Kwirabosa, Kisonko, Bundibugyo, 12 June 2010
Celili Makoma, Kisinga, Kasese, 12 September 2007
Yeremiya Maliba, Busaru, Bundibugyo, 12 June 2010
Atenasi Masereka, Kasese town, 4 June 2010
Faith Masika, Kisojo, Maliba, Kasese, 30 May 2010
Metusera Mujungu, Kabutabula, Bubandi, Bundibugyo, 4 September 2007
Christine Mukirane, Kasese town, 29 May 2010
Yustasi Mukirane, Bwera, Kasese, 13 September 2007 and 3 June 2010
Edrana Kabugho Mukirania, Kitsutsu, Munkunyu, Kasese, 30 May 2010
Cosmas Mukonzo, Karambi, Bwera, Kasese, 13 September 2007
Yolamu Mulima, Kasese town, 11 September 2007 and 29 May 2010
Omusingha Charles Wesley Mumbere, Kasese town, 4 June 2010
Petero Mupalya, Fort Portal, 15 August 2005 and 28 August 2007
Eriya Ngobi, Rwimi, Bunyangabu, Kasese, 8 June 2010
Yoweri Nziabake, Kasese town, 17 June 2010
Paulo Rweibende, Hima town, 11 September 2007 and 29 May 2010
Muhindo Tembo, Lombo Joash, Mbabwiyahi Tofesi, and others, Rwenzururu
    Veterans Association office, Bundibugyo town, 3 September 2007

Books and Articles

Adelman, Kenneth. "The Recourse to Authenticity and Negritude in Zaire." *Journal of Modern African Studies* 13 (1) (1975), 134–39.
Adoko, Akena. *Uganda Crisis.* Kampala: Consolidated Printers, n.d. [1967].
———. *From Obote to Obote.* New Delhi: Vikas, 1983.
Alexandratos, Nikos. "Food Price Surges: Possible Causes, Past Experience, and Longer Term Relevance." *Population and Development Review* 34 (4) (Dec. 2008), 663–97.
Ali, Picho. "Ideological Commitment and the Judiciary." *Transition* 36 (1968).

———. "The 1967 Republican Constitution of Uganda." *Transition* 34 (Dec. 1967).

Allen, John. *History's Villains: Idi Amin*. Farmington Hills, Mich.: Thompson Gale, 2004.

Amaza, Ondoga ori. *Museveni's Long March from Guerilla to Statesman*. Kampala: Fountain, 1998.

Amin Dada, Al-Hajji Field Marshall Dr. Idi. *On the Middle East Crisis*. Kampala: Government of Uganda, January 1974.

———. *The Shaping of Modern Uganda*. Kampala: Government of Uganda, 1976.

Amin, Jaffar, and Margaret Akulia. *Idi Amin: Hero or Villain?* Kampala: Millennium Global, 2010.

Apter, Andrew. *The Pan-African Nation: Oil and the Spectacle of Culture in Nigeria*. Chicago: University of Chicago Press, 2005.

Asiimwe, Godfrey B. "From Monopoly Marketing to Coffee Magendo: Responses to Police Recklessness and Extraction in Uganda, 1971–79." *Journal of Eastern African Studies* 7 (1) (2013), 104–24.

Avirgan, Tony, and Martha Honey. *War in Uganda: The Legacy of Idi Amin*. London: Zed, 1982.

Barber, J. P. "The Karamoja District of Uganda: A Pastoral People Under Colonial Rule." *Journal of African History* 3 (1) (1962), 111–24.

Bigsten, Arne, and Steven Kayizzi-Mugerwa. *Crisis, Adjustment, and Growth in Uganda: A Study of Adaptation in an African Economy*. London: MacMillan, 1999.

Brisset-Foucault, Florence. *Talkative Polity: Radio, Domination, and Citizenship in Uganda*. Athens: Ohio University Press, 2019.

Bruce-Lockhart, Kate. *Carceral Afterlives: Prisons, Detention, and Punishment in Postcolonial Uganda*. Athens: Ohio University Press, 2022.

Careers in the Uganda Police. Entebbe: Government Printers, 1970.

Carney, J. J. "The Politics of Ecumenism in Uganda, 1962–1986." *Church History* 86 (3) (Sept. 2017), 765–95.

Chimurenga Collective. *FESTAC '77*. London: Afterall, 2019.

Codere, Helen. "Field Work in Rwanda, 1959–1960." In *Women in the Field: Anthropological Experiences*, ed. Peggy Golde. Berkeley: University of California Press, 1986.

Commission of Inquiry into Violations of Human Rights. *Report of the Commission of Inquiry into Violations of Human Rights: Verbatim Record of Proceedings*. Kampala: The Commission, 1995.

Decker, Alicia. "Idi Amin's Dirty War: Subversion, Sabotage, and the Battle to Keep Uganda Clean, 1971–1979." *International Journal of African Historical Studies* 43 (3) (2010), 489–513.

———. *In Idi Amin's Shadow: Women, Gender, and Militarism in Uganda*. Athens: Ohio University Press, 2014.

Donald, Trevor. *Confessions of Idi Amin: The Horrifying, Explosive Exposé of Africa's Most Evil Man*. London: W. H. Allen, 1978.

Donovan, Kevin. "Magendo: Arbitrage and Ambiguity on an East African Frontier." *Cultural Anthropology* 36 (1) (2021), 110–37.

Doornbos, Martin. *The Rwenzururu Movement in Uganda: Struggling for Recognition.* London: Routledge, 2017.

Doyle, Shane. *Crisis and Decline in Bunyoro: Population and Environment in Western Uganda, 1860–1955.* Athens: Ohio University Press, 2006.

Dyson-Hudson, N. "The Present Position of the Karamojong: A Preliminary General Survey with Recommendations." Entebbe: Government of Uganda, 1958.

Earle, Jonathon. *Colonial Buganda and the End of Empire: Political Thought and Historical Imagination in Africa.* Cambridge: Cambridge University Press, 2017.

Earle, Jonathon, and J. J. Carney. *Contesting Catholics: Benedicto Kiwanuka and the Birth of Postcolonial Uganda.* Rochester, N.Y.: James Currey, 2021.

Edel, May. *The Chiga of Uganda.* New Brunswick, N.J.: Transaction, 1996.

Englund, Harri. *Human Rights and African Airwaves: Mediating Equality on the Chichewa Radio.* Bloomington: Indiana University Press, 2011.

———. *Gogo Breeze: Zambia's Radio Elder and the Voices of Free Speech.* Chicago: University of Chicago Press, 2018.

Ford, Margaret. *Even Unto Death: The Story of Uganda Martyr Janani Luwum.* Elgin, Ill.: David Cook, 1978.

Gertzel, Cherry. "Uganda After Amin: The Continuing Search for Leadership and Control." *African Affairs* 79 (317) (Oct. 1980), 461–89.

Goldhagen, Daniel. *Hitler's Willing Executioners: Ordinary Germans and the Holocaust.* New York: Vintage, 1996.

Government of the Republic of Uganda. *The Birth of the Second Republic of Uganda.* Entebbe: Government Printer, 1971.

Grahame, Iain. *Amin and Uganda: A Personal Memoir.* London: Granada, 1980.

A Guide to the External Service of the Uganda Broadcasting Corporation. Kampala: Uganda Press Trust, n.d. (but 1975).

Gunner, Liz. *Radio Soundings: South Africa and the Black Modern.* Cambridge: Cambridge University Press, 2019.

Gwyn, David. *Idi Amin: Death-Light of Africa.* London: Little, Brown, 1977.

de Haas, Michiel. "Rural Livelihoods and Agricultural Commercialization in Colonial Uganda." Ph.D. dissertation, Wageningen University, 2017.

Hancock, I. R. "Patriotism and Neo-Traditionalism in Buganda: The Kabaka Yekka Movement, 1962–62." *Journal of African History* 11 (3) (1970), 419–34.

Hansen, Holger Bernt. "Uganda in the 1970s: A Decade of Paradoxes and Ambiguities." *Journal of Eastern African Studies* 7 (1) (2013), 83–103.

Healy, Thomas. *Soul City: Race, Equality, and the Lost Dream of an American Utopia.* New York: Metropolitan, 2021.

Hofmeyr, Isabel. *Ghandi's Printing Press.* Cambridge, Mass.: Harvard University Press, 2013.

Hunt, Nancy Rose. *A Nervous State: Violence, Remedies, and Reverie in Colonial Congo.* Durham, N.C.: Duke University Press, 2015.

International Commission of Jurists. "Violations of Human Rights and the Rule of Law in Uganda." Geneva, May 1974.

Isaacman, Allen. *Cotton Is the Mother of Poverty*. Portsmouth, N.H.: Heinemann, 1996.

Jørgensen, Jan. *Uganda: A Modern History*. New York: St. Martin's, 1981.

Kaberuka, Will. *The Political Economy of Uganda, 1890–1979: A Case Study of Colonialism and Underdevelopment*. New York: Vantage, 1990.

Kambere, Amos. *Celebrating Literacy in the Rwenzori Region*. Victoria, British Columbia: Trafford, 2010.

Karugire, Samwiri. *The Roots of Instability in Uganda*. Kampala: Fountain, 1988.

Kasfir, Nelson. *The Shrinking Political Arena: Participation and Ethnicity in African Politics, with a Case Study of Uganda*. Berkeley: University of California Press, 1976.

Kasozi, A. B. K. *The Social Origins of Violence in Uganda, 1964–1985*. Montreal and Kingston: McGill-Queens University Press, 1994.

———. *The Bitter Bread of Exile: The Financial Problems of Sir Edward Muteesa II During His Final Exile, 1966–1969*. Kampala: Progress, 2013.

Kassimir, Ronald. "Complex Martyrs: Symbols of Catholic Church Formation and Political Differentiation in Uganda." *African Affairs* 90 (360) (1991), 357–82.

Kasule, Joseph. *Islam in Uganda: The Muslim Minority, Nationalism, and Political Power*. London: Boydell and Brewer, 2022.

Kato, Wycliffe. *Escape from Idi Amin's Slaughterhouse*. London: Quartet, 1989.

Kembabazi, Doreen. "The State of Morality: Sexual, Reproductive and Sartorial Politics in Idi Amin's Uganda." Ph.D. dissertation, University of Michigan, 2020.

Khanakwa, Pamela. "Reinventing Imbalu and Forcible Circumcision: Gisu Political Identity and the Fight for Mbale in Late Colonial Uganda." *Journal of African History* 59 (3) (2018), 357–79.

Kivengere, Festo. *I Love Idi Amin: The Story of Triumph Under Fire*. Old Tappan, N.J.: Revell, 1977.

Kiwanuka, Semakula. *Amin and the Tragedy of Uganda*. Munich: Weltforum Verlag, 1979.

Kodesh, Neil. "Renovating Tradition: The Discourse of Succession in Colonial Buganda." *The International Journal of African Historical Studies* 34 (3) (2001), 511–41.

Kondlo, Kwandiwe. *In the Twilight of the Revolution: The Pan Africanist Congress of Azania (South Africa)*. Basel: Basler Afrika Bibliographien, 2009.

Kyemba, Henry. *State of Blood: The Inside Story of Idi Amin*. New York: Ace, 1977.

Landau, Paul. "'Religion' and Christian Conversion in African History: A New Model." *The Journal of Religious History* 23 (1) (Feb. 1999), 8–30.

Larkin, Brian. *Signal and Noise: Media, Infrastructure, and Urban Culture in Nigeria*. Durham, N.C.: Duke University Press, 2008.

Lawoko, WodOkello. *The Dungeons of Nakasero: A True and Painful Experience.* Stockholm: Förtarres Bokmaskin, 2005.

Leopold, Mark. *Idi Amin: The Story of Africa's Icon of Evil.* New Haven, Conn.: Yale University Press, 2020.

Levey, Zach. "Israel's Strategy in Africa, 1961–67." *International Journal of Middle East Studies* 36 (2004), 71–87.

Macoun, Michael. *Wrong Place, Right Time: Policing the End of Empire.* London: Radcliffe, 1996.

Makinda, Sam. "Leadership in Africa: A Contextual Survey." In *Debating the African Condition: Governance and Leadership,* ed. Alamin Mazrui and Willy Mutunga. Trenton, N.J.: Africa World Press, 2003.

Mamdani, Mahmood. "The Colonial Roots of Famine in North-East Uganda." *Review of African Political Economy* 25 (Sept.–Dec. 1982), 66–73.

———. *Imperialism and Fascism in Uganda.* Trenton, N.J.: Africa World Press, 1984.

Mazrui, Ali. "The Sacred and the Secular in East African Politics." *Cahiers d'Études Africaines* 13 (53) (1973), 664–81.

Mbiti, John. "The Snake Song." *Transition* 27 (1966), 49.

———. *African Traditions and Philosophy.* London: Heinemann, 1969.

———. *Concepts of God in Africa.* London: SPCK, 1970.

———. *New Testament Eschatology in an African Background.* New York: Oxford University Press, 1971.

———. "Diversity, Divisions and Denominationalism." In *Kenya Churches Handbook: The Development of Kenyan Christianity,* ed. David Barrett et al. Kisumu: Evangel, 1973, 144–52.

———. *Love and Marriage in Africa.* London: Longman, 1973.

———. "Death and the Hereafter in the Light of Christianity and African Religion: An Inaugural Lecture." Kampala: Department of Religious Studies and Philosophy, 1974.

———. *The Prayers of African Religion.* London: SPCK, 1975.

———. "The Future of Christianity in Africa." *CrossCurrents* 28 (4) (Winter 1978–79), 387–94.

Meert, Abigail. "Suffering, Consent, and Coercion in Uganda: The Luwero War, 1981–1986," *International Journal of African Historical Studies* 53 (3) (2020), 389–412.

Melady, Thomas, and Margaret Melady, *Idi Amin Dada: Hitler in Africa.* Kansas City, Mo.: Sheed Andrews and McMeel, 1977.

Mirzeler, Mustafa, and Crawford Young. "Pastoral Politics in the Northeast Periphery in Uganda." *Journal of Modern African Studies* 38 (3) (Sept. 2000).

Moorman, Marissa. *Powerful Frequencies: Radio, State Power, and the Cold War in Angola, 1931–2002.* Athens: Ohio University Press, 2019.

Muhima, Edward. *Triumph of Faith: Uganda's Experience Under Idi Amin.* Kampala: Fountain, 2017.

Mujaju, Akiiki B. "The Political Crisis of Church Institutions in Uganda." *African Affairs* 75 (298) (Jan. 1976), 67–85.

Museveni, Yoweri. *Sowing the Mustard Seed: The Struggle for Freedom and Democracy in Uganda*. London: MacMillan, 1997.

Muteesa II, Kabaka of Buganda. *Desecration of My Kingdom*. London: Constable, 1967.

Mutibwa, Phares. *Uganda Since Independence: A Story of Unfulfilled Hopes*. London: Hurst, 1992.

Ngabirano, Evarist. "Beyond Ethnic Patriotism: A Comparative Study of Toro and Kigezi Districts in Uganda." Ph.D. dissertation, Makerere University, 2020.

Ng'weno, Hilary. "Letter from Nairobi." *African Arts* 1 (2) (1968), 66–69.

Niringiye, Zac. *The Church in the World: A Historical-Ecclesiological Study of the Church of Uganda*. Carlisle: Langham Partnership, 2016.

Nsibambi, Apolo. "Language Policy in Uganda: An Investigation into Costs." *African Affairs* 70 (278) (Jan. 1971), 62–71.

Nyabongo, Elizabeth. *Elizabeth of Toro: The Odyssey of an African Princess*. New York: Simon and Schuster, 1989.

Nyakaana, Laban Mukidi Aboki. "Agriculture Development Planning and Policy in Uganda." Ph.D. dissertation, University of East Africa, June 1970.

Obbo, Christine. *African Women: Their Struggle for Independence*. London: Zed, 1980.

Olupona, Jacob. "A Biographical Sketch." In *Religious Plurality in Africa: Essays in Honour of John S. Mbiti*, ed. Olupona and Sulayman S. Nyang. Berlin: de Gruyter, 1993, 1–10.

Omara-Otunnu, Ami. *Politics and the Military in Uganda, 1890–1985*. Basingstoke, Hampshire: MacMillan, 1987.

Opello, Walter. "Pluralism and Elite Conflict in an Independence Movement: FRELIMO in the 1960s." *Journal of Southern African Studies* 2 (1) (Oct. 1975), 66–82.

Otunnu, Ogenga. *Crisis of Legitimacy and Political Violence in Uganda, 1890 to 1979*. London: Palgrave MacMillan, 2016.

Ouma, Joseph. *Evolution of Tourism in East Africa (1900–2000)*. Nairobi: East African Literature Bureau, 1970.

Park, Emma. "Infrastructural Attachments: Technologies, Mobility, and the Tensions of Home in Colonial and Postcolonial Kenya." Ph.D. thesis, University of Michigan, 2017.

———. "'Human ATMs': M-Pesa and the Expropriation of Affective Work in Safaricom's Kenya." *Africa: The Journal of the International African Institute* 90 (5) (Nov. 2020), 914–33.

Parsons, Timothy. *The 1964 Army Mutinies and the Making of Modern East Africa*. Westport, Conn.: Praeger, 2003.

p'Bitek, Okot. *African Religions in Western Scholarship*. Kampala: East African Literature Bureau, 1970.

Peterson, Derek R. *Ethnic Patriotism and the East African Revival: A History of Dissent.* Cambridge: Cambridge University Press, 2012.

———. "Violence and Political Advocacy in the Lost Counties, Western Uganda." *International Journal of African Historical Studies* 48 (1) (2015), 51–72.

———. "A History of the Heritage Economy in Yoweri Museveni's Uganda." *Journal of Eastern African Studies* 10 (4) (2016), 789–806.

Peterson, Derek R., Kodzo Gavua, and Ciraj Rassool, eds. *The Politics of Heritage in Africa: Economies, Histories, and Infrastructures.* Cambridge: Cambridge University Press, 2015.

Peterson, Derek R., Emma Hunter, and Stephanie Newell, eds., *African Print Cultures: Newspapers and Their Publics in Modern Africa.* Ann Arbor: University of Michigan Press, 2016.

Peterson, Derek R., and Richard Vokes. *The Unseen Archive of Idi Amin: Photographs from the Uganda Broadcasting Corporation.* Munich: Prestel, 2021.

Peterson, Derek R., Richard Vokes, Nelson Abiti, and Edgar Taylor. "The Unseen Archive of Idi Amin: Making History in a Tight Corner." *Comparative Studies in Society and History* 63 (1) (2021), 5–40.

Peterson, Derek R., and Darren Walhof, eds. *The Invention of Religion: Rethinking Belief in Politics and History.* New Brunswick, N.J.: Rutgers University Press, 2002.

Pirouet, M. Louise. "Religion in Uganda Under Idi Amin." *Journal of Religion in Africa* 11 (1) (1980), 13–29.

Publicity Division, International Secretariat. *FESTAC '77 General Programme.* Lagos: Supercolour Productions, 1977.

Quinn, Joanna R. "Constraints: The Un-Doing of the Uganda Truth Commission." *Human Rights Quarterly* 26 (2) (May 2004), 401–27.

Raaberg, Gwen. "Beyond Fragmentation: Collage as a Feminist Strategy in the Arts." *Mosaic: An Interdisciplinary Critical Journal* 31 (3) (Sept. 1998), 153–71.

Reid, Richard. *A History of Modern Uganda.* Cambridge: Cambridge University Press, 2017.

"Report of the Commission of Inquiry into the Disappearances of People in Uganda Since 25 January 1971." Entebbe: Government Printer, 1975.

Roberts, George. "The Uganda-Tanzania War, the Fall of Idi Amin, and the Failure of African Diplomacy, 1978–79." *Journal of Eastern African Studies* 8 (4) (2014), 692–709.

Robinson, Cedric J. *On Racial Capitalism, Black Internationalism, and Cultures of Resistance.* New York: Pluto, 2019.

Rukikaire, Matthew. *70 Years a Witness: From Colonialism to Resistance and Beyond.* Kampala: Dominant Seven, 2019.

Rwehururu, Bernard. *Cross to the Gun: The Fall of Idi Amin and the Uganda Army.* Kampala: Netmedia, 2008.

von Schnitzler, Antina. *Democracy's Infrastructure: Techno-Politics and Protest After Apartheid.* Princeton, N.J.: Princeton University Press, 2016.

Schultz, Jason. "Supporting Capacity Building for Archives in Africa: Initiatives of the Cooperative Africana Materials Project Since 1995." *African Research and Documentation* 121 (2013), 3–12.

Scott, James C. *The Art of Not Being Governed: An Anarchist History of Uplands Southeast Asia.* New Haven, Conn.: Yale University Press, 2009.

Sembuya, Christopher. *The Other Side of Idi Amin.* Kampala: Sest Holdings, 2009.

Shaw, Rosalind. "The Invention of 'African Traditional Religion.'" *Religion* 20 (1990), 339–53.

Silverman, Ray, ed. *Museum as Process: Translating Local and Global Knowledges.* London: Routledge, 2014.

Smith, Jeffery K. *The Museum Effect: How Museums, Libraries, and Cultural Institutions Educate and Civilize Society.* London: Rowman and Littlefield, 2014.

Southall, A. W., and P. C. W. Gutkind. *Townsmen in the Making: Kampala and Its Suburbs.* Kampala: East African Institute of Social Research, 1957.

Soyinka, Wole. "Twice Bitten: The Fate of Africa's Culture Producers." *PMLA* 105 (1) (Jan. 1990), 110–20.

Sseremba, Yahya. *The State and the Puzzle of Ethnicity: Rethinking Mass Violence in Uganda's Rwenzori Region.* Kampala: Makerere Institute for Social Research, 2021.

Stacey, Tom. *Summons to Rwenzori.* London: Secker and Warburg, 1965.

Taylor, C. *Runyankore-Rukiga-English Dictionary.* Kampala: Fountain, 1998 [1959].

Taylor, Edgar C., Ashley B. Rockenbach, and Natalie Bond. "Archives and the Past: Cataloguing and Digitisation in Uganda's Archives." In *African Studies in the Digital Age: Disconnects?*, ed. Terry Barringer and Marion Wallace. Leiden: Brill, 2014, 163–78.

Thomas, Charles. "Uganda-Tanzania War." *Oxford Research Encyclopedia of African History*, 28 January 2022.

Tindigarukayo, Jimmy T. "Uganda, 1979–85: Leadership in Transition." *Journal of Modern African Studies* 26 (4) (Dec. 1988), 607–22.

Tshimba, David Ngendo. "Transgressing Buyira: An Historical Inquiry into Violence Astride a Congo-Uganda Border." Ph.D. dissertation, Makerere University, 2020.

Twesigye, Emmanuel Kalenzi. "Church and State Conflicts in Uganda: President Idi Amin Kills the Anglican Archbishop." In *Religion, Conflict, and Democracy in Modern Africa*, ed. Samuel K. Elolia, 151–99. Eugene, Ore.: Pickwick, 2012.

Uganda Protectorate. *Report of the Committee of Enquiry into the Organization, Policy, and Operation of the Government's Information Services.* Entebbe: Government Printer, 1958.

Van Beurden, Sarah. *Authentically African: Arts and the Transnational Politics of Congolese Culture*. Athens: Ohio University Press, 2015.

Wambuzi, Samuel. *The Odyssey of a Judicial Career in Precarious Times: My Trials and Triumphs as a Three-Time Chief Justice of Uganda*. Aberdeen: Cross House, 2014.

Ward, Kevin. "Archbishop Janani Luwum: The Dilemmas of Loyalty, Opposition and Witness in Amin's Uganda." In *Christianity and the African Imagination*, ed. David Maxwell and Ingrid Lawrie. Leiden: Brill, 2002, 199–224.

Weld, Kristen. *Paper Cadavers: The Archives of Dictatorship in Guatemala*. Durham, N.C.: Duke University Press, 2014.

Willis, Justin, Gabrielle Lynch, and Nic Cheeseman. "'A Valid Electoral Exercise?' Uganda's 1980 Elections and the Observers' Dilemma." *Comparative Studies in Society and History* 59 (1) (2017), 211–38.

Wooding, Dan, and Ray Barnett. *Uganda Holocaust*. London: Pickering and Inglis, 1980.

Zinn, Howard. *A People's History of the United States, 1492 to the Present*. New York: Harper and Row, 1980.

Index

Acholi District, 60–61, 68, 188
activists, 15, 25–26
    Idi Amin and, 55–57
    of the Buganda kingdom, 27–29,
        30–36, 42–46
    correspondence of, 44–45
    and journalism, 43–44
    outmoded, 61, 73–75, 249–51
    radio and, 80–81
    See also royalists
Addis Ababa, 171, 177, 178, 240
Adoko, Akena, 47–48, 50, 58. *See also* in-
    telligence
Adrisi, Mustafa, 135, 198–99
Africa Youth League, 176–84. *See also*
    Wankulu, Peter
African National Congress, 167. *See also*
    South Africa
African Traditional Religion, 17, 185,
    186, 201–5, 226, 267. *See also*
    religion
Ali, Picho, 48
Amin, Idi
    and anti-apartheid, ix, 166–71, 172–73,
        246–47
    attempted overthrow of, 4–5
    Black Americans and, 174–76
    and Britain, 63–67, 161
    and Buganda, 55–56, 66–70

children of, 18
correspondence of, 113–17
and cotton farming, 101
coup of January 1971 by, 57–58,
    59–62, 161
decorations of, 173
and FESTAC II, 225–26
and global affairs, 163–76
inauguration of, 60
and Israel, 161–63
in Lango, 63
as liberator, 120, 124
longevity of, 5
magnanimity of, 136
military career of, 51–57
and monuments, 207, 208, 211–18,
    221–24
pilgrimage of, 162
and racial justice, ix, 5, 15, 120–21,
    125–27, 171–72, 174–76, 246–47
on Radio Uganda, 77–78, 91–97
and religious unity, 192–205
reputation of, 2–3
rise to power, 4, 21
and Rwenzururu, 53–54, 229–30,
    236–51
and Scotland, 164
and "Secret Council," 55
as tyrant, 2

343

Amin, Idi (*continued*)
   and United Nations, 165
   and United States of America, 163–64
   See also Amin regime
Amin regime
   archives of, 12–13
   army and, 142–49
   Asian expulsion and, 119–24, 142,
      181–82, 185, 187, 207, 215, 268
   austerity and, 100, 104–11, 221,
      227, 230
   biography of, 53–54
   in Buganda, 61–62, 66–70
   bureaucrats and, 109–10
   campaigns and, 19–20, 100–103
   civil service in, 108–11
   deaths during, 156–57
   and demagoguery, 14–15
   diplomacy of, 164–71, 181–82
   and do-it-yourself, 22, 113–17
   and economic justice, 15, 120–24
   economic management of, 125–37
   economy of, 103–6, 121–37, 255–56
   elders and, 73–75
   enthusiasm for, 17–18, 60–62, 109
   fraudulence and, 110–11
   heritage industry in, 227
   historical reckoning with, 8–10, 261–62
   historiography of, 7, 9–10
   history and, 207–8, 211–18, 221–25
   idealism and, 5, 6, 179–81
   infrastructure of, 21–23, 83–97
   insecurity in, 88
   International Commission of Jurists
      report and, 1
   journalism and, 85–86
   Judiciary and, 112–13
   in Karamoja, 149–56, 268
   in Kigezi District, 60–61
   and kingdoms, 66–73
   in Lango District, 63–64
   memorialization of, 256–57, 261
   opposition to, 68–73, 142, 149, 200,
      229–30

   Organization of African Unity and,
      160, 167, 177–81
   ouster of, 5, 96–97, 229, 249–51,
      253–57, 263–64
   police in, 107–8
   and racial justice, ix, 5, 15, 120–21,
      174–76, 246–48
   radio and, 83–97, 230
   and radio, 16–17, 59, 91–98
   as restitution, 60–62
   Rwenzururu and, 236–37, 244–49
   self-sacrifice and, 6, 221–27
   speed and, 99, 121–22
   as "state of blood," 5
   Tanzania and, 253–55
   victims of, 20, 22–23, 68, 133–36,
      141, 198–200, 256, 261, 263–66,
      268
   violence of, 140–41, 156–57
Amba (people), 231–32
Amnesty International, 140, 156, 259
Anglican Church, 23, 39, 60, 186,
      191–94, 196, 197–98, 200–204,
      225, 237, 259
   and martyrs, 262
   See also religion
Angola, 166, 246
Ankole Kingdom, 25, 67, 191
anti-racism, 18–19, 160
apartheid, ix, 166–73, 246–47
Arafat, Yasir, 167
archives
   of Canada, 242
   of Central Police Station, 107–8
   dereliction of, 10–11, 107
   digitization of, 10–11
   fraudulence in, 110–11
   and historical memory, 12–13, 19
   of Hoima District, 11
   and intelligence, 50–51
   of Israel, 242
   of Judiciary of Uganda, 11, 111
   of Kabale District, 11
   of Kabarole District, 10, 133–34, 235

of Lira District, 139–40
reclamation of, xi–xii, 10–12
resistance toward, 13
of Rwenzori District, 12
of Rwenzururu, 14, 242–43, 248–49
secessionists and, 242–43
and self-promotion, 12
of State Research Bureau, 260–61
of Tooro Kingdom, 10–11
of Uganda Broadcasting Corporation,
   262–66
of United Kingdom, 242
violence in, 140–41
army. *See* Uganda Army
art, 160
and violence, 1–3
See also collage
Arua (town), 92, 176, 265–66
Attila the Hun, 2
Awori, Aggrey, 48

Bagaya, Elizabeth, 72, 284 n. 70
Baha'is, 186, 196. *See also* religion
Baker, William B., 95–96, 267
Bakonzo Life History Research Society,
   231–32, 250. *See also* Rwenzururu
Bar-Lev, Col. Baruch, 161. *See also* Israel
Bataringaya, Basil, 151
Bata Shoes, 129
Batwa (people), 189
Berlin, 84
Binaisa, Godfrey, 29, 256, 261
Bisereko, Tito, 114–16, 266
Black Americans, ix, 174–76. *See also*
   United States of America
Bokassa, Jean-Bédel, 173
Bolsonaro, Jair, 269
Botswana, 167
boycott (of 1959–60), 27–29, 34
newspapers and, 28–29
See also Kamya, Augustine
Britain, 38, 69, 70, 161, 165–66, 216,
   257–58
British Museum, 1

British officials
and Idi Amin, 64–65, 161
and decolonization, 29–33
and Ganda activists, 31–33
and history, 208–9
and radio, 79–80
Buganda (kingdom)
activists of, 27–29, 30–36, 42–46
and Idi Amin, 55–57, 61–62, 66–70
archives of, 11–12
Christianity in, 191–94
destruction of, 4, 21, 39–41, 81–82,
   191, 209, 235
ethnocentrism and, 70
independence of, 20–21, 26, 30–33
Islam in, 191
Kiwanuka administration and,
   33–36
Langi people in, 66
majority rule and, 30
museums in, 209–10
powers of, 25–26
regalia of, 40
self-government of, 32–33
Uganda National Liberation Front
   government and, 257–58
See also Kabaka
Bugisu District, 188–89
Bukedi District, 115
Bulwadda, Kizito, 67
Bundibugyo (town), 12, 95, 115, 125,
   129, 171–72, 232, 239
smuggling and, 130
Bunyoro (kingdom), 25, 38–40, 70,
   72–73, 211, 218
tombs of, 216–17
bureaucrats, 14, 27, 32, 105, 109–10,
   112–13, 136, 193–94, 233–34, 237,
   268
Burkina Faso, 6
Busoga (kingdom), 25
Busoga District, 80, 89, 90, 159, 182
Busoga University, xiii
Bwera (town), 197, 242

Cambodia, 164, 165
Cambridge University, 185
campaigns, 19–20, 21–22, 42–43, 51, 55,
    73, 99–103, 105, 115–16, 120–21,
    142, 153, 172, 201–2, 207–8, 215,
    253–54, 267–69
    and paperwork, 110–11
Canada, 123, 165, 242
Carmichael, Stokely, 175
Catholic Church, 17, 23, 39, 40, 60, 79,
    186, 194, 196, 259
    and martyrs, 262
    See also religion
cattle raids, 150–51
Center for Research Libraries, xi
Central African Republic, 173
chiefs, 93–94, 95, 103–4, 110, 147,
    148–49, 237
    and Rwenzururu, 233–34
Church of Uganda. *See* Anglican
    Church
citizenship, 36, 43, 109, 112–13, 174,
    251
civil service, 107–11, 144
clothing, 153–55, 187–88, 218–19, 220–
    21, 237, 268
collage, 160, 178–83, 267
"Command Post," 7
Commission of Inquiry into Violations
    of Human Rights, 8–9
commoners, 14–15, 20, 80, 100, 103,
    105–17, 153, 217
    liberation work of, 23–24
    See also activists
Commonwealth, 18, 69, 165–66, 257
Congo, 14, 26, 54, 197, 234, 263. *See also*
    Zaire
Congress of Racial Equality, 174–76.
    See also Black Americans
conservation, 19–20, 189, 207–8, 224
corporal punishment, 147–48
Costa Rica, 123
cotton farming, 5, 37, 95, 101–2, 110–11,
    147, 152–53, 293 n. 70

culture, 19, 21, 23, 74–75, 81, 122,
    187–89, 203, 208, 211–13, 218–21,
    224–25, 226–27, 251, 267
curatorship, 19, 207–8, 213–15, 218–27,
    265–66, 267–69
Czechoslovakia, 56

dance, 188–89, 220–21, 267. *See also*
    culture
Dar es Salaam, 44, 167, 229, 255
Dayan, Moshe, 161
Decker, Alicia, 271 n. 2, 297 n. 5
demagoguery, 6, 14–16
democracy, 6, 16, 34, 97, 268–69
Democratic Party, 33, 35–36, 51
    government of, 33–36
Departed Asians Property Custodial
    Board, 121–22, 136–37, 178, 224
Department of Antiquities, 207, 212–14,
    267
Dini ya Roho, 196
Double Production Campaign, 100–101.
    See also campaigns; economy
Du Bois, W. E. B., 176
Duhaga (king), 217. *See also* Bunyoro

East African Community, 242
Economic Crimes Decree, 131
Economic Crimes Tribunal, 22, 131–36,
    265–66
    complaints against, 135
Economic War, 15, 22, 119–37, 142
    propaganda of, 127–28
economy, 5, 100, 103–6, 121–37, 255–56
Ekangaki, Nzo, 180
elderhood, 73–75, 250–51
election
    of 1961, 29–34
    of 1962, 34–36
    of 1980, 258–59
Elizabeth, Queen, 164, 165, 257
engineering, 86–88
Engur, Yekosofati, 188
Entebbe raid, 173–74

Eritrean Liberation Front, 164
Ethiopia, 66, 84, 159, 164, 177

Farrakhan, Louis, 175–76
FESTAC II (Second World Black and
    African Festival of Arts and
    Culture), 218–20, 225–26
Fort Portal, 11, 39, 105, 125, 129, 133,
    135, 148, 172, 173, 232, 256
Fort Thruston, 208, 216. *See also*
    monuments
freedom, 13, 20, 25, 62, 171, 230, 247,
    251
Front for National Salvation, 255
funerals, 263–64

Gaddafi, Muammar, 162–63, 165, 203–4,
    254. *See also* Libya
Garvey, Marcus, 176
General Services Unit, 46–51. *See also*
    intelligence; police
Geneva, 242
Germany, 156, 163, 221–23
Ghana, 13, 30, 39
Guinea, 6, 166
Gulu (town), 56, 62, 83, 84, 176, 258

Hawaii, 164
Head, Bessie, 186
Heart Beat of Africa troupe, 188–89,
    226. *See also* dance
history
    as autopsy, 7–8
    lessons of, 9–10, 248–49
    as source of inspiration, 5, 23–24
    under Amin, 211–18
    under colonial rule, 208–9
    under Obote, 209–10
    See also curatorship; monuments;
    museums
Hitler, Adolf, 2, 14, 156, 163, 253
hoes, 102, 104, 127–29, 131
Hoima (town), 11, 211
hospitals, 115, 172, 174, 225

Indians. *See* Ugandan Asians
Indonesia, 242
inflation, 103–6. *See also* economy
infrastructure
    of dictatorship, 16, 83–98
    and maintenance, 16–17, 86–88,
    216–18, 221–25
    shortfalls in, 103–6
Innis, Roy, 174–76. *See also* Black
    Americans
intelligence, 27
    and Amin regime, 146–47, 166, 260
    Ganda activists and, 38–41
    and grift, 49
    indiscriminate character of, 49–50
    as public good, 47–48
    and state security, 46–51
Internal Security Organization, 261
International Commission of Jurists, 1,
    140
Islam, 161–62, 175–76, 191, 203–4
Israel, 56, 141, 161–63, 173–74, 247,
    268
Ivory Coast, 166

Jerusalem, 161
Jinja District, xii, 11, 51, 88, 113, 122,
    159, 172, 174, 176, 254, 257
journalism, 43–44, 85–86, 88–89
judiciary, 11–12, 111–13

Kabaka (king), 3, 46, 60
    Augustine Kamya and, 28
    and boycott (of 1959–60), 28–29
    deposition of, 40–41, 209, 235
    funeral of, 63–67, 161, 192, 245
    restoration of, 67–70
    return of, 46, 55, 56
    See also Buganda
Kabaka Yekka (political party), 34–36,
    37–38, 46, 49, 61
Kabale (town), xi, 11, 40, 94, 122, 218,
    225
Kabale University, xi

Kabalega (king), 207, 211–12, 213, 214, 217
Kabarole District, 10, 133, 235,
Kaberuka, Will, 7
Kakira sugar factory, 122
Kakungulu, Badru, 50, 60, 191
Kampala, x, 3, 4, 7, 13, 18, 23, 31, 32, 35, 37, 38, 41, 46, 53, 60, 62, 67, 69, 75, 78, 80, 89, 91, 94, 96, 101, 102, 104, 113, 114, 115, 119, 120, 123, 129, 130, 153, 160, 165, 167, 169, 183, 198, 214, 227, 237, 241, 259, 260, 265, 266
    Amin's government in, 126–27
    as center of pan-Africanism, 176–77
    fall of, 254–55, 263
    Organization of African Unity conference in, 177–78, 179
    urban crowds in, 27–29
Kamulegeya, Sheikh Obeid, 162
Kamya, Augustine, 20–21, 27–29, 31–33, 80
    death of, 119
    Ugandan independence and, 37–38
Karamoja District, 149–56, 268
Karugire, Samwiri, 7
Karwemera, Festo, 74–75
Kasese (town), 101, 102, 106, 107, 126, 129, 239, 242, 249, 250, 251, 258, 260
Kasozi, Abdu, 8
Kasubi Tombs, 207
Katasiha Fort, 216
Kaunda, Kenneth, 166
Kazairwe, Joseph, 72–73
"Keep Uganda Clean" campaign, 115–16. *See also* campaigns
Kembabazi, Doreen, 107, 292 n. 51
Kenyatta, Jomo, 159, 180, 239, 242
Kibedi, Wanume, 161
Kibuli Mosque, 161–62
Kiga people, 74–75, 220. *See also* Kigezi District; Kabale

Kigezi District, 60–61, 67, 81, 92–93, 106, 174, 189, 207
    curatorship in, 219–21
    monument in, 221–24
    museum in, 224–27
    Radio Uganda and, 94–95
    kings, 25, 40–41, 69–73. *See also* royalists
Kironde, Apollo, 31
Kissinger, Henry, 164
Kiwanuka, Benedicto, 33–34, 50, 51, 60, 276 n. 49
    murder of, 112
Kiwanuka, "Jolly Joe," 68
Kiwanuka, Semakula, 7, 141
Konzo people, 231–32, 250–51
Kuuya, Masette, 48
Kyemba, Henry, 50, 156
Kyeyune, Eli, 1–3, 5

Lagos, 218, 219, 220, 225–26, 227
Lake Albert, 213
Lake Edward, 213, 239
Lancaster House, 25
Land Reform Decree, 1975, 70–73
Langi people, 45, 62–63, 66, 235
    as victims, 142–43
Lango District, 35, 40, 43, 45, 59–60, 62–63, 66, 67, 90, 104, 155, 211, 235
"Lango Letter," 45–46, 59–60, 63. *See also* intelligence
Leballo, Potlako, 166–71. *See also* South Africa
Legislative Council, 33, 35, 80, 150–51
Leopold, Mark, 280 n. 154
Lesotho, 167
Liberation Committee, 172–73. *See also* Organization of African Unity
Liberia, 165
Libya, 162–63, 203, 247, 254
Lira (town), 40, 43, 63, 88, 89, 139, 176
London, 2, 25, 40, 44, 63, 75, 229, 242, 255, 258, 261
Lon Nol, 164

"Lost Counties" controversy, 38–40, 66, 72–73. *See also* Buganda; Bunyoro

Lubega, Henry, 66

Lule, Yusufu, 255–56. *See also* Uganda National Liberation Front

Lumumba, Patrice, 174

Luweero District, 259

Luwum, Janani, 198–202, 261, 262. *See also* Anglican Church; religion

Luzira Prison, 135–36

Maate, Blasio, 250. *See also* Rwenzururu

Mabunda, David, 177

Madhvani Sugar Factory, 181

maintenance, 78–79, 86–88, 216–18. *See also* infrastructure

Makeba, Miriam, 175

Makerere University, xiii, 1, 40, 47, 67, 109, 112, 133, 174, 185, 186, 195, 202–5

Makobore (king), 219–20

Mali, 6

Malire Regiment, 55–56, 145. *See also* Uganda Army

Maliyamungu, Isaac, 198–99, 263–64

Mamdani, Mahmood, 7

Masaka (town), 108, 168, 254, 263

Mayanja, Abubakar, 50

Mbale (town), 129, 176

Mbarara (town), 254

Mbiti, John, 17, 23, 185–87, 189–94, 198, 202–5, 267
   at FESTAC II, 225–26
   See also African Traditional Religion; religion

Mecca, 162

medicine, 115, 169, 170, 215. *See also* hospitals

Meir, Golda, 163

Mengo (palace), 4, 39–50, 58

Mobutu Sese Seko, 187–88, 213

Mondlane, Eduardo, 177

monuments, 3, 19–20, 201, 208–18, 221–24, 256, 257, 267
   toppling of, 15

See also curatorship; museums

Moroto (town), 31, 121, 153, 154, 155

Mountains of the Moon University (Fort Portal), xi, 10

mourning, 263–66

Mozambique, 166, 177

Mpambara, Mukombe, 74

Mparo, 211, 213, 217

Muhokya (town), 242

Mukirane, Isaya, 231–32, 233–35, 243, 248
   death of, 236
   See also Rwenzururu

Mulima, Yolamu, 241, 247–48

Mumbere, Charles Wesley (king), 236, 242–43, 244–51. *See also* Rwenzururu

Musazi, Ignatius, 123–24, 295 n. 28

museums, xiv, 1, 2, 7, 15, 17–18, 19–20, 74, 207–8, 212–13, 217–18, 224–27, 256. *See also* curatorship; monuments; Uganda Museum

Museveni, Yoweri, 8–10, 75, 136–37, 183, 223, 255
   historical remembrance and, 261–62
   war against Obote II regime, 259–60

Muslims, 162, 191, 192, 203

Muslim Supreme Council, 23, 186, 192

Mutahigwa, Cypriano, 200

Mutebi, Ronald (king), 66–67

Muteesa II, Frederick (king), 3, 35, 36, 39, 191
   funeral of, 63–66, 161, 192
   See also Kabaka

Mutibwa, Phares, 7

mutiny (of 1964), 51–54

Muwanga, Paulo, 255

"Muzinge," 29, 33, 42

Mwanga (king), 211–12

Nairobi, 2, 35, 75, 115, 176, 177, 229, 242, 255

Namanve Forest, 256

Namirembe Cathedral, 192–94, 263

Nasur, Abdallah, 126–27
Nation of Islam, 175–76
National Association for the
    Advancement of Muslims, 191
National Consultative Council, 256
National Literacy Campaign, 105. *See
    also* campaigns
National Resistance Movement, 75,
    259–62
National Tree Planting campaign, 102.
    See also campaigns
Ndagire, Sarah, 67
Nekyon, Apolo, 191
Neogy, Rajat, 186
newspapers, 21–22, 78, 80
    and boycott (of 1959–60), 28–29
    See also journalism; radio
New York, 242
Ngologoza, Paulo, 81
Nigeria, 69, 218–19, 226–27
Nile Hotel, 261
Nile River, 209
Nixon, Richard, 163, 164
Nkangi, Mayanja, 67
Nkrumah, Kwame, 30, 35, 37, 181, 183
Nomiya Luo Church, 196
Nyakaana, Labani, 71–72
Nyerere, Julius, 4, 159, 166, 253,
    257, 258

Obote, Milton, 8, 74, 153, 255
    alliance with Kabaka Yekka, 35–36,
        37–39
    and Idi Amin, 54–58
    assassination attempt on, 41
    biography of, 35
    and Buganda Kingdom, 35, 38–46,
        209–10
    ethnocentrism of, 45–46, 59–60, 63
    and history, 209–10
    Kabaka of Buganda and, 31, 40
    and Augustine Kamya, 37–38
    and "Lost Counties" controversy,
        38–40

    and Janani Luwum, 198–99
    and nationalism, 3–4
    nation-building of, 21, 26–27, 31,
        39–41
    overthrow of, 57–58
    political career of, 3–4, 36
    return to power (in 1980),
        258–59
    secret plans of, 38–39, 45–46
    and Uganda Army, 54–56
    weakness of, 26
    See also Obote regime
Obote, Miria, 153
Obote regime
    archives of, 50–51
    and Christianity, 191–92
    intelligence and, 27, 46–51
    Islam and, 191
    and Karamoja, 150–51, 153
    plots against, 46
    and radio, 78, 80–82
    and tourism, 208–10
    and Rwenzururu, 233–35
Oder, Arthur, 8
Odora, Chief Daudi, 211
Okigbo, Christopher, 186
Okinawa, 163
Okot p'Bitek, 186, 187
Ondoga, Michael, 266
Opolot, Shaban, 54–55
Organization of African Unity, ix, 23,
    122, 159, 166, 167, 171, 172,
    177–81, 239, 240, 242
Oryema, Wilson, 54
Ottawa, 242
Owor, Alex, 102, 254

Pakistanis. *See* Ugandan Asians
Palestine Liberation Organization, 163,
    167, 173, 247, 268
Palestinian people, 162, 165
Pan-Africanism, 176–84
Pan-Africanist Congress (P.A.C.),
    166–71

patriotism, 6, 14, 19–20, 24, 73, 82, 173,
    176, 182, 185, 186, 207, 208, 230,
    237, 251, 267–69
Pentecostals, 20, 68, 186, 195–96, 203.
    See also religion
photography, 131–33, 151–53, 168, 244,
    262–66
Pizarro, Francisco, 2
police, 107–8, 139–41, 148, 172
Pol Pot, 165
Pope Paul VI, 56. *See also* Catholic
    Church
populism, 6, 80, 236, 268–69
prisons, 12, 32, 35, 60, 64, 74, 88, 114,
    131, 135–36, 139–40, 146, 147,
    148, 191, 223, 236, 250
proprietorship, 14, 100, 114–17, 120,
    267–69
prostitution, 116
Public Safety Unit, 161

racial justice, ix, 5, 15, 120–21, 125–27,
    171–72, 174–76, 246–48
racism, 15, 18, 85, 160, 165, 168, 171–72,
    185, 187, 246
radio
    British officials and, 79–80
    and dictatorship, 22, 230
    fragility of, 78, 86–88
    moralistic programming of, 80–81
    and newspapers, 21–22
    reception of, 90–91
    resistance toward, 24, 80–81, 230
    transmission of, 85
    See also Radio Uganda
Radio Rwanda, 90
Radio Uganda, 59, 67, 122, 141, 162,
    166, 245
    Idi Amin and, 77–78
    anniversary of, 96–97
    archives of, 77–78
    censorship of, 81–82
    and dictatorship, 14, 16–17, 91–97,
    100, 266, 268

engineers of, 86–88
expansion of, 78, 85
external broadcasting service of, 85
languages of, 82
listeners of, 83–85, 89–90
and local government, 94–97
and murder of Janani Luwum,
    198–200
opposition toward, 238–44
origins of, 79–80
and pace of public life, 6
recording van, 74, 79
See also radio
Reeves, Jim, 84
religion, 23, 186, 189–98, 268. *See also*
    African Traditional Religion;
    Anglican Church; Catholic
    Church; Islam
Remembrance Day, 221–22
resistance councils, 260
Rhodesia, 69–70, 167, 246
royalists, 21, 66–70, 72–75, 257–58.
    See also activists
Rugumayo, Edward 142
Rugunda, Ruhakana, 48
Rujumbura (kingdom), 219–20
Rutakirwa (cultural leader), 40. *See also*
    Kigezi District
Rwagasore, Nelson, 177
Rwanda, 74, 143, 222, 241
Rwenzori District, 12, 13, 14
Rwenzori Mountains, 230, 248
Rwenzururu, 24, 26, 75, 229–30,
    315 n. 31
    administration of, 233–35
    Idi Amin and, 244–51
    archives of, 14, 248–49
    army of, 237
    assimilation of, 249–51
    Buganda and, 235, 245
    correspondence of, 239–41
    culture of, 237
    election of 1980 and, 258
    media of, 238–44

Rwenzururu (*continued*)
  military campaign against, 53–54
  origins of, 232–33
  and Radio Uganda, 238–39, 266
  support for, 236–37
  United Nations and, 241–42
  See also Mukirane, Isaya; Mumbere,
    Charles Wesley

Sabiti, Erica, 191–94, 195, 198. *See also*
    Anglican Church
Sanyu lya Buganda (the "Joy of
    Buganda"), 68
Scotland, 164
Second World Black and African Festival
    of Arts and Culture (FESTAC II),
    218–20, 225–26
"Secret Council," 43–46, 55, 59, 68. *See
    also* activists; Buganda; royalists
Selassie I, Haile, 159, 183
"Self Help Projects Decree," 105–6
self-sacrifice, 6, 100, 105–17. *See also*
    maintenance
Semliki River, 230
Semuliki District, 13, 104, 105, 106, 107, 122
Seventh Day Adventist Church, 186,
    196, 197. *See also* religion
Sihanouk, Norodom, 165
Singh, Charan, 194
Sithole, Ndabaningi, 165
Smith, Ian, 167, 169, 246
smuggling, 129–31, 135, 268
Sobukwe, Robert, 167
soldiers
  assault on Mengo, 40
  impersonators of, 144–45
  powers of, 22–23, 56–57, 142–49
  vendettas of, 144
  See also Uganda Army
Soroti (town), 176, 265
South Africa, ix, 70, 84, 166–71, 175,
    246. *See also* Pan-Africanist
    Congress
Soviet Union, 56, 103, 165

Soyinka, Wole, 186, 226–27
Speke, John Hanning, 209
Ssekintu, Charles, 214–15. *See also*
    Uganda Museum
Ssembeguya, Charles, 50
Stacey, Tom, xiii
State Research Bureau, 146–47, 196,
    199–200, 215, 256, 260, 261.
    See also intelligence
State Trading Corporation, 125
Suez Canal, 163
Suna II (king), 216. *See also* Buganda;
    Kabaka
Swahili (language), 127, 135, 146,
    150, 199

Tanzania, 4, 5, 74, 97, 159, 167, 198, 223,
    249, 253–55, 257, 260, 263
Thatcher, Margaret, 257–58
Theroux, Paul, 186
Tho, Nguyen Huu, 165
Time magazine, ix
Tooro Kingdom, 10–11, 26, 41, 72, 172,
    237
  Konzo people in, 231–32
  palace of, 210
  and Rwenzururu, 234–35, 248
  tombs of, 232
Tororo (town), 176
torture, 140
Toure, Sekou, 166
tourism industry, 105, 208–11
Transition magazine, 186
Trump, Donald, 15–16, 268–69
Turkana, 150

Uganda
  anthem of, 36–37
  Buganda's independence and, 32–33
  constitution of, 36
  decolonization of, 3–4, 29
  elections of 1961 in, 29–34
  election of 1980 in, 258–59
  economy of, 100

exiles, 229–30, 255–56
independence of, 3–4, 21, 25–27,
    36–37
Judiciary of, xii
kingdoms of, 25, 40–41, 70–73
monuments in, 210–18, 221–24
reconstruction of, 7–8
security services and, 55–57
Uganda Action Group, 255
Uganda Air Force, 167, 247
Uganda Army, 40–41
    campaign against Rwenzururu,
        53–54, 232–33, 247
    and government, 142–49
    and impersonators, 144–46
    indiscipline in, 53–54, 56–57, 143–44
    military honors of, 173
    mutiny of 1964 and, 51–54
    and state security, 51–57
    and training of Pan-Africanist
        Congress, 168–71
    war with Tanzania and, 253–55
    See also soldiers
Uganda Broadcasting Corporation,
    xi, 21, 77, 126, 131, 151, 153,
    262–66
Uganda Development Corporation, 122
Uganda Law Society, 47
Uganda Museum, 7, 17–18, 211, 212–13,
    267
    collections of, 214–15
    Museveni government and, 261–62
    photographic exhibition and,
        265–66
    See also curatorship; museums
Ugandan Asians, 15, 18–19
    boycott of 1959–60 and, 28–29
    economic role of, 121–23
    expulsion of, 119–24, 142, 181–82,
        185, 187, 207, 215, 268
    family histories of, 123
    and Uganda's independence, 37
    as victims, 20, 141
Uganda National Congress, 150

Uganda National Liberation Front,
    249–51, 255–58
Uganda National Records Centre
    and Archives, xii, 12, 256.
    See also archives
Uganda Patriotic Movement, 258
Uganda People's Congress, 31, 33, 74,
    255
    alliance with Kabaka Yekka,
        34–36
Uganda Revenue Authority, 201
Uganda Rifles. See Uganda Army
Uganda Television, 127, 135–36,
    189, 253
Uganda Youth Development
    Organization, 106
United Nations, 165, 240, 241–43
United States of America, ix–xi, 6, 28, 30,
    45, 47, 48, 84, 108, 123, 142, 163,
    164, 174–76, 268–69. See also
    Black Americans
University of the Redlands, 204
U Thant, 241

Vietnam, 93, 163, 164, 165
vigilantes, 19, 22, 116, 269
violence, xi, 2, 5, 8, 9, 22, 54, 56,
    112, 139–44, 146–57, 195,
    198, 230, 250, 261, 262, 263,
    265, 266, 268
Voice of Kenya (radio station), 90
Voice of Uganda (newspaper), ix, 86,
    91, 125, 133, 137, 168, 178,
    182, 188

Waldheim, Kurt, 163
Wankulu, Peter, 17, 23, 123, 159–60,
    176–84, 267
West Nile District, 35, 53, 56, 89, 142
Winyi, Tito (king), 217
women, 13, 20, 53, 66, 80–81, 116,
    127, 131, 148–49, 153, 169–70,
    194–95, 237
    attire of, 93–94, 188, 220–21, 268

Won Nyaci, 40. *See also* Lango
    District
World Council of Churches, 204
World War I, 207–8, 221–24, 267
World War II, 150

Zaire, 74, 115, 130, 132, 135, 172, 177,
    187, 229, 230. *See also* Congo
Zambia, 167, 223
Zimbabwe, 165, 166, 173, 246
Zinn, Howard, ix–x